Coxsackie

RECONFIGURING AMERICAN POLITICAL HISTORY
Ronald P. Formisano, Paul Bourke, Donald DeBats, and
Paula M. Baker, Series Founders

Other Books in the Series

Michael Goldberg, *An Army of Women: Gender and Politics in Gilded Age Kansas*

Mark Voss-Hubbard, *Beyond Party: Cultures of Antipartisanship
in Northern Politics before the Civil War*

Douglas B. Craig, *Fireside Politics: Radio and Political Culture
in the United States, 1920–1940*

Kate Weigand, *Red Feminism: American Communism
and the Making of Women's Liberation*

R. Rudy Higgens-Evenson, *The Price of Progress: Public Services,
Taxation, and the American Corporate State, 1877 to 1929*

Donald DeBats and Paul Bourke, *Washington County:
Politics and Community in Antebellum America*

Leigh Ann Wheeler, *Against Obscenity: Reform and the Politics of
Womanhood in America, 1873–1935*

Liette Gidlow, *The Big Vote: Gender, Consumer Culture,
and the Politics of Exclusion, 1890s–1920s*

Jeffrey O. G. Ogbar, *Black Power:
Radical Politics and African American Identity*

Robert E. Shalhope, *Bennington and the Green Mountain Boys:
The Emergence of Liberal Democracy in Vermont, 1760–1850*

Dennis Deslippe, *Protesting Affirmative Action:
The Struggle over Equality after the Civil Rights Revolution*

Williamjames Hull Hoffer, *To Enlarge the Machinery of Government:
Congressional Debates and the Growth of the American State, 1858–1891*

John R. Van Atta, *Securing the West: Politics, Public Lands,
and the Fate of the Old Republic, 1785–1850*

Coxsackie

The Life and Death of Prison Reform

JOSEPH F. SPILLANE

Johns Hopkins University Press
Baltimore

© 2014 Johns Hopkins University Press
All rights reserved. Published 2014
Printed in the United States of America on acid-free paper
2 4 6 8 9 7 5 3 1

Johns Hopkins University Press
2715 North Charles Street
Baltimore, Maryland 21218-4363
www.press.jhu.edu

Library of Congress Cataloging-in-Publication Data
Spillane, Joseph F.
Coxsackie : the life and death of prison reform / Joseph F. Spillane.
pages cm
Includes bibliographical references and index.
ISBN 978-1-4214-1322-8 (hardcover : alk. paper) — ISBN 1-4214-1322-1
(hardcover : alk. paper) — ISBN 978-1-4214-1323-5 (electronic) —
ISBN 1-4214-1323-X (electronic)   1. Coxsackie Correctional Facility.
2. Prisons—New York (State)—Coxsackie.   3. Prisoners—New York
(State)—Coxsackie.   I. Title.
HV9481.C69C697 2014
365′.974737—dc23   2013032123

A catalog record for this book is available from the British Library.

*Special discounts are available for bulk purchases of this book. For more
information, please contact Special Sales at 410-516-6936 or
specialsales@press.jhu.edu.*

Johns Hopkins University Press uses environmentally friendly book materials,
including recycled text paper that is composed of at least 30 percent
post-consumer waste, whenever possible.

CONTENTS

In February 2011, with the research for this book complete and well into its writing, I was surprised to find the reformatory at the heart of this book (the New York State Vocational Institution, more commonly known as Coxsackie) thrust unexpectedly into the news. Mike Stobbe, medical writer for the Associated Press, published a lengthy story reviewing the history of medical experimentation on prisoners in the United States. Stobbe uncovered some shocking examples for his article, including an experiment at Coxsackie in which researchers made young male prisoners swallow unfiltered stool suspension as a means of studying the transmission of a stomach illness. To employ something like the prisoners' own vernacular, they had been made to "eat shit" by institutional authorities. Of the many failings of Coxsackie and the reformatory system, it was one I hadn't come across before, but Stobbe had his facts right. In 1947, the results of the experimentation, conducted by doctors from the New York State Department of Health studying the transmission of epidemic gastroenteritis, were published in the *Journal of Experimental Medicine*. The fecal matter came from ill patients at Marcy State Hospital—one of New York's massive state mental hospitals—and was swallowed by young volunteers with no knowledge of what was being done to them. It made most of the young men ill, producing nausea, vomiting, and diarrhea, and it sickened readers all over again in 2011.[1]

Medical experimentation at Coxsackie, as elsewhere, is a troubling and significant aspect of the twentieth-century prison's history. But it is just one small part in a larger history of wrongs done, in the name of the state, at reformatories like Coxsackie. Fewer than a dozen prisoner-volunteers were made to swallow the fecal filtrates—but in the first two decades after Coxsackie opened in 1935, it was home to more than ten thousand young men, with several times that number being confined in New York's other reformatories for young male felony offenders. Although their stories have never been the stuff of national media attention, they deserve to be told and, in the end, are no less shocking.

This writing of this book began more than a decade ago, with my first review of Coxsackie prisoner case files held at the New York State Archives. Other projects undertaken during the intervening years delayed the completion of this study, but time has not diminished my recollection of the intense human drama revealed in every one of those files. Week after week, the inmate photographs that began every file (always attached to the inside cover) reminded me that the case records captured some small part of real lives, as full of youthful promise as they were riddled with deep and abiding conflict. Every case file offered unexpected connections to the past. When a discipline report cited an inmate for using a pack of cigarettes to prevent a cell from locking, I turned the page and found a neatly folded Camel cigarette pack—untouched since it had been placed there decades earlier. My time with the case files remains the most personally challenging research I have undertaken, and I made a commitment to document the experience of the reformatory prisoners as completely as I could. If they are still living, the oldest of the prisoners covered by my case file sample would now be over 90 years of age, while the youngest would be just past 70. Very few graduates of Coxsackie ever told their stories in a public way. Those who remained entangled in the criminal justice system moved onward and upward into the massive prisons for adult offenders, while those who avoided going back into the system undoubtedly wished to put that chapter of their lives well behind them. Should any of them read this account, I hope that they will recognize what it portrays, even as it inevitably falls short of the richness of their own personal experiences.

The completion of this work owes a great deal to inspiration and encouragement from a wonderful network of colleagues. I first encountered Coxsackie twenty years ago, while exploring the history of vocational education in American corrections with Steven Schlossman, then my doctoral adviser, now friend and valued colleague. My collaborators on other projects have, each in their own way, helped me refine my thinking about aspects of this book: John Burnham, Nancy Campbell, Trysh Travis, and David Wolcott are all innovative historians whose work has encouraged me to keep this project evolving. My "drug history" network, especially Caroline Acker, David Courtwright, and Eric Schneider, helped me shape my thinking about Coxsackie's engagement with heroin-using young men. I have also been fortunate to discuss aspects of this project in a variety of settings, including the Incarceration Nation conference held at the University of Florida in 2010; the Social Science History Association annual meet-

ing in 2011; the 2012 LSE IDEAS Conference on Governing the Global Drug
Wars; as well as the biennial conferences of the Alcohol and Drugs History
Society in 2011 and 2013. Over the course of the final years of this project, I
have been energized by my engagement with many outstanding entrants into
the field of prisons, punishment, and social policy, including Marsha E. Barrett,
Michael J. Durfee, Michael Fortner, Marie Gottschalk, Volker Janssen, Jessica
Neptune, Sam Roberts, and Heather Ann Thompson.

The staff of numerous archives and libraries helped facilitate the research for
this project; without their professionalism and energy, I could not have made
the progress I did. Working at the New York State Library and Archives was a
pleasure, and I am particularly grateful to Jim Folts for his assistance at every
stage of my research there. The M. E. Grenander Department of Special Collections and Archives, University at Albany, was a wonderfully congenial setting
for research, and I am particularly indebted to Supervisory Archivist Jodi Boyle,
whose willingness to dig through files in storage helped me uncover some critical sources. The outstanding special collections staffers at the Newton Gresham
Library at Sam Houston State University are the proud keepers of some remarkable manuscript collections, and I hope that these will continue to attract scholarly attention. Thanks as well to the staff of the Franklin D. Roosevelt Library as
well as to David Connelly for sharing some of the Osborne-MacCormick correspondence from the Osborne Family Papers at Syracuse University.

Critical financial support for this research came from the Larry J. Hackman
Research Residency Program of the New York State Archives; the small grants
program of the Spencer Foundation; and the Humanities Scholarship Enhance-
ment Fund of the College of Liberal Arts and Sciences at the University of Florida. I am also deeply appreciative of the support I have received from Johns
Hopkins University Press, and particularly the ever-patient Bob Brugger. I am
glad to have finally had the chance to show him what this prison project was all
about.

My academic home for nearly twenty years has been the University of Florida's Department of History. Among many wonderful colleagues, I am fortunate
to work with two of the finest historians of crime, law, and justice, Jeff Adler and
Elizabeth Dale. Among others, Sean Adams, Jessica Harland-Jacobs, Matt
Gallman, Howard Louthan, and Jeff Needell helped make my time as department chair just easy enough for me to keep moving forward with this book; my
successor, Ida Altman, has been an encouraging and supportive chair. The late
Robert Zieger encouraged my progress, and his untimely passing before this
book's publication is a source of great sadness for me. Prisons and imprisonment

have recently become a topic of much interest for historians, but Bob was among the few I knew a decade ago who found the subject compelling. Just as this book was completed, another valued University of Florida colleague, Alan Petigny, passed away suddenly. I am grateful for our many productive conversations about modern American politics and punishment. The Center for Studies in Criminology and Law was also an academic home for me for many years at the University of Florida, and I am thankful for the wonderfully supportive colleagues from that program, especially Jodi Lane, Lonn Lanza-Kaduce, Chuck Frazier, and Ron Akers (who was the first to push me toward pursuing this as a book project). Criminology and history graduate students have given me many insights over the years, in and out of the seminar setting. Among my graduate research assistants, the first and most important was Julian Chambliss, who shared with me the experience of working through the case files in Albany. My doctoral students, including Julie Baldwin, Erin Conlin, Hayden Griffin, and Bryan Miller, have done a magnificent job of charting their own scholarly paths and, in so doing, reminded me to keep following my own.

Above all, my family has provided the support necessary to sustain this project through to completion. Barbara and George Stackfleth remain outstanding consumers of history and always help me imagine my reading audience. Tara, Emma, and Howard Chilton were patient and kind hosts in New York. My parents, Joseph and Judy Spillane, were the first people to teach me how to value the past and appreciate it in the present—they both continue to be historians of the first order. My daughters, Maggie and Lily, have grown up around this project. They have shared time with my research trips and with my writing and have grown into thoughtful and remarkable young women despite my scholarly distractions. Finally, my wife, Jennifer, remains the most important influence on my work. I know of no one more committed to speaking truth and to hearing the voices of the unheard; this work tries to live up to that standard and, even where it falls short, is much the better for it.

Coxsackie

The Ashes of Reform

"Maybe this is the beginning of a new future."[1] The hopeful words of Leo Martinez, a prisoner in Coxsackie (pronounced "cook-sock-ee") Correctional Facility, stood in sharp contrast to the setting in which they were delivered. Martinez was a spokesman for roughly forty inmates who earlier in the day had taken three hostages and were now talking to four reporters brought into the prison that evening as part of negotiations with authorities. Both prisoners and prison staff were aware that the prison had been on the verge of an explosion well before the hostage crisis of December 2, 1977. The former reformatory for young male offenders—opened in 1935 as the New York State Vocational Institution and called Coxsackie throughout its history—had been through years of wrenching transition, as the rehabilitative and educational ideals that had inspired its construction waged a losing battle with punitive and custodial interests. The previous evening, a strongly negative announcement from program staff had informed inmates that formal education programs were being scaled back. Reacting to the news, prisoners staged a mass boycott of breakfast the next morning. The boycott turned into a hostage incident when authorities failed to secure the E-2 division, and inmates there seized a correctional officer, a lieutenant, and an investigator from Albany.

Any collective action within the prison setting poses a serious security threat, and never more so than in the super-heated political atmosphere of Coxsackie in 1977. Prison officials were already sensitive to the looming threat of prisoner action following a serious rebellion in August at Eastern Correctional Facility, another former reformatory. At Eastern, inmates protesting a history of Ku Klux Klan activity among the prison staff had taken eleven hostages as a way of securing a public airing of their grievances.[2] At Coxsackie, Leo Martinez and the prisoners of E-2 division likewise employed hostage negotiations as a mechanism for making public charges of racism and brutality. "We respect the system, but they [correctional officers] don't respect us," declared one of the prisoners. Instead, he told the reporters, "they treat us like animals and kids." While respecting the system may have seemed a curious turn of phrase, the demands of Coxsackie's hostage takers did not challenge the legitimacy of the prison itself, only the grossly deficient conditions of confinement and the refusal of the institution to recognize their basic worth as men and as citizens.

The hostage incident ended peacefully that evening. Before it did, Leo Martinez worried out loud to the reporters that his optimism might be misplaced: "Days like this happen, and then tomorrow it gets brushed off."[3] The day was not brushed off, but the "new future" coming was not the one for which Martinez had hoped. Instead, the hostage crisis became the occasion to bury the final legacies of Coxsackie as a reformatory. The state moved quickly to replace Coxsackie's reform-minded superintendent—who had started in prison work as a teacher—and to impose a stricter disciplinary regime. Corrections commissioner Benjamin Ward chided those who wanted to operate Coxsackie as "some kind of reform school spin-off" instead of focusing on custody and close supervision.[4] Coxsackie correctional officers joined in, with one observing, "We should forget rehabilitation and concentrate on security," and another pronouncing that "a prison should be a place of fear, not a hotel."[5]

That Coxsackie should be known as a "place of fear" was about as far, rhetorically, as could be imagined from where things had begun. The New York State Vocational Institution began life as the centerpiece of a large-scale prison-reform effort initiated in 1929 by New York governor Franklin D. Roosevelt and lieutenant governor Herbert Lehman. Coxsackie embodied the intention to respond to the problem of the young male offender through rehabilitative programs and humane confinement. When Lehman went to Coxsackie in 1935 to attend the dedication ceremony and seal the cornerstone of the New York State Vocational Institution, he pointed to the reformatory as a place of special importance; the new red brick institution featured a remarkable investment in prisoner education, employing more teachers and vocational instructors than any other prison in the United States.

Coxsackie's history since 1977 shows just how completely the original reform vision has failed to sustain itself. Indeed, the New York State Vocational Institution per se no longer exists—it was renamed the Coxsackie Correctional Facility in 1970, and only a small marker at the front driveway records the former name and identity of the institution. No longer designated a reformatory, Coxsackie more often serves as a vivid example of prison life in the contemporary age of mass incarceration and punitive punishment. Ted Conover, author of *Newjack*, visited Coxsackie along with his fellow correctional officer trainees to get a dose of life inside a "real" prison. *Newjack* offers readers a chilling description of the oppressive institutional environment in the former educational institution, a prison the trainees' tour guide called the "Gladiator School."[6] Documentary film-maker Tracy Huling used Coxsackie as the prototypical "prison town" in her 1999 film *Yes, in My Backyard.* For Huling, Coxsackie had become emblematic of the prison-industrial complex that supported rural economies while locking up masses of urban minority poor.[7]

What happened to Coxsackie? How and when did a cornerstone of reform become a conflict-ridden warehouse? The search for answers begins with a look inside the cornerstone sealed by Herbert Lehman on dedication day in 1935.

Reform's End

Coxsackie's cornerstone contains a few newspapers and coins from 1935, a copy of the 1932 legislation that authorized the prison's construction, and quite a bit of ironic history, for it also houses the contents of an older cornerstone—that of the New York House of Refuge. Coxsackie, by any definition a failed reform institution, was a legal successor to the House of Refuge, a far more famous failed reform institution. With the House of Refuge ready to be torn down in 1935, Coxsackie received the old prison's staff, its remaining inmates, a huge collection of case files, an institution bell, and the newspapers and in-denture papers that had been placed in the original cornerstone more than a century earlier.

The New York House of Refuge opened in 1825 as the nation's first juvenile reformatory, quickly gaining fame as the embodiment of the new republic's commitment to managing social disorder.[8] In 1854, the House of Refuge moved from Manhattan to pleasant farmland "far out of town" on Randall's Island facing the Harlem River. The Randall's Island location drew admiring visitors, including Alexis de Tocqueville and Gustave de Beaumont, who made the new "Houses of Refuge" a centerpiece of their argument that America's antisocial were being "saved from infallible ruin, and have changed a life of disorder for one of honesty and order."[9]

A century later, the House of Refuge on Randall's Island was a wreck, physically and functionally. It is astonishing in retrospect that there had been calls to close the House of Refuge as far back as 1873, and that these had sounded with some urgency since the 1880s.[10] By the 1920s, most buildings were part of the original 1854 construction, the dock landings needed to be dredged for fire boats, the coal-conveying belt needed to be replaced, and the motion picture machine dated from 1909. Inmates labored simply to keep the institution from falling apart around them. Despite a plan mapped out in 1917 for emphasizing vocational training over traditional military discipline, the needs of the institution thwarted the practical achievement of that goal. Whether assigned to the masonry class, the tinsmith, the painter, or the carpentry shop, every "student" ended up working on the physical plant.[11] The "class" in steam fitting worked in the boiler and engine rooms twenty-four hours a day, on eight-hour shifts, suggesting something other than dedicated instruction time. For the rest, intensive military drill—including a full hour of full-dress drill each day—was intended to give "a smart carriage to the boys" and to inculcate "habits of neatness and respect for discipline and esprit de corps."[12]

It was a motley collection of boys and young men consigned to the dreary walls of the House of Refuge, seemingly drawn at random from the great mass caught up in the nets of the criminal justice system in New York City. New commitments from the children's courts were older than they had once been, averaging sixteen years old. Nearly 80 percent had been convicted of criminal rather than status offenses, a departure from nineteenth-century patterns, in which criminal convictions were never more than 50 percent of the prisons population.[13] Still, it was hard to say exactly why anyone was sent to the House of Refuge. A study of 251 young offenders in the city shows that just 5 of these were sentenced to Randall's Island: an 11-year-old for stealing pigeons; a 19-year-old for violating parole (his fourth offense); an 18-year-old charged with possession of burglar's tools (his first offense; he was transferred to Elmira Reformatory within months after assaulting a guard in an attempt to escape); a 16-year-old convicted of attempted robbery (his fourth offense); and a 19-year-old convicted of attempted robbery (his sixth offense).[14]

The results of time spent on the island seemed to confirm that the institution was as unsound programmatically as it was structurally. Interviews with adult men in state prisons produced unsettling reminiscences about the House of Refuge: "Bad company and the House of Refuge; that's where I learned to be a real professional thief. I went out of there with the ambition to become a great thief and wound up here with 7 years." From another state prison inmate: "A better name would be deformatories, for unless a youngster has an exceedingly strong character, he is well on the road to the 'Gray Brotherhood'." And further along these lines: "A kiddie learns more wicked things in a year in this institution than he could possibly learn in five years outside."[15]

Despite decades of misery at the island reformatory, its closure was ensured only by a proposal from New York City parks commissioner Robert Moses to turn Randall's Island and nearby Ward's Island into an extensive public park. The East River Islands—Randall's, Ward's, and Blackwell's (also known as Welfare Island)—were first targeted for redevelopment in the Sage Foundations Plan of New York. A 1924 exhibition of the plan in progress drew a circle around the three islands, with a caption: "Within the line live a million people who now can make no use of the islands. Meanwhile most of the unfortunates who crowd the islands probably would be better off elsewhere."[16] Urban planners saw the great appeal of the islands in their being "entirely dissevered from or outside of the close network of the city's traffic-ways. This is their unique quality." This made them desirable locations for a series of parks and recreational facilities, a sentiment reiterated in the 1928 published volume on recreation, which designated Randall's Island as a future "municipal amusement park."[17] Randall's Island also figured into the planning for the proposed Triborough Bridge. Conceived at least as far back as 1916, plans for the Triborough Bridge construction were formally announced in 1927 and included Randall's Island as the central juncture point for the project's series of highways.[18]

In effect, Randall's Island had become too valuable to be "wasted" on the young delinquents who bided their time at the House of Refuge. At the same time, the State of New York was conducting a new round of investigations and inquiries into the operations of the House of Refuge, an institution largely supported by state funds though still run by the same private corporation that had founded the institution more than a century earlier. Governor Al Smith, supported by the state's leading reform organization, the Prison Association of New York, labeled the House of Refuge a failed institution. An investigating committee determined in 1928 that the institution either required closer state control or should no longer be funded by the state. The committee found unsanitary living conditions, classrooms that "would not be tolerated in any public or private school in the state," and work assignments that were "merely supplying the labor that might go to the upkeep of the institution." The report concluded, "It is a disgrace for the sovereign body of the State to acknowledge ownership therein, and the fact that they are confining the youth, whether delinquents, minor criminals or otherwise, in such a place is inexcusable."[19]

When Franklin D. Roosevelt took office as governor in 1929, he reiterated that same position, though he pledged to continue state funding for the House of Refuge until new institutions could be constructed. The next year, Moses's plan to remake the East River Islands was formally given the go-ahead; all public institutions, including the House of Refuge, would be razed to make way for new parks.[20] Boys between the ages of 12 and 15, and therefore subject to the state's juvenile courts, would be sent to a new juvenile reformatory under construction at Warwick. Inmates over 16 would go to what would be the New York State Vocational Institution, for which Roosevelt eventually approved the purchase of seven hundred acres in Greene County.[21]

The venerable institution's final year was one of its worst. With the younger inmates already transferred to Warwick, the older inmates who remained gave full vent to their frustrations and unrest. Tensions reached a critical point on a warm late summer Sat. in 1934, in the worst outbreak of rioting the House of Refuge had ever seen. The inmate baseball team was playing its regular Sat. afternoon game, squaring off against the visiting team of the Seventh District Republican Club. Four guards stood watch over the 365 inmates in the bleachers watching the game. The visiting Republicans took an early 2–0 lead in the game, and they were about to take the field after batting when one inmate stood up and lit a cigarette. A guard approached and ordered the inmate to put the cigarette out. The young man pushed the guard, and within moments dozens of inmates had jumped up from their seats and begun running for the dugouts and the bats. Yelling, waving the bats over their heads, they made a general rush for the south end of the field and the prison gates. A young Italian inmate had somehow procured a key to the gate, and forty-five young men made it through before guards were able to shut it again.

Immediately the institution's alarms started blaring. Running and stumbling, the boys raced through a rough three-quarters of a mile to reach the Bronx Kill River, where they faced only 150 yards of water separating them from the Bronx and freedom. The faster boys made it to the Bronx Kill and jumped in the water. The slower boys never made it to the water and were met by marine police and guards. The marine patrol, brandishing rifles, ordered the boys in the water to swim back. One of the boys yelled to the gun-toting patrol, "Go ahead and shoot," and dove under the surface, but a few warning shots turned most back. The weaker swimmers were held afloat by their friends until police launches could pluck them from the water.

Back at the baseball field, guards launched tear-gas canisters at the remaining rioters and shepherded the frightened visiting team to safety. Superintendent Frederick Helbing waded through the tear gas to personally plead with the rebellious inmates: "Haven't I been square with you?" "Hasn't the food been all right?" Helbing and his chief disciplinary officer were both burned by the tear gas as they made their appeals in the midst of the uprising. Within a short time, most of the young men dropped their makeshift weapons and went back inside, while guards subdued the remaining rioters after a brief struggle.[22]

Although House of Refuge officers and city police had quickly suppressed the riot, and only two inmates actually made good their escape, the events on Randall's Island attracted considerable media attention. As so often happened in such cases, the state sent investigators to the House of Refuge, who quickly concluded that the disciplinary situation was terrible. The investigators, Philip Klein and Leonard W. Mayo, subjected Superintendent Helbing to an extensive questioning, making clear that they found excessive discipline, racial segregation, useless regimentation, and a failing rehabilitative program.[23] Whatever reform luster the House of Refuge may have once enjoyed was a faded and distant memory by the time carloads of inmates and employees began making the trip upstate to Coxsackie. On May 11, 1935, the last fifteen inmates left Randall's Island, leaving behind the shell of an old reform project for the new facility at the center of the state's latest reform project, the New York State Vocational Institution.

Prison Histories

The intertwined histories of the House of Refuge and the New York State Vocational Institution featured early days of great promise and grand ambition, followed by decades of actual practice that obliterated the promise and mocked the ambition. Reform visions of the well-ordered and disciplined prison gave way to disorder, violence, and racism. The gaps between correctional ambitions and prison realities have long been an object of scholarly interest. Reformers themselves, ever conscious of their real-world failings, published some of the earliest and most penetrating studies. The reformist tradition, however, consistently framed failure in terms of *implementation*—attributable to public hostility, baneful political influence, a lack of proper funding, inability of staff to meet appropriate professional standards, corruption, or any number of equally plausible factors.[24]

The most important challenge to the reformist emphasis on implementation gaps appeared in David J. Rothman's landmark 1980 study, *Conscience and Convenience.* Too often, Rothman's pioneering work is lumped together with the work of other revisionist historians of the 1970s, most notably Michel Foucault. This is unfortunate, for it obscures Rothman's distinct—and, for the purposes of this study, important—contributions to the historical study of the prison. *Conscience and Convenience* employed a broad overview of America's twentieth-century

prisons, mental hospitals, and juvenile reformatories to highlight a ghastly record of ineffective operations, inmate mistreatment and neglect, and an utter
failure to live up to the high-minded creeds that had justified their construction. Where Foucault and other revisionists found prisons to be a direct expression of the impulses that underlay their creation, Rothman offered up a far
more ironic history, in which the intentions and self-image of reformers were
wildly distorted in actual experience. Unlike most of his contemporaries,
Rothman was no stranger to the dreadful condition into which an institution of
confinement could degenerate; he had seen more than his fair share of horrors
in his own reform work "in the field" during the 1970s, and he demanded that
historians open their eyes to actual practice, and not just the intellectual evolution of reform.[25]

Having described what he regarded as a nearly universal gap between reformist
creed and institutional deed, Rothman then provided a powerful explanation—
the gap was *not* due to the contingencies of implementation failures that the
reformers themselves saw and bemoaned; the gap was inevitable and built right
into the DNA of institutions themselves. For this explanation, Rothman drew
heavily on sociologist Erving Goffman's conception of the "total institution."
Total institutions, Goffman argued, were uniquely self-enclosed environments
in which all forms of social interactions bent toward the bureaucratic demands
of institutional maintenance. Following this logic, Rothman concluded that no
amount of money, goodwill, or human effort could have remade the prison (or the
reformatory, or the mental hospital) along the lines of the reformist vision, for
the inherent dynamics of institutional confinement would always and inevitably
have defeated reformist intentions. The necessary "convenience" of institutional
administrators trumped the "conscience" of reformers every time.[26]

Conscience and Convenience appeared in the midst of, and reflected, the anti-
institutional politics of the 1970s, but some critics wondered why Rothman paid
any attention to reform creeds at all, given how predictably they appeared to wilt
in the heat of institutional bureaucracy. Andrew Scull, in his review of *Conscience and Convenience,* posed the question most directly: "If so many of these
changes were no more than cosmetic, how can he [Rothman] simultaneously
grant them such revolutionary significance?"[27] It was a good question, and
Rothman's work supplied a plausible answer—reformist "conscience" served as
justification, as a prop, for the assertion and expansion of state power and authority. Despite its real-world failures, creed mattered because it provided a
ready rationale for, and defense of, the institutional confinement of convicted
criminals.

This study affirms and builds on this element of Rothman's argument about the rhetoric of reform.[28] The House of Refuge and the New York State Vocational Institution were able to escape careful scrutiny for many years in no small part because outsiders (legislators, courts, media, and the public) accepted the argument that these places were run by experienced professionals who knew what they were doing, and who did what they did in the best interests of the inmates. The liberal idea of the reformatory wove together some ideas that, from the vantage point of our era of mass incarceration, seem remarkably attractive: the quest to cultivate in prisoners the qualities of civic participation and community membership, and the related view that most young men behind bars possessed those qualities; the emergence of adult education in its various dimensions as an influence on prisons; the identification of youth and adolescence as critical moments of personal development and thus for criminal justice intervention; and a critical stance toward the punitive impulse in criminal justice, and a corresponding privileging of decency and compassion.[29] Taken together, these threads constitute a liberal vision of the prison embedded in the broader universe of efforts to define and cultivate social citizenship.[30]

Liberal reform interests were able to deploy these ideas to assert some measure of control over New York State's prison system. In the wake of a series of prison riots in 1929, reformers used various political resources to embed themselves into the state's correctional bureaucracy and to create and legitimize new expansion and growth. Their successes came at the expense of competing visions of punishment: the punitive model, in which prisoners were made to suffer for their crimes in the name of retribution and deterrence;[31] and the managerial model, where prisoners were pacified, in the name of stable institutional management and secure confinement.[32] But there were spaces within the reformatory, and within the larger prison system (including entire institutions), over which liberal reformers were never able to exert any substantial influence.[33] Liberal corrections remained just one of several political visions, engaged in a constant battle for authority.

Conscience and Convenience made only a limited impression on the subsequent historiography of Western prisons, with scholars drawn to the far neater story of power's expression articulated by Foucault and other revisionists. Histories of the *colonial* prison, on the other hand, were far more attuned to the gulf that separated justificatory rhetoric from actual prison practice. An early, and outstanding, study of the colonial prison, Peter Zinoman's *The Colonial Bastille: A History of Imprisonment in Vietnam, 1862–1940*, made a convincing case that the prison philosophies of metropolitan France were scarcely in evidence in their colonial counterparts. Instead, a confused and corrupt colonial prison administration maintained order through brutal violence in prisons that were "repressive, not corrective."[34]

Histories of the colonial prison, then, strongly affirm Rothman's attention to the distance between rhetoric and practice. In doing so, however, they have developed explanations for that gap that go well beyond Rothman's emphasis on the universal imperatives of institutional convenience. Colonial studies have laid considerably more emphasis on the integration of prison practice with three interrelated aspects of political economy: race and racism, labor control, and the overtly political nature of colonial criminal justice. Zinoman and others have made the case that these dimensions of colonial prison practice distinguished it from metropolitan prison practice.

But just how far does that distinction go? Most colonial historians have contented themselves with asserting the difference between colonial practice and metropolitan *rhetoric* and have rather uncritically assumed the real-world existence of "rational and disciplined" institutions in Europe and the United States.[35] This study argues, in contrast, that the conceptual frameworks of colonial historians are essential for comprehending prison practice generally, including the New York State Vocational Institution. The question of prison labor, for example, remained central to United States prison regimes—and not simply in the South.[36] Likewise, scholars interested in the history of modern mass incarceration in the United States have turned their attention directly to labor exploitation, racism, and politics.[37] We may now finally be realizing a new history of imprisonment in the United States, in which prisons are understood as fields of conflict rather than instruments of order.[38]

Building this new narrative will require close attention to the lives and actions of all those who lived and worked behind bars, whose struggles for influence and survival powerfully shaped the world of the prison.[39] Accounts of correctional policy or politics cannot afford to neglect this level of analysis. At Coxsackie, young men arrived at the reformatory with complex family lives, educational histories, and not infrequently with established institutional and delinquent careers.[40] Their encounter with Coxsackie's extensive educational and vocational programs produced, at best, mixed results for liberal reform. Implementation matters, and no social policies can be fairly evaluated if they are never given a chance to work.[41] Coxsackie's rehabilitative programs often simply foundered on the shoals of internal division, staff conflict, resource shortages, and personnel limitations.

The failures of the New Deal–era reformatories in New York cannot be evaluated solely in terms of program implementation; for the tens of thousands of young men who went through the system, imprisonment left a legacy of racism and brutality. At the Woodbourne Reformatory, Coxsackie's sister institution, an inscription from the Book of Ecclesiasticus (2:4–5) was placed above the mess hall door: "Whatever is brought upon you, take cheerfully and be patient: for gold is tried in the fire, and acceptable men in the furnace of adversity."[42] The furnace of adversity was precisely what the state created by placing young men from all over New York in a social setting as fraught as it was isolated. The reformatory experience was both an ongoing conflict between custodial staff and prisoners and one in which prisoners contested among themselves (often violently) for control of prison space and resources. While reformers spoke of social citizenship, they created a space in which young men were stripped of the most basic legal protections of citizenship and subject to the unbridled powers of the courts and institutional personnel. At its worst moments, Coxsackie replicated the very forms of torture and abuse that the reformers so abhorred.[43]

Like New Deal liberalism generally, reform at Coxsackie spent the postwar years embattled and under siege. The mission to "save" the reformatory produced increasingly desperate efforts to cordon off ungovernable youth into separate spaces within the penal system, and ungovernability itself was increasingly defined by gang membership, heroin use, and racial conflict. As reformers abandoned the idea that every young man could benefit from prison programs, large numbers of young men were removed from the frying pan of Coxsackie into the fire of a new end-of-the-line reformatory at Great Meadow. Great Meadow, in turn, became ground zero for a newly organized prisoner resistance movement. Long before the Attica riot of 1971, the obvious failures of the reformatory system had helped politicize a generation of young men. The roots of the liberal prison crisis, as for liberalism more generally, reach back to the earliest postwar years.

By the end of the 1960s, the reformist structure was in tatters, and by the 1970s, it was gone entirely, replaced in the short term by institutional chaos, and in the longer term by a massive new apparatus of control and mass incarceration. The reformatory and the very concept of rehabilitation were subjected to withering attacks from all ends of the political spectrum, while veterans of Depression-era reform programs increasingly retreated to a rigid and defensive posture that became self-defeating. The collapse of the liberal model of the prison ran parallel to a collapse of the position of the reformers within the prison bureaucracy, as control-oriented interests gained the upper hand within Coxsackie and the New York Department of Corrections. As it brought the story of the reformatory to a close, the new politics of punishment paved the way for the modern era of mass incarceration.

PART ONE

THE RAPID RISE OF PRISON REFORM IN NEW YORK, 1929–1944

CHAPTER ONE

The Reformer's Mural

The Liberal Penal Imagination

Building the New York State Vocational Institution would have been impossible without an underlying reform vision that led the state to embrace educationally oriented prisons as the centerpiece of a correctional strategy aimed at the young male offender. The ideas that informed Coxsackie's construction in 1935 were deeply rooted in progressive-era critiques of the industrial prison, embraced New Deal–era visions of adult education and social citizenship, and rejected punitive and moralistic approaches to crime and punishment. This bold, comprehensive vision has largely been forgotten today, remembered only in the most general terms, as a commitment to the rehabilitation of the criminal offender.

Reconstructing the vision begins with Austin H. MacCormick, for no one meant more to prison reform in New York. His published work provided the intellectual basis for Coxsackie and the entire network of institutions for young male offenders in New York, and he was instrumental in helping reformers navigate their way through the state's complicated political landscape. Little remembered in correctional circles today, MacCormick was among the best-known prison reformers in the United States by the time Coxsackie opened in 1935. Appointed New York City commissioner of corrections by the newly elected mayor Fiorello LaGuardia at the start of 1934, MacCormick received nationwide publicity for his efforts to clean up corruption and prisoner mistreatment in the city's prisons and jails. The epicenter was Welfare Island, site of the city's jail, hospital, reformatory, and other facilities—most notoriously, the Welfare Island Penitentiary. On January 24, 1934, MacCormick led a sensational raid on his own penitentiary, revealing lavish treatment for well-connected gangsters and repellent conditions for the less fortunate. A wave of positive press coverage, including an admiring *New Yorker* profile ("The Four-Eyed Kid") by Arthur Bartlett, gave MacCormick an enviable platform to promote his vision for prisons.[1]

Bringing that vision to life led MacCormick, in the spring of 1934, to meet with muralist Ben Shahn at the still-under-construction Rikers Island Penitentiary. Construction of Rikers under the previous mayoral administration had ground to a halt, and with weeds growing up through the unfinished buildings, MacCormick recognized the chance to use Shahn's work to publicize his reform efforts and speed up the completion of this planned replacement for the decrepit Welfare Island facility.[2] He and Mayor LaGuardia gave Shahn, who just the previous year had played a critical part in the creation of Diego Rivera's ill-fated Rockefeller Center mural, and artist Lou Block permission to produce a mural for Rikers Island, to be funded by the Temporary Emergency Relief Administration (TERA).

If the MacCormick and Shahn made an odd pairing—the slight, stiff prison administrator, son of a Congregational minister from "wholesome but sterile" Maine, and the theatrical social realist, brought to New York City as a child by Jewish-Lithuanian immigrants—they shared a boldness in outlook and action, and a shared commitment to the left-liberal reform program.[3] For Ben Shahn, the project was his most ambitious personal public work to date. Beyond his work with Rivera, Shahn was already well known for his series of twenty-three paintings, *The Passion of Sacco and Vanzetti*. Created during 1931 and 1932, the series blended a powerful indictment of the system that condemned Sacco and Vanzetti to their deaths with a compelling portrait of the two men's humanity.[4] For the Rikers project, Shahn hoped to extend this vision of social justice, conscious as ever of the need to work within a conventional liberal framework. He and Lou Block wrote to Mayor LaGuardia, using language they hoped would appeal to the new city administration: "What we would like to suggest is the possibility of a full realization of reform direction as it affects a convict both in prison and after his release, reacceptance without stigma by society, the opportunity for employment, and a general readjustment calculated to prevent a return to crime."[5] And, indeed, over the course of several meetings between MacCormick and Shahn, the mural became an expression of the reformist vision of prison, present and future.[6]

Once Shahn's proposal was accepted, and funded by TERA, MacCormick gave the artist the freedom to move about the soon-to-be-closed jail complex at Blackwell's Island, taking photographs of inmates and the facility that would be inspiration for the mural to come. For more than a year—from May 1934 to June 1935—Shahn and Block worked on the project plans.[7] Block focused on a series of images to be installed at the new Rikers chapel, while Shahn developed the massive murals that would run along both sides of a 100-foot corridor leading to the chapel. One side of the corridor would feature scenes of "traditional" degradation and violence in punishment, while the other side would employ images highlighting the promise of reform.

Shahn's mural is a roadmap to the liberal penal imagination, with four central themes predominating. The first was an emphasis on social citizenship as the pathway to individual reform and self-improvement, a vision deeply rooted in a progressive-era vision of promoting social citizenship through education.[8] The second was a focus on the idea of adult education, aiding the intellectual, social, and vocational development of the prisoner. A third theme was the problems of youth—particularly the young men ages 16 to 21, caught in a liminal state between the worlds of school and industrial employment. The final element, too often forgotten today, highlighted the powerful reformist critique of punitive punishment. Even as Shahn and MacCormick advanced their own vision for the future of the prison, they were keenly conscious of the competing "get tough" approach to the criminal offender. Taken together, these four threads of the liberal reform vision would inspire substantial programmatic changes in years to come.

Thomas Mott Osborne and Social Citizenship

On the wall above the entrance to the Rikers chapel, in between the two long hallway murals, Shahn proposed to place a large image of the only real person depicted in the project: the late prison reformer Thomas Mott Osborne. Osborne would literally point the way, in the words of Shahn and Block, "toward proper prison methods" that went down one side of the corridor. The choice of Osborne is unsurprising, for he had been an early mentor of, and active collaborator with, Austin MacCormick. Before his death in 1926, Osborne inspired an entire network of younger reformers and prison administrators with his strongly held views regarding the potential for social citizenship to transform the lives of prisoners.

Osborne is best known for his early efforts to promote his vision through the establishment of an inmate self-government organization, the Mutual Welfare League. As a young man, Osborne had become involved in the work of the George Junior Republic, an innovative new private reform school for younger delinquent children, operating on the principle of self-governance. As a trustee of the fledgling institution in 1896, Osborne saw and was deeply impressed by young men (and women) working as an independent community, exercising the self-control he deemed essential to productive citizenship.[9]

In summer 1912, ill and confined to bed, Osborne picked up and read Donald Lowrie's newly published memoir of life behind bars at San Quentin Prison.[10]

The opening of Lowrie's indictment of the prison experience posed a troubling question: "As I look back I wonder what has been accomplished by my imprisonment. Perhaps before this series of sketches is done some of you may discover what has been accomplished in my individual case. But what is being accomplished in the thousands of other and more unconscionable cases?"[11] The answer, it seemed, was a good deal—but nearly all negative.

Osborne's encounter with Lowrie's text set him on the path of full-time prison reformer, on which he would continue until the end of his life. The object of his interest was the one closest at hand, Auburn Prison—the oldest of New York's trio of ancient prisons, which also included Sing Sing and Clinton—in his hometown of Auburn, New York. His opening came with the election of Democrat William Sulzer to the governorship in 1912. In 1913, Osborne first pressed Sulzer to appoint one of his own close political associates, Charles Rattigan, as the warden of Auburn Prison, and then secured an appointment for himself to the State Commission on Prison Reform.

In this role, Osborne famously had himself committed to Auburn Prison as inmate Tom Brown, an account of which was quickly published as *Within Prison Walls: Being a Narrative of Personal Experience During a Week of Voluntary Confinement in the State Prison at Auburn, New York*. Not long after the work's publication, Osborne accepted the wardenship at Auburn for himself. The next year, 1915, he assumed the warden's position at Sing Sing Prison. In both institutions he established a Mutual Welfare League, a program of inmate self-governance based to some extent on the old George Junior Republic model. A master of promotion, Osborne brought Donald Lowrie (who addressed a meeting of the guards and officers) and other reformers to both Auburn and Sing Sing, to review and praise the work he was doing.[12]

Osborne, long an enemy of Tammany Hall, quickly became the target of a campaign to discredit and remove him (Governor Sulzer himself had been impeached by a Tammany-influenced state legislature in 1913, after too many appointments along the lines of Osborne). With a personal style that even his closest allies would have characterized as blunt and impolitic, Osborne also made enemies of local politicians near Sing Sing, who lost their influence over institutional matters, the state prison superintendent in Albany, and certain well-connected Sing Sing inmates. All of this conflict inevitably spilled over, first into the newspapers, where Osborne's experimental regime was constantly being challenged, and then into the courts, where political opponents secured a grand jury investigation in Westchester County. Osborne took leave of the warden's office to wage a legal fight that he ultimately won, but though he professed to relish the battles ("When I'm in a very small minority then I know I'm right"), he resigned the Sing Sing wardenship not long after returning to the job, having served only eighteen months.[13]

The story of Osborne at Sing Sing has been seen as the high-water mark for progressive prison reform, with prisons post-Osborne era featuring the "severing of progressive disciplinary techniques from their higher, moral purpose (of reform)"; by the 1920s, "the goal of social justice would be more or less fully eclipsed by that of institutional stability."[14] Osborne's best-known successor at Sing Sing, Warden Lewis Lawes, has been exhibit A for the emergence of post-progressive prison administration. Lawes's twenty-one year tenure (1920–1941) was predicated on the managerial notion that reform was merely a helpful instrument of control (and that, consequently, "the best prison was one in which the prisoners were well-fed, well-exercised, and frequently entertained").[15]

Osborne's career in prison reform, however, continued for another decade after he departed Sing Sing.[16] During this time, he continued both active work as a prison administrator and typically aggressive efforts to create nationwide organizations that could sustain the campaign for genuine prison reform. In the course of this decade, Osborne would inspire and mentor an impressive network of younger reformers.[17] One so inspired was a Bowdoin undergraduate, Austin MacCormick. MacCormick recalled reading everything that Osborne had written as well as all the newspaper and magazine publicity surrounding his work. This was work, he would later recall, that "aroused my humanitarian impulses." Reflecting on that moment, MacCormick had felt "a desire to crusade—I suppose being small and so on—and I was captivated by this great man and what he was doing."[18] He was moved to write his senior thesis on Osborne's famous work at Sing Sing and his penological ideas, and delivered his commencement address on the same subject.[19] In the audience for the Bowdoin commencement speech was future senator Paul Douglas, himself a Bowdoin graduate, who was then conducting an extensive survey of Maine civic and public institutions. Douglas asked MacCormick to make a survey of Maine jails and the state prison. Consciously emulating Osborne, MacCormick had himself committed anonymously to a Maine prison in order to understand the inmate's predicament firsthand.[20] This led to a well-received report on prison conditions, a report that brought MacCormick to the attention of Osborne himself.

In 1917, Osborne and MacCormick began a period of intense collaboration that would last until Osborne's death in 1926. With the support of his old partner in anti-Tammany politics, assistant secretary of the navy Franklin Roosevelt, Osborne secured from Navy Secretary Josephus Daniels an invitation to investigate conditions prevailing in the U.S. Naval Prison at Portsmouth, New Hampshire.[21] Osborne wrote to "My dear Fellow-criminal" MacCormick and invited him to do "as I did in Auburn and you did in Thomastown . . . The Secretary of the Navy has given me carte blanche; and I should like to have you join me in what I think may turn out to be a very important work."[22] "Tom Brown" and "John Austin" went back to prison (this time posing as navy deserters). They recreated the Mutual Welfare League as the Naval Welfare League at Portsmouth and attempted to introduce it onto several ships (including the USS *North Dakota*, on which MacCormick spent three months in early 1920, under Executive Officer Harold Stark, later chief of naval operations).[23] When Osborne left Portsmouth and the navy in 1920, MacCormick followed shortly thereafter. In 1922, the two men founded the National Society of Penal Information, which, after Osborne's death in 1926, became the Osborne Association.

MacCormick's collaboration with Osborne profoundly shaped his views on prisoners and prisons. The two shared a reform vision predicated on several critical assumptions. First, they consistently argued against any bright-line method of differentiating between the prison population and the adult population more generally. In this respect, Osborne and MacCormick were challenging two distinct perspectives: the popular moralism that we can distinguish between the decent and the depraved individual, and the quasi-medical approach believed to explain criminality by reference to physical and psychological defect. Indeed, they detected that these two points of view had more in common than most suspected, as Frank Tannenbaum had also suggested: " 'Good' may have been translated into 'normal.' And 'evil' may have come to be described as 'abnormal' . . . but the contrast in absolutes still pervades the air of criminological discussion."[24] In place of moral and criminological absolutism, Osborne and MacCormick offered a view that the criminal was "just like us" and "differs less than the layman thinks from the ordinary run of humanity."[25]

The second element of Osborne and MacCormick's shared vision was a strong but tempered faith in individual capacity for self-transformation, aided by education for social citizenship and community membership. Their faith, in other words, drove them to seek out the power of *internal* transformation over external discipline. The less said about criminal past, about the causes of crime, the better. Instead, inmates were regarded as "hungry and eager" for the good to drive out the bad, and to respond to the "right condition and the right appeal."[26] The Mutual Welfare League and the Naval Welfare League were both understood by Osborne less as forms of institutional democracy and more as exercises in (and training for) self-government in the most fundamental sense—self-awareness, self-control, and self-discipline.[27]

In the Osborne-MacCormick worldview, self-mastery had to involve meaningful integration into a larger system of social relations. Of the Mutual Welfare League idea, MacCormick would later write (after Osborne's death), "The primary aim and result of this method of prison organization is to transmute the 'gang' spirit, whose essence is loyalty to the local group, into a spirit of loyalty to the larger group which constitutes the prison community."[28] In this respect, Osborne and MacCormick's work was something of a precursor to later and more comprehensive studies of inmate social systems. Unlike those studies, which tended to describe a fixed and inherent quality to social life within "total institutions," the Osborne-MacCormick view of prison social organization was far more dynamic and socially contingent. Properly organized, the social world of the prison could be a force for positive change.

This element of the Osborne-MacCormick program extended to include social adjustment after release, and the preparation for re-entry into the community. At Portsmouth, they restored an unprecedented number of men to duty. "Men who had been discarded" were able to complete their service and were "saved from the disgrace of a dishonorable discharge."[29] Osborne put it succinctly: "The prison must be made primarily—not a gate of exit, but a gate of re-entrance."[30]

The Education of Adult Prisoners

A trip down the "reform" side of Ben Shahn's Rikers mural revealed many scenes focused on the education of prisoners. A multiracial group of adult inmates were shown in a classroom, seated at traditional school desks, while an instructor and an inmate-student stood at a blackboard. Just beyond the classroom, a pair of inmates laid bricks, while next door other inmates engaged in auto repair work. The auto shop is clearly a vocational training experience, with an instructor and three inmates gathered around a large diagram of an automobile; the instructor, in coat and tie, uses a pointer to explain certain features of the motor.[31] Further down, inmates worked an institutional farm; an early Shahn study for the mural, "Prisoners Milking Cows," presents industrious inmates, alert and upright, focused on various dimensions of industrial milk production, from milking to bottling.[32] There is a sense of productivity and pride in the working figures, a theme played out in most of Shahn's New Deal–era mural projects.[33]

Education was central to MacCormick's conception of the prison; it was both the essential need of every inmate and the highest purpose of the institution. As he famously wrote, society must regard "the prisoner as primarily an adult in need of education and only secondarily as a criminal in need of reform."[34] MacCormick's formal training in the field of education began with the ideas he encountered as a graduate student at Teachers College, Columbia University. There, he came under the dual influences of the two titans of "scientific" educational reform in early twentieth-century America, Edward Thorndike and John Dewey.

From the educational psychologist Edward Thorndike, MacCormick internalized a lifelong commitment to the principle of "individualization," translated into the prison setting as an effort to "diagnose" inmates' needs, desires, and innate capacities in order to provide them with finely calibrated opportunities for learning and rehabilitation. Psychological instruments were a component of diagnosis, though MacCormick's attraction to environmentalist and learning theories limited his full embrace of Thorndike's emphasis on formal testing.[35] Resisting reductionist assessment tools, MacCormick explained that testing results should be seen as indicating something that was "probably true" but should not be understood as indicating anything about the prospects for growth and development. Cultivating human potential, he argued, was "a more complex problem than that of merely determining intelligence and achievement levels by scientific tests."[36]

The other lesson of Thorndike's work was the need to focus educational energies on the things that mattered to students. Thorndike questioned the value of the traditional academic curriculum and was an influential voice in encouraging a vocational orientation to school training. This focus on the practical and the relevant was among the most hotly debated questions at Teachers College. One of the foremost advocates of this practical approach—social efficiency— was David Snedden, who joined the Teachers College faculty the same year that MacCormick arrived as a student.[37] There are some echoes of Thorndike and Snedden in MacCormick's admonition that educators should be on guard for wasting students' time with "useless" or irrelevant subjects, and in his advice to modify educational programs based on the social situation of the student.

From John Dewey, MacCormick absorbed the essentials of the early twentieth-century "progressive education" movement. Two articles of faith in that movement were especially important to MacCormick: first, the pedagogical principle of "learning by doing," and second, the democratic view that "culture," rather than an elite preserve, could and should be made accessible to all because of its inherently life-enhancing, morally uplifting qualities (the Deweyan notion of popularization without vulgarization). Dewey's argument in *Human Nature and Conduct* that a positive line of interest or action was the key to changing behavior—in contrast to one that focused on the bad behavior itself—was entirely consistent with the line of thought that Thomas Mott Osborne had already been encouraging. For MacCormick, as for both Dewey and Osborne, the key to improvement was to find a way of responding or reacting to circumstances and situations that would draw on a person's better instincts.[38]

It may have also been at Teachers College that MacCormick began to think of himself not simply as a professional educator, but as an *adult* educator. This was a distinction with considerable meaning. When MacCormick arrived at Teachers College in 1916, adult education was on the verge of achieving success and recognition as a distinct field. In that year Dewey published *Democracy and Education*, which focused on learning as a process that continued throughout life—the human potential for growth was neither fixed nor finite.[39]

World War I proved a critical turning point for the adult education field. Mass intelligence testing carried out through the army Alpha and Beta IQ tests, devised by Robert Yerkes, electrified the world of adult education. Less well known, but equally important, the military undertook a massive training and education program for its recruits. In just over two years, more than one hundred thousand soldiers went through programs that trained in basic academics and literacy as well as vocational and social subjects. Simultaneously, Congress passed the Smith-Hughes Act, providing funds for vocational training in agriculture that could be used for adult as well as school-age learners.

The twenties were a fertile and exciting period for adult education.[40] The many hundreds of practical experiments included service organizations for labor, like the Workers Education Bureau, and "labor colleges," like the Bryn Mawr Summer School of Women Workers. The former was organized in 1921 to work for social reform and citizenship education.[41] The latter, founded by Hilda Worthington Smith in 1921, was an important innovator in workers' education. The eight-week residential program brought women factory workers to the campus each year for intensive classes. (Smith self-consciously borrowed Osborne's ideas regarding self-governance for the school as part of teaching the skills of democratic participation.)[42] These and similar programs coupled a goal of personal transformation with an ambition that students become agents of broader social change.[43]

The Carnegie Corporation emerged as the center for funding and support of adult education research. In 1923, Frederick Keppel began serving as president of the corporation and brought with him an eager interest in expanding the foundation's work in adult education. He was acquainted with the Workers Education Bureau (for which the Carnegie Corporation would come to provide substantial support) and had some association with the World War I army education programs as third assistant secretary of war.[44] Carnegie money helped start the American Association for Adult Education (AAAE).[45] Its executive secretary, Morse Cartwright, had been Keppel's administrative assistant at the Carnegie Corporation. Cartwright was a firm supporter of what he called the "live and learn" model of education, in which educational programming was linked in a direct way to the lives of students. The substantive goal was to assist adults in various settings to adjust themselves to life in a modern democracy.

Carnegie/AAAE investments supported a wave of empirical research and investigation. Perhaps the best-known fruit of that effort was Edward Thorndike's *Adult Learning* (1928), which utterly demolished the popular notion that adults could not be taught as effectively as children. Some of Thorndike's research had been conducted with inmates at Sing Sing prison, and the study deeply impressed MacCormick. "It is safe to consider," MacCormick wrote, "the older prisoner, as well as the younger, a prospective student." The Carnegie/AAAE modus operandi was to fund experimental programs in a wide range of settings and demonstration projects, and this support produced a series of important studies.[46]

Along these lines, the AAAE recommended to the Carnegie Corporation that a grant be made to Austin MacCormick, so that he might conduct a survey of educational and library programs in the nation's prisons and reformatories. The AAAE intended that MacCormick's survey generate not merely descriptive detail, but practical and specific recommendations for institutional administrators. The grant sent MacCormick on a grueling ten-month tour of the United States, from November 1927 to August 1928, during which time he visited approximately 110 penal institutions. He submitted his final report to Carnegie/AAAE in 1929 and eventually published the study as *The Education of Adult Prisoners*.[47]

The first conclusion of the book was that there was little, if anything, that qualified as decent educational programming in U.S. prisons. In the spatial and social geography of the prison, education was an entirely marginal activity. Few prisons had adequate space for it, and many had none at all. Educational materials were outdated, of poor quality, or inappropriate for adult learners. As for staff: "The teacher is the chaplain, an underpaid guard, a city school-teacher who has already done a hard day's work in his own school, or an inmate who got the job because he has somewhat more education than his fellows."[48] Educational programs bore the "stamp of unimportance and mediocrity."[49] And these were the *average* practices. The worst situations MacCormick encountered, he found almost tragically bad for prisoners.

The Education of Adult Prisoners took a broad view of the potential pool of educable prisoners. In general, the book spent little time on the causes of crime. MacCormick allowed that there was "a direct correlation between vocational incompetence and crime," but he contended that this incompetence was only one dimension in a larger environment of poverty.[50] Whatever deficits prisoners had were common to the communities from which they came. MacCormick acknowledged that inmates were an "especially unpromising" group of potential students, but he felt certain that the prison experience could open inmates up to the possibilities of education and self-improvement. Giving students some knowledge of "what lies beyond the horizon" was fundamental education, MacCormick argued, and practicable for educated prisoners as well as those "of very limited education."[51]

The book gave MacCormick the opportunity to integrate the diverse strands of educational thought into his own coherent vision of what education should be. He straddled the theoretical divide between those who wanted adult education to be purely practical and vocational (the social efficiency model) and those who embraced the less tangible values of classical education and personal enrichment. Toward the latter, MacCormick argued that adult education should eschew a narrowly utilitarian approach. He cited with approval the Danish folk schools' orientation away from pursuing narrow technical competencies: "The Danish farmer reads the literature of his country and studies philosophy with no idea that they will increase the productivity of his farm."[52] In any event, MacCormick pointed out, a strictly utilitarian approach would fail prisoners, since so few of them had a specific direction (vocational or otherwise).[53] The larger and more fundamental project was to extend educational opportunity to prisoners, "that they may thereby be fitted to live more competently, satisfyingly and cooperatively as members of society."[54]

But *The Education of Adult Prisoners* also championed the practical and the relevant for prisoner education: "The curriculum of fundamentals must be cut down until everything that remains has real significance for the prisoner." The inmate "has the right not to be interested" in the parts of speech or the number of soldiers at the Battle of Gettysburg. Instead, basic education should be linked in every instance to the inmate's interests.[55] The same pragmatism informed MacCormick's approach to vocational education, which, he argued, should not be about skills alone, but should address the larger questions of "steady jobs, regular pay, homes, families, and economic stability."[56] *The Education of Adult Prisoners* displayed an aversion to external discipline and habit. These had been hallmarks of New York State policy: one committee praised the "moral advantage of the machine" and urged that the task itself become the boss, while another pronounced of the prisoner that "it seems obvious that the best way to fit him for hard work outside is to give him hard work inside."[57]

MacCormick condemned the "social losses" that came from the quest for productive prison industries. These, he argued, utterly failed to "fit men for free life." His criticisms were consistent with the conclusions (if not the reasoning) of the broad-based movement away from profit-making prison industry and agriculture. In place of prison factories and farms and their rigid systems of habitual labor, he hoped would emerge a broadly educational approach to work.[58] "Only when the individual knows what his proper relation to the social order is and wishes to assume it," wrote MacCormick, would the prisoner become fully socialized and achieve "conformity with understanding." Linking the inmate mentally and morally to the body politic was essential to counteract attitudes that most prisoners had internalized since childhood. MacCormick observed that most prisoners were non-social rather than anti-social, rarely aggressive and plotting when it came to criminality.[59] Social education could replace mechanical obedience with self-help and community engagement.[60]

At the intersection of MacCormick's educational philosophy and his work with Osborne, we find the essence of his vision of rehabilitation—willing conformity, based not on subordination in a power relation, but on an understanding of self and society.[61] The importance of this vision helps explain why MacCormick (and Osborne) opposed Lewis Lawes' managerial prison at Sing Sing, for there, they felt, "the general emphasis is on making good prisoners, rather than good citizens."[62] Rehabilitation of prisoners took place in the largely hidden world of motivation and inspiration—where the critical question was not whether, but *how* and *why* a man would be moved to change the conduct of his life, "to feel dissatisfaction with his former mode of living."[63]

And Now, Youth!

Ben's Shahn was given permission to roam about the old penitentiary at Welfare Island, as well as the newer New York City Reformatory in New Hampton, to take photographs of prisoners for use in developing the studies for his mural.[64] Shahn's photographs highlighted the difference between the older Welfare Island institution and the apparently more promising reformatory; photos from the latter institution feature a clear visual emphasis on the vitality and promise of youth. Shahn scholar Deborah Martin Kao observes that the photos show him "sympathetically allied" with the young men in these photographs—young men "not to be feared but regarded as rebellious adolescents."[65] Shahn's focus on youth was consistent with MacCormick's own observation, that "the problem of the prison, as of crime in general, is a problem of youth."[66]

Of course, the problem of the younger prisoner was hardly a discovery of New Deal–era New Yorkers. The reformatory movement of the nineteenth century had first brought attention to the problems of the young first-time offender, and the juvenile court movement had focused attention on the judicial handling of delinquent and incorrigible children. But a newer element in the reformist language of the 1930s was the growing focus on "youth" or "adolescence" as a formally defined period of transition between childhood and adulthood, and to use this period as a meaningful concept in criminal justice practice. The problem of the adolescent in the thirties was largely defined by the growing gap between the end of formal schooling and the start of full-time productive labor, a concern made more pressing with each passing year of the Great Depression. Efforts to bridge this period of enforced idleness gave rise to two significant New Deal programs, the Civilian Conservation Corps (CCC) and the National Youth Administration (NYA), both of which focused on the problem of employment for adolescents *after* they left public schooling. The American Youth Commission, organized by the American Council on Education in 1935 to consider the needs of youth (defined as between the ages of 16 and 24), concluded, "All aspects of a healthy transition from youth to adult life depended" on successful employment and work experiences following school.[67]

MacCormick would come to embrace the CCC model and the transformative power of work experiences. He observed that CCC youth "didn't want to go at first, they were pretty pale when they went, they didn't look much like workers, but when they came back they had esprit de corps, their muscles had begun to develop, they stood up straight, they were brown and a great many of them weathered some terrible years in which they would have otherwise got into trouble." For MacCormick, the CCC was one model of what the state could do to fill the gap between youth and adulthood.[68]

In 1936, MacCormick partnered with the Osborne Association in developing a vocational demonstration project, for the purpose of placing young prisoners "in worth-while jobs, preferably on the basis of their interests and their training."[69] He recruited Viola Ilma, former head of the American Youth Congress and author of *And Now, Youth!*, to direct the demonstration.[70] But the problem of enforced idleness was not simply a concern *after* release, but a condition of confinement as well. Here, the problem of youth idleness was linked to the more general problems of prisoner idleness related to the long campaign against for-profit prison industries. For the reformers, the lack of productive labor produced a throwback to retrograde conditions.[71] MacCormick seconded the criticism, writing that "nothing has been more harmful and shameful in our recent penal history than the idleness in our prisons for all age groups . . . the young prisoner, particularly, needs to have his day full to the brim with work and training, balanced by recreation and a variety of character-building activities that use up his energies to the limit."[72]

The push for engaging the energies of the delinquent adolescent was coupled with an important, though little-remembered, effort to extend the concept of the juvenile court upward into the realm of the adolescent offender.[73] Harry M. Shulman's 1931 study of the sixteen-to-twenty-year-old offender in New York City bluntly stated that it was "without logical or scientific foundation" to handle young men in this age range in the same fashion as adult offenders.[74] MacCormick summarized the argument in favor of such an arrangement:

> Too many youths who should be given probation are committed to an institution for punitive reasons, while youths who require institutional training are put on probation as an act of misguided leniency . . . The surest way to reduce the margin of error is by a thorough presentence investigation. This should not only include complete information on the current offense and the offender's previous criminal record, but also his family history, his personal history and community background, pertinent data from medical, psychiatric and psychological examinations, and so forth. The judge should give careful consideration to all this material before passing sentence.[75]

Without a coherent process, MacCormick argued, "the hapless delinquent is passed from one to another like lumber through various processing plants. Almost inevitably the mass-produced end result proves a perverse failure, for unfortunately the delinquent boy is not lumber."[76] The cure for mass processing was to embrace the individualized model of the juvenile court and dispense with the patterns of routine characteristic of the criminal courts.

Against Cruelty: Machine-Gun Criminology and the Conditions of Confinement

Not long after Ben Shahn and Austin MacCormick began discussing the Rikers Island mural, Shahn abandoned the original concept for the mural, which would have emphasized more broadly historical developments in the history of penology. Instead, the focus became quite contemporary. Shahn and Block argued to LaGuardia, "The murals would have more force" if they examined only "prisons of our own time." As a consequence, the "archaic" side of the Rikers mural, the one featuring scenes of retrograde punishment and inhumanity, was drawn not from scenes of ancient ritual or obviously bygone moments, but from present-day conditions.[77] Shahn gave a sharply political edge to these observations, consistent with his previous explorations at the intersections of social injustice and the criminal justice system (in the Sacco and Vanzetti series, and his series on imprisoned labor leader Tom Mooney). His notes on the Rikers project show him deeply immersed in contemporary criticism of criminal justice, including John Spivak's devastating 1932 account of the Georgia chain gangs, *Georgia Nigger*; the 1932 Warner Brothers film *I Am a Fugitive from a Chain Gang;* and the memoir of the same year, on which it was based, *I Am a Fugitive from a Georgia Chain Gang*. Shahn also maintained a file of images related to the notorious Scottsboro case, for which retrials were still ongoing.[78]

The final rendering of the mural reflects Shahn's immersion in the causes of social justice. In the center of the north end of the mural, between the two long hallways, two prisoners appear in a lineup. Standing somberly in front of an institutional setting, bundled up in overcoats and visibly handcuffed together, they appear to have been taken directly from similar images of Sacco and Vanzetti that Shahn had prepared a few years earlier.[79] Just outside the lineup scene, homeless men sleep on newspapers with screaming crime-related headlines partially visible, and a line of unemployed men confront a "No Help Wanted" sign—all ironically juxtaposed against the Centre Street courthouse and the words along its façade, "The True Administration of Justice is the Firmest Pillar of Good."[80]

The mural echoed the manner in which reformers defined the harms of punishment in terms of both body and mind. There were scenes focused on the mistreatment of the body: images of southern chain gangs (in front of what sharp-eyed observers would have recognized as the Morgan County Circuit Courthouse in Alabama, site of the ongoing Scottsboro trials), poor prison conditions, and even Delaware's whipping post (known as Red Hannah, a potent symbol of the forms of corporal punishment still extant). Scenes of mental suffering appeared throughout—images of hopelessness, overcrowding, and idleness. In a preliminary sketch, "Prisoners in Bed," Shahn showed an endless row of inmates packed together in dormitory bunks, restless, disturbed, their individual differences washed out by the setting.[81] The program for his final sketches listed the scenes: "idleness and the milling about of prisoners," "dreary, unproductive labor," and "overcrowded dormitories."[82] All scenes seem to consciously echo what MacCormick called "Paregoric Penology": "As long as these institutions were kept nice and quiet, with the prisoners drifting in half or total idleness through the day and locked snugly in their cells at 5:00 p.m. for 14 hours, their wardens were perfectly willing that the prisoners deteriorated like vegetables rotting in a bin."[83] The wall ended with a strong intimation of a revolving-door criminal justice system, with lines of released inmates queuing first at an employment station, then into jail.

Shahn's mural perfectly captured the prevailing sense within reform circles in 1934 that tremendous abuses and cruelties remained within the American prison system.[84] Frank Tannenbaum put it most forcefully: "Imprisonment is negative. It takes all. It gives nothing. It takes from the prisoners every interest, every ambition, every hope; it cuts away, with a coarse disregard for personality, all that a man did or loved, all his work and his contacts, and gives nothing in return."[85] And few reformers had seen more than Austin MacCormick. Since the early 1920s, MacCormick had traveled throughout the United States making prison inspections under the auspices of the National Society of Penal Information (NSPI), the organization Osborne has founded in 1922, following a nationwide speaking tour on which he raised funds for the new enterprise. The purpose behind the NSPI was to conduct systematic surveys of prisons and prison conditions, much like other privately funded surveys were doing with other dimensions of the criminal justice system.[86] These surveys would, in turn, provide a basis for pressuring states to reform prisons where reforms were needed, and to give an accounting of best practices and standards to follow.[87]

The NSPI surveys (eventually organized and published as the *Handbook of American Prisons*, the first edition of which appeared in 1926) exposed horrific conditions. Frank Tannenbaum made some of the first NSPI-sponsored visits to southern prisons, prison farms, and road camps. He incorporated some of these experiences into *Darker Phases of the South* (1924), where he asked the reader to "believe the unbelievable" regarding the conditions of confinement.[88] MacCormick reported from Mississippi that conditions were "very primitive" and that the dormitories were "like the holds of slaveships . . . what goes on in there better not come out in the light of day." In addition to ghastly conditions of confinement, NSPI surveys helped demonstrate that torture continued to be commonplace in southern prison systems, including the use of the strap ("fastened to a short handle so that some of the clever boys can make it come down edgewise"), stocks, sweatboxes, and similar instruments of abuse.[89]

Even as the NSPI exposed the brutality of punishment in the South, the surveyors cautioned readers against "the delusion that the rest of the country is so much better."[90] Throughout much of the United States, the same conditions of confinement that had inspired progressive-era indictments by Donald Lowrie, Kate Richards O'Hare, and others remained stubbornly resistant to change by the early 1930s. The Wickersham Commission's investigation of prison conditions, published in 1931, revealed many appalling practices.[91] To his colleagues in 1933, MacCormick observed that many "rotten old penitentiaries" deserved to be "turned over."[92]

MacCormick and fellow reformers tried to explain the consequences of brutality and torture. Their writings harkened back to Donald Lowrie's progressive-era declaration: "You cannot make a saint out of a man by confining him in a church, but you can make a devil out of him by treating him like hell . . . fear has no legitimate place in the training of men."[93] The mechanisms of imprisonment generated cruelty, even evil, all in the name of virtue and under sanction of the state. The personal transformations it produced were damaging for both the keeper and the kept, "the sufferer and the perpetrator both being unfortunate souls caught in a vortex of passion and hate that drives them to madness and brutality."[94]

In Portsmouth, MacCormick had encountered a prison overcrowded with wartime inmates, forced to house more than half of its men in wooden barracks, guarded largely by other inmates. Touring confinement facilities at California's Mare Island Naval Shipyard with Captain Clark Stearns (an ally of Osborne's), MacCormick observed the men being treated "like dogs" in isolation cells called "coke-ovens."[95] Locking up a man for twenty hours a day, MacCormick would later write, "puts an intolerable strain on the physical and mental health of every man so confined."[96] The "vicious phases of Naval discipline," disgusted MacCormick, who wrote to Osborne from Guantanamo Bay, describing a scene in which a boatswain's mate had been convicted of breaking and entering and was being led off the ship: "We were all kept aft while he marched across the deck under guard and went into the boat which started him on his way to prison. It was all very dramatic and very stupid and very ineffectual and unspeakably cruel."[97]

Even as MacCormick and others attacked the cruelty and waste of punitive imprisonment, they firmly believed that these conditions derived *not* from any universal quality of the prison, but from case-by-case decision making. By implication, the mitigation of cruelty was also a matter for case-by-case intervention and control. There was no inherent defect in prisons, nor any inevitably positive quality. The 1929 NSPI survey put it this way: "It is too sweeping a statement to say that American penal institutions are steadily getting better . . . Waves of public opinion, caused by general excitement over crime or by some bit of local scandal or maladministration, cause temporary changes for better or worse." It was therefore true, MacCormick argued, that "an institution might be a fine place in 1930 and a bad place in 1935; or it may be a bad place in 1932 and a good one in 1937."[98]

Conditions could not be changed by good intentions alone, but good intentions backed with political influence could defeat punitive interests. The critics of reform presented a formidable obstacle to changing prisons, as they had for Thomas Mott Osborne. MacCormick reflected on his mentor, "The prison field does not . . . attract his like, except in rare instances. When it does, it often crucifies them."[99] The navy had been MacCormick's most personal lesson in the politics of punishment. Although he and Osborne enjoyed the patronage of Navy Secretary Daniels and Assistant Secretary Roosevelt, they suffered from officers' resentment of the "soft" treatment being meted out at Portsmouth. Near the end of their navy work, MacCormick warned Osborne of the animosity he and Daniels would face: "I can't impress upon you too strongly how great and widespread the hostility to you is among officers. It is partly because of the way in which they despise the Secretary. There is no other way of describing their attitude toward him. He is accorded the same respect that Emma Goldman and Berkman get when their names come into a consideration—no more."[100] Captain Joseph K. Taussig, former navy director of personnel, unleashed a series of violent attacks on Osborne and MacCormick in the *Army and Navy Journal*, precipitating a lengthy and public battle pitting Daniels and Roosevelt against the navy brass and the Republican press.[101] Under pressure, Osborne and MacCormick resigned in early 1920; the next year President Warren G. Harding's newly appointed navy secretary systematically purged the remaining elements of Osborne's reforms.[102]

MacCormick spent much of 1924 helping Osborne and Colorado governor William Sweet remove Warden Thomas J. "Golden Rule" Tynan, in what MacCormick later recalled as "one of the most exciting and dangerous experiences I ever had in my life."[103] Replying to Osborne's invitation to survey Colorado, MacCormick replied: "You bet I will go. Thrilled to pieces."[104] "Hopelessly rusty on prison work," MacCormick saw Colorado as "a great chance to get back in the traces." The initial survey found Tynan's prison to be in bad shape, a mix of equal parts torture and corruption.[105]

The battle engaged, Osborne warned Governor Sweet that those who fought "crooked politics" confronted two essential problems: "the utter unscrupulousness of his opponents, and second, the ignorance and indifference of right-minded people." When the State Board of Corrections failed to act on the survey, Sweet brought charges before the Civil Service Commission (for which MacCormick returned to testify). At one point, Governor Sweet (strongly anti-Klan in a state where Ku Klux Klan activity was near a peak in 1924) arranged a secret meeting between himself, Osborne, MacCormick, and the prison chaplain (who also happened to be the local Klan leader).[106] They persuaded the chaplain to permit Klan members (virtually the entire guard force) to testify at the hearing against Tynan.

The weakness of the reform position in the state meant that neither Osborne nor MacCormick was willing to take an administrative position and "serve under a bunch of low-down trimmers like that prison commission." MacCormick wrote to Osborne: "I am not a combined Napoleon and Caesar. I would be badly handicapped, as you would, in a state where we could not use a lot of people whom we know and trust. Out there we would have to go it blind."[107] Still, MacCormick observed to Osborne, "We certainly kicked over the milk pail. If Tynan has time enough he will prove every charge we made against him." In the end, Tynan outlasted Sweet, but not for long—he was ousted in 1927 (though not until attracting national attention by barricading himself behind machine guns to prevent legal papers being served).[108]

Reformers like MacCormick took an expansive view of prison politics, understanding that it included national, state, and local politics as well as prison administration and staff. Reform politics could not afford to stop at the prison gate. While MacCormick was at the Bureau of Prisons, the bureau established the United States Training School for Prison Officers, based at the Federal Detention Headquarters in New York City; according to its director, "The School is not only informative in the essentials of prison management, but is also a test period to weed out inferior characters whose service in an institution would be hazardous to the organization." The school eliminated one of every six would-be officers who arrived during its first two years.

Reformers were also forced to confront their opponents' powerful rhetoric in public debates over punishment—what MacCormick once referred to as the "machine-gun school of criminology."[109] One of the foremost proponents of that school, FBI Director J. Edgar Hoover, assailed the advocates of parole and rehabilitation as the "cream puff" school of criminology, whose views "daily turn loose upon us the robber, the burglar, the arsonist, the killer, and the sex degenerate."[110] MacCormick was in attendance for a speech in which Hoover assailed "sob sister wardens, country club prisons, and convict coddlers"; MacCormick later lamented to a meeting of the American Prison Association that he "had to sit within six feet of the speaker and didn't have a gun on me."[111]

Years earlier, Donald Lowrie had observed that, as soon as he began making his public criticisms of the prison, he had been accused of "sentimental twaddle," "maudlin hysteria," and "lackadaisical neurasthenia"—all suggesting a lack of true manhood.[112] Prison reformers were often attacked on the basis of their supposed homosexuality or sexual practices. This had certainly been true of Osborne, at whose 1916 trial Assistant District Attorney William Fallon proclaimed: "We have numberless affidavits, testimony that we have not introduced, that shows this man to be the worst kind of degenerate."[113] MacCormick knew that these charges had "hurt his [Osborne's] work immeasurably" and "could never have been given color if it were not for his decent and effective way of handling perverts as he encountered them in prison. He did not side-step the issue and paid for his honesty and courage with his reputation."[114]

The fate of the Rikers mural gave Austin MacCormick and Ben Shahn one more powerful example of prison politics. By early 1935, Shahn had completed his sketches and presented them to MacCormick and LaGuardia. By all accounts, the two men were well pleased with what they saw; both stopped by Shahn's Bethune Street studio to offer their personal congratulations on a job well done. As publicly funded art, however, the mural sketches still required the approval of the Municipal Art Commission, and here they ran into serious trouble. The commission, which had the previous year rejected a series of public murals from Shahn on the subject of Prohibition, now attacked the Rikers reform mural. They rejected the design, with its review of harsh punishments, as too disconcerting to prisoner sensibilities.[115] Among art historians, the commission's decision has been cast as an act of aesthetic conservatism against challenging modern public art ("lugubrious and unpleasant to look upon"), which it certainly was, but the rejection of Shahn's mural was also explicitly about the politics of prison reform. The commission branded the proposed mural as "antisocial propaganda."[116] Jonas Lie, painter and member of the commission, argued that it would "incite prison inmates to further an anti-social attitude" and to "increase their opposition to law and order."[117]

The art world bitterly protested the actions of the Municipal Art Commission. Audrey McMahon defended the mural sketches as "works of high artistic merit."[118] *New York Times* art writer Edward Alden Jewell praised the mural's depiction of a "New Deal in prison life."[119] Stuart Davis, in *Art Front* magazine, famously attacked commission member Jonas Lie: "We suggest that while the Commission was thinking along the lines of 'psychological unfitness,' it might have done well to look at its own painter member. For, wherever particularly stupid and reactionary acts are committed in regard to art matters, one seldom has to look far to find the person of [Lie] . . . Jonas Lie has proved himself unfit to hold a seat on the Municipal Art Commission, or to hold any public office, for that matter, outside that of a Fascist Censor."[120]

MacCormick and LaGuardia tried to help Shahn fight back against the Municipal Art Commission. Following the commission's preliminary rejection of the plans, in February, MacCormick went to so far as to persuade his friend and colleague, the psychologist Harry Shulman, to conduct a remarkable study of inmate reactions to the proposed mural. Forty inmates were selected and shown some of Shahn's drawings. They were then given a questionnaire that began: "Here is a set of pictures showing the good and bad sides of prison life. The small ones are sketches and the large ones will give you an idea of how it will look on the wall. This is planned for a mural in one of the halls of a brand-new and modern prison building. The artist would like to know what you think of these pictures." Inmates were also asked how they felt about having a mural on the walls of a prison, what they thought other prisoners might think of such a mural, and whether visitors to the prison would have any interest in them. The four questions for the forty inmates produced a total of 160 question responses. Shulman reported to MacCormick that out of a possible 160 answers, 97 were favorable, 10 unfavorable, 22 indifferent, and 31 left blank. The positive responses were encouraging: "They will certainly brighten the place up a bit and also give the inmates something to concentrate on besides the walls."[121]

LaGuardia and MacCormick offered the survey results to the Municipal Art Commission as evidence that the murals would not be overly disturbing to the inmates, but the commission remained unmoved. In its formal decision in May, the murals were definitely and finally rejected. At this point, LaGuardia and MacCormick gave in to the commission, formally abandoning the project. Theirs was a shocking decision for Shahn and his supporters, and there is no clear explanation for this reversal of course. MacCormick gave a statement to the press in which he lamely attempted to explain his new reasoning: "Although a number of prisoners submitted written opinions that were favorable to the sketches, we found afterwards that many of them expressed approval because they thought they were expected to do so."[122]

Disgusted at the politics of public art in New York, Ben Shahn left both the city and the prison project behind. It was never carried out. Shahn and Block briefly attempted to resurrect the mural by bringing it to one of the state prisons, but this seems not to have progressed very far.[123] The panels that composed the mural study were sold by weight as scrap—not until they were reconstructed for a 1999 exhibition would the full vision of the project be presented to the public. As for MacCormick, he had once confided to Osborne that he was sometimes "disgusted" with the "infernal muddle into which prison affairs seem to work themselves if anyone tries to do anything to change the status quo."[124] The killing of the Rikers Island mural had proved this yet again. Still, he remained firmly convinced that reformers needed to be ready to seize political opportunities when they presented themselves.[125]

Despite the failure to realize the mural, Shahn's collaboration with MacCormick produced a powerful distillation of the liberal reform vision. Rooted in educational theory, it deeply affirmed the citizenship of the offender in custody, strongly condemned physical and mental cruelty, and linked prison reform to political action. The mural's ultimate fate, of course, was a cautionary tale, reminding would-be reformers that regressive politics still had much to say about the manner in which prisoners would be kept. While MacCormick had engaged these political skirmishes in New York City, he had been aiding the opening of another front in the battle for reform, this one in the prison system of New York State.

CHAPTER TWO

A New Deal for Prisons

The Politics of Reform in New York

Austin MacCormick liked to tell stories from the time he spent as a young member of the Boothbay Harbor volunteer fire department, entertaining audiences with tales of the ways in which the small-town firefighters used to attract notice. "We first chop a hole in the roof," he explained, "and then someone kicks in a cellar window. This provides sufficient draft to make the blaze worthy of our attention." Prison politics, MacCormick found, worked in much the same way. Without a blaze worthy of public attention, it was prone to inattention and drift. In his experience, there were no bigger blazes—or what policy scholars term "focusing events"—than prison riots.[1] On a bitterly cold morning in December 1929, inmates of Auburn Prison launched a violent uprising, one that would give reformers the political opportunity they needed to initiate an ambitious restructuring of the correctional system for the adolescent male offender.

That the Auburn riots would be a political tipping point for reform interests in New York was not immediately obvious, nor is it self-evident in retrospect. The decade of the twenties had featured a rapid expansion of punitive crime-control policy, as popular sentiment and political expediency led New York to "get tough" with criminal offenders. Prison riots the previous summer at both Auburn and Clinton prisons had produced only a hesitant, unfocused response from Governor Franklin Roosevelt and the legislature. But the December riot shifted momentum in the public debate and provided an opening for the educational reformers. Roosevelt and Lieutenant Governor Herbert Lehman placed the direction of correctional reform in the hands of two successive commissions, both of which embraced a focus on reformatory construction and educational programming.

The consequences of Roosevelt and Lehman's choice were real. New York constructed several new prisons—including Coxsackie—as the basis of a distinct system for young male offenders, designed to deliver an ambitious program of education and vocational training. Inspired by Austin MacCormick's work, correctional educators assumed critical administrative roles in the new prisons. They also established an administrative beachhead—the new Division of Education—within the Department of Corrections, from which they would dominate rehabilitative programming for the next thirty-five years. From within the prison bureaucracy, they advanced a range of ambitious plans to infuse reformist ideas throughout the prisons, including creating one of the nation's earliest and most comprehensive prison guard training schools. And, finally, reformers succeeded in wresting from the criminal courts the control of institutional assignment, through the Youthful Offender Act and the creation of the Elmira Reception Center.

Coxsackie and the larger system for adolescent male offenders were fundamentally products of this reform moment. In effect, a rehabilitative regime assumed control over significant parts of the prison system and helped legitimate an impressive expansion of the correctional bureaucracy and infrastructure.[2] The reformers' victory was far from complete, however; they remained largely frozen out of the state's "big house" prisons, and substantial elements of the reform program were never realized or were short-lived. But Coxsackie was, to a great extent, the realization of their ambitions. To judge what Coxsackie became in practice, one must return, first, to the moment of its creation.

The Pot Boils Over: The Auburn Prison Riot and Its Aftermath

The inmates of Auburn Prison awoke, on the morning of December 11, 1929, to weather that was bitterly cold, even by the standards of upstate New York. Despite the deep freeze outside, tensions inside the old state prison had reached a boiling point. All three maximum-security facilities for adult male offenders (the other two were Sing-Sing and Clinton) were experiencing varying degrees of crisis in prison management. The warden of Clinton Prison was shockingly blunt in his annual report at the end of 1928, warning the State that it was not a matter of if, but when, his prison would face a riot: "When the inevitable trouble does come, we will be prepared and trust that, with the aid of the machine guns, cyclone fences, etc., we will be able to handle the situation in a satisfactory manner."[3] The predicted violence broke out in July, with a significant prisoner uprising at Clinton.[4] Within a week, inmates at Auburn Prison staged their own uprising. Learning of the destruction at Clinton through the prisoner grapevine, Auburn's inmates did their best to recapitulate the effort, before their eventual surrender in the face of gathering forces of well-armed state troopers and national guardsmen.[5] The rioters were placed in segregated cells at Auburn following the July riot; from among this same group, the uprising of December 11, 1929, would begin.

The wardens of Clinton, Auburn, and Sing Sing agreed, the crisis of prison administration had been brought on by two factors. The first was the complicated question of prison labor. Since the end of contract labor in New York State in the 1890s, the need to keep inmates busy and at work had been the central problem of administrators and would-be reformers.[6] At Sing Sing, the highly idiosyncratic Warden Lewis Lawes had embraced "penal managerialism," with a highly structured set of inmate privileges and rackets that were anathema to Austin MacCormick and like-minded prison reformers who as yet remained on the sidelines of state politics.[7] Clinton and Auburn prisons were only lightly touched by Lawes's managerial approach. Inmates languished in these large-scale disciplinary institutions, little expected but obedience to institutional rules, and little offered but strict discipline. The industrial labor regimes of years past had faded, leaving large numbers of idle prisoners with little more than resentment to fill their days.

Overcrowding was the second critical management problem facing New York prisons in 1929, and every warden could agree on the cause—more and longer prison sentences imposed by the courts under the so-called Baumes Laws passed by the state legislature. The Baumes Laws were named for Caleb Baumes, under whose leadership the New York Crime Commission had initiated a raft of highly popular "get tough" policies between 1926 and 1928. Most focused on ending the "breaks" that offenders supposedly got from the criminal justice system: convictions not appealed within thirty days would become irreversible; limitations were set on bail; and a provision was made for smaller and non-unanimous criminal juries. Above all, the commission successfully pushed for stricter sentencing, such as large increases in the mandatory sentences for burglary and armed robbery, and the most famous of the Baumes Laws—the "fourth strike" mandatory life sentence provision.[8]

The philosophical principle behind the Baumes Laws was simple and well described by one district attorney: "The only cure for crime is the cure for sin. Crime is a concrete manifestation of sin." The only logical response to criminal conduct was efficient arrests, prompt detention, immediate trials, successful prosecutions, and the imposition of a harsh sentence. Criminals, as more than one commentator explained, should be "put away and put away for good."[9] The Crime Commission itself praised the good effect the new laws were having, observing that they had pricked "that foolish bubble" that punishment was not a deterrent to crime. As for prisons, the main thrust of the Crime Commission's work was to ensure that they did nothing that would coddle inmates, instead putting them to constant and hard labor while in confinement, as a means of demonstrating that crime did not pay.[10] New York City police commissioner Enright echoed the condemnation of "too much prison reform" and "too much ease and comfort in the penal institutions."[11]

There was precious little ease or comfort to be found in New York's state prisons, with the success of the Baumes Laws in stark contrast to the general failure of reform proposals in the twenties.[12] The New York state legislature was not inclined to buck the public mood for getting tough on crime and criminals, and bills promoting rehabilitation went nowhere fast. A 1922 attempt to expand the use of parole and promote the early release of prisoners by virtue of good behavior came under withering attack. The district attorneys of New York State were among the most reliable critics of such legislation (and equally reliable supporters of the more punitive approach) and provided ample testimony against the bill at a public hearing in Albany. Although the 1922 bill finally secured a positive vote, the governor vetoed it.[13] For E. R. Cass, secretary of the venerable Prison Association of New York, the state's oldest and most important reform organization, these were the wilderness years, a time when "little hope was entertained by those interested in the administration of prisons and in court procedure for the enactment of progressive legislation," and his organization spent most of its effort combating "reactionary and severe legislation which was introduced to cope with the so-called crime wave."[14]

As the Baumes Laws packed ever-larger numbers of prisoners into the aged Auburn, Sing Sing, and Clinton prisons, younger inmates fared scarcely better in the state's two other, ostensibly reform-oriented, institutions for men. The state's old "honor prison," Great Meadow, was officially written off as a failure in the twenties; inmates spent the second half of the decade building a three-thousand-foot concrete wall to enclose themselves into the former prison without walls.[15] The old Elmira Reformatory, opened in 1876, operated largely as a site of industrial labor and military drill, and it received unsparing criticism from prison reformers. A German criminologist, visiting Elmira in 1928, concluded, "It is nothing better than a poor prison, not in any sense a model educational establishment."[16] The most devastating review came from Austin MacCormick who found illustrated in Elmira every fault that had been charged with reformatories in general. Elmira was an "educational treadmill" designed to do nothing more than keep inmates busy. "Here then," he concluded, "is the institution in which the reformatory idea in America had its birth and in which it is now slowly and surely going to its death."[17]

The tensions of the tough-on-crime twenties came to a head on that brutally cold December morning at Auburn Prison. At around ten in the morning, the well-coordinated uprising began, initiated by a group of fifty inmates who had been held in solitary confinement in an "emergency isolation block" since their participation in the events of the previous July. At the "box office" that controlled the gates to the outside, an inmate with a gun nearly seized control, thwarted only by a last-second lockdown by a fleeing guard. The principal keeper was shot down outside his office, killed by several gunshots to the chest. Warden Edgar Jennings was taken hostage and led to the isolation block, where the July rioters were then freed.

Local officials, including Auburn mayor Charles D. Osborne (the son of Thomas Mott Osborne) and chief of police Chester Bills, called in state troopers and the national guard after receiving a distress call from the prison. Outside the prison, swarms of local residents gathered in the chill, many armed, some wearing hunting caps with licenses affixed, perhaps anticipating the response to come.[18] The prisoners took eight hostages to bargain for their freedom, demanding safe passage from Auburn in exchange for allowing the hostages to live.[19] Mayor Osborne apparently proposed to Albany officials that some consideration be given to the demands, in the interest of protecting lives. Lieutenant Governor Herbert Lehman (acting governor while Roosevelt was out of town), however, declared that on this "taxing and unhappy day" that "there will be no compromise"—Warden Jennings and the other hostages would simply have to take their chances. Meanwhile, the troopers and guardsmen were given simple instructions: "If they come out shoot them down; if they don't come out, go in and get them." As the day wore on, Lehman was impressed with the need "to return the prisoners from the yard where they were milling about to their cells as darkness was rapidly coming on."[20]

Accordingly, a plan was hatched to deceive the leaders of the revolt. State troopers set three cars, engines running, outside the front gate (which they left slightly open) and tricked the Catholic chaplain (whom the inmates had made a kind of go-between at the start of the standoff) into going inside to tell the hostage takers that their demands had been agreed to. Looking out the window of the principal keeper's office, the hostage takers observed the cars and the entire group headed for the main gate. When two of the riot leaders made a fatal run for the cars, forty guns blazed away, ripping their bodies apart and killing them instantly. The hostages and remaining rioters were attacked with tear gas, and they retreated. With darkness falling, and floodlights sweeping the grounds, Troop D of the state police led the final assault. With orders to shoot to kill, troopers rushed the building, gassing the guards and hostages, and gunning down six more prisoners, five by machine-gun fire.[21]

For the inmates of Auburn Prison, the aftermath of the uprising brought a wave of retaliation. Authorities placed the prison on extended lockdown while inmates were beaten and tortured in bloody reprisals. In less than two months, three Auburn prisoners—William Force (already serving a life sentence for his role in the July riot), Claude Udwin, and Jesse Thomas (a fourth-strike prisoner)—would be sentenced to death for their roles in the riot, following a hasty and questionable criminal trial. The three were executed six months later in the death chamber at Sing Sing Prison.[22]

The Auburn riot came to a violent end, but the drama upstate reopened the public debate over the Baumes Laws and punitive punishment. The riot itself became the basis for a hit Broadway drama, *The Last Mile*, which opened at the Sam H. Harris Theatre in February. Although playwright John Wexley moved the setting out of New York, the play's stark and sympathetic depiction of prisoners being impelled to riot through the brutality of their keepers was unmistakably derived from the Auburn experience. The published play included a foreword penned by Lewis Lawes: "To me it is a story of those men within barred cells, crushed mentally, physically and spiritually between unrelenting forces of man-made laws and man-fixed death." Several months later, MGM released a film adaptation of the Auburn story, *The Big House*, featuring another generally sympathetic tale of inmates facing repressive institutional conditions.[23]

The newly energized debate in the wake of Auburn was given additional momentum with a second widely publicized incident, the Ruth St. Clair case. Exactly one week before *The Last Mile* opened, the twenty-nine-year-old shoplifting defendant faced Judge Max Levine for sentencing. St. Clair had three times before been convicted of theft, each a similar case of stealing clothing from department stores, and she was now the first woman in New York State to face the new fourth-strike provision of the sentencing laws, which mandated life imprisonment. In a moment captured by newsreel photographers, St. Clair pleaded for mercy in sentencing, as Judge Levine went ahead and imposed the life sentence. "I had no alternative under the Baumes law," protested the judge, who declared that he would be "the first to sign a petition asking the Governor to commute or reduce sentence."[24]

At that, Ruth St. Clair fainted in the courtroom, and the movement against mandatory sentencing and multiple-offense laws gained a potent symbolic figure. The St. Clair case became an immediate cause célèbre and a test of one's liberal mindedness (or toughness, depending on point of view) with regard to the problem of crime and punishment. All over New York City and, indeed, across the entire state, voices were raised in protest of this case (many doubtless moved in part by the fact that the defendant was an attractive, young white woman).[25]

The backers of the status quo aggressively defended their ground. In March, Eleanor Roosevelt presided over a public debate in New York City, in which one-time Osborne assistant Spencer Miller and ex-convict George Hudson debated Baumes Commission member Thomas S. Rice.[26] "The sentimentalist," Miller argued, "is not the man who would utilize science as an ally in dealing with the criminal but the man who is making illogical demands for severe dealing with him." Rice claimed that New York City before the Baumes Laws had been "worse than a frontier mining town," with criminals facing "joke sentences." In the absence of frontier lynch law, Rice argued, the state needed the deterrent effect of harsh sentences. Rice went so far as to invoke the Ruth St. Clair controversy, defiantly asserting that he did not think "there was a more fit subject for the Baumes laws" than this young women who had been "an ingrate to her family."[27] And yet, for all its seeming moral clarity, Rice's aggressive defense of toughness began to give way to the rhetoric of reform and rehabilitation, and at that point, Governor Roosevelt finally gave prison reformers their opportunity.

Choosing Reform: Roosevelt, Lehman, and the Elmira Project

Critics of Franklin Roosevelt often made the case that he was a politician of no great convictions, beyond furthering his own success as a politician. When it came to prison reform, Roosevelt spent much of 1929 seemingly determined to prove his critics right. That summer, following a post-riot inspection tour of Clinton Prison, Roosevelt blamed the Baumes Laws for the rioting while in the same breath affirming his continued support for the harsh sentencing provisions.[28] Not content to contradict himself in the immediate instance, Roosevelt soon took to protesting that he had never made any criticism of get-tough sentencing laws. His eyes firmly on national politics and the Democratic nomination for president in 1932, Roosevelt and his office spent the subsequent weeks and months in a tough-on-crime mode. They assured the *Lexington (KY) Leader* that "sentimentality will have to be ruled out in dealing with such dangerous parasites and the most severe measures taken to put the fear of the law into them. Punishment is the only thing they dread."[29] To the *Goshen Democrat*, Roosevelt's office likewise averred that the Baumes Laws *were* an effective deterrent to crime.[30]

Not long after the July riots, in a "Dear Frank" letter, Felix Frankfurter urged Roosevelt to establish a "very strong" commission of inquiry into the riots and the future of prison administration in New York.[31] Roosevelt replied that the world had already had altogether too many prison inquiries, "almost every year for the last twenty or twenty-five years." "We have," Roosevelt complained, "volumes of reports from expert penologists. Almost every penologist has an individual theory and it is difficult to get any unanimity of opinion." Instead, the governor proposed having the Baumes Commission push for more prison construction, "to take care of the overcrowding."[32] The lack of enthusiasm produced not one but *four* ineffectual investigations into the July riots, shambling along, simultaneous, uncoordinated, and for the most part unfocused.

Roosevelt's waffling and dissembling on the subject of the Baumes Laws and prison conditions were particularly surprising in light of his long connection with prison reform. He had been one of Osborne's most important political allies more than a decade earlier and remained in close contact with the network of prison reformers.[33] The two most important of his reform connections were New York industrialists Adolph and Sam Lewisohn. Both father (Adolph) and son (Sam) kept up a steady stream of correspondence to Roosevelt, following the July prison riots. From Adolph Lewisohn came copies of Lombroso's *Criminal Man*—with its support for non-institutional responses to younger, non-dangerous offenders—and *Five Hundred Criminal Careers*.[34] From Sam Lewisohn (an old Columbia Law School classmate) came commentaries on reform projects for adolescent boys in minimum-security facilities.[35]

Perhaps disingenuously, Roosevelt wrote to Adolph Lewisohn, "I honestly believe that we shall get some very constructive legislation this coming year. Those [July] prison riots accomplished more in one summer than many years of legislative hearings!"[36] The following day, December 10, Roosevelt was in Chicago, delivering three speeches in one day—an act of political showmanship that quite unmistakably amounted to throwing his hat in the ring for the 1932 presidential nomination. As Roosevelt rode home on the train, his primary political adviser, Louis Howe, mimeographed copy after copy of the governor's Chicago speeches to be mailed to Democratic members of Congress—and the Auburn prisoners began their revolt.[37]

The Auburn uprising of December 11 threatened to undo much of what Roosevelt had been trying to accomplish in laying the groundwork for 1932. At a minimum, it made a more definite approach to the crisis of prison administration all the more imperative. Still, even at this juncture, there was confusion and delay. Eventually, in May, Roosevelt fired the incumbent commissioner of corrections, declaring, "New York State can no longer tolerate prisons like Dannemora and Auburn," and hired Walter Thayer. Thayer was a dedicated liberal in prison politics, in step with the reformers; he had previously denounced New York prisons as "archaic, crowded, filthy; their inmates idle, disgruntled, inflamed."[38] The liberal press praised Thayer's appointment, in the face of "such vestiges of medievalism as the Baumes Fourth Offender Act, which defies every principle of the newer criminology."[39] Thayer would be a champion of rehabilitative approaches until his sudden death in 1936.[40]

Roosevelt also finally determined to follow Frankfurter's advice from the previous summer and appoint a strong reform commission. The first versions of the proposed commission were focused almost entirely on the question of prison labor, and the commissioners were to come primarily from industry and organized labor (indeed, the commission was originally to have had two prison experts, two labor representatives, and two industry figures).[41] Roosevelt wrote to Marshall Field in March, pitching the idea of his participation. We must keep prisoners "occupied," and the solution to the "prison labor problem" was possibly "the establishment of trade schools rather than in factories to turn out finished articles . . . In my judgment, the right answer can only be found by a meeting of those understanding the needs of the prisoner, of those representing the State's workers, and of those representing the manufacturing interests of our Commonwealth."[42]

As the process of actually naming the commission dragged on and on, however, negotiations between Roosevelt and the state legislature grew increasingly tense. So, at the end of July, Roosevelt jumped the gun and announced that Sam Lewisohn would head the commission, and irritated legislators simply acceded.[43] The Commission to Investigate Prison Administration and Construction spent the next six months putting together their initial report. In their deliberations, the commission was greatly influenced by the work of the Osborne Association and Austin MacCormick (who was at that time completing *The Education of Adult Prisoners*), supported by the Prison Association of New York and its secretary Edward R. Cass, and given political weight by Sam Lewisohn (whose name was generally attached to the commission and its work).

The Lewisohn Commission immediately became the center of policy development in the state. Roosevelt praised Sam Lewisohn, his "old classmate," calling him "the godfather of the finest constructive report and the finest prison

policy that any State has ever had."[44] That report urged repealing the most punitive of the Baumes Laws, particularly the fourth-strike law (a repeal that happened in 1932). The commission attacked the "monstrous" old "battleship" prisons of the state, calling the 1929 riots the state's "day of reckoning" for years of
"harsh, repressive measures."[45] When the Lewisohn Commission laid out a
vision for the new prisons it wanted for the state, it got right to the point: "The
new prison policy which your Commission proposes for the State of New York,
is the replacement of mass treatment and routine organization by a system of
constant personal study, individual treatment and training of every prisoner."[46]
In 1932, the state legislature authorized a prison bond for the new construction
of multiple institutions, smaller in size, to be used to house younger inmates
and first offenders, and to relieve overcrowding at the existing prisons.[47]

The Lewisohn Commission's reports marked the beginning, rather than the
end, of its work. The commission now turned its attention more directly to the
question of prison programs, setting up an experiment in new educational programming at the Elmira Reformatory—the very institution where MacCormick
had declared the obituary for the reformatory movement, but also the only reformatory institution available to the commission as a proving ground. Using
its own privately raised funds, the commission was empowered to begin making
programmatic reforms, with a particular focus on the younger male offender. To
conduct the Elmira experiment, the commission hired a Teachers College Ph.D.
candidate, Walter Wallack.

The Elmira experiment introduced much of what would become standard
elements in the rehabilitative program of the thirties. A classification committee
reviewed the program placements for each inmate at Elmira, with new arrivals
to the institution being given a thirty-day "reception" period for this purpose.
During the reception period, inmates were given a tour of the institution, in
order to better express their preferences for assignment—in the classrooms, the
traditional grade lines were eliminated in favor of students of varying abilities
working together. The curriculum reflected the desire to integrate the vocational
and the general, and social education courses were developed as well.[48]

The educational program followed MacCormick's goal of "adjustment to life"
through its rejection of overly formal and structured educational programs.
Wallack brought with him a pedagogical commitment to the project method, by
which inmate-students would pace their own instruction and work on areas of
interest to them. "The formal instruction which used to prevail," according to
Wallack, "was totally unfitted to help them face their problems on release." Boys
in Elmira were rebels against society, Wallack argued, and formal academic in-

struction disconnected from their real-world feelings and experiences would be a tremendous waste of time. Instead, one of the keys to the Elmira program was the attempt to cultivate a "community consciousness"—a sense of the common good to which they could contribute.[49]

Within Elmira, Wallack moved quickly to reorganize institutional routine and to bring existing staff on board with the new program. Inmates were given a vocational and classroom assignment, split between morning and afternoon (with the classroom assignment split into three fifty-minute periods). Teachers were made to attend a training class for institutional instructors, at which they were coached in the new curriculum and pedagogical approaches. Three "model" shop classes were set up (the machine, sheet metal, and carpenter shops), in which instructors were explicitly freed from other supervisory and maintenance responsibilities that were normally typical of a shop instructor's assignment.[50]

The Lewisohn Commission presented its report on the Elmira experiment in February 1933. By statute, the commission ended its work on March 1, 1933. By the end of the year, however, Governor Herbert Lehman appointed a new commission with the explicit purpose of extending the Elmira experiment into a more broad-ranging revision of the state's handling of the young male offender. Lehman's decision reflected a general sense that the Elmira project had been a success.[51]

The focus of the new body couldn't have been clearer—it was named the Commission for the Study of the Educational Problems of Penal Institutions for Youth—when it was placed under the chairmanship of N. L. Engelhardt of Teachers College. Writing to the members of what would generally become known as the Engelhardt Commission, Lehman made it clear that the Elmira experiments were to be the basis of the commission's work, and that this work was to be extended in a tangible way into more of the prison system, with a particular focus on the young offender. The commission took this as a broad mandate, one that ultimately spoke to every aspect of prison administration: "The educational problem of penal and correctional institution is co-extensive with the entire life of the institution and cannot be met by any narrow, formal educational scheme."[52]

The Engelhardt Program: Building New Prisons

As the Lewisohn Commission had done, the Engelhardt Commission pursued private funding for specific program development, this time on a substantially larger scale. The commission approached Frederick Keppel in late 1934, through Sam Lewisohn, to secure funding from the American Association for Adult Education and the Carnegie Corporation.[53] The AAAE, in its response, wanted to be sure that they weren't simply helping to fund the Teachers College graduate program, but providing funds for specific program developments, ones that could then be transferable to other states. Toward that end, Walter Wallack aggressively promoted his work at Elmira, inviting the members of the commission, the AAAE, and Carnegie to visit this institution and inspect the educational programs.[54]

The site of the Engelhardt Commission's educational experiments was Wallkill Prison, the first of three reformatory institutions that the state would open up between 1933 and 1935. All three were designed by architect Alfred Hopkins and self-consciously embraced an idealistic notion of the rural idyll and an old-fashioned sense of place. Hopkins chose an English country appearance for Wallkill—one former inmate recalled that it "looked just like Oxford University."[55] Walter Wallack observed that the new prison, built without perimeter walls or fencing, bore "almost no resemblance in either its exterior or interior to the typical penal institution."[56] The premise of the arrangement was a greater freedom of movement for inmates—no plumbing in the cells, but rather a bathroom on each gallery that could be accessed from the unlocked cells. Inmate accounts seem to bear out that the Wallkill experience *was* different—George Malinow, transferred from Sing Sing to Wallkill in 1939, recalled that the switch was "like coming out of a desert into a lush rain forest."[57]

To administer the Wallkill experiment, the Engelhardt Commission recruited two more Teachers College doctoral candidates, Glenn Kendall and Howard Briggs. Kendall, who supervised the academic and social education programs at Wallkill, had begun his career at the Boys Industrial School in Kearney, Nebraska, followed by five years as a school principal and another four as superintendent of schools before heading to Teachers College and Wallkill. Howard Briggs had begun his career as an electrical shop teacher at the Irwin Avenue Industrial School in Pittsburgh before moving on to administrative positions in vocational education at El Paso and later Cleveland.

Programming at Wallkill was exclusively designed for education, extensive vocational shops and training, social education programming and both academic and commercial education. Kendall developed a course in modern social and economic problems, with lessons prepared in accessible, "peppy" language; the course was taught in the vocational shops, on a rotating basis. Specific units included "Modern Ways of Doing Business," "Satisfying the Customer," "History of Labor Organization," and "Getting a Job Today." The latter unit examined the difficulty inmates would have in securing a "Square Deal" after their release, honestly reckoning with the challenges to securing a job after prison—

not just "the first job needed for the [parole] Board" but satisfying and long-term employment.[58] The results of the experiments were encouraging, but they also revealed the limitations of the reform program to that point. There were worries about whether teachers would take the new material and "kill it with old teaching methods."[59] More important, the commission determined to use the other reformatories under construction to sort and classify young men on the basis of educational ability.

Toward that end, the second of the three new reformatories was intended for younger male prisoners of borderline intelligence, of the sort that were thought to have had difficulty with the Elmira and Wallkill programs. Alfred Hopkins' design for the Woodbourne Reformatory was perhaps his most distinctive; the architectural vision it embraced echoed nothing so much as a medieval monastery. Construction began on Woodbourne in 1932, under the auspices of the Works Progress Administration, and the first inmates arrived in 1935. In its first years, Woodbourne functioned as a receiving institution for the more "hopeful" cases among sentenced "defective" delinquents (those diagnosed with more serious intellectual deficiencies were given indefinite commitments to the Institution for Defective Delinquents at Napanoch), although it often received "normal" inmates because of prison population pressures.[60]

Coxsackie was the third of the new reformatories constructed by New York and designed by Hopkins. Of the three, Coxsackie had the most traditional institutional look. A quarter-mile-long driveway, flanked by open fields and divided by a grassy mall, led visitors to the central administration building. The administration building (which also housed the reception cells) formed the west side of a courtyard, with a dining hall on the east, and two cell buildings on both the north and south sides, each with three cellblocks (two more cell buildings were added to the north side in 1940, making a total of eighteen cellblocks). Behind the dining hall were the vocational shops. As with the other two prisons, Coxsackie was constructed without a wall. Coxsackie superintendent Helbing, a veteran of more than thirty years in the New York prison system, observed: "I have spent all my life behind four stone walls twenty-two feet high. When I went to this institution without a stone wall, I wondered what was going to happen. But you see a different atmosphere in that institution today."[61]

Staffing for Reform

The Lewisohn and Engelhardt programs were important, but the most pressing matter for reform interests was securing a foothold within the state prison bureaucracy. Toward that end, the most notable development was legislative support for a Department of Corrections proposal to create the position of director of education in 1935. The following year, the legislature funded two assistant director positions as well as several new teaching positions to staff educational programs at institutions throughout the prison system. Walter Wallack left his position at Elmira to become director of education, while Glenn Kendall and Howard Briggs left their Wallkill experiment to assume the two assistant director positions.[62]

The Division of Education became the center of rehabilitative programming leadership within the Department of Corrections, directing the educational experiments already under way and extending the reform influence into other institutions. As Wallack, Kendall, and Briggs saw it, "the relationship of the Division to an institution is very similar to that of a staff or supervisory department in a public school system."[63] The division gained authority over all appointments to educational positions in the state's prisons, to prepare or approve all instructional materials, to oversee institutional program budgets, and to inspect and oversee educational programs. The three men logged thousands of miles and spent six months of the year on the road visiting each state institution, meeting with wardens and teachers, inspecting schools, and reviewing educational materials and records. The director of education position became the link between the division and institutions as well as between the educational program and other institutional dimensions.[64]

There were limitations to the influence of the Division of Education within the Department of Corrections. The division was largely frozen out of the maximum-security, old-line institutions for adult male offenders—Attica, Auburn, Clinton, Great Meadow, and Sing Sing. Albany-based reformers simply could not exercise effective influence over every institution in the "confederation of autonomy" that was the New York prison system.[65] Raymond Corsini described Auburn prison, circa 1942, as "an old-line, repressive, unprogressive institution, with a minimal treatment program and a minimum in the way of professional staff . . . The warden, an ex-police chief, was almost completely unapproachable by the prisoners and discipline was very strict. The men were kept under constant surveillance and a comparatively large percentage of their week was spent locked in cells."[66]

As the Division of Education struggled for influence at these prisons, its staff complained (to little effect) that institutional education directors were frequently shut out from assignment decisions, inmates were regularly and easily allowed to drop out of educational assignments, and the local prison administrators failed to provide institutional support for educational directors' annual budget

requests. The same report concluded that no "valid" vocational training was offered at the high-security institutions.[67] In fact, the Department of Corrections
employed more than 75 percent of its civilian educational staff in just four of
the state's twelve correctional institutions.[68] In the old-line, big house prisons,
inmates taught other inmates in a handful of remedial courses, while everyone
else worked on prison industries and maintenance. While Wallkill, Elmira, and
Coxsackie enrolled 69, 89, and 86 percent of inmates in educational programs,
Attica, Auburn, and Sing Sing enrolled just 18, 31, and 23 percent of their prisoners. Most of the Attica inmates assigned to "class" were "men assigned to the
idle groups who were usually unfit for other services."[69]

Within "reform" institutions, the creation of service units was an attempt
to strengthen the relative position of rehabilitative interests. The first such unit
emerged at Wallkill Prison in 1936, followed somewhat later by Elmira and Coxsackie. The service unit—Walter Wallack selected the name because inmates
were prone to shunning programs too closely connected with treatment—aimed
to consolidate all prison services in a central location and to integrate those services with parole decision making. The unit became the surveillance apparatus
for the reformers, collecting reports from classrooms, shops, and custodial
personnel as well as helping to promote like-minded staff. Walter Wallack described the unit director as the "liaison officer of the Warden in his relationship to all activities which in any way relate to training, or the social and general
welfare."[70]

Few efforts at directing the prison bureaucracy toward reform were more
ambitious than the attempt to train new prison guards to become part of the
educational program. Opened in November 1936, the Central Guard School remains one of the most innovative and pioneering aspects of New York's reform
regime. Begun at a time when formal job training for prison guards was virtually nonexistent in the United States, the Central Guard School put recruits
through an eight-week residential training program and offered extensive in-
service training for members of the existing guard force. It remains one of the
most far-reaching programs ever designed to produce a custodial force oriented
toward rehabilitative interventions.

The origins of the Central Guard School idea can be traced to the evaluative
stages of the Wallkill Prison programs sponsored by the Engelhardt Commission. Presiding over a Commission meeting at Columbia University in 1935,
Engelhardt had quizzed Walter Wallack and other representatives of the Wallkill
program about the response of the guards to the new educational programs.[71]
Finding a general concern that prison guards were not adequately prepared to

accept, much less participate in, rehabilitative work, the commission created a committee on personnel training. As Wallack observed, "Inasmuch as the guard is the man who comes into closest contact with the prisoner, it is highly essential that he should be carefully chosen, that he should possess the right traits of personality."[72] The Division of Education followed up this interest with a proposal for a Central Guard School, responsible for training all new recruits.

The proposal likely would have gone nowhere, however, without a concurrent development in the state legislature, which finally adopted an eight-hour workday law for state prison employees in 1935 (effective July 1, 1936).[73] For more than a decade, prison guards had been pressing for an eight-hour workday law; many worked twelve-hour shifts, seven days a week.[74] In order to fulfill the law's mandate, the Department of Corrections estimated that it would be necessary to hire approximately five hundred new prison guards in the coming twelve months.

The school opened with its first group of eighty recruits at Wallkill Prison on November 7, 1936, graduating the class the following June.[75] The Division of Education placed the school under the supervision of Walter Wallack, who designed the training curriculum around the rehabilitative program. Prospective guards took a ten-course training sequence, with most of the courses designed to introduce custodial officers to the latest in modern penological thought.[76] Supplementing the regular course sequence were a parade of well-known reform figures: criminologist Nathaniel Cantor from the University of Buffalo, Engelhardt from Teachers College, MacCormick from his position as commissioner of corrections in New York City. MacCormick advised the trainees to take an enlightened approach to their work, saving their prisons and themselves in the process: "You can brutalize yourself if you want to . . . but it won't get you anywhere and it won't get the prison anywhere . . . Be the right kind of guard, not just a club swinger." Elmira superintendent Frank Christian warned the recruits to be mindful of prisoners' humanity: "Don't say anything to a man that will in any way humiliate him."[77] Reformers sensed that the school presented a unique opportunity to shape the future of corrections; in the words of Glenn Kendall, named the supervisor of general courses, the new venture into guard training packed "all the thrills of pioneering."[78]

The Central Guard School is one of the great forgotten chapters in the history of prison guard–training programs. By 1940 two-thirds of the active guard force had been through the Central Guard School as a trainee or as part of in-service training.[79] Did it work? Division of Education officials never examined (and there is no longer any definite way to measure) the question of how many guards-in-training ignored or rejected the reform message drilled into them at the Central Guard School. Certainly many of the graduates received a different sort of on-the-job education as soon as they graduated and were assigned to an old-line state prison. On the other hand, the school functioned as a kind of classification and reception center, not unlike the one the reformers wanted for the prisoners. Prospective guards were given a battery of intelligence, educational, physical, and psychological tests. Their IQ scores, scholastic achievements, age, and parentage were all carefully recorded and summarized. Much as the service units did, the Central Guard School allowed reformers to identify and promote like-minded custodial personnel, and thus to perpetuate the reform leadership.

In the end, however, the fate of the Central Guard School illustrates just how tenuous the reformers' gains could be. A round of late Depression-era state budget cuts led the department to shutter the school for the 1939–1940 fiscal year. The Division of Education secured temporary funding for the 1940–1941 fiscal year through the federal George-Deen Act, which offered states matching funds for job training in the public service sector. The permanent closure of the school arrived with U.S. involvement in World War II—wartime manpower shortages created a sudden demand for new guards, and the state found the Central Guard School an obstacle to filling the large number of new positions. Neither affordable nor immediately helpful to the Department of Corrections, the guard school closed in April 1942, less than six years after it had begun. To "keep the idea of training alive," an introductory course consisting of seven correspondence units was compiled, but the Department of Corrections had no good way of ensuring that guards actually fulfilled even this limited training requirement.[80] Well into the 1940s, the Division of Education looked forward to the "reopening" of the Central Guard School, but not until 1965 would the state undertake systematic training of correctional officers again, and nothing on the scale of the Central Guard School would be attempted until after the Attica riots in 1971—indeed, current training requirements are not notably stricter.

Youthful Offender Act and the Elmira Reception Center

When the New York Department of Corrections (NYDOC) established its network of specialized institutions for the young male offender in the mid-1930s, it did so without any ability to control the assignment of convicted felony offenders to specific institutions. Instead, criminal court judges across the state were at liberty to sentence young men to whatever institution they saw fit, as long as the offenders met whatever basic age and offense guidelines were laid out by the legislature. This lack of control was a constant source of frustration for correctional administrators, and it inspired the pursuit of an ambitious two-part reform: legislation that would allow them to take adolescent offenders directly from the courts and make institutional assignments from within NYDOC, and additional legislation that would authorize creating a distinct reception center where evaluation of newly received inmates could take place. By 1945, the correctional reform interests had succeeded on both counts, achieving the high-water mark in their campaign to remake the correctional system in New York.

The origins of this last project can be traced back to a 1935 decision by the chief city magistrate in New York City to allow a magistrate's court in Brooklyn to give its exclusive attention to the hearing of criminal charges (both misdemeanor and felony) against boys ages 16 to 18, following years of agitation from the Criminal Courts Committee of the Brooklyn Bureau of Charities. The Brooklyn Adolescent Court, as it was known, was able to circumvent the absence of any legal foundation for this specialized court by extending the wayward minor designation used for juveniles to this older age group. The authors of *Youth in the Toils* proudly observed, "This court has exercised power and followed procedures which are frankly admitted to be extra-legal. The penal code has been 'flung out the window' and the protective wayward minor act has been substituted therefor."[81]

The Brooklyn experiment remained an isolated (though well-publicized) example until 1940, when New York district attorney Thomas Dewey promoted his own comprehensive plan for adolescents between 16 and 18, in which defendants would waive a public arraignment and trial in lieu of a wayward minor designation and supervision until age 21. The publicity-conscious Dewey proclaimed his plan the first of its kind in the country (which immediately drew protests from Brooklyn), as he posed for reporters next to a 17-year-old defendant who had been indicted for auto theft and was now being accorded the celebrity of appearing in court as the first case processed under the new rules.[82] At the same time, however, Dewey called for a new and comprehensive policy from the 1941 state legislative session, to bring the handling of adolescent offenders into line with actual law.[83]

That same year, the American Law Institute (ALI) published a model Youth Correction Authority Act. The ALI had committed itself to this project after receiving early copies of *Youth In the Toils* in late 1937, establishing a working committee on criminal justice comprising several notable figures in liberal correctional thought.[84] Their plan featured the first comprehensive model of both a youthful offender designation and a centrally located reception center that would receive convicted offenders directly from the courts and hold the authority to assign them to an institution.[85]

The ALI report received considerable attention in New York State, and a joint legislative committee (the Young Committee, chaired by Fred A. Young) was formed to review its recommendations and make a proposal for the state.[86] The first recommendations went before the legislature in early 1942 and included establishing a Youth Court Division in the New York City Domestic Relations Court, where 16- to 19-year-olds would be designated as "youthful offenders." The New York City model would then be employed throughout the state.[87] Young's bill sparked intense opposition. The New York State District Attorneys Association joined some legislators in denouncing the proposal as "pampering" and "coddling" serious criminals, while Mayor LaGuardia and the New York City magistrates objected to the cost of a new court (the bill, in its own way, sided with Dewey and against the chief magistrate in their ongoing turf war—Dewey broke from his fellow district attorneys to support the bill "in principle").[88]

The legislation was delayed less by the objections of coddling than by the conflicts between those who wanted a distinct youth court and those who wanted to continue a Brooklyn-style approach, in which youth were handled by regular criminal court judges under different rules. The Youthful Offender Act would not be signed into law until early 1943, after Dewey had taken office as governor. Dewey acknowledged that the final legislation was a compromise that did *not* provide for distinct youth courts, but it did allow 16- to 19-year-old criminal defendants to be designated as youthful offenders. This designation would spare adolescent offenders the lasting consequences of a felony conviction and would provide them with the "protective cloak" of the less-formal process that juvenile defendants typically received.[89]

That protective cloak was a substantial one, at least in strictly legal terms. Defendants could be adjudged a youthful offender either directly by the judge or on the recommendation of a prosecutor or grand jury. Once that determination was made, the disposition of the case would not result in a felony conviction, and all proceedings and outcomes would be outside the public record. Youthful offenders would then receive an indeterminate sentence with a three-year maximum limit.[90] As an ALI report later concluded, New York's Youthful Offender Act probably established more legal fictions than any other legislation dealing with offenders over the age of juvenile jurisdiction: "that an arrest shall not be deemed a criminal prosecution, that an adjudication shall not be considered a conviction, and that a finding of guilt on a felony charge either may or may not be 'certified' as a felony."[91]

The youthful offender designation also gave courts considerable discretionary authority over adolescent defendants. In essence, New York State was placing the young adult male in the same procedural category as juvenile delinquents and, in the process, rendering them just as vulnerable. In a telling letter, Austin MacCormick made just this case: "There is one point many people never think of: if you handle a case in juvenile court, you can get an adjudication of delinquency with very little evidence, even if it is a felony case which an adult could and would fight to the limit. If you put the case in criminal court, you run into the rules of evidence, clever defense lawyers, and frequently into juries more lenient than the juvenile court judge would be."[92]

Dewey's election to governor in 1942 gave an important boost to the other component of the youthful offender reform package: a centralized authority within the Department of Corrections that would receive youthful offenders directly from the courts for assessment and institutional assignment. The department, particularly the Division of Education, lobbied hard for the creation of such an authority, "more keenly aware each year of the absolute necessity of scientific classification of inmates if education is going to be most effectively administered."[93] Dewey regarded the ALI "youth authority" model as the best opportunity to make something of a legislative mark in this field, and he supported the creation of an interdepartmental committee, which issued two reports endorsing the idea of a reception center to be housed at the Elmira Reformatory, for 16- to 21-year-old offenders committed to the Department of Corrections. The overlap between the proposed reception center and the Youthful Offender Act was not exact—the reception center would handle inmates up to age 21, and it would handle all inmates in that age range, not simply those who had been designated youthful offenders.[94]

Dewey placed the proposal for the Elmira Reception Center (ERC) before the Republican-controlled legislature in the 1945 legislative session at just the right moment. He was near something of a political high point in New York, enjoying a streak of success with his legislative proposals.[95] The reception center proposal also benefited from apprehension over a looming postwar juvenile crime wave, the subject of intense public discussion in New York during the war years.[96] Dewey packaged the reception center legislation alongside a series of juvenile delinquency measures, most of which focused on prevention programs. Reformers within the Department of Corrections were savvy enough to sell the proposals in similar terms; Glenn Kendall warned that the ERC was "the final attempt by the State to understand and rehabilitate young offenders before they become seasoned to a life of crime."[97]

The Elmira Reception Center opened in November 1945, as a separate unit within the Elmira Reformatory, with a capacity of 352 inmates. The ERC staff numbered seventy-four, which included twenty-two professional personnel, fifteen clerical employees, and thirty-seven guards, giving the ERC the highest ratio of treatment personnel to custodial personnel in the NYDOC. Each inmate received from the criminal courts spent sixty days in the ERC, undergoing a series of examinations. As it was originally constituted, the ERC program had four stages: reception (two to three days), orientation (two to three days), examination (seven to ten days), and program.[98] Staff claimed that "a careful analysis can hardly be prepared in less than sixty days," and that "under ideal conditions, three months at the reception center would be a more suitable length of time," but any longer of a stay would meet objections from reformatory superintendents for cutting too far into the short sentences of most youthful offenders. The ERC operated a high-volume, high-intensity workload, with more than one hundred young men arriving each month—the center "celebrated" its twenty-five thousandth case in 1961 (the young prisoner asked, "If it's such an honor, why don't they send me home?").[99]

The public philosophy of the ERC was that the inmate should "make time serve him" by using these two months of assessment to explore his interests and capacities.[100] In theory, the conclusion of this evaluation period would then produce a report indicating the optimal institutional assignment. Inmates were then shipped off to serve their sentences (about twelve to fifteen arrived at Coxsackie each week), accompanied by the full ERC report (averaging about twelve pages), which included specific recommendations with respect to subsequent institutional treatment programs.

A sign of the importance of the Elmira Reception Center for the reform regime in New York State was Glenn Kendall's move from the Division of Education to lead the Elmira Reception Center (much as Walter Wallack had earlier been shifted to Wallkill Prison). Kendall was fully invested in the ERC and made it clear that the program there required ongoing promotion to politicians and to the general public "through talks, radio addresses, motion pictures, and other media in order that there will be the type of general understanding that will accept and support the work of the center." At the same time, Kendall was realist enough to know that the ERC faced "serious hazards from some of [their] overzealous and overoptimistic, uncritical advocates . . . too much may be expected from classification itself, with too little effort in the total process of handling the offender."[101] The challenge of integrating the ERC within institutional programming in New York's prison system, of defending it against the critics of coddling, and sustaining the integrity of its own processes would become Kendall's consuming mission.

The Elmira Reception Center's 1945 opening marked the final piece in the construction of a new system for the young male offender in New York. The reform project begun fifteen years earlier, in the wake of the Auburn Prison riot, had realized many of its ambitions. The educational reformers first brought together by Austin MacCormick and Sam Lewisohn had assumed control of the Elmira Reformatory and helped build and administer Wallkill, Woodbourne, and Coxsackie. The Division of Education gave the reformers a vital administrative foothold in Albany, and the appointment of institutional educational directors gave them a toehold (though no more than that) in the state's maximum-security prisons. The opening of the Elmira Reception Center (also administered by the educational reformers) and the passage of a youthful offender law promised a future in which adolescent males could be rationally distributed within the Department of Corrections. Most notably, the reform project that had been explicitly endorsed by governors Roosevelt and Lehman seemed likely to continue under Governor Dewey, giving the reformers continued and critical executive support in state government.

Nonetheless, the reformers' victory was far from complete, and it would be wrong to describe a "rehabilitative regime" in control of the entire prison system, even in this ostensibly most progressive of states. New York's prison landscape remained dotted with big houses, holding the majority of the adult male prisoner population, which largely ignored reform interests. The coming of World War II further weakened the reformers' position, with the closure of the Central Guard School and the movement of inmates from structured programming to wartime industrial and agricultural production. The new prison at Coxsackie, then, would operate within a criminal justice system (and a state political system) that challenged and even undermined the reformist premises upon which it was built.

PART TWO

PRISON LIVES AND THE WORLD OF THE REFORMATORY

CHAPTER THREE

Adolescents Adrift

Young Men on the Road to Coxsackie

For Karl B., the road to prison—the road to Coxsackie—ended just short of his seventeenth birthday.[1] Months earlier, he had broken into a Westchester County food market after hours, taking some merchandise and cash. Well known to the local police, Karl was quickly arrested and charged with breaking and entering. In court, Karl pled guilty to the offense, in exchange for consideration as a youthful offender, which resulted in a three-year maximum term and commitment to the Elmira Reception Center. After four months at the reception center, he was sent along to Coxsackie, with a recommendation that he serve twelve to fifteen months of the three-year term (he ultimately served fifteen months).

Karl's time at Coxsackie began, in an official sense, with the creation of a case file. Every case file began with an institutional photograph (profile and facing, in the style of a police mug shot), taken at the start of the quarantine period, pasted on the inside cover. The photographs at the front of Coxsackie case files show new arrivals wearing various expressions, youth their only common feature. Despite their prisoners' young age, Coxsackie officials were certain that the road to prison for Karl and the rest had begun long before their arrest, so the case files each began by working backwards. By the time Karl departed Coxsackie, he left behind a case file dense with observations on the evolution of his physical and mental health, social behavior, educational strengths and weaknesses, work habits, spiritual values, and family relationships over his first seventeen years.

In one sense, the men who ran Coxsackie were right—most prisoners, despite their youth, or perhaps because of it, arrived at prison following years of surveillance and scrutiny from child welfare agencies, schools, police, juvenile courts, and juvenile reformatories. Karl B.'s life as an object of state interest began when he was just 3 years old. Abandoned by his parents, Karl and his sister were placed with the New York Foundling Hospital, where he spent the next several years and where, according to the hospital, he "did not do well." Sent to Bellevue Hospital at age 10 for psychiatric observation, Karl was passed along to the Sisters of St. Dominic in Blauvelt, New York—his first trip "up the river" to a new institution, one intended for the care of "destitute, homeless, and unprotected children." Karl fiercely resisted remaining there and ran away as many as twenty-six times. He never got far, generally breaking into local restaurants after hours, stealing food, and setting fires to keep warm.

Karl's final escape from St. Dominic's, when he was 12, led to his being adjudged delinquent and sent to the Rockland State Hospital for psychiatric observation. A month later, he escaped from Rockland, was caught again, and this time was sent to the State Training School for Boys at Warwick, which had opened in 1932 to replace the House of Refuge. Designed in the cottage style of youth reformatories, the quasi-familial environment of Warwick proved no more congenial for Karl than any other place where he had been made to reside, and he made several more escapes over the next four years, before finally being released to a foster home on his sixteenth birthday.

Karl's time with his new foster family was short. He enrolled in the Bronx Vocational High School, the same city school where Evan Hunter's brief experience as a substitute teacher (the following year) provided the raw material for his novel *Blackboard Jungle*. Hunter's fictional principal delivers a lecture to the teachers, setting out his expectations in ways that were not far from the truth of most New York City vocational high schools: "So here's what I want. I want a well-disciplined school because we can't teach a disorderly mob. That means obedience, instant obedience. That does not mean delayed obedience, or tomorrow obedience, or next-week obedience. It means instant obedience! It means orders obeyed on the button. The teacher is boss, remember that! . . . If there's trouble, fine and dandy. If there is, we step on it immediately. We step on it the way we would step on a cockroach."[2]

When Karl entered Bronx Vocational, testing indicated that he had an above-average intelligence, but he had precious little time in which to demonstrate his capacity for learning. Before his first term concluded, Karl had dropped out, fleeing the school just as quickly as he had fled the Sisters of St. Dominic, the state hospital, and the reform school. Now Karl was truly on his own, with no one to take him back to Bronx Vocational. His freedom lasted less than one month before the police arrested him for breaking and entering, the charge for which he would arrive months later at Coxsackie.

As the basis of fully realized life history, Karl's case file has clear limits—as do all the case files sampled for this study (see the "Essay on Sources" for details on the sample itself). Case files record the lives of penal and welfare subjects, and they include only those elements of young lives that would have seemed relevant to a prison counselor, a youth court judge, or a school principal. There are many silences in these files, but none more obvious and important than the voices of the young men themselves. We will never know just how Karl felt about a life defined by institutions, though running away and escaping tells us just how much effort he expended in trying to make himself heard. Still, these case files do help reconstruct three critical points along the road to Coxsackie.

First, for many of the young men who were sent to Coxsackie, their most significant points of social interaction—family and school—were also sources of sustained personal conflict. Written out of socially disorganized lives, the prison's case files were packed with the sort of material that would have filled (and did fill) the pages of mid-century social scientific studies of the urban slum and ghetto. But to understand that the prisoners of Coxsackie were the products of difficult circumstances is to grasp only a portion of their reality. Like many other young people in the communities from which they came, they devised creative and adaptive ways to manage the social reality of their environments. The crimes these 16- and 17-year-olds committed generally occurred at this complicated intersection between their own expressions of autonomy and the continued authority of family, school, and the state.

The second common point of experience is the criminal justice system. If this seems an obvious point to make about state prisoners, it is by no means well developed in the historical literature. Prison studies tend to begin at the prison gate and ignore the fundamental truth that confinement was merely the final step in a longer process of criminal justice. In fairness, the reformers tended to ignore this point themselves, rarely taking time to consider how the experience of arrest, interrogation, jail, and trial might have affected their subjects. Looking more closely in retrospect, we can see that the criminal justice system offered adolescent offenders cruelty, mistreatment, and arbitrary decision making, all wrapped up in a process that was largely incomprehensible. Prisoners arrived at Coxsackie deeply hostile to criminal justice authority, convinced that they were victims of an unjust system, and suspicious of the motives of those who claimed to have their best interests at heart.

The case files also reveal, finally, the sorting process by which the courts sent young men to Coxsackie. Predictable though the outcome of imprisonment might seem in light of long histories of family instability, educational failure, and institutional entanglements, Coxsackie received only a small fraction of New York's adolescent criminal offenders. This final game of chance confused defendants and troubled reformers, but it persisted in the face of every effort to remake the state's prison system. In its first decade, Coxsackie received prisoners based solely on the varied judgments of the state's criminal court judges; after 1945, the creation of the Elmira Reception Center gave the reformers greater control over institutional assignment—but left prisoners as bewildered as ever about the decisions that would shape their lives.

Adolescents Adrift—Family, School, and Work

In 1955, Glenn Kendall looked back on the more than twelve thousand young men who had passed through the Elmira Reception Center in the first decade since its opening. Trying to capture some sense (his sense, in any event) of their life experiences before the reception center, and how it influenced their behavior, Kendall offered this gloomy portrait: "And so they become the empty ones, the disinherited, with no ties to any constructive group or activity, with no standards or goals, with little hope, covering their discouragement and despair with bravado or happy-go-lucky clownishness. They feel wanted by no one, they know no one whom they can call friend in the true sense of the word. I call them 'Adolescents Adrift'—no rudder, no compass, no motive power, no beckoning harbor."[3]

These young men would not have shared Kendall's portrait of their interior states of mind, but his assessment of their life experiences would probably not have raised many objections. Kendall believed that most young men had experienced some form of family disruption or conflict, that "in school these boys either could not or would not respond to ordinary procedures and methods," and that "having rejected school, or been rejected by it, they either loaf or get part-time or low-level jobs of which they soon tire and in which they find little satisfaction."[4] That critical confluence of family, educational, and work conflicts appears time and again in the case histories of Coxsackie inmates and offers some important context for comprehending just what young men brought with them to the reformatory.

Family

Not long before Karl B. was to be released from Coxsackie, he received a letter from his sister, requesting that he not come to visit or identify himself to anyone as her brother. She had developed a close and constructive relationship with her own foster parents and was thought in her community to be their birth daughter. Karl read the letter in the company of the prison psychologists (incoming correspondence from authorized relatives was screened in advance by Coxsackie officials), who reported that Karl "became extremely tense and emotional and broke down on two occasions and cried profusely."[5] Cut off from his last remaining family tie, Karl was paroled to a YMCA in New York City, to work as a general helper in a manufacturing plant.

The family ties of Coxsackie's other inmates were not often cut off as severely as they had been for Karl B., but only about one-third (36%) of prisoners in the case file sample had lived with both parents prior to the arrest that sent them to Coxsackie. Another third of the inmates had lived with a single parent (in cases where this information was reported in the files, 60 of 336, or 17.9%, of fathers were recorded as deceased at the time of commitment, as well as 56 of 343, or 16.3%, of mothers), while the remaining third resided with other relatives, with friends, in foster homes, or in institutions of various kinds. One study of Coxsackie inmates found that 62 percent did not live with their fathers in the years before their conviction, compared with 51 percent of young drug addicts in treatment, and just 37 percent of a "non-delinquent" control group. Strained family connections appear to have influenced prisoner attitudes—the same study found that 42 percent of the non-delinquent group identified one or both parents as the adult whom they most wanted to think well of them, compared to just 10 percent of the Coxsackie inmates.[6]

Long before their criminal careers (or general delinquency) brought Coxsackie inmates to the attention of public authorities, many of these young men had been entangled in complicated family interventions related to alleged dependency and neglect. The case file sample is suggestive—in cases where this information is clearly noted one way or the other, fully one-quarter of the files contain some formal record of child abuse or family neglect (numerous others contain less explicit suggestions of harsh physical discipline). An additional one-tenth of the case files record a period of institutionalization for one or both parents, or interventions centered around parental drug and alcohol abuse (these are files without formal records of abuse or neglect—a subset of files contain both). A later study of Coxsackie inmates found that 40 percent had one immediate family member with a police record (compared to just 10 percent of a comparison group).[7]

Of course, the simple facts of family poverty just as frequently exposed young men to the operations of private and state welfare agencies. The case file sample contains numerous examples like that of Ronald T., 16 years old when he was committed to Coxsackie. Ronald had lost his father as a young boy, then his mother remarried and died in childbirth, and his stepfather was sent to a tuber-culosis hospital. With his stepfather's departure, Ronald was sent to live with his grandmother, and subsequently to live with a maternal aunt. By the time he became a prisoner of the state, Ronald's case file contained detailed reports from the New York City Department of Welfare, the magistrate's court, the Salvation Army, and Harlem Hospital.[8]

The young men sentenced to Coxsackie had also experienced the failures of those agencies. James H. lived in the Bronx with his drug-addicted mother (his father was deceased) and a man reported to welfare agencies as his "grand-father" but who was actually one of his mother's addict boyfriends. His mother had spent time in the House of the Good Shepherd after being caught selling drugs, but otherwise she apparently received no treatment interventions or assistance. James left school at age 15 and spent his time keeping other "boy-friends" away from his mother; finally he headed for a YMCA when another of these was returning from the Lexington Narcotic Hospital. After James and two co-defendants were arrested for robbing a man at gunpoint and forcing him to perform oral sex, officials reported that he was "bitterly anti-social when social agencies were mentioned."[9]

Coxsackie administrators were not without sympathy for such young men, "more sinned against than sinning": a Rockland County boy abandoned to St. Agatha's Home in Nanuet and "totally rejected by a mother who just didn't care"; a New York City youth "literally dumped" at Lincoln Hall (run by the New York Catholic Protectory) by parents who had "no understanding of his person-ality"; another who lived with a violent father and an ill mother in a "depress-ing" household.[10] Of course, expressions of sympathy only went so far; family dysfunction remained just one more justification for prison authorities to sub-ject young men to a period of confinement. Moved by the plight of Edgar G., convicted of assaulting his abusive and cruel father, the vice principal of his public school urged the reformatory to consider that any criminal tendencies had "been embedded there by years of loneliness and physical suffering." Edgar was hungry for kindness and callous to punishment, the vice principal urged. But the Coxsackie superintendent, while conceding that Edgar was not really responsible for his present situation, observed that such boys had usually "ac-quired a few warped points of view." Edgar would, therefore, remain behind bars while Coxsackie worked on assisting him in correcting his past mistakes.[11]

Parental correspondence to Coxsackie authorities frequently sounded notes of frustration or bewilderment at their sons' behavior. The mother of Gordon G. wrote to the superintendent: "I don't understand my son in the last two years.

Before that time he was a grand child . . . then generally he was skipping school, ran away, anything he saw and wanted he just took, and you could not believe a word he told you. I feel that I have failed somehow in making him see right from wrong so perhaps someone else can succeed."[12] Still other parents added their belief that bad associates had caused an otherwise good boy to go astray. The mother of Vernon J. blamed the "wise guy" and "devotee of the zoot suit" who had exercised an unwholesome influence on her son, as they loafed around their Brooklyn neighborhood.

While Alfred C. was in Coxsackie, prison officials confiscated an incoming letter from his older sister, who had also run away from home. In a letter Alfred would never read, she reached out to him with a mix of anger and hope: "What in the world happened to you? Aren't you ashamed . . . Did Pa turn you in? Ma doesn't know yet that you are gone. I don't know what it will do to her when she does find out . . . learn something good while your [sic] there so you can be a good boy when you come out."[13] Letters like these remind us that at least some families placed their faith in Coxsackie to "turn around" adolescents' lives, particularly through the exercise of a strong masculine influence. The mother (nearly all correspondence sent to the institution came from mothers) of Alfred D. wrote to Superintendent Helbing in 1940, full of regret: "He is of weak will and strong head. By that, I mean that he can be easily influenced to do the evil or weaker things, than the good and strong or finer things . . . he is lacking fatherly love since he was a baby he never had the love of a father. It is possible that all this trouble is due to that."[14] The mother of Melvin D. struck a similar note: "He needs someone to take an interest in him or be sort of a father or big brother to him . . . his father died three years ago and he needs someone to teach him to do what is right and to work."[15]

School

The greatest irony of Coxsackie—an irony that, in fairness, correctional educators fully acknowledged—was that the "correctional school" housed students for whom school had been the most notable failure of their lives to that point. The case files frequently contain assessments from teachers and school administrators, collected by the court before sentencing, and they are universally critical. A small sample of the summary terms from the case file sample tells the tale: "lack of ambition"; "indifference"; "smart aleck"; "lazy and indifferent"; "untruthful and undependable"; "quite anti-everything connected with school"; "persistent truant, lazy and indifferent"; "sullen, careless, disobedient, and untruthful"; "insolent, impudent, lazy and truant"; and "a real menace."[16] Max N. had been asked to leave his Buffalo parochial school where, "because of his annoy-ing behavior, his teacher is supposed to have suffered a nervous breakdown." Sent to public high school, Max fared little better. An "impossible" student, he was eventually expelled from school. His principal wrote directly to Coxsackie officials: "We tried hard to do something to change his attitude" but "could not appeal to him, neither reason nor threat were effective."[17] Inmate Willie G. summarized his school experience succinctly: "They couldn't do nothing with me so they stopped trying."[18]

Few Coxsackie inmates were active enrolled students at the time their most recent offense had been committed. The largest number in the case file sample (33%) ended their school careers sometime during the ninth grade, usually co-inciding with their sixteenth birthday, when they were no longer subject to compulsory attendance laws. An even larger number (44%) of Coxsackie inmates had never even attended high school, leaving school at grades before ninth. Only 23 percent of prisoners had attended school past the ninth grade (not surpris-ing, given the young age of prison commitment).[19] It should be noted that the young inmates at Coxsackie *did* have longer records of schooling than the older inmates at New York's maximum-security prisons, at least initially—an educa-tional survey of prisoners conducted not long after Coxsackie opened showed that 21 percent of all Sing Sing inmates had never made it past the fourth grade, while only 3 percent of Coxsackie inmates left school that early.

In many ways, the adolescents of Coxsackie were one of the earliest genera-tions of state prisoners for whom a majority possessed some high school experi-ence, consistent with the general expansion of high school attendance among American teens in this era. The salient point for correctional educators, of course, is that the experience had left prisoners "almost universally resistant to school." They described school attendance in terms not unlike prison.[20] Part of that resistance derived from a strong sense that the school system was indiffer-ent or hostile to them. One survey of the state's adolescent male offenders under confinement revealed that their primary complaint about school was not exces-sive discipline or academic rigor, but teachers with "no interest in students." Returning the favor, prisoners reported that being "bored with school" was the primary reason for leaving.[21] One former prisoner described the "monotonous memories of instruction" that had characterized his days spent at vocational high schools (attended by many Coxsackie inmates), places "where all the re-jects were sent."[22] George H. offered the simplest summary: "I just didn't like it. That's all."[23]

Work

If educational reformers understood that adolescent offenders carried with them records of educational failure, they were also correct in assuming that these young men had been only loosely attached to the labor market prior to entering the reformatory. Coxsackie opened in the midst of the Great Depression, at a point when "young men left school and became available for employment far, far more quickly than the clogged labor market could extend jobs to them."[24] Kingsley Davis, author of 1935's *Youth in the Depression*, recorded that "the machinery by which young people [were] drawn into the work of the nation had broken down; and youth, bearing the burden of this breakdown, was seeking blindly for some way out."[25] The case file sample reveals a fairly even three-way split in work experience: one-third had never worked at all, one-third had worked irregularly at odd jobs, and one-third had some experience with regular, unskilled employment—consistent with a published study of Coxsackie parolees that found over half (461 of 829) had never had "regular" employment.[26]

Reformatory inmates had a complicated relationship to work. On the one hand, they disdained the world of work as constraining and uninteresting. Coxsackie inmates generally expressed the sentiment that "only saps work" and that those who did were "working stiffs" who lacked a spirit of independence. The case files are replete with spotty work histories. Ernest N.'s working career began at a Brooklyn bakery, at a job secured for him by his father when Ernest left school (seventh grade) at age 17. He lasted just three weeks before quitting because he "did not like to be bossed." Ernest spent five weeks in Connecticut remodeling a house, work that ended when the remodeling was finished. Following that, he picked up a job at a manufacturing enterprise but left the job "in a huff" after less than one month of employment—Ernest's own stated reason for leaving is that he was "working too hard."[27]

For all their resistance to the working life, Coxsackie inmates like Ernest were constantly returning to work—even for short periods—as a way of supporting themselves and obtaining the things they desired. Eric Schneider, in his study of postwar New York gangs, makes the same observation: "They expressed their distaste for the low-skilled, low-wage jobs available to them, but, driven by poverty, they desperately hunted for work."[28] The only trade experience Coxsackie inmates brought with them was the small number who worked as helpers for carpenters, painters, mechanics, and electricians. Most of the jobs young men located, in contrast, were to be found at the fringes of the labor

market, working as delivery boys, farm hands, stock boys, messengers, dish-
washers, busboys, and shoe shiners—and the case file catch-all term, laborers.
Essential and objectionable, the world of work they had experienced held little
appeal for the young men who arrived at the reformatory as subjects for vocational training.

Crime and Delinquency

The place of crime and delinquency in the lives of the adolescent boys who
served time in Coxsackie and similar reformatories has never been given a full
accounting. If the educational reformers were reasonably clear eyed when it
came to educational and work histories, they generally missed the significance
of criminal histories. That this should be overlooked is not entirely surprising;
after all, the chief selling point for the state's focus on the adolescent male offender was the promise of early intervention—that confinement at the first signs
of serious criminality would interrupt the start of a potentially serious criminal
career. Through youthful offender laws New York simultaneously suppressed
and denied serious criminality among teenage boys.

Subsequent critical histories of the reformatory tend to share this notion of
the naïve youthful offender, arguing that progressive reforms tended to have a
"net widening" effect, as the state expanded its reach over otherwise stable patterns of youthful behavior. New York's intensified focus on the adolescent offender *did* widen the net of surveillance and control, but there is no reason to
assume that underlying patterns of adolescent behavior were static. The ability
of young men to cause trouble has a historical specificity that, combined with
criminal justice system behavior, produced the patterns of adolescent criminal
careers.

The case files reveal that most of Coxsackie's prisoners had been arrested
prior to the arrest that sent them to the reformatory. In the case file sample,
more than four of every five prisoners arrived with prior arrests—far more than
the general population of adolescent criminal defendants.[29] The average number of prior arrests per inmate in the case sample was quite stable over time
(table 3.1), as was the relative distribution of the number of arrests. There may
have been a slight rise in the proportion of never-arrested inmates in the postwar years, although this difference may well be accounted for by a decline in
"unknown" cases that could generally have been cases of no record of arrest.

Coxsackie's prisoners had far more previous institutional experience than
the designers of the reformatory would have imagined. The case sample of Coxsackie inmates shows 118 (31.8%) having some prior institutional commitment

TABLE 3.1
Prior arrests of Coxsackie inmates, 1935–1956, case file sample

Dates of admission	No prior arrests (%)	One arrest (%)	Two arrests (%)	Three + arrests (%)	Unknown (%)	Average number of arrests (%)
1935–1939	18 (15.5)	36 (31.0)	22 (19.0)	31 (26.7)	9 (7.8)	1.83
1940–1944	18 (17.0)	29 (27.4)	18 (17.0)	35 (33.0)	6 (5.7)	1.93
1945–1949	15 (23.1)	21 (32.3)	12 (18.5)	17 (26.2)	0 (0.0)	1.60
1950–1956	19 (22.6)	24 (28.6)	21 (25.0)	20 (23.8)	0 (0.0)	1.80
TOTAL	70 (18.9)	110 (29.6)	73 (19.7)	103 (27.8)	15 (4.0)	

(table 3.2), a number that does not count jail time that might have accompanied previous arrests. Unlike prior arrest patterns, the experience of institutional commitment clearly declines over time in the sample. The percentage of Coxsackie prisoners with no prior commitments rises with each five-year group, capturing part of what may have been an even longer historical decline—fully *one-half* of new commitments to the House of Refuge in 1925 had already spent time in another institution.

The decline has two plausible explanations. One possibility is that the opening of the Elmira Reception Center in 1945 diverted prisoners with institutional experience from Coxsackie. A second possibility, made more likely by the House of Refuge data, is that young men after World War II were simply less likely than previous generations to be committed to an institution before they turned 16 years old. Certainly this is most plausible in the case of private institutional confinement, as the numbers of children in foster care began to surpass the numbers in institutional care. To the extent that these developments may have also depressed public institutional commitments, it may well help explain the declines shown in table 3.2.

The case file sample does suggest, however, that Coxsackie inmates with institutional experience frequently found themselves in a kind of revolving door of placements within the complex of public and private institutions that governed New York's adolescent boys. Willie G., growing up in New Rochelle with his immigrant parents, first encountered the legal system just after his thirteenth birthday, when a juvenile court judge sentenced him to probation because of persistent delinquency. Two months later, Willie made another juvenile court appearance, again because of his refusal to attend school regularly. Six months passed before the next court appearance; this time, the judge sentenced Willie to the Children's Village, a private juvenile institution where he lasted only four months before being returned to the courts as "ungovernable." Unwilling to

TABLE 3.2
Prior institutional commitments of Coxsackie inmates, 1935–1956, case file sample

Dates of admission	No prior institutions (%)	Private institutions (%)	Public institutions (%)	Both (%)	Unknown (%)	Total in institutions (%)
1935–1939	61 (51.7)	22 (21.6)	16 (13.8)	3 (2.6)	14 (12.1)	41 (35.3)
1940–1944	60 (56.6)	17 (22.6)	16 (21.7)	7 (6.7)	6 (5.7)	40 (37.7)
1945–1949	47 (72.3)	3 (4.6)	12 (23.1)	3 (4.6)	0 (0.0)	18 (27.7)
1950–1956	65 (77.4)	5 (5.9)	8 (9.5)	6 (7.1)	0 (0.0)	19 (22.6)
TOTAL	233 (62.8)	47 (12.7)	52 (14.0)	19 (5.1)	20 (5.4)	118 (31.8)

return the young man to his parents, the court adjudicated him a neglected child and sent him to St. Benedict's Home for Colored Children in Rye, New York. He lasted two months before the administrators of St. Benedict's returned him to the court, where he was adjudicated delinquent again and sent to his first "state" institution, the New York Training School at Warwick. At Warwick, Willie made three escape attempts before being released. Following this, he was adjudicated delinquent yet again (at age 15) and sent to Industry, where he was paroled in February 1940. His freedom lasted just six weeks before an arrest for assault sent him to Coxsackie.[30]

Loafers, Drifters, and Thieves

Nothing was more consistent in the criminal records of Coxsackie inmates than convictions for petit larceny and burglary, which together account for more than one-third of the case file sample (if youthful offenders whose original charges were petit larceny and burglary are included, the total becomes closer to one-half of the case sample). Petit larceny was a serious misdemeanor that could result in a reformatory sentence, and burglary was a felony crime; both offenses were heavily overrepresented by adolescent boys. In 1950, for example, 16- to 18-year-olds accounted for 17.2 percent of all major crime arrests, but 35.7 percent of all burglary arrests.[31]

Perhaps the most critical factor in most of the petit larceny and burglary arrests was theft as a form of work and survival among young men. One 16-year-old explained his offense: "I was hanging around the block and they said did I want to go out and get some money. I said all right. We went to a house and got some lead pipe. We did it about a week before I was caught. The others got away."[32] To "get some money" was the eternal quest of the Coxsackie's inmate's life before prison.[33] Whether caught stealing from cottages on Ballston Lake, apartments in Auburn, or mailboxes in Binghamton, young men arrived from across the state from burglary and larceny convictions.[34]

Petit larceny and burglary arrests are best understood as the legal tip of a much larger iceberg of police and community interactions with adolescent boys living between school and work. In a survey of Coxsackie inmates, most reported that their time prior to the reformatory was spent "just hanging around" with friends and "goofing off."[35] Hanging around, young men became well known to the police; as a consequence, a burglary or petit larceny charge was often just the culmination of a long series of encounters. Jerry O. was sentenced to Coxsackie after being caught breaking into a building and stealing a typewriter, but he was already well known on the streets of Rochester as a "petty thief and tough, a corner loafer and the leader of a gang of tough street urchins." While in school, Jerry had appeared in school court three times, for truancy, insubordination, and fighting. After leaving school at 16, Jerry worked irregularly as a messenger boy but mostly spent his time roaming the streets with his friends. Picked up and released numerous times by the Rochester Police Department, the causes of Jerry's contacts with the police give a sense of how he spent his time: for walking on the railroad tracks; for stealing; for hanging around girls' houses; for swimming in a forbidden river; and for morals violations. Only one of these police contacts resulted in a formal adjudication of delinquency, before the theft of the typewriter led Jerry to Coxsackie.[36] For most reformatory prisoners, the police were simply a part of everyday experience; their Coxsackie sentence just a culmination of a process of control and discipline deeply embedded in their lives.[37]

Joyriders

Over time, no category of criminal activity became more closely associated with the adolescent male offender than auto theft, a linkage described as "well established" in the mid-century criminological literature.[38] Auto theft was the second most common crime among New York City adolescent offenders when Coxsackie opened, and that age group accounted for a disproportionate percentage of total auto theft arrests (in 1950, for example, 16- to 18-year-olds accounted for 17.2% of all major crime arrests, but 43.1% of the auto theft cases).[39] Nearly all adolescent car thieves were boys. Nationally, male auto arrests outpaced female arrests by a 40:1 ratio; in New York City between 1937 and 1938, all but 5 of the 408 adolescents arrested for auto theft were boys.[40]

The case file sample from Coxsackie reveals that the proportion of admissions having stolen a car steadily increased over time, from just 6 percent in the first five years of the sample, to over 25 percent of cases in the last five years of the sample (table 3.3). The percentage of car thieves was growing most dramatically

TABLE 3.3
Coxsackie inmates sentenced for auto theft, 1935–1956, case file sample

Dates of admission	Number of cases	Number of auto thefts	Auto theft (%)
1935–1939	116	7	6.0
1940–1944	105	17	16.2
1945–1949	64	12	18.8
1950–1956	84	24	28.6

at the end of the sample period—of the final thirty sampled cases (covering 1954 through 1956), nearly half (14 of 30) had stolen a car. The increase over time is hard to explain simply with reference to behavior, in that the overall rates of auto theft did not have a comparable growth during this period. It may be that adolescent offending did increase within the auto theft category, but this does not seem to be borne out by the data that show adolescents heavily over-represented in this category both before and after World War II. More likely, the numbers reflect a greater determination of judges to treat the misappropriation of autos by young people more seriously than before.

Arrests for auto theft among the Coxsackie inmates reveals a fascinating intersection of youth attitudes with police behavior. On the one hand, while public discussions of auto theft were warning that this category of crime was becoming "scientific and organized" in support of a multimillion-dollar illicit market in cars and their parts, the adolescent offenders' approach to auto theft seems to have been quite the opposite.[41] For adolescent boys, auto theft was often a spur-of-the-moment act, with little expertise required. To the extent that young men had some notion that the auto would eventually make its way back to an owner, they may not have regarded its taking as a "real" criminal act at all. Joseph T. described the circumstances of his crime in these kinds of muddled terms: "Did not have no money to take the train to go home. It was a 14 mile walk so I stole a car and drove home. Was asked for my license and ownership of the car and found out that the car was stolen."

Joseph's notion that he "found out" that the car was stolen only after he had taken it and driven home seems quite consistent with David Wolcott's observation: "Boys approached auto theft with the same casual disregard they displayed toward lesser criminal behaviors."[42] Almost without exception, the auto theft cases in the sample involved appropriations of cars for immediate needs or simply for joyriding (of the sixty cases involving a stolen automobile, only two contained any suggestion of a commercial purpose).[43] As one study of adolescent offenders put it, cars were a powerful symbol of youthful independence: "Cars are symbols of many longings, secret signs of things forbidden."[44]

Police took the crime far more seriously than the joyriders. Taking a car, for whatever purpose, meant appropriating an item of great value (far more so than the small-value petit larcenies and burglaries that appear in so many Coxsackie cases), as well as appropriating an item of great power and potential hazard to public safety. While not a bona fide theft in some respects, joyriding, as one study put it, were "important for the reason that there is the constant possibility and probability that the car may be partially or totally wrecked or may be the cause of serious property damage or personal injury."[45] Arresting joyriders took on the same kind of opportunistic quality as joyriding itself. Police also went after joyriding and auto theft because they *could*—by simply being on the lookout for groups of adolescents driving around in the "wrong sort" of cars, officers could readily spot young men breaking the law.

Gangs and Fighting

After burglary and larceny, the third most common offense among Coxsackie inmates was assault, and many of the case files connected the assaults to "gang" activity of some sort. Reports of gang associations go back to the earliest case files in the sample, and of course, groups of young men being identified or self-identifying as gangs long preceded Coxsackie's opening. But the problems of adolescent youth, and adolescent criminality, were rarely defined in terms of gang membership or gang violence. During World War II, however, the organization of adolescent youth gangs in New York City began to assume a newer, more distinct form, emphasizing highly visible gang cultures (gang names, clothing, language), interethnic fighting and the use of weapons, and a strong rejection of school and work authority.[46]

Jack E., who arrived at Coxsackie in 1943, is "case one" of the new youth gang culture at the prison, the first case of the sample who fit the new profile. Jack, the son of West Indian immigrants living in Harlem, had been arrested for possession of a knife, which he claimed to be carrying out of fear for his life. He was a member of the Socialistic Dukes and had previously been shot in the arm by a member of the Comanches. These are the first named gangs in the case file sample; indeed, Coxsackie administrators did not yet grasp the emerging concept, referring to the Socialistic Dukes as a "Harlem social club characterized by the Police Department as a troublesome gang." All of Jack's friends were members of the Socialistic Dukes, and he had been arrested with another member.

Jack was among the first of many products of an emerging gang culture to reach Coxsackie, and the Socialistic Dukes were the first of many named gangs to be represented there.[47] In the remaining thirteen years of the case file sample, Coxsackie received adolescent members of the Young Politics, Slicksters, Bankers, Turks, Copians, Nomads, Imperial Lords, Comets, Happy Gents, Imperial Counts, Tigers, Garfields, Seven Saints, Dragons, English Lords, and the El Mambo Reys, to name just some of the gangs represented. Gang members most often arrived following arrests and convictions related to gang fights, usually involving weapons; postwar gang convictions generally account for the rise of crimes involving weapons in the Coxsackie case sample, which rose from 8.6 percent of the pre-1945 cases to 19.6 percent of the post-1945 cases.

The public visibility of intergang violence in wartime and postwar New York City elevated youth gangs to a public policy issue of prime concern. Day-to-day interactions with gang members helped to establish the boundaries—spatial and behavioral—of what the city would tolerate from young men. Arrest and prosecution, on the other hand, arose from police chasing the violence. In the wake of violent confrontations, particularly those in which gang members were injured or killed, police tracked down young men they believed responsible, initiating the process that led to Coxsackie. Albert J. came to Coxsackie following a large gang fight in the Morrisania neighborhood of the Bronx, between the Comets and the Happy Gents. The two gangs gathered outside PS 55 during negotiations over a truce; at some point, members of the Happy Gents became convinced that the truce was not real, and a large-scale fight ensued, during which Albert reportedly fired a revolver. In a similar vein, Ralph C. came to Coxsackie following another Bronx rumble, this time between the Dragons and the Rockets, in which three Rockets were shot and wounded with a .22 caliber rifle. Ralph was just one of several Puerto Rican members of the Dragons who were arrested by police in the roundup that followed.[48]

Sexual Violence and Sexual Delinquency

Few Coxsackie inmates in the sample were ever formally convicted of crimes of sexual violence (1 rape conviction in the 372 cases) or of sex and morals offenses (only 8 of 372 cases). The paucity of sex offenses among the convictions that sent young men to Coxsackie should not be taken to mean that these categories of behavior have little relevance to their life histories. In fact, the case file sample reveals a rather extensive policing of boys' sexual behavior, rather more than one might expect in light of the general emphasis in the historical literature on the policing of *girls'* sexuality, and the construction of female delinquency as sexual deviance. As Tamara Myers has observed, "One is hard pressed to find mention of boys' sexuality—or the corporal dimension of their designation as delinquents—in the literature on boys and juvenile delinquency." In her own work, however, Myers observes a "more widespread policing of boys sexuality" over the course of the first half of the twentieth century, and the Coxsackie sample certainly seems to confirm this.[49]

The single rape conviction, for example, obscures eleven other cases (3.0% of the sample) in which an original indictment for rape was changed to a youthful offender designation, or where the elements of an indictment for rape were present, or where past juvenile histories included a crime of sexual violence.[50] In every one of these cases, the sexual act in question was committed against a younger person. Seven of the cases involved sexual relations with 14- or 15-year-old girls; the remainder involved sexual contact with very young children (both boys and girls) including two 4-year-old girls. Alongside these cases were three cases of incest, in which the defendants had sexual relations with their sisters (in two instances resulting in a pregnancy).

The Coxsackie case files also include sixteen cases (4.3%) that cover a variety of sex and morals offenses, including public exposure, impairing the morals of a minor, bestiality, indecent advances, and unspecified sex delinquencies. Some were obscured by a youthful offender designation, as in the case of Earl F., sent to Coxsackie following an arrest for "manipulating his penis in full view of women subway passengers." Others in this category had records of arrests or convictions for sex offenses as juveniles; Jacob G., for instance, had been picked up by local police several times for indecent exposure and "peeking in windows" (including one arrest for which he was sent to the county jail) prior to his being sent to Coxsackie at age 18.[51]

Homosexual activity was also the subject of state interest, and ten cases in the sample included some prior monitoring of same-sex sexual activity. Although these generally appear in juvenile court records, the "cases" were initiated in various ways, mostly by parents, upset at discovering their son's sexual behavior. Sixteen-year-old Alfredo A., for example, was committed to Coxsackie as a wayward minor on the complaint of his mother. Recently arrived from Puerto Rico, Alfredo had dropped out of school because of his poor English and had no employment (though he hoped that his father might help him find work with an electrician). He seems to have spent much of his time fighting with his mother (who "called him names" and "made him feel unwanted"), smoking marijuana, and hanging out on the street. But it was not until Alfredo's mother discovered that he had been having sexual relations with an older man that she went directly to the court. Although charged as a wayward minor, Alfredo went to Coxsackie because he had recently turned 16.[52]

A final group of cases in the Coxsackie case file sample record instances in which adolescent boys committed acts of violence against homosexual men.[53] In these cases, the adolescent defendant beat or robbed another man seeking a sexual encounter. Adolescent boys understood that gay male vulnerability to arrest and official harassment made them attractive targets as victims. One former prisoner recalled his habit of "sneaking into the all-night pictures around Broadway and Forty-Second Street where all the fags hung out." His friend would lead a customer down the street, whereupon he would run up and loudly accuse the man of soliciting his "little brother" for sex: "The fag would beat it quick, but usually he got so scared we might make a scene he would throw money at us before he took off."[54]

Solicitations for sex served as the basis for criminal victimization. Donald J. and his friends severely beat a man when he asked them for sex after picking them up on a Rochester street corner and purchasing alcohol for them. Complicating many of these cases, many of the young men involved also earned money providing sexual favors to other men, and only in certain instances did robbery or violence follow. Coxsackie prisoners Raymond E. and Jack J. spent many of their days hanging around the Times Square area, looking for men from whom they could earn money for receiving oral sex. But Raymond and Jack also carried with them a .32 caliber revolver, and when the opportunity arose, they used it to rob their customers (both were convicted and sent to Coxsackie on charges of illegal possession of a firearm, when they tried to sell the gun).[55] In similar fashion, Harvey L. (sent to Coxsackie as a wayward minor) earned money for allowing homosexuals to fellate him in Greenwich Village while carrying with him an unloaded gun to use in robbing some of the men he encountered.[56]

Narcotics

For the reformatory system, no change to inmate criminal histories was more sudden than the rise of adolescent heroin use in the late 1940s. In 1937–1938, New York City recorded only *a single arrest* on narcotics charges among adolescents. By the end of World War II, however, an aging population of long-term opiate users began to give way to a younger group of "hip" heroin users attached to the city's jazz scene. In the late 1940s, these hipster trendsetters helped precipitate a surge of heroin initiation among high school–age youth. The first wave of heroin addicts arrived in the reformatory system in 1948, particularly as arrests for violations of drug laws rose. Glenn Kendall reported that the Elmira Reception Center had received "very few users" before 1948, but by 1951, prisoners reporting some previous heroin use accounted for 22 percent of the ERC intake.[57]

The first heroin user to appear in the Coxsackie case file sample, 17-year-old Walter M., went through the Elmira Reception Center in May 1948. He cannot have been the first user of all cases, as Coxsackie had already prepared a "Narcotic Addiction History" form for Walter to complete. The form was a first step toward creating a bureaucratic mechanism for dealing with drugs, a process agencies in New York City and elsewhere were also undertaking in earnest. Walter was asked to report "age when first began to use drugs" "narcotic used" "daily quantity-minimum" "daily quantity-maximum" "cause of habit" "source of method of obtaining supply" "number of months or years taken" "occupation during narcotic period" "effect on earning capacity" "treatment received" "present condition" "criminal history during narcotic period," and "family history as to narcotic addiction." Generally, these forms yielded little in the way of particularly useful information—for "cause of habit," Walter responded, "It is a popular thing; a lot of people use it."[58]

The simplicity of Walter's assessment of heroin's appeal masked the extent to which heroin use—and the public response to that use—presented the reformatory system with a distinct set of challenges for which it was not at all prepared. The first wave of postwar heroin use peaked around 1951, after which the proportion of heroin users gradually declined to about 10 percent of prisoners received at the Elmira Reception Center.[59] A second wave of adolescent heroin use would begin to arrive at the ERC at the start of the 1960s. Heroin users made up 19 percent of ERC commitments in 1962, then 25 percent of new commitments in 1965, and an astonishing 43 percent of all new commitments in 1968. These waves of heroin-using and, in some cases, heroin-addicted adolescents presented the reformatory with a problem it was wholly unequipped to solve, and that ultimately helped undermine the reformatory itself (see chapter 7).

Youth in the Toils

From initial arrest through detention, interrogation, trial, and sentencing, every Coxsackie prisoner had experienced "the system" in action at least once. These experiences included police brutality, harsh interrogations, lengthy pretrial incarcerations, filthy and dangerous jails, and confusing judicial procedures, all of which would profoundly influence the manner in which adolescent offenders understood the criminal justice system and the reformatory they entered. Few prisoners accorded the criminal justice system any legitimacy at all. One described an impenetrable game of chance: "Everything that ever happened to me with cops and courts and boards and commissioners was confusing . . . Maybe the law don't punish or reform you, but they certainly keep you guessing."[60]

Arrest was the first step in the formal criminal justice process. Police acted less frequently on the complaint of parents or family members than they did in the juvenile justice system, where such referrals were quite common. Instead, the police initiated most of the arrests on a victim's criminal complaint, or after officers made their own observations of criminal behavior. Pending a first appearance before a magistrate, young men accused of more serious crimes would be subject to police interrogation. For adolescents in the system, the interrogation not infrequently mirrored the physical brutality of the informal "nightstick justice" they faced in the streets from the police. The Wickersham Commission had exposed, only a few years earlier, widespread use of the third degree by law enforcement, and the NYC Legal Aid Society's review of 1,500 indigent prisoners found that nearly one-third (405) had claimed to have been beaten by the police. Of the 398 adolescent offenders in Manhattan in 1937 defended by the Voluntary Defenders Committee of the Legal Aid Society, approximately 1 in 5 claimed to have been beaten by the police.[61]

Even allowing for some overclaiming on the part of defendants, the journey to Coxsackie often began with police violence.[62] It appears with disturbing regularity in the stories of Coxsackie prisoners. John Valletutti was picked up from Coxsackie on the day of his scheduled release from the institution, taken by police to Brooklyn, where he was interrogated for thirty consecutive hours, during which time his requests to notify his parents or to use the telephone were refused. Valletutti claimed that he was "brutally and continuously assaulted" throughout the interrogation, and a jail physician's investigation days later confirmed the presence of wounds likely from having been beaten.[63] Another prisoner recounted an extensive third-degree interrogation after being picked up on suspicion of burglarizing a school, in which he was handcuffed to a chair while three pairs of police officers spent five hours beating him.

Police violence affected vulnerable adolescent defendants, regardless of race, but brutality against African American defendants emerged as the most troubling public issue by the time Coxsackie opened. As the last carloads of young men headed from the House of Refuge to the new institution, Harlem exploded into rioting over the rumored beating by police of a young black shoplifting suspect. The protests of 1935 presaged years of community conflict in New York City over the dilemmas of policing and police violence, particularly for young black men. Mass rallies against police violence were commonplace by the 1940s, and police-community conflict was both spark and tinder for the Harlem riots of 1943.[64] For black prisoners at Coxsackie, police violence loomed large in the experience of criminal justice. Caught by police following a supermarket theft, one former prisoner recounted his experience in the police station: "He called me a nigger, and some unkind things about my ancestors, and then began hitting me all over my body with his fists—punching, grabbing, kicking. I could never go all the way down because I was handcuffed to the top of the radiator and finally that resulted in my head hitting the radiator and me losing consciousness . . . a couple of hours later, my father, who was sent for, arrived and obediently promised to give me a beating when I got home. And so I was released—on the promise of good behavior."[65] The stories of Coxsackie's prisoners underscore historian Dominic Capeci's conclusion that "most blacks viewed policemen as the boldest examples of northern racism."[66]

For the young men in the hands of the police, of course, any time to reflect on the larger injustices of their treatment would have to be found while the wheels of justice continued to turn for them. While in police detention, young men were generally held without access to family or to legal counsel, with anxious parents also denied access and information.[67] A prewar Coxsackie prisoner recalled the precinct house experience:

> The precinct house was like all precinct houses—old, run-down, with the smell of linseed oil they treat the floors with, and stale vomit where some old drunk had thrown up. And there's that strange feeling like it's deserted, except that there's life there somewhere, always behind the closed doors, and plenty of lights on inside the desk room, but nobody there. Empty. Off in the distance, behind a closed door, was the clatter of a teletype machine, every now and then the ring of a telephone and the sound of someone talking. Then the desk sergeant came in and Pete and I got tied up again with the machinery of the law.[68]

For these young men in custody, the next step was the police lineup, during which they were questioned again. Facing the bright lights, unable to make out the people standing in front of them, the adolescent defendant could begin to feel the fear of an uncertain fate. As one boy put it, "I don't know why, but suddenly I got very scared. Everything inside of me sort of curled up."[69]

Once the initial interrogation and lineup had been completed, the adolescent offender generally went to a detention facility to await arraignment before a magistrate. These facilities varied enormously across New York State, from small police holding cells in rural upstate counties to massive jails in urban centers.

In the largest jails, young offenders were confined with others of their age group—on the top tier of the Queens City Prison, the fifth floor of the Bronx County Jail, or the south annex of the Tombs in Manhattan. At times, "institutionally experienced" inmates were held in separate sections from young men without such experience.[70] At the Tombs in Manhattan, for example, those who had "done time" went to the north annex of the facility, while homicide cases went to the main building. A rough racial separation was enforced at the larger facilities. At the Tombs north annex, for example, the "colored boys" usually spent their time on the top tiers; below, a rough assignment by nationality prevailed, with small numbers of non-English speakers assigned together when possible.[71] "In the eyes of the keepers who run the place," recalled one inmate, "you were guilty the minute they locked you up in the Tombs. They treated you like the crap the joint stunk of . . . To them you were guilty and this meant you were the scum of the earth."[72]

Cases that did not end at magistrate's court (and about half of all cases did end there, with a dismissal or reduction of charges) meant continued confinement while young men awaited final trial and disposition. Pretrial release was not at all the norm—nearly eight in ten adolescents were denied bail, a figure that is roughly the same even for defendants who would eventually be discharged, acquitted, given suspended sentences, or placed on probation.[73] The amount of time spent in pretrial detention declined over time but remained substantial. In 1929, the New York State Crime Commission evaluated time elapsed from arrest to final disposition in 3,907 cases: 969 in one to five days; 1,362 from six to thirty days; 822 from thirty-one to sixty days; and 752 more than sixty days. In 1937–1938, fewer than 10 percent of inmates were confined for five days or less—most still spent more than one month in confinement awaiting trial.[74]

For the prisoners of Coxsackie, the arrival of their day in court meant only a brief appearance to accept a plea bargain (often, after 1945, under the terms of the youthful offender statute). The court appearance rarely seemed, to young defendants, to embody anything other than a process of deal making that they barely understood. Failure to comprehend the proceedings could not have been helped by the relatively poor quality of legal counsel. Coxsackie inmates were rarely able to afford private defense attorneys. Most adolescent defendants were provided court-appointed counsel, but generally not until immediately before the final disposition of their case. Few were under any illusions about the quality of their legal representation. George Malinow, who faced armed robbery charges as a 17-year-old in 1938, felt that a lack of legal assistance worked against him and his fellow defendants: "We weren't given that kind of consideration, simply because our parents were poor. None of us had any money to pay a lawyer."[75]

As inadequate as court-appointed counsel might have been in some instances, worse still were times when adolescent defendants ended up facing adjudication without any legal representation. Dominick Losacco was a 16-year-old inmate at the Warwick reformatory, where staff members caught him tampering with the wires of a truck. Just four days later, the state indicted Dominick on charges of attempted grand larceny. The indictment was handed down on a Fri.. By the following Mon. morning, counsel was assigned to the defendant, and he pleaded guilty to the charges—but Dominick had never actually *seen* counsel. It later came out that the court hadn't bothered to notify the assigned attorney, and court personnel had simply entered the plea—one that resulted in a sentence to Coxsackie.[76]

Judges and prosecutors were not above manipulating defendants and their parents to secure a guilty plea. The hard reality of serving prison time left Coxsackie prisoners feeling duped by the plea negotiation process. Jerry O. claimed that he had been "tricked" into being sent to Coxsackie: "I pled guilty to a burglary charge to get a lighter sentence."[77] The youthful offender law proved to be a powerful device by which judges could encourage guilty pleas. The judge hearing the cases of Joseph Giacco and Eugene Panzella, charged with robbery, grand larceny, and assault, carefully explained to both boys the benefits of pleading guilty as a youthful offender. Going further, the judge also met privately with both of their mothers. He assured the concerned parents that, by pleading guilty, Joseph and Eugene "could go to Elmira and [they] would be studied for 75 to 90 days, and they would then go to a vocational training school."[78] In court, the judge reiterated, "It is not a crime to be a youthful offender. The law so provides, so that, even if you were to plead guilty as a youthful offender, it is nevertheless, not a crime . . . It is not a crime at all now." For all of the judge's assurances that pleading guilty as a youthful offender was not a crime, it masked the reality that they were facing punishment—just as his assurances that the boys would be sent to a "vocational training school" masked the reality that they were heading to a state prison for up to three years.[79]

Few cases illustrate the casual indifference of the criminal courts toward the adolescent defendant more clearly than that of 16-year-old Marvin Gayes, sent to Coxsackie in 1938 for burglary and petit larceny. Gayes had been born in Savannah, Georgia, before his parents moved the family to Rochester. At some point prior to his arrest, Gayes had been removed from his home by the

Rochester Society for the Prevention of Cruelty to Children and taken to an SPCC shelter in the town of Rush, just south of the city. On July 13, 1938, Gayes and a friend broke into the Pontiac Garage in Rush and stole some cigarettes, two flashlights, and some cash. The entire value of their heist was just four dollars and seventy-five cents. Arrested and brought to court two days later, his initial appearance was quick and to the point:

ASSISTANT DISTRICT ATTORNEY: You spell your last name G-a-y-e-s?
DEFENDANT: Yes.
ADA: Do you have a lawyer?
DEFENDANT: No, sir.
[The content of the indictment is then read]
COURT: Do you need a lawyer before you enter a plea of guilty or not guilty
    to this indictment?
DEFENDANT: No, sir.
COURT: What is your plea?
DEFENDANT: Guilty
COURT: You have not received any promises from the district attorney or any
    member of this staff as to what disposition will be made of your matter?
DEFENDANT: No, sir.

And, with that, Gayes's trial concluded. In just a few minutes, he had waived his right to an attorney and pled guilty to felony burglary charges. Gayes's sentencing two weeks later was, if anything, an even more cursory affair:

ASSISTANT DISTRICT ATTORNEY: The People move this matter for sentence.
CLERK: Have you any legal cause to show why the judgment of the court
    should not now be imposed upon you?
COURT: Have you anything to say?
DEFENDANT: No, sir.
COURT: It is the sentence of this court that you be committed to the New
    York State Vocational School at West Coxsackie, New York, and dealt with
    there according to law.

Having uttered just nine words on his own behalf—four "no, sir" responses and "guilty"—Marvin Gayes was shipped off to Coxsackie, two hundred and fifty miles away.

The same year Gayes headed to Coxsackie to serve his sentence, Leonard V. Harrison published a scathing indictment of the criminal justice system's handling of the adolescent defendant. How, Harrison asked, could a reformatory hope to accomplish any good after the brutality and indifference to which young men were subject on their way through the system? "It is a poor beginning for the reform process," he wrote. "Although the state seemingly believes in the possibilities of reform after an offender's conviction," Harrison concluded, "it nevertheless begins with procedures of accusation, arraignment, and detention which militate against the task of reform."[80] Few challenges to the moral authority of the reformatory were greater than its connection to the rough justice meted out at the lower levels of the criminal justice system.

The Final Sorting

The record in Marvin Gayes's 1938 case is silent on at least one important question—why Coxsackie? Just as with the old House of Refuge, Coxsackie received a relatively small number of cases chosen from the great mass of young men caught in the legal system. Most could have received sanctions short of incarceration in a state reformatory, such as the five-year suspended sentence handed down to Marvin Gayes's co-defendant. Were there any patterns to the decision making that led young men to be sentenced to Coxsackie or, after 1945, being sent to Coxsackie from the Elmira Reception Center?

Most sentencing judges before 1945 used Coxsackie as an option for what they considered to be younger versions of more dangerous adult offenders. Rather than adopting the reformer's position that Coxsackie should house the more hopeful cases in the state prison system, judges more often used a reformatory sentence to send a message to the most intractable adolescent defendants. As noted earlier, Coxsackie inmates were more likely to have prior records of arrest or conviction than the general population of adolescent offenders. Marvin Gayes, for example, had been convicted of breaking and entering earlier that year in Toronto, while his co-defendant had no prior criminal record.[81]

Judicial speechmaking at sentencing reveals many instances of "getting tough" on defendants who had run out of chances. One defendant headed to Coxsackie heard the judge declare him "a dangerous, incorrigible little gangster, a nuisance to society."[82] A Nassau County judge lectured Jack B. at his sentencing for burglary: "You are a tough boy, aren't you? We have been talking to each other here for a year and trying to get along and trying to straighten you out, and we go from bad to worse all the way along the line."[83] A Brooklyn youth was called "a moral consumptive" who should not be allowed to "go back to the same pest-hole that caused his original condition."[84] Three Utica boys were told: "Probation is for boys who have made a mistake and who have a conscience, but you boys have no conscience." The defendants, the judge averred, were "a disgrace to their families."[85] Still another sentencing judge made it clear what the reformatory sentence meant: "Wrong. Wrong in your attitude, wrong in the company you keep, wrong in your whole approach to life . . . Further leniency in your case is useless. You've already had three chances to prove that you wanted to reform, and each time you've gone out to commit another offense. I hereby sentence you to an indeterminate term of one to three years."[86]

Less often, judges embraced the reform narrative that a sentence to Coxsackie constituted a positive point of intervention for promising youth less experienced in crime. Though the case file sample is hardly comprehensive in revealing judicial decision making, this attitude seems to have been more prevalent among judges in rural upstate counties. John M., from a farm family in Cortland County, was sent away "to a state Institution for boys" on his first criminal offense, because "he has been inclined to chaff off the supervision of both his father and grandparents."[87] Arthur G. faced his sentencing judge in rural Montgomery County with no prior arrests or convictions and with the support of his parents, minister, and family friends. In light of this positive record, the judge concluded, the defendant would be sent to Coxsackie: "This is not a penal institution but an institution, if you do cooperate, you will leave in much better condition and health than you are in now."[88]

The variability of judicial opinion meant that Coxsackie housed an odd mixture of cases. A population largely composed of tougher adolescent offenders with longer juvenile and criminal records than most resided alongside smaller numbers of genuinely naïve first-time offenders. Above all, the case files from Coxsackie's first decade (before the Elmira Reception Center opened) highlight just how discretionary sentencing was, and how much an adolescent's future truly hung in the balance in the courtroom. Three cases from the sample illustrate his highly contingent process at work.

In the first case, Antonio S. and his parents made a court appearance on Thanksgiving Eve, 1945, before Judge Saul Streit in the Manhattan General Sessions Court. Antonio had been arrested for stealing an automobile to go joyriding, and his exasperated parents were insisting that he be sent to "jail" in order to "teach him a lesson." Judge Streit hesitated to do so and, perhaps hoping to spark a familial reconciliation, reminded Antonio's parents that the next day was Thanksgiving. Unmoved, the parents insisted that something be done with their son. His appeal to holiday harmony being unsuccessful, the judge decided to send Antonio to Coxsackie, where he remained for about a year.[89]

In the second case, Stanley M., a 16-year-old defendant from Poughkeepsie convicted of breaking and entering, faced three distinct alternatives at sentencing. In light of Stanley's previous juvenile conviction for breaking and entering, the judge expressed an intention to commit him to Coxsackie. He stipulated to the presentencing examiner, however, that if the boy's home was deemed adequate, then Stanley could return home and serve probation. Alternatively, if Stanley's intelligence was "too low for training" at Coxsackie, then he was to be committed to the Wassaic State School for Mental Defectives (one of New York State's newest training schools for the mentally disabled). The home was quickly judged unsuitable, which ruled out probation. The previous year the juvenile court had measured his IQ at 68, which would have sent him to Wassaic, but his retested IQ was 70 ("slow, dumb cooperation but good effort"), the minimum needed. For his "good effort" and the two extra IQ points, Stanley began serving twelve months at Coxsackie, rather than an indefinite assignment to Wassaic.[90]

In the third case, Melvin P. arrived from a Brooklyn court that "could think of no other institution except the New York State Vocational Institution." It wasn't for lack of trying. Melvin had been charged under the wayward minor law, for breaking dishes in his home and refusing to attend school. His mother brought him to the court; living alone with Melvin, she felt unable to control his behavior—indeed, she had tried to have him committed as mentally ill earlier in the year. The court's welfare worker first attempted to place Melvin in a vocational school "in the South," but Melvin resisted, and the placement fell through. The court psychiatrist found no evidence of mental illness and recommended that the young man be placed with the Urban League's Home for Friendless Boys, but this placement, too, fell through. Having run out of options for Melvin, the court sentenced him to Coxsackie.[91]

With the opening of the Elmira Reception Center, the sorting process theoretically became more rational. While the decision to sentence young men to prison (the ERC received 16- to 21-year-olds) remained with a trial court judge, making particular institutional assignments became the job of reception center staff. Every week, an average of thirty young men took the "big train ride" to Elmira to begin a three-month period of assessment and observation. Jacob Miller gives an interesting account of the ERC from the inmate's perspective:

> When we finally got to Elmira, a bus was waiting for us at the train station that transported us to the prison . . . Once we left the bus and were taken inside, we had haircuts, crew cuts, marine style, were stripped, showered, after which they had us bend over and spread our butt cheeks and sprayed our anuses with some type of disinfectant that burned. After that they gave us a sack of toiletries and a

bologna sandwich and a water-down coffee . . . The job in that three months for a prisoner, I quickly gathered, was to convince the authorities you wouldn't be a problem. Every day was another test, seeing doctors, shrinks, taking IQ tests. Knowing that the outcome of their evaluation at the end of the three months would determine where I would be imprisoned the next several years, I stayed away from fights and tried to keep a low profile, hoping to be assigned to a less intense prison than Elmira."[92]

As Miller understood, the job of the ERC staff was to make a decision about institutional assignment, based on a "Classification and Recommendations" document that would then be forwarded to the prison with the inmate. The report consisted of a summary sheet for the receiving prison, which highlighted the psychologist's report; the psychiatrist's report; reports on general education, vocational education, physical education, and religion; the custodial report; and general parole recommendation (which usually grouped inmates into one of several classes that suggested either longer or shorter periods of confinement).

The specific reports were attached to the summary sheet and were remarkably detailed documents. In the ERC psychologist's report were the results of intelligence testing, often multiple test scores including the Otis Beta, Army Designs, Kent Kohs, and more; school achievement scores, listed as a general grade-level achievement and broken down into reading vocabulary, reading comprehension, arithmetic reasoning, arithmetic fundamentals, and language; mechanical ability tests, including most often the Minnesota Paper Form Board Test, the Stenquist Mechanical Aptitude Test, and the Bennett Mechanical Comprehension Test; a personality test score (Bell Personality Test or the Minnesota Multiphasic Personality Inventory); and the Brainard Occupational Preference Inventory. Given the large caseload, a psychiatrist's report was prepared only when observation suggested the possibility of mental illness. General and vocational education reports included detailed educational and work histories, along with preliminary assessments of the inmate's trial work at the ERC and some qualitative summaries. The physical education report was shorter, listing recreational activities pursued at the ERC (basketball, softball, etc.) and briefly summarizing "attitude in program." The chaplain's report covered their church attendance history, parent's church activity, attitudes toward religion, and a set of comments and recommendations. The "custodial adjustment" report brought the custodial officers into the process, and their report generally focused on personal habits, work habits, behavior, and respect for authority.

So who went to Coxsackie from the ERC? The phrase "more hopeful cases" was part of the ERC's formal language for Coxsackie assignment, but what made for a more hopeful case? Despite all the testing and observation, the most important factors were nothing more complicated than age and prior record. Coxsackie's inmates were considerably younger than those in the rest of the ERC; just over half of 16-year-olds and just under half of the 17-year-olds at the ERC were assigned to Coxsackie, but only one-quarter of the 18-year-olds and virtually no inmates aged 19 or older.[93] Among reformatories, Coxsackie also housed the lowest percentage of prisoners with a previous adult criminal record. In 1962, 50 percent of Coxsackie inmates had a previous adult criminal conviction, and although this was certainly much higher than the general population of adolescent felony offenders in New York, it was a lower proportion than any other reformatory: repeat offenders made up 60 percent of the populations at Woodbourne, 74 percent at Elmira, and 76 percent at Great Meadow.

The sentence handed down by the trial court made a difference as well. ERC inmates who had received five-year terms under the Youthful Offender Act were far more likely to go to Elmira or Great Meadow / Comstock than the inmates sentenced to "zip-three" (inmate shorthand for a three-year youthful offender sentence), who generally went to Coxsackie or Woodbourne. Along the same lines, Coxsackie was the institution of choice for ERC inmates who had been sentenced as misdemeanants or as wayward minors. After 1948, the state limited sentences for Coxsackie inmates to no more than five years, although most were already arriving with three-year terms.[94] This held steady over time; in 1962, 83 percent of all Coxsackie inmates were there on three-year terms, compared to only 19 percent of Elmira inmates.[95]

In general, a youthful offender designation (recalling that the ERC received *all* 16- to 21-year-old convicted felons, not just those convicted under the youthful offender laws) tipped the balance toward Coxsackie. Many borderline or troubling cases seem to have been directed to Coxsackie simply because they were youthful offenders. Wendell M. arrived at the ERC in 1945, having run away to New York City from Wisconsin (after his parole from the State School for Boys at Waukesha). He had spent most of his free time hanging around Times Square, where he was arrested for breaking a store window and stealing some clothes. ERC staff found Wendell to be deeply disturbed, referring him to the psychiatrist, who diagnosed him as having "profound personality disorganization" and placed him "tentatively" in the group to be committed to a mental hospital. Instead, "because of his commitment as a Youthful Offender," he went to Coxsackie.[96]

Did "hopeful" have any meaning beyond age and sentence? The case files suggest that it was also related to attitude and aptitude, though not in the ways that reformers originally imagined. Coxsackie tended to receive the "immature" inmate—young men possessed of essentially normal intelligence and without specific mental illness, but who were too childish for Elmira or Wallkill Prison. Walter P., a Brooklyn youth who arrived at the ERC in 1949 on a robbery conviction, was regarded as "an accidental offender with a fairly normal makeup" whose high intelligence made him a natural candidate for Wallkill. But Walter ended up at Coxsackie, largely because of his immature world outlook, influenced "by the need for flashy clothing and . . . a fairly strong impulse to play the role of becoming affluent."[97] A zoot-suit attitude, in other words, might be sufficient to direct young men to Coxsackie.

Likewise, when Earl W. arrived at the ERC in 1946 from Queens, he managed to annoy everyone who observed him. The psychologist reported that he had "acted in an irrational, peculiar manner, continually drawing attention to himself by constant talking, getting up, asking all sorts of silly questions and in general acting in a peculiar, irrepressible manner." The general education counselor predicted Earl would "be a problem in the classroom" and the vocational education report expressed the hope that he would move back down South to live and work on a farm. Until that day came, because of his youthful offender status and his "immature personality," Earl would serve his time at Coxsackie.[98]

The games of chance that brought Earl and other prisoners to the reformatory marked a critical juncture in young lives already well worn by conflict. Breakdowns within the family, hostility and indifference at school, and frustration with work ran alongside growing levels of contact with the police. On their journey to institutional confinement, whether for the first time or just the most recent of many times, reformatory inmates had too often experienced the worst of what the criminal justice system had to offer. They arrived hungry for opportunity yet profoundly skeptical of what they felt Coxsackie stood for. Placed behind bars by the state, young reformatory inmates would soon face an even more serious game, one of survival and adaptation.

CHAPTER FOUR

Against the Wall

Survival and Resistance at Coxsackie

Years before Rocky Graziano, the fiercely competitive boxer with a powerful punch, became middleweight champion in 1947, he was just another anxious teenager awaiting transportation from the Tombs to Coxsackie. An older prisoner, perhaps to taunt the younger Graziano, warned him: "Don't kid yourself . . . that's a state prison, that ain't no reform school. They put kids in there for life, kids that are too young to send to the chair."[1] While no one actually went to Coxsackie for life—nearly everyone had a three-year maximum term—the warning echoed the general tenor of pre-arrival advice: be careful, be aware of how little you are prepared, focus on survival, and understand that you are headed to a real prison. For all of their legal entanglements and institutional experience, few new arrivals to Coxsackie had ever been in a state prison before, and few had been as far removed from family, neighborhood, and home as they were when they reached the reformatory nestled in the rural Hudson Valley. Graziano recalled the train trip up from New York City: "I suddenly felt sick . . . They were taking me away from New York City for the first time in my life. Every minute I was farther away from the East Side . . . It would be a beautiful day on the East Side. It was almost June. The sun would be beating down on the roofs, shining on the wings of all the pigeons. The streets would be full of stickball games and everybody's windows would be open and the crap games would move outdoors to the stoops and you would feel wonderful."[2] Feelings of being uprooted from home mixed with anxiety about the institutional life ahead of new arrivals.

For the teenage boys sent on "the big train ride," finding and maintaining their place in the social system of the prison became the key to survival.[3] This struggle, far more than any educational or vocational program, defined life behind bars at the reformatory. In this respect, the "rehabilitative" prison at

Coxsackie looked very much like its more punitive contemporaries. Historian David Rothman once observed that progressive prison reforms were ultimately "up against the wall"—by which he meant that efforts at rehabilitation were inevitably subordinated to the demands of secure custody and discipline. As a way of expanding on this insight, it may be helpful to observe that, at Coxsackie, the inmates were literally up against the prison wall. Every day, they gathered along the walls of the prison yard during their outdoor time, in space starkly divided by race and ethnicity. Against these walls, prisoner survival required constant displays of toughness and masculinity, preying on the weak without violating the boundaries set by institutional authorities.

Just how reformatory life at Coxsackie came to be defined by a racially segregated and violent social system is the sort of question that has occupied correctional researchers for many decades. Some of the earliest and most important work on prison life stressed what would come to be known as "deprivation," or "prisonization," theory: that the artificial world of the prison created its own distinct (and equally artificial) social system. Prison life, from this perspective, could be accounted for solely by reference to prisons themselves. Later scholars rightly challenged the overly determined character of deprivation theory, making the case that a richer account of prison life had to consider the values and identities that prisoners imported into the institution. Importation theory emphasized the pre-prison context, arguing that social experience and individual personality were more determinative of behavior behind bars.[4]

Coxsackie's history suggests that historians can most profitably try to integrate elements of both models, taking care to understand the historically dynamic elements of each. On the one hand, what Graziano and his fellow inmates carried with them into Coxsackie mattered a great deal. As chapter 3 has already shown, they brought with them pronounced ideas about school, family, work, and authority. They imported into Coxsackie models of dominant masculinity that would define power relations between them, filtered through deep interracial hostility. On the other hand, Coxsackie *was* another world from the one they knew. The reformatory gave young men precious few outlets for expressing masculinity, offered near-constant challenges to its maintenance, and responded with brutal violence to those who became too assertive or resisted authority. In the very act of removing thousands of adolescent boys from across New York and housing them in a rural upstate prison, the state created an environment that could not help but represent a distinct lived experience.

Every prison was not Coxsackie, and Coxsackie was not every prison—what it came to be emerged from a specific mixture of adolescent experiences and attitudes, prison space, and institutional policies (both formal and informal). Life behind reformatory bars is told here, as much as possible, in the words of those who lived it. They include a surprising number of well-known figures, but also many prisoners known only through the words and actions recorded in their case files. Individual voices, brought together once again, tell a story far removed from the ambitions of the liberal reformers who built Coxsackie. Their accounts include memories of abuse, humiliation, and victimization that constitute a shameful legacy for New York State. This legacy remains largely hidden from public memory; we have forgotten not only the painful consequences of imprisonment at Coxsackie, but also what the experience itself was like.

Quarantine: Adolescents Uprooted

Every prisoner spent the first two weeks in quarantine at Coxsackie, during which time he tried to assess what the prison experience would mean. The process certainly emphasized the distinctiveness of reformatory life. New arrivals came into Coxsackie and immediately exchanged their street clothes for a state prison uniform (brown or green or gray at varying times over the years) and their number—a number that "none of those who spent time at Coxsackie would ever forget."[5] As for quarantine itself, it was, in the words of Rocky Graziano, "a two-week deal, while they give you medical exams, shots, interviews, all that."[6] For all the care that reformers took with the planning of the quarantine period, few prisoner accounts acknowledge much more to its rehabilitative aspect than Graziano's indifferent summary.[7]

Prisoner accounts of quarantine do not dwell much on the vocational interviews or the psychological assessments because, for new arrivals, these were far from the most salient matters to which they had to attend. More than anything else, the young men in quarantine worried about their survival at Coxsackie, and the process by which they could navigate a social universe as novel as it was artificial. Few brought with them definite ideas. Some had been given advice by older friends, gang members, or neighborhood ex-prisoners, advice that usually emphasized how tough the place was compared with the experience of a juvenile reformatory. Coxsackie inmates sought to get the word back home to friends, even as they remained behind bars. Two inmates attempted to communicate with a mutual friend in New York City by adding a message to a letter written to one inmate's mother. The advice was direct and to the point: "Take it slow old man because this is tough slamers [sic] to be in, its hard."[8]

Like so many letters by and for Coxsackie's prisoners, this word of warning was confiscated by prison censors and placed in the case file. The great physical distance between prisoners and home was accentuated by the rigid limitations on contact with networks of friends and family on the outside. Every inmate was allowed to include a short list of immediate family members on a visitation and correspondence list; institutional authorities forbade prisoner contact with anyone else while in prison. The case files suggest that even the family members on the visitation list were not able to visit often. Travel from New York City, or upstate cities like Buffalo and Rochester, involved considerable time and expense, and few prisoners' families had enough of either to allow for frequent visits. Dhoruba Bin Wahad had only a single visitor at Coxsackie before being transferred to another prison, and he recalled: "The Bureau of Prisons [sic] made it so difficult and costly for a person of limited means to navigate the prison bureaucracy and get to the facility that visits were rare to nonexistent."[9] Past lives and imagined futures were, for the most part, replaced by the overwhelmingly alien and forbidding present of the quarantine cell.

The experience of quarantine emphasized the new sense of isolation, and their only contacts with the general prison population reinforced their sense of entering a new world. Frankie Moreno encountered this sense in the daily trips to and from the mess hall, "marching in columns of two (military style with an angry guard barking orders, 'eyes front,' 'about face,' 'halt')." As the new arrivals marched, Moreno recalled, "we were eyed by the hawks looking for easy prey . . . Anyone showing too much sensitivity was a target; the ones wearing their fear on their sleeves would have it the hardest. I marched with just enough of a 'screw you' swagger that I hoped they got the message not to mess with me."[10] One inmate thought about the cars passing by on highway 9W as the gate closed behind him, hopefully imagining that their drivers, given a chance to go behind bars, would sympathize with Coxsackie's "sorry load of humanity."[11] Another young prisoner found no such comfort in an imagined solidarity with the drivers in the distance: "All I could do was think and look out to the open area before me, where I saw crops growing on a farm and seven houses that I thought were farmhouses but found out later were the residences of the warden and the staff. The best view of all was of highway 9W where the cars rushed by, all having destinations, oblivious to this one black soul who could do nothing but look and wonder where they were off to."[12]

In the Yard: The Shock of Segregation

Inmates began their first day in general population by moving their personal items to the assigned cell block or dormitory space, and then heading to their school or shop assignment for the morning (most new arrivals divided the day between school and vocational shop, with one assignment in the morning and one in the afternoon). After the morning's educational and vocational work had concluded, new prisoners joined the rest of the prison population in heading to the cafeteria for lunch. After lunch, it was time to move outdoors to the prison yard, the space that—more than any other—would define the Coxsackie experience for inmates.

Although Coxsackie was touted at its opening as a prison without walls, the with-or-without walls distinction must have been lost on the prisoners themselves, as few of them ever had much time to spend outside (those assigned to work the prison farm were the biggest exception). Instead, Coxsackie fashioned its outdoor space from a massive courtyard (about the size of a football field) formed by the surrounding cellblocks. The outdoor space was just as walled off as any prison space could be, probably more so given the great height of the imposing cellblocks that surrounded the hundreds of young men who gathered below. And to reinforce the point, armed guards patrolled the rooftops, looking down on the gathering prisoners.[13]

The yard, then, was hardly the pastoral setting one might have imagined from how the new reformatory had been promoted. The real shock of the yard, however, had less to do with the grimness of the space. Rather, young arrivals were taken aback by the absolute racial segregation imposed in the yard. Long-time Brooklyn-based activist Abubadika Sonny Carson, who was launched into black nationalist politics by his experience in the reformatory, described "the [segregated] way the inmates gathered there" as absolutely shocking. In his memoir, Carson recalled, "All of the blacks were concentrated on one side and all the whites, with Puerto Ricans intermingled, gathered on the opposite side. As I walked down the steps, I perceived what segregation was all about. So I headed into a particular direction on the side of the yard where all the blacks were located."[14] Prisoners gathered against the walls of the yard, and all new arrivals found themselves forced to assume their assigned place in the racial geography. Former inmate, and later political activist, Ronald Casanova recalled the futility of resistance to the racial order as a black Puerto Rican: "When I first went into Coxsackie I even walked the middle for a little while because I didn't believe in segregation. But as a means to survive, once again I decided I'd better join a group."[15]

Casanova's reluctance to submit to the racial division at Coxsackie highlights some important interpretive questions: Was the yard's organization a product of the prisoners or their keepers? Was Coxsackie's yard historically contingent or part of some more timeless and universal way of ordering prison space? To the former question, the racial segregation does not seem to have been imported into Coxsackie by the prisoners; at least, the separation of the reformatory yard was unlike anything that most adolescents had ever experienced. On the contrary, most accounts suggest that the yard seemed, in the words of one inmate, "like a sick kind of joke" at first encounter.[16] Eric Schneider's insightful work on postwar gangs in New York City reminds us that "interethnic" gang conflicts were often waged by gangs with a multiethnic composition, and that in rapidly changing environments, "rigidly drawn lines demarcating one ethnic group's turf from another's simply could not be maintained."[17]

At Coxsackie, on the other hand, racial lines appear to have been rigidly drawn and aggressively maintained, as they had been back in the House of Refuge, and this almost certainly had the approval of the institutional administration, particularly the custodial staff.[18] One inmate saw prison segregation as an instrument of survival, but one that was distinctly sharpened in the prison environment: "You talk about segregation, prison is the place to find it because that's how you stay alive."[19] Every prisoner account of Coxsackie from this period makes at least some reference to the race and racism behind bars as well as the overwhelming barriers the institution raised between white and black inmates. A black prisoner from Buffalo recalled Coxsackie as his "first experience with segregation that was officially reinforced and encouraged."[20] A white prisoner at Coxsackie recalled that he and black inmates "could not talk to each other. Couldn't look at each other at one of these institutions. They have separatism right down to the water you drink. You have separatism in your eating and job areas . . . I was very fortunate. I was white, for one thing, and this is status in a prison."[21]

Separation bred hostility. Ronald Casanova observed: "Coxsackie was a very prejudiced place. Not only were there guards against the inmates, but also the inmates against each other. You lived under that pressure all the time."[22] The racial divisions among the inmates, and their use of violence to enforce solidarity, were an essential fact of life from the moment the reformatory opened. A visiting researcher in 1937 took note of the "constant antagonisms that prevail between the two color groups." "If a colored boy hits a white guy, even a creeper," the researcher reported, "all the white guys, regardless of benches, go over and beat the Negroes."[23] The domination of the white inmates was easier to maintain at Coxsackie, where black inmates were a minority of the population throughout this period. Charles McGregor, who went on to have an active career acting in films such as *Super Fly* and *Blazing Saddles*, recalled that when he entered the reformatory in 1940, "there weren't enough of us blacks to win any fights against the white inmates, so for a long time we didn't pick any fights . . . In New York State, racism is institutionalized in prisons."[24]

Puerto Rican inmates, universally referred to as "spicks" at Coxsackie, suffered from both their small numbers and their ambiguous racial status in the prison. As one terrified young inmate confided to an investigator, "They don't like fellows they call Spick."[25] Their side of the prison yard was called "Spain," in keeping with the habit of Puerto Rican youths in New York City self-identifying as Spanish, at least in part to reject any common identity with the city's African Americans.[26] The case file sample includes only thirteen Puerto Rican inmates (3.5% of the total sample), reflecting what appears to have been a deliberate policy of steering Spanish-speaking inmates away from Coxsackie and toward institutions for inmates of lower intelligence. This trend continued after the period covered by the case file sample. By the mid-1950s, nearly 25 percent of new commitments to the Woodbourne reformatory—for adolescents of "borderline intelligence"—were Puerto Rican, as opposed to roughly 6 percent of new commitments to Coxsackie.[27] Those who did make it to the Coxsackie reformatory found themselves dealing with the hazards of their unstable place in the institution. Their status, recalled one inmate, "was like a pendulum and when the system had a problem, say [with] one pole, Black or white, the pendulum would swing one way or the other depending on what the onus was. So the Puerto Rican was either white or Black given the circumstances . . . And this was sort of a control mechanism because there was no unity."[28]

Bop City: Masculinity, Violence, and Inmate Life

For Coxsackie's inmates, life in and beyond the prison yard involved a series of challenges to their masculinity. Reformatory boys took advantage of every opportunity, therefore, to demonstrate their manhood and earn the respect of their peers. In the yard, this took the form of constant bragging and storytelling, either about crimes committed (or to be committed in the future) or sexual exploits. One young braggart was future middleweight boxing champion Jake La Motta. LaMotta recalled in his memoir *Raging Bull*, "All we did was gather up in little groups and yak—even in a place like that the guys break up into gangs, most of which hate each other's guts, and they talk about breaking out or lie about the number of broads they've laid or other things they haven't done."[29]

Clothing and personal style were, as on the outside, the other great signifiers of status. In the fifties, the "diddy-bopper walk"—the defiant strut of the gang member—became known on the streets of New York City as the "Coxsackie shuffle" in honor of the reformatory where it was so well practiced.[30] Disciplinary reports in the case files show constant thefts of oil for prisoners to use in slicking back their hair, as well numerous citations for inmates modifying their uniforms in unapproved fashion. These small gestures of independence carried real meaning in the reformatory environment.

Two prisoners from the case file sample, both transferred from Coxsackie as "incorrigible" in 1945, show the maintenance of a masculine identity at work. Donald M., sent to Coxsackie in 1943 for auto theft, had attempted an escape. While in solitary, he attempted to pass a series of notes that were confiscated and placed in his case file. They reveal Donald's efforts to maintain his peer status. His note to the superintendent was pleading and full of remorse, while notes written to fellow inmates were full of bravado. In them, he bragged about how thoroughly the guards had been beating him and threatened the prisoner responsible for informing authorities of his escape plan: "If I get the rat, he'll get knifed." In another letter, Donald urged someone to smuggle him "smokes" and some lard from the prison kitchen so that he could slick his hair. Prison guards also confiscated a booklet of poems Donald had written. Entitled *Prison Songs 1944*, they included a number of reflections on taking prison discipline with courage, including "21 Years in Sing Sing."[31]

Gary R. was also a prison poet, though his work played up his dominance over women, including "Pimping Sam" and "Miss Bitch"—both of which were also confiscated. Like Donald, Gary had been sent to Coxsackie in 1943 for stealing a car—though unlike Donald, a white inmate from Duchess County who had been adjudicated a wayward minor, Gary (a black inmate from Brooklyn) had been given a ten-year sentence for grand larceny. Like Donald, his file contains threatening notes to other inmates (including short communications like "I will get you") side by side with pleading notes to the prison administration for release from solitary: "I am trying to get out of here. I have a wife who's going to the hospital on the 5 of September to have a baby do you think I would go out of my way to start trouble that don't make any sense." Declared "an agitator among the colored inmates," Gary was declared "not a fit subject for this institution" and transferred to Clinton Prison.[32]

During Coxsackie's early history, boxing was the highest legitimate form of expressing toughness at the reformatory. In odd contrast to the underfunded classrooms and poorly equipped shops, the reformatory opened with a completely finished, top-of-the-line gymnasium. Jake LaMotta began his boxing career at the gym, encouraged by the reformatory priest, and he marveled at the quality of the space: "a real, full size gym, with polished hardwood floors, a regulation ring set up in the middle, a whole series of punching bags down at one end, plenty of weights and barbells and dumbbells and those pulley weight systems all along one wall and even a row of rowing machines. In other words, the whole works." LaMotta recalled that the gym was "one of the favorite spots for the guys" and that "you almost always found someone there and a few of them were pretty good at fighting."[33] The reformatory organized bouts between inmates, and between prisoners and visiting groups of young fighters through groups like the Catholic Youth Organization. Cheering on the reformatory boys against the CYO fighters proved a rare, ultimately illusory, moment of solidarity for keepers and kept at Coxsackie.[34]

Most of the fighting at Coxsackie took place outside the ring.[35] To maintain a reputation for toughness was essential to defend oneself against abuse, the primary currency in the economy of prison social life. Conversely, displays of fear and weakness marked a young man as vulnerable prey for stronger inmates. One prisoner explained, "You are on trial" at Coxsackie: "Prison don't break a man, but if he has any yellow it will show." Another observed, "New fellows are tried out in a variety of ways in the first days of admission to the yard . . . Within a week they know what kind of guy you are. If you pass, they invite you to a bench."[36] Passing that test required at least some public display of a willingness to use violence to defend oneself. Piri Thomas made the point directly: "At the first sign of shit coming your way from a con, bust him in the mouth. Better to win or lose fighting than cop out and earn a punko rep."[37] As another inmate told prison officials, "Even if God hit me, I'd swing back."[38]

Frankie Moreno, spending his first night in general population, overheard some other inmates "talking in low, gravelly voices, messing with another guy's head, threatening what they were going to do to him, how they were going to do it to him; and I thought I heard this guy kind of whimpering, like a scared dog, and I thought how I had to make it clear fast how I was not to be messed with." The next day, Moreno picked out a large African American inmate and, without provocation, began punching. For this, he earned two weeks' solitary, but "what I wanted was achieved; the other inmates sized me up as someone not to be messed with, and that was all that mattered to me in my first days in general population."[39]

For white inmates, who made up the majority of the population throughout this period, fighting was first and foremost a way to shed the status of "creep." New arrivals at Coxsackie (save for those prisoners with strong preexisting gang or neighborhood ties to other inmates) were classified as creeps until they proved otherwise. This classification system appears to have been in place from the opening of the prison in 1936, and it continued to be used through the

1960s, particularly among the white inmates.[40] The goal of the creeps was to join the "gees," who gathered along the walls, while the creeps had to wander the middle of yard. The gees dominated prison life. Joseph Sullivan, a white inmate, recalled that the gees "were not permitted to speak to the so-called Creep at all. That was immediate expulsion!" The creeps had, Sullivan noted, "no wall to lean against and no place to sit." Instead,

> they stood in the middle of the yard . . . When they got bored standing still, all
> they could do was keep walking in circles, even in the winter when all the snow
> was pushed out in the middle of the yard. It really hurt me to look at them on the
> really bitter cold days; no wall to protect them from the cutting winds or galoshes
> to protect their feet when the snow piles they stood in began to thaw. We didn't
> have to go through this because we shoveled all our snow out on them. In reality,
> we treated ourselves with more disrespect as human beings than the cops did, but
> it was a result of what they and their fathers created for years.[41]

For a long time at Coxsackie, the gees's policy for the creeps was simple—they could join the gees at the wall by attacking a black inmate in the yard to prove their courage. As Sullivan observed, "most of them did, usually by japing the dude when he wasn't looking."[42] All Coxsackie inmates, white and black, were keenly aware of the policy. Lucky, a dark-skinned Puerto Rican inmate at Coxsackie, knew that creeps were "generally white inmates who had not proved their toughness, who were preyed upon homosexually or beaten regularly or made to run errands for the dominant prisoners. A creep could shed his humiliating role by picking a fight with a tough black." One day, Lucky was walking in the prison yard when a creep spotted him walking along the prison wall and yelled, "Get the hell back where you belong, black boy." He knew a confrontation was inevitable, and later, when the creep walked by Lucky's open cell door, Lucky "hit him hard in the face, knocked him down and jumped on him."[43]

The effects of prison violence should not be understated. Although many of the confrontations involved little more than a few thrown punches or wrestling another inmate to the ground, weaker or more vulnerable inmates could face terrible acts of physical harm. William Rodriguez's story seems notable more for having been recorded in some detail than for being truly exceptional. On the day before Thanksgiving 1936, William had been left alone in his cell by a guard who, for reasons unknown, kept the door unlocked. An inmate named Inglis entered William's cell, while two other inmates kept watch for the returning guard. William was beaten with an iron pipe and knocked unconscious. His jaw fractured and several teeth missing, he spent a month in the prison hospital. Paroled the following year, William was returned for a parole violation—he had gotten married in defiance of the parole officer's instructions not to do so. Distraught at having to return to Coxsackie and the scene of his attack, he attempted to commit suicide not long after being re-imprisoned. A Greene County judge declared William to be mentally ill and ordered him sent to the Hudson State Hospital.[44]

If fighting was a means of proving one's toughness and shedding creep status, it was also the chief mechanism by which yard turf was defended. Every section of the wall was "owned" by a small group of inmate leaders, and it was their job to ensure that no one crossed into their section of the yard without a physical challenge. As Sullivan recalled, each area of the yard (called "pads" by the time he was in Coxsackie) were defended by "five to twenty guys" whose duty it was to " 'go up' on any dude who crossed that line unless he had permission from the 'pad owner' to do so." Coxsackie officials were for many years tolerant of these yard arrangements; at best, they proved themselves utterly incapable of penetrating the social networks of the yard, as in this fruitless exchange from a 1957 parole board hearing, concerning Lloyd G., who had twice been in fights over violations of pad boundaries:

q: What was that [fight] over?
a: A colored guy came up on me.
q: Was the fight over that section of the yard you control?
a: I don't control no section of the yard.
q: Who does?
a: The guy who owns it.
q: Are you a part owner?
a: No, I don't own anything in the yard.
q: They don't let you stand there unless you are a member.
a: You have to be a member of the group, but you don't own it.
q: How do you get in?
a: A guy brings you in.
q: What do you pay him?
a: Nothing.
q: But once you are in, nobody else comes in unless somebody brings him?
a: Yes, unless you ask somebody you know in.
q: Who asked you?
a: The guy who owns it.
q: Who owns it now?
a: I don't know.

An early critic of Coxsackie pointed to the reformatory's "yard culture" as "a good example of the horns of the dilemma with which the administrator . . . is faced . . . Either he utilizes the repressive, controlling measures which are natural to the type of institution he must run, or he attempts to introduce a degree of individual freedom that is the prerequisite to effective treatment, and then he reaps the consequences of having a population which is too large and too heterogeneous and which is reacting to the total repressive atmosphere at the institution."[45]

Punking: The Prison Sexual Economy

Fighting constituted one of the primary fields of action in the social system of Coxsackie's inmates. The other was same-sex sexual intimacy and same-sex sexual violence. Here, too, scholars have sought to comprehend inmate behaviors by reference to deprivation and importation theories. Studies employing deprivation theory are far more common in the corrections literature, in part because incarceration rather obviously results in the deprivation of different-sex sexual intimacy. Scholars, therefore, long defined same-sex sexual behavior behind bars to be as unnatural as the institutional conditions within which it takes place.

Regina Kunzel's insightful work on prison sexuality, however, challenges the "timelessness" of deprivation theory and the curious way in which it makes prison sex "stand outside history." She makes a compelling case that sexual behavior behind bars at mid-century was far more "imported" than prison officials and scholars were willing to accept; indeed, she argues that it was fear of accepting just this proposition that pushed observers toward the deprivation model. The sexual characters in men's prisons—"wolves," "fairies," and "punks"—were, Kunzel writes, "recognizable figures in the urban working-class milieu from which prison populations were disproportionately drawn. Far from insulated, singular, and timeless, the sexual customs that evolved inside the prison roughly followed those on the outside."[46]

Kunzel presents a compelling importation argument and an important corrective to the literature on prison sexuality. As I suggest in chapter 3, the young men of Coxsackie did indeed bring with them distinct ideas about, and experiences with, same-sex intimacy. Most notably, they carried with them the idea that dominant masculinity (the "wolves") and same-sex relations could go hand in hand, as long as one performed the dominant or penetrative role in sex. What Kunzel understates in her work, however, is the extent to which adolescent offenders also regarded sexual violence as normative, as well as the ways in which institutional authorities played a role in channeling behavior by rewarding, ignoring, or punishing certain conduct. The great paradox of Coxsackie was that consensual intimacy, and there was a great deal of it, was strictly disciplined, while the perpetrators of sexual violence and coercion were all too often tolerated or ignored.

Consensual sexual intimacy between prisoners at Coxsackie makes little or no appearance in published accounts by former inmates, but it shows up repeatedly in prison disciplinary reports and in the confiscated notes that made their way into case files. A prison guard disciplined Alfred D. after walking to the rear of a dormitory and finding Alfred and another inmate "lying together": "They were definitely 'in the mood,' for I stood there fully two minutes before either of them saw me."[47] The fact that the guard chose to watch the two young men without making himself known is itself suggestive of the prurient interest officers took in the relationships between prisoners.[48] Love notes were regularly confiscated and filed. Warren D., known to officers as a "big shot around the yard," was written up for passing notes regarding "immoral and sexual perversion," and it was noted with some concern that he had prostituted himself to men before coming to Coxsackie. Leonard P.'s case file contained what officials described as "love letters": in one, the writer declared, "You are the sweetest thing I have ever seen. I would like to know the answer to that question I asked you the other night . . . your loving one," and a second letter writer signed his note, "dearest of all."[49]

Jake LaMotta recalled a time when he "almost triggered off a riot"—by which he meant a race riot—by confronting a black inmate over his sexual demands on a white inmate: "There was this white kid that used to hang around the gym, one of those kids that the world is always picking on because he doesn't fight back enough and he looks like he's dying in front of your eyes, and I found out that one of these black kids is forcing him to be his girl. I dug up the black kid and told him, 'If a guy wants to do it, that's okay by me, but any of this forcing and I'll personally take you apart bone by bone, you understand that?' "[50] LaMotta's threat, of course, explicitly acknowledged that it was "okay" by him if a white inmate wished to "do it" with a black inmate at Coxsackie, and that those wishes were entirely comprehensible within their social world.

Locating consensual sexual intimacy is complicated by the fact that it constituted a disciplinary violation. Being caught by prison authorities meant having to come up with a way of excusing sexual behavior and passing blame. In such cases, stories of bullying and victimization could serve a useful purpose, by allowing a prisoner to deny desire and consent and thus avoid penalty.[51]

Terrence B., for example, had already been cited for performing acts of mastur-
bation and "oral sodomy" when he was interviewed by prison officials. Terrence
protested that other inmates in his dormitory were threatening him with a
"frame-up" that would cost him his upcoming parole unless he complied with
their sexual demands; they also threatened to spread lies among prisoners in
the yard that he was "queer."[52] Even ordinary gestures could demand explanation. Marco W. patted another inmate on the rear end only to be stopped by a
guard and questioned as to whether "he was bothering the inmate along sexual
lines." Marco protested that "this was all in fun," and he was warned to "quit
clowning around and acting in a childish manner."[53]

Sexual coercion, however, was commonplace at Coxsackie. In a prison economy that left inmates with little to bargain with, or for, sex became a primary
currency, along with magazines, cigarettes, food, and protection.[54] Piri Thomas
recalled being warned not to accept "loans or presents from stranger cons" at
the risk of incurring obligations that could only be paid off in sexual favors.[55]
Guards cited Vincent C., serving time in Coxsackie for assault and robbery, for
"homosexual activities": he had been paying for money owed and for cigarettes
by masturbating various inmates, having anal intercourse with others, and performing "sex shows" for others.[56]

To occupy the subordinate position in the world of prison sex was, as it was
on the outside, to be a "punk." In Coxsackie, to be called a punk was a grave in-
sult, and even a remark that one "travelled with punks on the outside" was enough
to spark fights among inmates.[57] Although prison did not create the role of the
punk, it attached to it a particular idea of punking, in which punks were not
simply taking on the passive or feminine role as sexual objects but were subject
to acts of sexual violence.[58] New arrivals were immediately sized up as potential
punks. Jake LaMotta recalled the taunts he received as a new inmate: "Hey, boy,
they're gonna soften you up good, then you'll be a nice little girl for somebody
here . . . Yeah, she's ugly enough to be my type. Boy, you gonna be my girl, you
hear?" Confiscated notes in the case files could strike a similarly threatening
tone, as did the note Frank W. sent to another inmate: "Are you prepared to get
down with the action the last period. I mean are you prepared to drop your
pants. Now remember no bullshit because I want some ass. I have the place
already picked out."[59]

Gang rapes of young, vulnerable prisoners figure prominently in the retrospective accounts of Coxsackie prisoners. Ken Jackson stated that, "In this institution there were a lot of things that weren't mentioned. You learn about gang
rapes and maybe take part in them."[60] Charles McGregor echoed the sentiment,

observing that Coxsackie taught him about just two things: "gang rapes and racism."[61] Felipe Luciano recalled one incident in vivid terms: "Though I never saw him, I heard a newly arrived inmate raped by several guys on my floor. The screams were unbearable, high-pitched, furious and then suddenly, there was silence. I heard the grunts of their passion. I heard the body hit the floor."[62]

The role of the prison guards and Coxsackie administrators in dealing with prison rape seems ambiguous at best. On the one hand, punking and rape were disciplinary offenses within the prison, and the case files contain several instances in which inmates wrote to prison officials for help in defending themselves. Jerry O. wrote a note in 1939 to the assistant superintendent, complaining that inmates in his division were "bulldozing" him "for cigarettes and desserts" and that a "sex maniac" had asked him to "do a hand job and to punk him." He expressed a fear that they would find him out to be a "squealer" and would beat him up, so he asked to be moved to another division.[63] Howard G. asked to be sent to solitary confinement for his own protection in 1943: "I would rather stay locked up in a cell block than to get my ass beat every night and that is that . . . they want to make me give them hand, and they say they are going to fuck me and I am no girl . . . that new guard doesn't know what is going down."[64]

On the other hand, punks do not appear to have been regarded as anything but a problem by prison staff, and the victims of serious sexual violence found little or no recourse. Piri Thomas put the matter bluntly: "Nobody from the warden on down gives a damn, as long as it's just cons eating up cons."[65] Fighting back meant certain punishment by prison authorities; Stanley Telaga, a former Coxsackie inmate, recalled being placed in solitary for eleven days for defending himself from an attempted rape.[66] Thomas believed that "the victims had no recourse. If they complained to the guards, they would condemn themselves to the lowest wrung [sic] on the prison ladder . . . if they had to endure the contempt of the guards and inmates alike for having succumbed to being girl-boys, being squealers was even worse."[67] Weaker inmates were described, as Peter Y. was in his case file, as "very meek . . . no pride whatsoever . . . absolutely spineless."[68]

Disciplinary notes regarding predatory inmates were matter-of-fact regarding their role, giving the impression that little thought was given to attempting to seriously control their behavior. Vernon K., sent to Coxsackie from Buffalo for auto theft, was a "ring man"—the term used for inmates who played a dominant role in the underground economy. Vernon had been cited for having a "bad influence on younger boys" and for his sex activities. He was also known in the case file as the prisoner who ran the "Buffalo pad," collected "tribute" from Buffalo inmates while he was there, and controlled the trafficking of contraband cigarettes. Although he was cited five times while at Coxsackie, he was never placed in a punishment cell.[69]

Ring men often attained that status by virtue of choice institutional assignments that allowed them to bestow favors and to aid fellow inmates. One Coxsackie ring man recalled being given the position of hospital clerk by the officer in charge, "as he hated to see a nice Irish lad like myself in trouble." From this position, he admitted, "I was in a position to admit men to ward x of the hospital and keep them there (by crooked means of course) as long as I wanted to . . . I have gotten 'punks' into the hospital to be used by other inmates, when my whole being revolted at the idea of young kids that couldn't stand the gaff, yellow, just without friends and willing to do anything to keep from getting beat up." One punk was kept for sixteen days, during which time approximately fifty other inmates had sex with him. Coxsackie officials learned of this and did send the ring man to solitary but, inexplicably, later promoted him to the prison's number one ring man position, chief clerk of the record office.[70]

Faced with little aid or sympathy from the prison administration, some inmates broke down entirely. Frankie Moreno recalled two victimized inmates, on different occasions, committing suicide, while another rape victim killed his attacker, turning his three-year sentence into a life term.[71] Leonard P. was identified as an "overt homosexual" in his case file, because he had assumed a "fairy" identity even before being sentenced to Coxsackie in 1940.[72] Paroled in 1941, he was returned to Coxsackie for homosexual behavior in his rural hometown ("immoral actions" was the euphemistic charge). During his second stay at the prison, he was repeatedly the victim of sexual assault. Depressed and suicidal, the young man told Coxsackie officials, "I have nothing to live for. It is hopeless. I have nothing to lose by dying." After a suicide attempt, he was transferred (as suicide attempters often were at Coxsackie) to a state mental hospital. Returned after a short time, he attempted to hang himself, and on another occasion, he broke a window and slashed his wrists. Leonard's case file notes "unstable, impulsive, hysterical, and at times destructive behavior" before authorities sent him back to the mental hospital (and eventually on to another prison).[73]

Ceaseless War: Prisoners Face the Guards

Within a day of arrival, often in the afternoon of the first day, new prisoners would be taken from quarantine to the administrative offices for an interview with the warden. Coxsackie's first warden was Frederick Helbing, a longtime veteran of institutional work (he started in 1899) and the final superintendent of the House of Refuge on Randall's Island. In talking with new arrivals, Helbing tried to make clear that the promise of rehabilitation could only be fulfilled by the observance of prison rules and a respect for uniformed authority. When Jake LaMotta refused to make eye contact during his interview, Helbing made it clear where institutional power lay: "There's only one tough guy up here, and that's me. And I'm undefeated. I've had a lot of young punks in here who thought they were tough, and I'm undefeated."[74]

Helbing's interview reflected his personal vision for the young men under his supervision. What they lacked, he felt, was male authority and strong masculine role models. "If only," Helbing said of his new arrivals, "some real he man had gotten hold of this boy a year or so ago."[75] His views on their behavior were simple—every young man had the choice to behave well or to behave poorly. Addressing the prisoners on the occasion of his retirement, Helbing told them, "Many of you have been arrested three or four times and I don't understand why. There isn't a feebleminded fellow in this room . . . Every lad in this room has something in the upper story that God gave him and I don't understand why lads get into trouble when they know the difference between right and wrong."[76]

Helbing's vision, in which young men needed the strong hand of male authority to help them choose between right and wrong, was one he repeated many times in public speeches and lectures, and it served as the basic philosophical framework for the custodial staff of the reformatory. Although Helbing was publicly sympathetic to the reform program at Coxsackie, his version of institutional governance was not entirely consistent with that anticipated by the educational reformers, who had always intended for the prison guard to play a quasi-therapeutic role. The Central Guard School (see chapter 2) was to be the cornerstone of this effort, a place where the reformers themselves could train new generations of custodial officers to fully participate in the process of correctional rehabilitation. There is evidence that some officers did take on these roles at Wallkill Prison, at Elmira Reception Center, and even at Coxsackie, but in many instances, members of the custodial staff at the reformatory engaged in patterns of behavior that exemplified the most regressive traditions of punitive prisons.

One might account for this failure of the reform project by the rapid demise of the Central Guard School, but this is only one part of the story. Perhaps as important was the importation of the custodial principles of the old House of Refuge, along with many of the former House of Refuge custodial staff. A state board of inquiry had blamed the 1934 riot on Randall's Island (described in the introduction) on the "custodial environment" at the institution, an indirect way of expressing their view that conditions were overly repressive. The board urged the state not to import the House of Refuge custodial staff to Coxsackie, singling out assistant superintendent and principal keeper George Cochrane for criticism.[77]

Of course, the custodial staff *were* brought into the new prison at Coxsackie. As for George Cochrane, although he did not assume the title of principal keeper at Coxsackie, he was captain of the guards and stayed on at the new prison until his retirement in 1949. Sonny Carson recalled the old man clearly:

> I beheld an old, old man in a uniform not unlike the other uniforms of the guards . . . this honky had gold braid and captain's bars on his shoulders. He was so old, he stooped with age but I later found out that this old man was deceiving and could move with the speed of a jackrabbit when he wanted to get his point across. His name was Captain Cockroach. He was in charge of all the hacks, and the only person that had more authority was Assistant Superintendent Conrad [Conboy], who next to Cockroach was, for most, the most hated man in that institution . . . Captain Cockroach and Assistant Superintendent Conrad were to shape my thoughts of white people in years to come."[78]

Not every guard at Coxsackie embraced the old Randall's Island focus on maintaining order through force and dominance; some officers wrote hopefully of a time "—and not in the too distant future—when the old-time prison guard with his stringent rules and set demands, his hard demeanor, and even his brutality, will be a thing of the past."[79] But at Coxsackie, where one early evaluator observed the manner in which "ceaseless war is waged with the keepers, their natural enemies," neither side ever called a halt to the hostilities.[80] Coxsackie guards treated the "resisters" among the prisoners with physical brutality, and this was true of black and white inmates alike. Jake LaMotta was given a thorough and brutal beating by a group of three guards: "The trouble is when guys are afraid maybe they're going down they start fighting for their lives, and then when they've got it won, they got so much adrenalin running that they can't stop, they just keep on beating."[81] Ken Jackson remembered Coxsackie (which in his time was known as Cack or the Bucket of Blood) as a place where "they use lumber to educate you when you step out of line":

> Coming from Brooklyn I have a bad habit of saying 'yeah' in response to a question. I did, anyway, until that point in my life when a so-called correction guard asked me a question, and I said 'yeah' and he hit me in the face with a bat, and I

had to have most of my teeth taken out. So that started my introduction to 'reha-bilitation,' at the end of this stick . . . I went through Coxsackie as an incorrigi-ble, I was termed that on release because I didn't become the vegetable like they make most guys in the institutions. I fought their system inside, and they didn't like it.[82]

One of Rocky Graziano's first encounters with a Coxsackie prison guard re-sulted in what might be best described as a modified version of the superinten-dent's lecture: "I thought you were one of them East Side Guinea punks. Well, kid, you open your mouth around here and you're dead, understand? The war-den got a personal dislike for East Side Guinea punks, understand?"[83]

From the outset, Coxsackie's guards relied on punishment cells as a device for disciplining resistant and troublesome prisoners. Although most prisoners never went to solitary, the use of punishment cells was not exceptional but was part of the basic disciplinary framework of the reformatory. In the case file sample, fully 49 of the 370 cases (13.2%) explicitly record an assignment to a disciplinary cell at some point during incarceration, a number that almost certainly undercounts the actual percentage of inmates who received such an assignment.[84] Disciplin-ary cases were sent to C3, which was one step above being sent to pure solitary confinement. C3 prisoners occupied cells with nothing but a toilet; they slept on the cell floor; and they were provided one meal a day (lunch, with bread and coffee substituting for the other two meals). Moving to the most extreme level of disci-pline involved going to solitary, or "the hole," as it was universally known. Here, prisoners were given bread and water for all three meals, allowed no contact with other inmates, and given no clothes save for a pair of underwear.[85]

The idea of solitary at Coxsackie was to break down the tough, resisting prisoner. "Let's see how goddam tough he is when he comes outta there" is what Jake LaMotta heard as he was taken to solitary. Frankie Moreno gave this ac-count of two weeks in Coxsackie solitary:

> Solitary—two weeks. Solitary—fourteen days. Solitary—three hundred and thirty-six hours. Solitary—twenty thousand one hundred and sixty minutes. Stripped and left in your underwear in the cell behind the sliding iron door, in the cell with no furniture, no bed, no lights, no newspapers, no cigarettes, no tooth-pick to chew on for those hours when you give in to cursing through your clenched teeth—whatever else it is, it's enough time to see every calculation of your time alone. Two weeks was one million two hundred and nine thousand and six hun-dred seconds.

Solitary, sitting on the cold concrete floor shivering in winter only in your underwear, waiting for the night when they toss a thin blanket into your cell, which they'll take out the next morning.[86]

The solitary aspect of disciplinary confinement was rigidly policed, as Stanley Telaga later testified: "You have no mirror. You have nobody to look at. If you hum, whistle, or talk to yourself you are beaten by the guards. The only time you see a face is about every two days when toilet paper is given to you."[87] John Mack, recalling the "sadistic savagery I had to live through," would years later observe that "a nervous tension enters my system whenever I think back to the terrible beatings, the many 30 days I spent naked in a 'stripped cell,' with only one meal every third day, the rest of the days with only bread and water, and the long silence of day and night, and all of this when I was just a teenager."[88]

Nearly every account describing the punishment cells at Coxsackie in this era confirms that prisoners were routinely beaten while being taken to solitary. The case file of Melvin H., a frequent occupant of solitary in 1944 and 1945, contains a confiscated note written to another inmate, which indicates that prison officers "jacked me three times yesterday my face is cut up pretty bad . . . I got the shit kicked out of me."[89] Joseph Sullivan described the process in painful detail:

For serious offenses like a bad fistfight, you were automatically beaten up with clubs from the place the fight took place to the "box" up in "A-3." There, surrounded by eight or ten officers, you were made to strip (if you were still conscious), get down on all fours and bark, meow or moo, according to what type of animal Capt. Follette desired to hear. When they all tired of this, everyone that was in the box would be told to get up on their doors and watch another of their "Gees" slide by. They didn't want you to simply crawl on your hands and knees, you were beaten until you got on your belly and pulled yourself along the floor with your hands and forearms while they continued to beat you across your back and legs. If you didn't scream, "I'm a punk, a faggot and a motherfucker" for everyone to hear, they'd feel cheated and indignant. This is the point where many kids, 16 or 17 years old, could get their heads split open, crying not from the pain but the unbelievable humiliation. I was in the box on a number of occasions when this took place, and cried like a baby every time I was forced to watch it. If you didn't watch, you were forced to join them out there.[90]

Sullivan noted that several of "that one sadistic crew" at Coxsackie later became wardens in the New York State prison system by the early 1970s. "I would bet that they are proud and their families are proud of how they 'worked' their way to the top," Sullivan bitterly recalled. "My God, how they worked!"[91]

Racism among some Coxsackie prison guards was as overt as the violence and left a lasting impression on the prisoners. John Mack reflected on the extent to which the Coxsackie experience "made me aware of the fact that I am an outsider, that I am alienated and permanently exiled from ever becoming an integral part of American society." At age 18, Mack got into a fight with a white inmate who had called him a nigger: "When I was brought before the warden, and when I told him the fight started because the white inmate had called me a nigger, he rose halfway out of his seat, leaned over his desk, and with his eyes blazing with hatred, screamed in my face, 'Well, I call you a nigger! You're a nigger, nigger, NIGGER! Now hit me! Hit me!' I had never seen such an open, naked, official hatred before, and the impact of it crushed me. I have never forgotten it."[92] Claude Brown, in his memoir *Manchild in the Promised Land*, remembered that his friend Dunny, who served time in Coxsackie, "told me a lot things" about racism within the reformatory:

> The guards—the hacks, as they called them—were hillbillies. These hillbillies disliked anybody who came there and acted too suave or had handkerchiefs that were expensive, anything like that. According to Dunny, a Negro who was too suave had a hell of a hard time to go. The hacks were always kicking his ass for no good reason . . . he described a fellow Coxsackie inmate who had spent time in Texas and Alabama, who said that "the jails in New York were no better, and maybe a little worse, than some of those he'd been in in the South." Dunny said, "Yeah, Sonny, don't ever go to jail in this state, because they even have segregated jails." I didn't know this about New York State, but I believed he was telling the truth. He said, "Yeah, they put the white boys in one place and they put the niggers in another section. The niggers get all the shitty jobs, and white boys . . . man, they live good. It's just like it is out here . . . everybody isn't doing the same kind of time. There's white time in jail, and there's nigger time in jail. And the worst kind of time you can do is nigger time."[93]

Another detailed account of racism comes from Dhoruba Bin Wahad, who was sent to Coxsackie ("a prison full of gangbangers") in 1962 on a felony assault charge (stemming from a gang shooting) for a five-year indeterminate sentence:

> The racism that existed in the prison system was an advanced stage of what existed in the street; it was overt. The guards and commissary employees were mostly inbred country boys from upstate, and they were racist to the core. They

had no problem calling you nigger, but they would only do that when they were all massed together in a goon squad. "Nigger, get in that cell!" They only said that when there was a whole group of them whipping on you. One on one, they wouldn't dare use the word. Because if they said nigger to a brother who was a Nation of Islam militant, they got knocked the fuck out. A brother would submit to the group ass-whupping he knew was coming later just to land one good blow.[94]

Prisoners believed that Coxsackie guards generally tolerated interracial fighting as a means of keeping inmates' hostility directed toward one another. As Sullivan wrote in his account of life at Coxsackie: "This fucking place destroyed any sense of feeling I had in me for quite some time to come. It was a racist institution because it was kept that way by a sick administration. Their philosophy was that as long as they can keep blacks and whites at each other's throats, stabbing, fighting and fucking one another like animals; they knew we would never have the time to wonder why certain things were as they were or who our real enemies were." The toleration of interracial conflict had limits, however, and was quickly stopped whenever it threatened to spread beyond one-on-one violence and endanger the order of the reformatory. Above all, reformatory officials feared systemic or organized racial conflict, race riots, and anything that threatened to fan the flames of racial hostility into uncontrollable institutional conflict. Prisoners worried about being accused of "instigating a race riot."[95] Even before World War II, case files from the sample reveal reformatory officials constantly working to head off uncontrolled racial conflict. Several cases from the prewar period highlight disciplinary action designed to head off wider conflicts: a black inmate from the Bronx was punished for having "attempted to turn another colored boy against the white boys," and a white inmate was sent to a disciplinary cell for "instigating trouble between blacks and whites."[96]

By 1940, the tensions among Coxsackie inmates exploded into a series of racial incidents. The case files record the experience of Gino M. at the center of one such incident in the summer of that year. Originally sentenced to Coxsackie in 1939 for having stolen "cigarettes, gum, and pie valued at five dollars," Gino and another white inmate had given orders to the black inmates not to go to the counter in the dining room for seconds; the black inmates went anyway and precipitated a serious melee in which several inmates were apparently injured. Superintendent Helbing found Gino's behavior to be so serious, he took the highly unusual step of writing to the commissioner of corrections. Noting that "the result of this disturbance has caused bad feeling between the white and colored boys," Helbing asked that Gino be transferred to a state prison, a serious step for a young man who had stolen five dollars' worth of pie. Commissioner John Lyons refused the transfer request; Gino's case file indicates that he instead spent a remarkable nine months in a disciplinary cell at Coxsackie.[97]

By the start of the 1950s, the tenuous racial and disciplinary order that Coxsackie's officers tried to maintain would come crashing down around them, and the reformatory system would drift toward ungovernability (see chapter 7). Increasingly, the threats of prisoner violence would direct themselves toward the prison system itself. The rage that burst into full public view in the 1971 Attica riot had been near full boil within the reformatories for years, and it would ultimately destroy the reformatory system and liberal prison reform. Until then, the racism of the yard and the brutality of the custodial regime at Coxsackie made confinement a transformative experience, but only in a profoundly negative sense. It was within this disciplinary context, then, that the agents of the rehabilitative program would undertake their efforts at realizing the transformative power of education, vocational training, and counseling. It is to their efforts that we now turn.

CHAPTER FIVE

Reform at Work

Ideas into Action at Coxsackie

The New York State Vocational Institution, built from the ground up as a model institution for correctional education, symbolized the rapid progress of liberal reform. The men who carried the flag for the new rehabilitative programs saw themselves blazing a new trail, of sorts, through the prison landscape. Sam Lewisohn proclaimed correctional education to be "one frontier which is by no means closed . . . almost as full of possibilities for improvement as was the land first cleared and cultivated by the pioneers."[1] Winning this new frontier, reformers believed, demanded a new prison culture and a new set of organizing principles. Price Chenault, a correctional educator who began his career at Coxsackie and eventually assumed leadership of the Division of Education, believed that the reformatory must "venture forth into strange territory," led by men who dreamt about "the golden opportunities that lie ahead." Experimentation and discovery could never flourish, he added, under the influence of prison traditionalism, which "held sacred the things of the past."[2]

In contrasting the bold vision of the educational project with a countervailing conservatism within prisons, Chenault made it clear that reform would have to take root in institutional contexts not congenial to the rehabilitative ideal. In effect, he offered an early version of Ann Chih Lin's more recent observation that the context of prison programs—the "struggles and accommodations"—so often decides their fate.[3] The fulfillment of the educational mission of the New York State Vocational Institution would be a challenge of *implementation*, understood to mean both the practical challenge of securing the necessary resources to carry out a program and the development of an institutional culture within which those resources can accomplish their intended purpose.

Evaluating the reform programs at Coxsackie reveals extensive failures in both areas of implementation. Serious resource limitations continuously undermined the effectiveness of educational and vocational programs, starving them of qualified staff and imposing daunting logistical challenges. Institutional culture and politics proved to be just as much an obstacle to success. As chapter 4 revealed, the struggle for dominance and survival among inmates, and the brutal conflict between prisoners and the custodial force, defined much of the reformatory experience. Rehabilitative programs and personnel struggled heroically to find space within the conflicts at Coxsackie, and to resist being subordinated to the demands of custody and order. At times, on a case-by-case level, program interventions achieved notable successes, transforming young prisoners' lives for the better. The larger picture, however, reveals gradually diminishing expectations and uneven results.

Budget Failures

Educational reform at Coxsackie registered impressive achievements by some measures. State investment in reformatory education programs easily outpaced the rest of the prison system. For the fiscal year 1936–1937, the first full year of operation, Coxsackie employed thirty-seven educational professionals, second only to the much larger Elmira Reformatory. In contrast, the four old-line prisons (Attica, Auburn, Clinton, and Sing Sing) provided for only thirteen educational positions combined. Elmira and Coxsackie in fact accounted for two-thirds of all educational positions in the state's male correctional facilities.[4] During that same fiscal year, per-inmate spending on education at Coxsackie was the highest in the New York system at $158.42, compared with $27.20 throughout the system as a whole, and a low figure of $3.09 at Sing Sing (none of the four old-line prisons spent more than $7.00 per inmate on educational programs). The per-pupil cost of education at Coxsackie (educational spending per inmate actually enrolled in educational programs, rather than per inmate) was $173.37, which compared rather favorably to the New York State public school average per-pupil spending of $133.00.[5]

Coxsackie not only outspent the old-line prisons, it also enrolled far more of its inmates in formal educational programs. Not long after it opened, Coxsackie reported to the Division of Education that 82 percent of prisoners were actively engaged in some form of organized vocational training. None of the old-line prisons enrolled even 10 percent of inmates in vocational programs (the figures ranged from a high of 9% at Sing Sing, to a low of *zero* at Auburn Prison). The same gap held true for general education, with 64 percent of Coxsackie inmates enrolled in classes, which contrasted with far lower numbers at the old-line prisons (3% at Attica, 6.5% at Auburn, 21.4% at Clinton, and 15.7% at Sing Sing).[6]

During the war, the press of military production lowered vocational (59%) and educational (50%) enrollments at Coxsackie, but over time, the level of inmate participation remained steady. About three-quarters of the case file sample, for example, record some sort of formal educational or vocational assignment.

As impressive as these numbers are, they cannot tell the whole resource story by themselves. Even as Governor Lehman sealed the Coxsackie corner-stone, the reformatory faced serious budget problems. The state-funded public works program ran out of funds before the reformatory was finished. As a cost-saving measure, the intended school building was not built, forcing classes to be held in the library, a small inmate reading room, and the recreation rooms in individual cellblocks. Several of the vocational shops were also left unfinished, lacking basic equipment. While Coxsackie's auto, masonry, and barber shops were fully supplied, the carpentry shop opened without proper equipment, and the painting and plumbing groups were put to work finishing construction work that the state's crews had failed to complete.[7]

An early warning sign for reformers that state budget issues would be an ongoing concern arrived with the passage of the Feld-Hamilton state pay law in 1938. The Feld-Hamilton law required the state to adopt a comprehensive set of pay classifications for state employees. In the spirit of economizing, head teach-ers were placed in the same category (Grade 7-1; $1800 to $2300) as regular teachers, a move that seriously compromised the Department of Corrections' ability to hire or promote individuals into the challenging head teacher role. Worse, from the point of view of the Division of Education, instructors were given a much lower classification (Grade 2-2b; $1650 to $2150), a pay downgrade that the division claimed would make it almost impossible to secure qualified vocational instructors.[8] Even regular teacher salaries posed a problem—Coxsackie salaries were, on average, just over half as much as the average for public school teachers in the New York City metro area.[9]

Another major budget blow arrived with the passage of the state budget for 1939–1940. In the summer of 1939, the legislature met in special session to pro-pose major reductions in public spending (a move that echoed a similar push for fiscal retrenchment by the Roosevelt administration in 1937–1938).[10] Under the new economy program, the state pledged to eliminate positions, starting with those that were currently vacant. For the Division of Education, their high rate of employee turnover—exacerbated by the pay-grade decisions—had left a large number of professional positions vacant. As a result, the division lost thirty-one educational positions, with a corresponding "lowering of morale" through-out the system.[11]

In the wake of these developments, the Engelhardt Commission and the Division of Education self-published a booklet entitled *Future Plans and Costs for Education in Institutions in the New York State Department of Correction.* The booklet took the unusual step of directly taking to task the Department of Corrections' Budget Division for failing to appropriately support all aspects of educational reform, and for failing to provide adequate salaries for correctional teachers. The report insisted on a long-term commitment of 5 percent of the annual corrections budget (a commitment, it might be noted, they did not receive).[12] Meanwhile, Howard Briggs found himself spending time shopping in used tool supply houses in Albany and New York City, trying to secure the light tools that his vocational shops needed, and salvaging scrap iron from the old cellblocks being demolished at Clinton Prison.[13]

Not long after publication of the *Future Plans and Costs* booklet, the Engelhardt Commission—the most important source of external political and financial support for the reform program—ceased to function. The writing was on the wall in the spring of 1939, when Morse Cartwright called Frederick Keppel to let him know that the Carnegie Corporation had "done enough" in the prison field.[14] Without Carnegie and AAAE support, the Engelhardt Commission could not continue to function. The Division of Education glumly observed that the end of the commission "would result in the loss of moral support, mature guidance, and material aid so essential to the growth and direction of the program."[15]

Coxsackie finally opened a school building in 1940, but the new construction brought more problems, for the Public Works Administration project that provided the classrooms also extended the reformatory's north wings. The new cellblocks raised the capacity of Coxsackie from five hundred to roughly eight hundred inmates, without any corresponding increase to the number of educational personnel, all of which led one critic to observe, "The State would not for a moment consider enlarging a population from 500 to 800 without adding custodial officers, but the institution has not been successful in securing budgetary allotments for the reforming effort at the Reformatory."[16]

The coming of World War II added to the resource challenges facing Coxsackie and the other state reformatories. Although the immediate demands of wartime industrial production essentially solved the problem of inmate idleness in the adult prison system, it also meant that reformatory inmates were often drawn out of educational programs to contribute to the production effort. Moreover, military service began to draw out substantial numbers of classroom teachers and vocational instructors, resulting in ever-larger numbers of position vacancies. The Division of Education reported that Coxsackie in mid-1943 had four teaching vacancies and seven temporary teachers: "During the past year no problem has been more time-consuming, and at times, more discouraging, than that of trying to keep the educational positions filled with adequately qualified persons."[17] Among the leaders of the pioneer reform group, Walter Wallack worried about the impact of war, and what the end of the war would mean for correctional education: "That there has been progress I think no one can dispute. Then along came the war . . . in considering post-war problems, we should not forego the gains we have recently made."[18]

The postwar years brought no relief. In the mid-1950s, the commissioner of correction concluded that, because of the state's salary schedule, "there is little hope of securing the services of fully qualified teachers and instructors." Nearly every postwar report on Coxsackie produced by the state Commission of Correction (charged with conducting annual surveys of institutions) highlighted the problems caused by high levels of staff turnover and position vacancies. This problem seems to have never been resolved: during 1961, nine of the thirteen general education teachers left the reformatory, replaced by eight new hires.[19] The constant vacancies and high turnover rates played a critical role in weakening the position of educational programming at Coxsackie. Hard pressed to attract the best teachers, struggling to provide the support they needed, and unable to retain them for more than a short time, the reformatory's budget challenges presented a perpetual challenge to program implementation.

Social Education

If education was to provide the spark for personal transformation at Coxsackie, most of those hopes were pinned on the effectiveness of social education. The basic premise of social education was to employ educational activities in the development of positive attitudes toward institutions, and an interest in acceptable social living, without which no amount of skills training could presume to have an effect. Social education was embraced early on by the Lewisohn Commission, which framed it in terms of the "building up of community consciousness," and promoting "adjustment to life." The Engelhardt Commission likewise stipulated, "The basic and ultimate aim of the correctional institution may be stated to be 'the social and economic rehabilitation of inmates.'" The commission made it clear that social education was the device by which negative forms of social learning could be countered. Young prisoners, products of a "confused society," had developed "contempt for the factory and office worker," but these feelings could be redirected in the classroom setting.[20]

For forty minutes a day, reformatory inmates attended a course in social and economic relations. Class units included, "The Boy and His World," "Respect for Property," and "Social Protection for the Individual." The latter unit's objectives included learning "that society does not require an individual to be a law unto himself," and "that physical prowess is only one evidence of social worth."[21] Course units reflected a moderate New Deal liberalism, critical of the inequities of capitalism, but also looking for ways to integrate the worker into a reformed and regulated industrial system. The unit on the history of labor organization, prepared by Coxsackie teacher George T. Drojarski in a "peppy, conversational" style, gave the young reformatory inmates an overview of modern labor relations:

In 1913, the President of the United States appointed a Secretary of Labor to his Cabinet, so labor organizations could feel that their problems were being well considered. The first eight-hour day law (for railways) was passed by Congress in 1916. In 1919, Communists led a big strike on the Steel Industry, and the unions lost much in money, reputation, and membership. The membership built up, however, up to 1929, when the big depression came. That cut down the membership greatly, and unions lost a lot in power. Then the N.R.A., the National Recovery Act, pepped them up because the government was trying to do by law what they had just been trying to get. The Supreme Court said the N.R.A. was unconstitutional and threw it out, but the unions were still pepped up by the "shot in the arm" that the N.R.A. gave.

Still, it looked as though the unions would slip again. Then John Lewis grabbed the chance to do things at the right time. He broke from the A.F. of L. to start the C.I.O., as described in the last lesson. Whether it will turn out to be a good thing or not, no one knows, but it has put a fighting spirit into labor. In late 1936 and 1937, strikes were started everywhere, and great numbers of men joined unions. They must control themselves, however, for public opinion is getting sore at so many strikes.[22]

The unit included substantive discussion questions on labor issues, such as "Which is better, 'help those who help us,' or, 'form a new political party'?"

Discussions of broader social issues within the framework of New Deal worker education, however, were almost always linked in the reformatory setting with questions of personal behavior and responsibility. At Coxsackie, the Social Studies Committee quickly began mapping out the inmate attitudes that social education needed to correct.[23] These ranged from "only saps work" to "all landlords are profiteers and grafters." One lesson, for example, featured a 16-year-old who refused a job paying 70 cents an hour because it did not pay enough. Students reading the story were required to answer specific questions, with correct answers like, "roaming around will get you nowhere." True or false questions asked prisoners to evaluate statements like "Quitting jobs every now and then can make a person drift into the ranks of the vagrant and often into the ranks of the criminal."[24]

Social education remained central to the Coxsackie program throughout its life as a reformatory. Over time, though, the program drifted further from broad-based consideration of social and economic issues (though these remained a part of the curriculum) and closer to individual behavioral issues. In 1946, for example, the reformatory replaced, "An Individual in a Democracy at War" with "Institutional and Parole Problems of Inmates." In 1952, the corrections commissioner, noting the "obvious . . . disintegration of the moral and ethical fiber essentially to sustain integrity in our political, economical and social order," announced a new social education program called successful living.[25] Based on the military's character guidance program, the successful living series included: "Worship," "Clean Speech," "What is Right," "Honesty," "Sincerity," "Development of Character," "Constructive Thinking and Purposeful Living," "Self-Control and Chastity," "My Example," "Home," "As You Would Be Done By," and "Sense of Duty."[26] Taught at Coxsackie by the educational staff (except for "Worship" and "Chastity," taught "on a nondenominational basis" by the institutional chaplains), social education began to embrace the language of postwar psychology. As Glenn Kendall observed, in 1954, the educational reformers were "becoming more aware of the personality and social adjustment phases of their work."[27]

The challenges for historians evaluating the social and general education programs at Coxsackie are formidable. Even if one were to arrive at a satisfactory definition of what it would have meant for correctional education to "work" in the reformatory setting, there are no historical data that would allow for any firm connections to be made between institutional programming and the postrelease lives of prisoners. It is possible, however, to reconstruct some of the basic issues involved in implementing educational programming at Coxsackie.

Reformatory teachers found Coxsackie hard ground to plow, partly because of the tension between undertaking educational programming and the custodial setting in which those efforts took place. Teachers could find easily find themselves in the position of resisting the demands of prison routine and thus coming into unresolvable conflict with institutional administration. "Some of the most capable correctional educators I have known have been killed off and forced to leave the service," observed Price Chenault, because they had a "questioning mind" that refused to accept existing policies and rules crafted in the name of maintaining a secure environment.[28] On the other hand, Chenault was at times frustrated by the inability of some prison teachers to adapt. "Many capable teachers," he concluded, "make miserable failures because they paid too little attention to the basic principles of winning friends in the correctional environment."[29]

Teachers also had to find ways of reaching students with a high level of antipathy for formal schooling and of modifying traditional teaching methods that had already failed their students.[30] Reformatory inmates, when surveyed, indicated a strong dislike for public schools, for nagging and disinterested teachers, for work whose purpose they did not understand, and particularly for testing.[31] Poorly done, the self-paced instructional methods on which the Coxsackie program was designed threatened to degenerate into thoughtless routine. Glenn Kendall eventually concluded, "The so-called worksheet . . . is a very deadly procedure . . . an inmate can complete a thousand worksheets without very much interest on his part or without gaining much that will help him make a good adjustment after release."[32] Motivating the prisoner to embrace the educational experience would require more than simply worksheets, teachers argued, such as enough time and space to engage students in specific learning projects. The project method of learning, however, more often than not fell victim to the demands of institutional routine.[33]

Coxsackie's young prisoners presented myriad difficulties in the classroom setting, and even the best-prepared teachers found themselves challenged daily by their students.[34] Of reformatory students, Glenn Kendall observed, "They act like six year olds . . . they are full of lies, excuses, and constantly project their faults or misdeeds on others."[35] The case file sample from Coxsackie includes a great many similar observations recorded by classroom teachers: Edward B. "does not care whether he passes or not"; Richard F. "could not do anything with the school work" and "did little more than pass time"; Herman M. was "carrying on as usual"; while Hector P. "accomplished practically nothing in the school program . . . a puzzle to those who came into constant contact with him . . . very lazy, no interest in work, unable to follow directions or obey orders . . . seems to take delight in doing the wrong things."[36]

The educational staff, almost immediately, began lowering their expectations for prisoners and narrowing the definition of educability. Even before World War II, Coxsackie's program staff had concluded that only about 15 percent of the prison population had the "native ability" required to "settle down and make the best of what the institution has to offer in the way of an educational program." The largest group (65%) of reformatory inmates possessed "less ability" and "considerable crime experience," as well as being generally more resistant to the educational offerings at Coxsackie. The staff concluded that these young men could be reached, but they framed the challenge in a way that reflected their unease over the chances of success. To show progress among the prisoners in this group, they concluded, a teacher "must possess a high degree of ingenuity, untiring energy and devotion to the cause of education."[37]

Lowered expectations notwithstanding, the case file sample certainly does reveal instances of real educational success. Louis W., a white inmate from Albany removed from his home at age 12 as a neglected child, was only five credits short of graduating high school at the time of his arrest; his teachers actively tried to keep him from being sent to a prison, but to no avail. At Coxsackie he was assigned to an all-day school program, where an instructor worked with him on regents courses (English, history, and algebra) and commercial law; he also completed an individual study program in which he studied and critiqued fiction and poetry. His teachers reported, "This inmate was an exceptional student in his conduct and willingness to work," and he was paroled after just twelve months at the institution.

Steven K., a black inmate from Westhampton Beach, was committed to Coxsackie for an armed robbery, despite favorable recommendations by the chief of police and the victim, a community petition, and a positive pre-sentencing report. In a note to the Coxsackie superintendent, Glenn Kendall expressed his hope that Steven would be given some advanced courses and released soon. "If the home situation were not so bad economically," wrote Kendall, "there is no doubt that this boy could go on to achieve his ambition of becoming a physical education director. We would be very interested in knowing how this case works out and also your feeling as to whether we made the proper disposition." Steven was paroled after just six months, and his time in the educational program at Coxsackie made it possible to quickly complete his high school degree after release.[38]

Retrospective accounts of the Coxsackie experience from former prisoners, almost universally negative in their assessment of the reformatory, tend to reserve some praise for the interventions and influence of individual educators. Joe Bataan, a pioneer of Latin soul following his release from Coxsackie in the early 1960s, developed his musical talents while imprisoned at the reformatory on an auto theft charge. He studied under Mark Francis, a black music instructor trained at Julliard, whose guidance helped inspire Bataan to pursue his interest in music more formally and extensively. Felipe Luciano recalled Bataan as

a reformatory celebrity, especially in "Spain" (the Puerto Rican sector of Coxsackie): "His appearances at the annual talent shows in Coxsackie, where he would
accompany himself on the piano singing both commercial and original songs,
are still talked about by the inmates."[39] One of Bataan's earliest successful com-
positions, "Ordinary Guy," featured a title and lyrics he "brought back" from
Coxsackie.[40]

Abubadika Sonny Carson's otherwise devastating account of racism and brutality at the reformatory reserved a few words of appreciation for his English
teacher:

> Another white gentleman I owe a great deal to. Because of his ardent belief in me,
> I was able to graduate from high school while incarcerated and also took courses
> in the Rutgers mail catalogue program . . . My first meeting with Mr. Buchbinder
> resulted in a steadfast friendship that lasted my entire stay at this institution, dur-
> ing which time I was challenged by him to use every bit of intelligence I could
> muster. He provided the kind of academic challenge that caused me on many
> occasions—sometimes late at night—to search through books for answers to
> many questions . . . on many occasions he brought books in especially for me
> when, often, it was against the rules to do so. So there was a genuine effort on his
> part to assist me in using my mind.[41]

Forging individual connections kept educators hopeful and motivated but
could not (and cannot) serve as measures of program effectiveness. At the reformatory, however, such stories were as close to program evaluation as one could
get. A bibliotherapy program for young drug addicts, begun in 1963, illustrates
both the good intentions and the vague assessments that characterized educational programming. Price Chenault partnered with New York's library extension on the project, and he personally came to Coxsackie to introduce the program to the initial participants. Chenault explained that a successful trial could
mean the extension of the project to other inmates and other institutions. Of
the thirty men selected, twenty-seven elected to participate. The group divided
into four reading groups, which met to discuss short stories and poems from
Harry Golden, O. Henry, Poe, and others. The students' favorite poem was
"Cocaine Lil and Morphine Sue," which had escaped the notice of the librarian
in her inspection of *The Silver Treasury of Light Verse.* "Since everyone wanted to
copy it," the teachers ruefully admitted, "the only graceful thing to do was to
provide paper and pencils and let them." The program directors, moved by the
teachers' "faith in our ability to reach these men as fellow human beings," believed that this reading could help men "though periods of discouragement,

stress or temptation." "We wanted them to listen to what the authors were say-ing," they reflected, "but to think for themselves." The program was evaluated by interviewing the young men afterward to gain some sense of what the exer-cise meant to them and "how it might help them after they leave the Institu-tion." This was exceedingly casual evaluation but enough to keep the program running.[42] There is much to admire in the motivations of the instructors—the attempt to recognize the humanity in their students and to use the forces of creative inquiry to promote self-development. By the time of the bibliotherapy project, however, correctional education at Coxsackie had been operating for nearly three decades, and time was rapidly running out to justify the invest-ment or to document its effectiveness.

The World of Work

Vocational training was by far the most substantial part of the reformatory pro-gram at Coxsackie. Prisoners spent forty minutes in social education classes, but most spent at least three hours in a vocational shop, often with an additional class period of related trade instruction. Consistent with the vision developed by Austin MacCormick and others, vocational training became less a means of developing specific work skills (though it was that as well) and more a method by which young men would develop a capacity for earning a constructive living after release. It was, in effect, about inculcating appropriate attitudes toward work in a modern society: "The worker released from prison should have ac-quired not only usable skills but that pride in high-grade performance which enables one to 'get a kick' out of doing a job well. He must be trained to the point where he gains more satisfaction from the performance of legitimate work than from criminal activities."[43] These attitudes could not be taught through mindless repetition and habit, or from simple tasks traditionally associated with prison industrial production.[44]

Coxsackie was consequently one of the few correctional institutions, along with Woodbourne and Wallkill, with no prison industry at all. At large old-line prisons like Auburn, hundreds of prisoners manufactured furniture, brooms, beds, clothing, blankets, license plates, and road signs, all for state use—even the Elmira Reformatory had a small coffee-roasting program. Although none of Coxsackie's shops were run by the Division of Industries, this does not mean prisoners engaged in purely nonproductive training projects. On the contrary, most of the reformatory shops spent their time on institutional maintenance and the production of goods for institutional use. The carpentry shop generally spent about half of its time on these sorts of projects; the upholstery shop spent most of its time recovering and renovating mattresses, pillows, and chairs; and the print shop—one of the most capable in the state system—handled the printing of the Department of Corrections newsletter, a probation officers' manual, state documents, and so forth.[45] Reformatory inmates would have been hard pressed to explain what it meant to operate outside the Division of Industries, other than the fact that, at Coxsackie, no one was paid for their work, since it was defined as education.[46]

Inmate vocational preferences, recorded in the case files, offer a window into the hopes and expectations young men held for their training and future employment. At times, their statements reflect a weary resignation. Milton C. explained why he chose the institutional farm: "Why I like farming is because that is about all I can do. That is all about I did in my life time so I might as well finishing my life time on farming that is taking care of cow and milk them too and drive the team of horse."[47] Other shop requests display a kind of youthful vagueness: "My choice of work is to be a baker where I could make bread, cakes, and cookies and others things . . . By learning a trade and to like work just as you like play have a job so that you can earn your own money and [not] depend on your mother or father to live and eat, have pepol talk about you that you are a good worker hang around whit good fellows and have a fin family."[48]

Most reformatory inmates offered up a fairly clear-eyed assessment of what constituted desirable work behind bars and what it might take to secure a job back home: Max N. chose the machine shop because "I think there is a greater possibility for me securing a job at home. There are many factories being built at home"; Alex A. requested welding because "welders are needed" during wartime, and "I could marry and settle down with a job like that."[49] Benjamin F., the son of West Indian immigrants, selected carpentry to "take after my father, and when the war is over I will go overseas and get a job as a carpenter building all the wreckage over there. Or else I could stay right here with carpentry that is needed right here in our city."[50] The most popular choices were the auto, carpentry, and electrical shops—all of them connected to interesting, project-based work at the reformatory. One study found that these three shops accounted for roughly 50 percent of all expressed vocational preferences.[51]

Inmate interest, however, was not matched by the actual patterns of vocational assignment at Coxsackie. One survey indicated that fewer than 10 percent of prisoners were assigned to these popular choices. The majority of prisoners labored at an assignment focused largely on institutional maintenance and state production. The dining room and the laundry employed seventy prisoners at tasks with little vocational appeal. Approximately one hundred young men worked on the reformatory farm, the largest number of reformatory inmates on any one assignment. Coxsackie, built on excellent farmland, operated one of the largest and most productive state farming operations. It produced milk, eggs, pork, beef, poultry, potatoes, and other vegetables and fruits, with work-year patterns that would have been familiar to farm boys entering the institution. In the spring, plowing, harrowing, and planting of the fields, with harvesting and canning operations commencing in the summer and building into the fall, and a winter of brush cutting and equipment repair and maintenance (farm crews also handled snow removal during the winter).[52] Ironically, new inmates who actually requested a farm assignment were rarely accommodated, since the outside work presented an escape risk. Instead, the farm became dependent on laborers selected on the basis of behavior, rather than vocational preference.[53]

In theory, each shop endeavored to consider the basic operations and jobs of the trade, and the specific set of skills required to conduct those operations. In practice, the most talented vocational students were also generally those who were released quickly from the institution, meaning they had precious little time to develop their skills. State officials observed, "As soon as one becomes competent in any field and the attitude is such that he seems to be willing to work, [Coxsackie] authorities feel that it is then time to make plans for his release on parole."[54]

Still, the case file sample includes some clear vocational success stories coming out of Coxsackie. Timothy W., sentenced to Coxsackie from a Bronx court on a disorderly conduct charge, expressed interest in both the auto shop and the machine shop. Assigned to the latter, Timothy showed a "cooperative spirit . . . excellent mechanical skill" and was judged "a very good candidate for vocational training." By virtue of his behavior, he was paroled after only seven months. Barry I., arriving from Chatauqua County on a burglary charge, demonstrated "superior intelligence and excellent mechanical skills" and "appears quite serious minded and very desirous of obtaining vocational training." Officials assigned Barry to the machine shop, where the instructor assessed him as "one of the best prospects" he had seen in his fourteen years in corrections. Barry was also released after just seven months, after which he took a position back home at a machine works.[55]

More typical were those cases where prisoners picked up some minimal trade experience that could be helpful after release but nothing remotely approaching what might be required for skilled positions. Walter M. spent seven months in the electrical shop, where he managed modest progress in the trade training, completing twelve of fifty-six units in electricity science and twenty-three of fifty-nine units in electricity. Instructed in fundamental circuits, armored cable, and conduit wiring, he was rated average in work and class, "a very slow worker, but willing and follows instructions readily. His rating is average. His ability is fair. He has no difficulties in getting along with his fellow workers. Should be able to work as an electrician's helper in house wiring."[56]

Training for "helper" status was typical in the case files, which reveal a dispiriting combination of prisoner disinterest, weak work evaluations, and routine institutional work. Herbert D. was assigned to the kitchen every afternoon, where he cleaned the potato steamer and the sinks, and then served dinner. According to his supervisor, "He has avoided work wherever possible, likes to fool around and engage in horseplay unless closely supervised and is inclined to be sneaky. He has shown no particular aptitude for kitchen work, but could function as a bus boy or porter at the present time."[57] James T. spent some time in the reformatory laundry, operating the extractor, tumbler, and the flat work ironer, performing work "he had no interest in, and very little ability for," so he was switched to the garden squad, hoeing, weeding, picking vegetables, cutting grass, and loading hay. He showed "no particular aptitude for farm work" either "and at best could function as a farm laborer under rather close supervision."[58] Warren F. worked in the paint shop in the mid-1950s, where he refinished reformatory furniture and painted walls. He showed good skill at painting walls, and his instructor determined that he might "develop into" a journeyman painter at some point in the future. The related vocational education materials included fifty-one units, of which Warren completed just four—on sanding, furniture refinishing, setting up scaffolding, and placing drop cloths.[59]

The possibility that a young reformatory inmate might advance to the skilled level of their trade came to be regarded by staff as increasingly unlikely. In 1947, shops were reorganized to accommodate slower students, "by having the substandard pupil do the shop work on . . . a helper's level." Another correctional educator concluded, by 1951, that vocational training should "consist primarily of vocational guidance and exploration," given that few reformatory youth "have the mental endowment to become master craftsmen." The State Commission of Correction observed, in 1954, "There is no particular magic in teaching a boy to be a good plumber . . . without the strength of character to adjust himself to the community." "Perhaps," the commission's report concluded, "there has been too much emphasis on the potential of the vocation."[60]

Faced with the reality that most reformatory inmates would be leaving Coxsackie with no certificates, diplomas, or any other tangible proof of training that would have practical value in helping them to secure post-release employment, along with trade training that had only a questionable link to the process of obtaining and holding a job, shop instructors were understandably concerned with getting inmates to buy into the program. Glenn Kendall advised them to focus on faith and good salesmanship—if administrators and teachers believed, then inmates might as well, and programs might then do what they were intended to do.[61]

If salesmanship was the order of the day, many inmates were not buying. Piri Thomas recalled how hollow the promises of future employment seemed: "Us blacks and Puerto Ricans in prison took our courses and studied our brains out, but without much hope of ever really working at the trade outside, we were the wrong-colored race and now we were also ex-cons."[62] The teachers were not necessarily the enemy, but neither did they appear able to overcome the institutional environment of which they were a part. "The consensus among the prisoners," recalled Thomas, "was that [the teachers], too, were frustrated by the poorly equipped shop and classrooms and by the pressure put on them to perform miracles . . . But we resented their indifference and felt they were only there to collect a paycheck. It was a laugh to watch them making out fabulous reports on our progress."[63]

Many Coxsackie inmates were never even given the opportunity for vocational training. Racism played at least some role in excluding prisoners. Some was subtle, taking the form of low expectations. Melvin D., for example, was judged to be a "rather immature, naïve boy who should adjust in one of the lower type shops," and ended up assigned to the farm. Robert Y.'s case file records him as having a "fairly good background for a colored boy," but he was nonetheless assigned to the kitchen, and then to work as a houseboy in the superintendent's home, before being paroled to his parents in South Carolina.[64] Some of the racism in work assignments was far less subtle; work at the institutional power plant, for example, was almost exclusively reserved for black inmates. Austin G., 18-year-old from Schenectady, started in the plumbing shop but requested an assignment to the powerhouse. He was warned, "Work in this assignment would be harder and there would only be a few white boys working with him." Eventually, Arthur requested a transfer back, claiming that he had "trouble with the colored boys down there being I am the only white boy."[65]

Disciplinary cases were also shut out of vocational training, generally being assigned to all-day labor squads. David M., tired of the classroom, requested assignment to the labor squad; his final vocational report scarcely concealed the nature of the "training" he was receiving: "Had 650 hours of training in road building and repair work, learning to use pick and shovel, wheelbarrow and rake."[66] Randall E., sent to Coxsackie after he stole a 1950 Ford convertible coupe, drew a fortunate assignment to the auto shop but failed every one of his unit work assignments. Thereupon followed a series of transfers down the ladder of reformatory work, first to hall janitor duty (a constant problem to authority figures) and then to cell block janitor (couldn't stay out of other people's lockers), and finally to dining hall janitor.[67]

Vocational education at Coxsackie never lived up to the hopes or expectations of the reformers who had helped design the institution. Within a structure that was nominally fully distinct from systems of agricultural and industrial labor that prevailed in adult prison systems around the country, Coxsackie nonetheless managed to produce strikingly similar day-to-day conditions. While less exploitative in some dimensions—few inmates labored all day as they might have in the industrial big houses or on southern prison farms—the gap between theory and practice was more fully apparent at the reformatory, where inmates resented the dull routines of institutional labor being dressed up in the guise of vocational training. In this sense, then, the reformatory was never able to separate itself from the labor issues that defined mid-century prison life.[68]

The Bug Doctors: Weeding Out the Uneducable

Mental health professionals occupied a curiously marginal place within the rehabilitative structure at Coxsackie. Psychology and psychiatry had the bad fortune of receiving state investments in treatment programming prior to the 1929 riots. The riots discredited much of the old system, including mental health services (even the prison commissioner fired by Roosevelt was a psychiatrist). By the 1930s, psychiatrists and psychologists found themselves working in a treatment bureaucracy dominated by correctional educators.[69]

Mental health professionals often held reservations about the merits of educational programming and took a dim view of educators' attempts to understand what they regarded as the complex problems of the young criminal. At the House of Refuge in 1929, psychologist Pauline Trapp explained that her job was to "interpret the child to his teachers and his shop instructor; so that they will be [able to] understand him and develop his special abilities." As if this backhanded treatment of the educational staff were not enough, Trapp further claimed that only a small percentage of prisoners were really able to take advantage of educational opportunity. "Let us recognize the fact," Trapp opined, "that vocational guidance, as such, has long been seen as a fraud. It does not and cannot offer choice of vocation to the proletarian child ... our problem boy is little shaped by schools."[70] Hyman Goldstein, Coxsackie's first psychologist, constantly reiterated the point that reformatory youth were poor prospects for trade training, owing to their unstable personalities and their disorganized backgrounds.[71] Goldstein offered less-than-inspiring encouragement for his educational colleagues: "We must not be discouraged if we fail to see tangible results in a year or two or even ten ... we are working with individuals who are retarded mentally, handicapped educationally, and dulled emotionally. It is need-less to state that the end will be more than worth the means if we can convert failures in crime into shoemakers or electricians, no matter how mediocre they may be as tradesmen."[72]

While educators celebrated their pioneering efforts, prison psychologists settled into a stultifying routine of administering tests, usually of mental age and IQ. A postwar survey of prison psychologists nationwide found that "mea-surement of intelligence" and "measurement of personality" were the two most prominent professional activities.[73] Intelligence testing administered by refor-matory psychologists generally ended up providing a kind of justification for decisions that were made at other levels, when an inmate presented a series of problems or did not do well in the program at Coxsackie. By helping to classify a prisoner as uneducable, intelligence testing provided a mechanism by which such inmates could be transferred from the reformatory.

Before World War II, the transfer mechanism Coxsackie employed most often (roughly one in every twelve prewar cases in the case file sample) was the Institution for Defective Delinquents. Napanoch, as the institution was gener-ally known, was the nation's first prison dedicated to housing the "feeble-minded" criminal, a status it assumed in 1921.[74] Ironically, this wasn't the first time the prison at Napanoch had served as a safety-valve institution; it had orig-inally been constructed in 1900 to house troublesome inmates from the Elmira Reformatory.[75] Although Napanoch could receive commitments directly from the courts, the majority of "Nappies" (as they were known in the prison system) were transferred to the institution from other state prisons, or from state schools for the mentally disabled. In *Creating Born Criminals*, historian Nicole Rafter demonstrated that Napanoch became a kind of "dumping ground" for the un-governable and the exasperating inmates of other institutions.[76]

The disciplinary basis for transfer was never formally acknowledged. Quite the opposite, as authorities claimed that transfers to Napanoch served a double rehabilitative benefit. Napanoch would provide a more therapeutically appropriate setting for the treatment and supervision of the "defective" delinquent, while "normal" prisoners in the Coxsackie classrooms and shops would not suffer needless disruption and distraction. Best of all, the ubiquitous IQ testing of prisoners provided a scientifically precise and administratively convenient mechanism for establishing defective delinquent status.[77]

The closer one looks at the case files of Napanoch transfers, however, the more evidence one sees to support Rafter's disciplinary dumping ground argument. In the first place, not every prisoner with low measured intelligence was sent to Napanoch; not even a majority of them were transferred. Instead, such prisoners could be (and were) assigned to an all-day "general duty" assignment that would keep them out of the classrooms and shops. In fact, by 1938 Coxsackie housed eighty-five inmates (11.7% of the population) whose IQ scores were below 66. Every one of these eighty-five *could* have been transferred to Napanoch, which would accept prisoners with IQ scores below 70. But many were not, generally because they were "good" prisoners. Morris V., admitted to Coxsackie on a joyriding charge in 1943, was flagged for transfer to Napanoch because of his low intelligence and inability "to progress academically while in the Institution." But Morris stayed at Coxsackie working general duty and on the farm, because his "conduct [was] very good" in his dormitory, and he was an "excellent inmate."[78] As Glenn Kendall noted, such an inmate was "usually assigned to some simple laboring job and, as long as he does not cause any trouble, little attention is paid to him."[79]

Transfer was a device by which the troublesome inmate could be removed. James L. McCartney, Coxsackie's first institutional psychiatrist, employed revealing language in his transfer recommendations. Urging the transfer of Homer K. in 1937, McCartney concluded, "He will not profit from trade training, will be a constant problem at this institution and should be returned to court without delay so that he will be committed to a feeble minded institution and kept under supervision for the rest of his life." Likewise, Hector P.'s Napanoch transfer was based nearly entirely on bad behavior: "He is very lazy, no interest in work, unable to follow directions or obey orders. Seems to take delight in doing wrong things."[80] Many other prewar cases feature similar language: "a recidivist who will continue to get into difficulty," "behavior problem," "in constant difficulties with the other inmates," "the boy will get into much trouble while here."[81]

The cases of Maurice W. and Robert E. help illuminate the decision making of Coxsackie officials. Both young men were among a group of eight prisoners transferred from Coxsackie to Napanoch in July 1936. Maurice was 17 years old, convicted of petty larceny for stealing brass pipe and copper tubing from General Electric's Schenectady works. Robert was also 17, convicted of unlawful entry for entering a Brooklyn home and stealing some lead pipe. Both boys were given general duty assignments on their arrival at Coxsackie but were quickly designated for transfer. Maurice had a long criminal history, even by the standards of Coxsackie inmates: first adjudicated delinquent at age 10; six subsequent juvenile court appearances; stays at St. Coleman's Home, the Troy Catholic Orphanage, the Catholic Male Orphan Asylum; and two commitments to the State Training School at Industry (from which he escaped twice). McCartney's report concluded, "He is suggestible, easily led and entirely without insight." Robert's criminal record was shorter, but he demonstrated homosexual tendencies ("he is definitely antagonistic to the opposite sex . . . he emphatically states that he will never get married"), and, McCartney opined, "This feeble-minded individual has a hopeless prognosis and undoubtedly will be again led into delinquency when he is paroled, consequently he should be transferred to Napanoch where he may be kept under supervision the rest of his life."[82]

The rest of his life—McCartney was a true believer in New York's defective delinquent law, which allowed Napanoch inmates to be held on purely indeterminate sentences (literally one day to natural life), regardless of the conviction offense.[83] Inmates transferred from other prisons would be evaluated at the expiration of their original sentence, at which point they could be either released or committed indefinitely beyond that sentence. A young prisoner like Robert E., who had stolen some lead pipe, could nonetheless be held for years, even decades, if institutional authorities decided he posed an ongoing danger to society.

One can only imagine the dread of Coxsackie inmates, who only served an average of sixteen months, facing the prospect of many years with the rest of the Nappies in their gloomy Ulster County prison. Years later, one recalled the shock of being transferred to Napanoch ("a joint for retard criminals") with a group of other Coxsackie prisoners: "Most of them [Napanoch inmates] had 'one day to life' sentences for bullshit beefs, but these cats were really insane. They had all kinds of bugs there—you name it! . . . We quickly forgot our Coxsackie [racial] prejudices and agreed that we would stick together in this joint . . . Because, frankly, 90 per cent of these guys, white and black, weren't playing with a full deck."[84]

Historian Nicole Rafter has shown that years of confinement would have been the worst-case scenario (or best-case, from McCartney's point of view), and that "the practicalities of prison management" required Napanoch to parole most inmates fairly quickly or risk being hopelessly overcrowded. Still, there is no denying that Coxsackie's transfer decisions—based more on institutional convenience than on particular diagnoses of mental disability—almost surely cast some young men into a long and nightmarish maze of state control. Maurice and Robert were both paroled from Napanoch by 1939. Robert avoided a return trip (his record indicates only a subsequent twenty-day sentence to the New York City workhouse on a disorderly conduct charge), but Maurice was re-arrested in 1940 and committed directly to Napanoch on an indefinite sentence. There is no record in his file that indicates when, or if, he was subsequently released.[85]

While psychologists churned out intelligence tests, reformatory psychiatrists—at least when Coxsackie actually had one on staff—were composing personality profiles, particularly on the lookout for the psychopathic personality (or, later, the "sociopathic personality").[86] There is no evidence, however, that these sorts of psychiatric diagnoses had any effect whatsoever on classification, assignment, or parole—and efforts to provide the recommended programs of psychotherapy were rare. James McCartney glumly reported that correctional psychiatry was "at a standstill," with little in the way of programmatic influence.[87]

Psychiatric services became relevant to the reformatory only when a diagnosis of serious mental illness might serve as the basis for removing seriously disturbed or violent inmates to either the State Hospital for the Criminally Insane at Matteawan or another state mental hospital. As with the psychologists' program of intelligence testing, the psychiatrists' assessment was generally a response to decisions made at other levels of reformatory administration. The number of inmates transferred to Matteawan or mental hospitals was not large (generally fewer than ten cases a year), but nearly every one presented deeply disturbing questions of how the criminal justice system dealt with mental illness.

Morris C. arrived at Coxsackie in 1939, on a petit larceny charge. Within weeks, he began sleeping under his bed, muttering to himself, hallucinating, and complaining of persecution. Officers placed him in a bare room after he became violent, and he was finally transferred to Matteawan two days after he attacked four officers.[88] Raymond B., who told the Coxsackie psychiatrist, "I think I am a little cracked," was a serious discipline problem at the reformatory on his return for a parole violation in 1938; he stayed in lockup nearly the whole time, talking to himself and claiming to hear voices. The psychiatrist, Frederick Patry, concluded that Raymond was potentially homicidal and "too disturbed to be taken care of here." Patry petitioned the Department of Mental Hygiene to send Raymond to the Hudson River State Hospital (from which he subsequently escaped).[89]

In 1954, the Elmira Reception Center passed along John H. to Coxsackie, an 18-year-old from the Bronx, despite the fact that he had "broken down" in his final month at the center, refusing to leave his cell. He had been given phenobarbital as a means of controlling his behavior, but Kendall hopefully suggested to Coxsackie authorities that John might "regain his equilibrium on transfer and operate satisfactorily in the population as he did during the first part [of] his stay here rather than crawl into his cell and stay there as he did during the latter part of his stay here . . . you'll probably decide that Dr. Hersloff should see him soon." Indeed, Nils Hersloff was called in within two days of the inmate's arrival—John was refusing to eat or to leave his cell and insisting upon a transfer to Matteawan. In obvious torment, John pleaded, "Can't something be done for me? A lobotomy. I can't go on like this." Although doctors concluded that John presented a case of incipient schizophrenia, "exerting a tremendous amount of control over his slowly slipping contact with reality," he was held at Coxsackie for seventeen months. By the time of John's release, Hersloff had concluded, "It is not felt that this institution can offer this boy anything further. He probably has received the maximum benefit of his incarceration." Paroled to his mother, John was committed to Bellevue Psychiatric Ward (and then to Rockland State Hospital) less than a year after his release.

As with commitments to Napanoch—indeed, even more so—commitments into the mental hospitals or Matteawan presented reformatory inmates with the real prospect of an indefinite commitment lasting many years beyond the original sentence. Joseph P. Scott had been sent to Coxsackie in 1949 on a minor criminal charge of malicious injury to property and was transferred by the reformatory to Matteawan the following year. At the expiration of his original three-year sentence, Matteawan officials determined that he was still insane, and therefore his confinement was continued. He was finally released from the state's custody in 1966 and eventually sued the state for damages related to his long period of incarceration.[90]

The most publicized case coming out of Coxsackie concerned William Jones, sentenced to the reformatory at age 17 as a wayward minor, following a purse-snatching incident. Jones arrived at the reformatory in December 1947, and by the following October, Coxsackie officials began to suspect some form of mental illness. According to his case record, Jones "began imagining that his name was called and that inmates were making fun of him. Suspicious powder was blown at him. Fought imagined persecutors and threatened to kill an inmate. Change of behavior past three days; quiet, depressed, preoccupied. Strange behavior. Suspicious. Thinks people regard him as going crazy." On one occasion, Jones attacked an inmate and held him by the throat against a wall; on other occasions, he fought inmates who "looked at me and I didn't like it," or who "gave him the evil eye." Although Jones furiously denied any mental illness, he was diagnosed at Coxsackie as paranoid and "too dangerous to others and self to maintain in New York State Vocational Institution at this time." Transferred to Matteawan at the end of 1948, he was released as recovered from the state hospital after fifteen months. That the system had failed Jones became all too evident when, just four days after his release from Matteawan, he went on a murderous rampage on a Brooklyn street, stabbing seven people and killing four, prompting a wave of public criticism of the state's system of handling mentally ill offenders.[91]

Actual treatment programs at Coxsackie, as opposed to testing and diagnosis, were only sporadically attempted, particularly since the positions of institutional psychologist and psychiatrist were often vacant. In 1950, Charles C. Cuccio, the institution's psychologist, began what appears to have been the first formal group therapy program at the institution.[92] The program began after a newly received inmate in the quarantine division regaled Cuccio with tales of "freak parties" in his Bronx neighborhood, in which a dozen or more youths would gather to smoke marijuana and engage in a "variety of sexual perversion." Intrigued, Cuccio continued the conversations, eventually discussing the reformatory itself. The young man viewed Coxsackie "almost exclusively in terms of punishment" giving "no indication of recognizing the present philosophy of a reformatory type of institution." The inmate mentioned that several friends in quarantine held the same view, and Cuccio suggested the formation of a group for newly arrived inmates.

The young man never made it to group therapy—days later he smashed his fist through a window, the first in a series of troubling incidents that culminated in the young man's attempt to commit suicide by hanging himself in his cell. Cut down in time to be saved, the inmate was eventually transferred to Matteawan State Hospital. Despite the sad outcome, Cuccio pursued the idea of group therapy, and the project was begun in August. The new group met once a week for ninety minutes. Early volunteer participants included Alexander G., "the most verbally aggressive member within the group . . . he seems to thrive by entertaining the group and making an occasional funny remark." In the third session, Alexander began to talk about his background, and the remainder of the group surprised Cuccio by raising some possible reasons for his stealing, some of which the inmate argued against, and some he conceded (he "appeared to gain some insight"). In an early assessment, Cuccio observed that Alexander was "adopting a more serious attitude toward the discussions and his comments are becoming less superficial and immature."

The positive moments kept coming. Donald S.—like Alexander, sent to Coxsackie at 18 for auto theft—opened up during the group's fourth session, speaking for a full half-hour about the conflicts he had with his father and "the rejection he felt at home." The group was sympathetic, recounting their own experiences with family conflicts. A third participant, Paul T., had also been sent to Coxsackie at 18 for auto theft, after he took a 1946 Dodge sedan from the street for a joyride in his Queens neighborhood. Paul was the most withdrawn and reserved of the group, but like Alexander and Donald, he appeared, to Cuccio, to grow more trusting over time and displayed "genuine remorse for his past action." Alexander, Donald, and Paul all received positive pre-parole reports from Cuccio and were released after serving twenty-six, fifteen, and fourteen months, respectively.[93]

As with many of the interventions and programs staged at the Coxsackie reformatory, there is little to document the effectiveness of Cuccio's group therapy project. From his perspective, the young men involved (those in the case file sample, at least), appeared to respond to the opportunity to open up with one another and to explore their past, present and future. The case files themselves offer relatively little to help assess any longer term effects. All three successfully completed their parole supervision. Alexander joined the army a few years later; Donald (who had been trained in the electrical shop) became an electrician's helper and joined the union; but Paul's record offers no indication at all of his postparole history. More to the point, Cuccio—like nearly all Coxsackie psychologists, was soon on the move, heading to Saratoga County and a long career in school psychology. His group therapy sessions might well be added to a substantial list of small moments of success and hope facilitated by the reformatory staff over the years, but these were never able to translate into sustained or systematic programmatic achievement.

The teachers, shop instructors, psychologists, and psychiatrists who worked at Coxsackie during the reformatory years really were, in some ways, the pioneers they imagined themselves to be. Coxsackie made an investment of time and resources in educational programming that no other institution in the state could match—few institutions anywhere in the United States had comparable staffing and programs. Moreover, program staff labored to overcome the adversarial environment of the prison, to encourage inmates' desire to learn and grow as young men. Their individual successes should not be discounted. But the many obstacles to implementation meant that reform at Coxsackie would remain episodic. All too often, good intentions lacked resources, or were buried under layers of institutional conflict.

CHAPTER SIX

A Conspiracy of Frustration

Coming Home

Like thousands of other young men, Kenny Jackson departed Coxsackie wearing his "State-O" suit, issued to released prisoners, and carrying his "State-O-20"—the twenty dollars (and bus ticket) the reformatory provided. A prison car drove Jackson to the bus depot on a rainy Wed., where the driver left him with a mocking "so long for now." "I had only one fear," Jackson recalled, "fear that now you had to make good on all the talk you'd given yourself in the yard all those years, and that dreams weren't going to come true."[1] Many other accounts of leaving Coxsackie describe the same mix of hope and fear. Abubadika Sonny Carson looked around at the familiar faces of the reformatory, "and felt an unexplainable emotion: a reluctance to leave them."[2]

Young men leaving Coxsackie now found themselves "home," only to find that home was not exactly the one they had left behind. Prisoners without family connections were released to living arrangements ranging from upstate farm families to a New York City YMCA. More often, prisoners returned to their old homes, where families, neighborhoods, and social networks had changed since they had departed. A former reformatory inmate marveled at the differences in his Bronx neighborhood of Morrisania: "The Third Avenue elevated subway line had been completely demolished; the area was now dominated by two massive new housing projects . . . everything in my life before then was like a dream. Now, I was another person in another place and time."[3] The challenges of reintegrating into communities were obvious to friends and family. Claude Brown wrote of his friend Alley Bush, who departed Harlem for Coxsackie at 16 and returned three years later: "He seemed real backward, as though he hadn't grown any . . . seemed to think that the world had just waited for him, just stood still while he was in Coxsackie."[4]

Ex-prisoners were all too aware that the reformatory had scarcely delivered on its promise to return them to their communities with the kind of education and training they would need to make a future for themselves. As Howard P. left Coxsackie for his Bronx neighborhood, he offered some wry reflections on what the reformatory had taught him: "During my stay here I have learned many useful things, such as how to shoe a horse and to bend steel into all different angles . . . I have learned how to mind my own business and leave other people alone." Imprisoned at 16 for stealing a Buick to joyride, released just after his 18th birthday, Howard returned to New York City to live on his own, eventually taking a job as a hospital maintenance worker before his parole supervision period ended when he was 19.[5]

Case files and other sources offer a rich picture of the short-term transitions involved in coming home from the reformatory. They provide ample support for the conclusion Leonard Harrison and Pryor McNeill Grant reached back in 1938: "However broken a boy may be by what he has been through [in the reformatory], his release finds him full of hope for the future. Yet possibly the aftermath of a prison sentence is more discouraging and embittering than what has gone before." They argued, "There is a veritable conspiracy of frustration to defeat the boy released from prison." These young men were out of the reformatory, but they were still criminals.[6] Thirty years later, this same conclusion would lead Kenny Jackson to become one of the first counselors of the Fortune Society, dedicated to aiding newly released prisoners. During the intervening thirty years, however, more than ten thousand young men departed Coxsackie for the uncertain future that lay ahead.

The Release Decision

Most inmates arrived at Coxsackie on what prisoners called a "zip-three"—by which they meant a reformatory sentence that carried with it a maximum term of three years, with no minimum. The average time served was a comparatively short sixteen months, which meant that Coxsackie released nearly as many prisoners every year as it held on any given day. Excluding parole violators, the number of prisoners held for their maximum term was small, less than 5% of the case file sample.[7] For most reformatory prisoners, the route to release was the parole board.

During the reformatory's first decade, it had its own institutional parole board and associated parole officers. After 1945, Coxsackie's parole functions were consolidated into the State Division of Parole. In both cases, parole authorities had nearly unlimited discretion to hold or release an inmate. Sixteen-year-old Paul Glowacki, sentenced to Coxsackie on a petit larceny charge, challenged his indeterminate zip-three sentence in 1940, only to have the appellate court vigorously affirm the release powers of the reformatory: institutional authorities "should be in a position to determine when, in [the offender's] own best interests as well as the interests of society, they should be released. Some criminals reform for life, before they have even been convicted. For others, the first sentence is the formal and recorded social noting of a series of disasters. Only those in the institution can tell when release is wise in one case and unwise in another. The sentencing court certainly cannot."[8]

The court in Glowacki's case was deferential to correctional expertise, as most mid-century courts were, but no one attending a Coxsackie parole hearing would have been impressed. The public dimension of a typical case involved a cursory review, featuring the sorts of brief, random exchanges between inmates and officials that led historian David Rothman to characterize parole as a game of chance. This exchange, between parole head William Cashin and William B. (an 18-year-old from Harlem, convicted as a wayward minor), from a 1944 hearing, is typical:

Q: [Inmate name], have you attended the pre-parole classes?
A: Yes, sir.
Q: Do you understand what parole is?
A: Yes, sir.
Q: What is it?
A: Trust put on us boys to go out and try to do the best we can.
Q: Do you think you can do that?
A: I will try to do it.
Q: What will happen if you don't?
A: I will be brought back.
Q: If you are brought back you will probably serve more time than you have served this time. Do you understand that?
A: Yes, sir.
Q: Are there any questions you want to ask concerning parole?
A: No, I haven't any, Mr. Cashin.
Q: You are recommended.
A: Thank you, sir.[9]

The next month, the parole board's consideration of the case of Louis V. (a 17-year-old from rural Tompkins County, convicted of driving a car without a license while on parole from a juvenile reformatory), consisted of the following dialogue:

Q: Louis, have you attended the pre-parole classes?

A: Yes, sir.

Q: What do you understand parole to be?

A: Chance to get out and start a new life.

Q: You have to live up to the rules and regulations of the institution and do what your parole officer tells you. Do you think you can do that?

A: Yes, sir.

Q: If you had straightened out you probably would have been home before this. If you violate we will bring you back and you will serve more time than you have this time. Any question you want to ask?

A: Could I go to see my brother if my father goes with me?

Q: You will have to get permission from your parole officer.

A: Yes, sir.

Q: You are recommended.

A: Thanks a lot.[10]

And so it went. For a time after World War II, inmates attended a pre-parole class and prepared essays to accompany their parole cases. The essays can most charitably be described as exercises in telling institutional authorities what they wanted to hear. Murray C. declared, "I sincerely promise to do what is expected of me, and live the life of a respected citizen," while Warren W. affirmed that, "I will be honest with my parole officer. I will also to the best of my ability try to become an honest and trustworthy citizen."[11]

These short exchanges and rehearsed essays are simply artifacts of the parole ritual, and historians should not take them as an indicator of how release decisions were actually made at Coxsackie. Parole rituals usually ended in affirmation of a decision regarding release already made by an institutional program committee. The program committee included, at various times, the superintendent, assistant superintendent, director of education, guidance supervisor, physician, psychologist, parole officer, and chaplains. Their first meeting with a prisoner took place four months into his sentence, at which point the committee could certify for a parole appearance, or set a date for reappearance before the committee.

The decision making of the committee, though less superficial than the official parole hearing, was still quite predictable. Every aspect of a young man's institutional life had been carefully documented and made available to the committee, but conduct trumped everything else. Even when school grades were good and shop work satisfactory, cases were still held up with admonitions like "your behavior needs improvement," "you have not got along well with other people," "stop the fooling around," "[stop] trying to be a big shot."[12] Oscar M. went to more than one Coxsackie committee hearing armed with good grades in the reformatory school and the tailor shop, along with job offers and letters from his church, the Brownsville Neighborhood Center, his parents, and his lawyer. Despite all the assurances of work, family, and community support, he was held until the maximum expiration of his sentence, for being "in constant trouble with the colored boys."[13]

Of course, reformatory prisoners still had to make an appropriate show of contrition and cooperation at a parole hearing. The program committee warned Clinton P. that he would be required to provide evidence concerning his role in the armed robbery that sent him to Coxsackie:

Q: Your record has been good enough here. One point should be cleared up. Who was the leader of the gang?
A: If there was a leader, I would tell you.
Q: Don't hedge. There has to be a leader where nine boys are involved.
A: I had a lot to say. I guess I was something like a leader.
Q: The parole board is likely to ask you the same questions. If you can't answer them, they will likely hold you.[14]

Drug-using inmates at Coxsackie were specifically reported to NYC authorities upon parole, and an effort was frequently made to persuade parolees to become informants.[15] Parole boards demanded correct answers to questions like, "Are we to believe that you are remorseful for your behavior and ready to handle the pressures of civilian life?"[16] Over time, as some prisoners became more self-consciously political, parole questions did as well, with young men being asked to disavow their identification with the Black Muslims or the politics of black nationalism. When correct answers were not forthcoming, neither was parole.[17]

Parole Supervision

Once released on parole, Coxsackie prisoners faced a brief but critical period of supervision. Since most had been sentenced to three-year maximum terms, serving an average of sixteen months, the usual period of parole supervision was just over one year. Like the reformatory itself, time spent on parole supervision produced inspired successes and terrible tragedies. Two 19-year-old parolees—one released in 1937 and one in 1938—illustrate the ends of the parole spectrum.

The experience of Martin E. shows the possibilities of constructive, supportive post-release supervision. Released to his parents in Brooklyn in 1938, Martin was described in his Coxsackie case file as "one of the most emotionally maladjusted persons ever in the institution," with eighteen disciplinary reports at the reformatory. Still, Martin had been interested in the trumpet while at Coxsackie and had been encouraged in this interest by the institution's music teacher, who provided him a recommendation for a job giving music lessons after release. His parole officer took a keen interest in Martin's music, discussing jazz and classical music during their meeting, providing him with tickets to a Carnegie Hall recital, and arranging an appointment at the Cotton Club with Benny Davis (then responsible for the club's popular Annual Revues). The parole officer even spent some time counseling Martin's younger brother about his grades in school and praised him when those grades improved. Although Martin's parole supervision ended in 1939, a brief note from 1952—when Martin was 33—found him married with two children, living in Queens as a "respected member of the community."[18]

The case of Cornelius N., in contrast, shows the extent to which young lives could be destroyed by the experience of imprisonment and parole. Cornelius was released to his hometown of Rochester in 1937, following twelve months in the reformatory for burglary. Bullied and abused by other inmates while in Coxsackie, Cornelius had been "badly damaged by his incarceration," according to reformatory officials, who recommended his release back to his parents and to his previous job at a city junkyard. Once home, Cornelius requested permission from his parole officer to obtain a driver's license in order to get to work. As was common practice for parolees, the request was denied—most parolees were ineligible for a driver's license. So Cornelius spent the next few weeks walking along the highway to and from the junkyard each day—until he was struck by a car and died from the resulting skull fracture one month before what would have been his 20th birthday.[19]

For most inmates, the experience of parole supervision was a routine of trying to satisfy the state's demand that they find appropriate work and residence as well as demonstrate good behavior. Arriving home, parolees were instructed to meet with their parole officers, hold a specific curfew, maintain their current residence, remain gainfully employed, and "not to frequent hangouts, candy stores, and street corners."[20] Initial weekly reporting could later be changed to semi-monthly and even monthly reporting, depending on how well parolees were adjusting. By the 1950s, young men from Coxsackie were being assigned varying levels of supervision from the outset of their supervision period, based on prospective risk assessments.

Parole supervision itself could be quite intensive, as parole officers sought to keep young men attached to work and family and away from negative influences. This was particularly true during the institution's first decade, when it employed its own officers. One officer, on his way to visit Sylvester T. at the bakery where he was employed, spotted the young man hanging out in a candy store with his friends. Waiting until the boys left, the officer found Sylvester hiding in the back of the store; questioned about his job, Sylvester appeared evasive and was promptly returned to the bakery.[21] Antonio S., whose case file paid some attention to his "sexual confusion," was returned for violation of parole after making a series of "lewd phone calls" in which he arranged to meet the subject of the phone calls in Times Square, where he was taken into custody by his parole officer. Antonio was furious, claiming that the officer was "out to get him."[22]

Despite the close level of surveillance, the actual practice of parole supervision was quite flexible in avoiding revocations of parole. Parole officers were encouraged to continue young men on parole if they could. When Binghamton police arrested Charles F. for standing and talking with someone who had stolen some junk—a technical violation of parole—his officer declined to send him back to the reformatory. Seven years later, Charles was happily married with children and working as a machinist (the trade he had been taught at Coxsackie); he was released early from his ten-year period of parole supervision at the request of his parole officer, who wrote that this "was an example of what this institution can do for a boy who has the desire to rehabilitate himself."[23] In similar fashion, when Irving T. was located after disappearing for nearly two years, his officer simple noted, "If as the report indicates he is on relief and has no prospect of employment, he should be returned . . . if he should be employed and living a decent law abiding life, consideration should be given to continuing him on parole."[24] Time and time again, parole officers sought to protect those who appeared hard working, cooperative, and conforming, even when they violated the technical rules of parole.

Still, parole officers returned approximately one in every six prisoners released from Coxsackie for violations of their parole. Why did so many fail this period of supervision? The desire of these young men for freedom of movement frequently led to parole violations, and no condition of parole seems to have grated more than the routine denial of a driver's license. The lure of the automobile and the conditions of release were fundamentally incompatible. Raymond M. was sent back to Coxsackie for the unlicensed operation of a motor vehicle, violating curfew, leaving town without permission, and purchasing an auto without permission. Similarly, Ronaldo C. was returned to Coxsackie from Spanish Harlem for having obtained a driver's license without permission, leaving New York State without permission, staying overnight away from his approved residence, and associating with persons of questionable character.[25]

Freedom of movement, of course, went hand in hand with freedom of association. Here, too, Coxsackie parolees found themselves repeatedly in trouble. Parole reports carefully monitored young men who spent too much time loafing or lounging with their friends. Indeed, occasional parole violations were for nothing more serious than "corner lounging with six other youths" and "staying out late" but more often involved actual arrest for more serious criminal charges. William D. was a concern to his parole officer almost immediately, after he left his post-release job through the Works Progress Administration (WPA) after just three weeks. Reassigned to an NYA position, William was dismissed because of his venereal disease and from that point on spent "most of his time loitering around the streets of Harlem, drinking and associating with low moral characters." Held as a material witness in a murder case, William was sent back to Coxsackie largely for his refusal to engage in respectable patterns of work or association.[26]

Some parole revocations simply reveal young men with a simmering post-release anger that occupied a complicated borderland between criminal activity and activism. Peter B., the son of West Indian immigrants to New York City, had been sent to the reformatory in 1940 for having snatched a camera. He spent nearly his full term at Coxsackie, for Peter was constantly fighting with authorities and twice placed in solitary confinement. Peter's disciplinary violations suggest the extent to which he resisted reformatory authority: disobeying orders; shirking work; being disrespectful, disorderly, and insolent; causing a disturbance; cursing loudly; breaking rules; possessing contraband; fighting; and more. In August 1943, on parole from Coxsackie, Peter found himself swept up in the Harlem rioting. Police found Peter with a knife in his possession, "near a location where stores had been broken into." Apparently his location and his knife were sufficient to be returned as a parole violator to Coxsackie, where he was cited nine more times for disciplinary violations before being re-paroled in 1944.[27]

Employers played a critical role in supporting parole supervision. Upstate farm families, for example, often agreed to take in Coxsackie parolees and provide frequent updates on their character and conduct. One farmer contacted the parole office whenever he needed new boys to work on his farm, "accustomed to milking cows, in preference."[28] Another farm in Schuyler County regularly accepted Coxsackie parolees when their families refused to take them back, or when they wished not to return home. Farmers' complaints about parolees sounded common notes: "keeping company with a girl . . . keeping late hours, he is not able to get up in the morning when he should and can not do his work satisfactorily. He also apparently has the attitude that he does not have to do as his employer orders unless he so desires."[29] The demands of employers clashed with the desire of young men for leisure—where the clashes were too great, revocation of parole could provide the needed lesson in the importance of steady labor.

Family members played an important role in parole supervision as well. Sons had a way of disappointing families with their behavior, and families looked to the parole officer as an ally. One mother wrote to her son's parole officer, asking him to "intimidate" the young man, who had begun spending time with his former "bad associates."[30] A father, whose son was "running around with a gang," went to the parole officer to demand that the boy be returned to Coxsackie; another father wept in the parole office, telling stories of a son who refused to work and stayed out late at night, asking the officer to help direct the boy into the Civilian Conservation Corps (CCC).[31] When family expectations for work and association meshed with parole rules, family members were another critical part of the process of post-release surveillance.

Home

Coming home most often meant returning to the parents or relatives with whom parolees had lived prior to Coxsackie, sources of both support and conflict. The case files certainly reveal instances of families who intended to assist young men in making a better life. One farmer wrote a poignant letter to a soon-to-be-paroled youth from rural Cortland County: "We know it isn't going to be too easy to come back here and sometimes I wish the farm was a hundred miles from Cuyler instead of four but we'll stand by to help in any way we possibly can because we want you to show the real stuff we know is there in you."[32]

Just as often in the case files, parolees appeared to be going back to precisely the sort of poor home situations that had preceded their commitment to the reformatory. One young parolee wrote to his parole officer in 1937 that he was again fighting with his father, who "throws me out of the house and calls me names . . . please take me back there I can't stand it any longer."[33] Parole officers spent a great deal of time simply trying to persuade family members to open their homes to paroled sons, grandsons, brothers, and nephews—and then persuading parolees to stay.[34] Paul G. "conducted himself poorly at home," according to his parole officer, and had "been miserable in his attitude toward his parents."[35] After persisting in a "questionable" association with a 14-year-old girl, ignoring instructions to save some money, changing jobs without permission, and failing to report, Paul's parole was revoked five months after his release.

For those without family connections, a patchy network of institutions housed recently released prisoners. The Chrystie Street House in New York City, since well before Coxsackie had opened, operated as a home for "young men who have neither the right kind of family or friends to receive them when they leave prison."[36] The YMCA was another go-to institution for paroled reformatory inmates without homes to return to, or for those who were barred from contact with their homes as a condition of their release.[37] Where those institutions failed, some former prisoners settled instead into a lonely and vulnerable existence. Wendell M. arrived at the small upstate town of Avon, New York, released to the supervision of a local farmer. He knew no one at all—his family was in Wisconsin, and he had run away to New York City, where he had largely hung around Times Square. Not long after he arrived in Avon, Wendell left the farm and began working at a local diner. That summer, the police arrested him for peeping in a house window. Although his parole officer felt that "he may just have been lonely," he was returned for violation of parole "because of prejudice in the community."[38]

Coxsackie parolees were also beginning to form their own families after their release from the reformatory. Benjamin G. came to Coxsackie in 1936 to serve a fifteen-year term for robbery (despite the sentence length, Benjamin served only a year). After his release, he enrolled in the CCC, and after his discharge from that work program, he met and married a young woman in his hometown of Troy. The parole officer was impressed with her as "straightforward who would undoubtedly have a good influence." Benjamin's wife "claimed that the marriage was a happy one," and the parole supervision was suspended when he enlisted in the army in 1943.[39] Not infrequently, parolees in the case files sought permission from their parole officers to marry after getting a girlfriend pregnant.

New families could also be the source of turmoil for former prisoners. Several parolees in the case file sample, for example, were arrested for physically assaulting girlfriends or wives.[40] An East Harlem parolee was given permission to marry his pregnant girlfriend, but she was soon writing to his parole officer,

"My husband has very bad conduct . . . doesn't come home nights. He beats me. Every time things don't come his way he argues with me and beats me up. He do it very often and I can't stand it, was acting that way ever since I got married to him . . . We don't love each other, I don't want him no where around me because I am not safe around him."[41] As had been true before they were sentenced to Coxsackie, the young men's family ties remained substantial sources of frustration and conflict as they moved further, yet uncertainly, toward adulthood.

Work

Reformers hoped that the New York State Vocational Institution would provide young men the sort of training that would enable them to secure skilled employment upon release, but in the short term, this was rarely the case. Only 30 percent of inmates in the case file sample sustained regular postrelease employment during their period of supervision, no better than the proportion of young men employed before the arrest that led to their reformatory sentence. What employment parolees did secure was rarely skilled or leading to skilled work and even less often directly connected to specific Coxsackie vocational training programs.

While the Great Depression spurred the public works programs that helped build the reformatories, it also provided a bleak economic backdrop for the first groups of released prisoners. The mother of one Coxsackie parolee complained that "jobs are very hard to get . . . now that the law is that a boy should have a job when he gets out then the state should find jobs for these boys."[42] Albert M., recently laid off, wrote to his parole officer about his steady girlfriend, complaining, "I feel like a heel not being able to take her to a movie or to a dance at least once a week."[43] Rearrested for stealing scrap metal, Albert was promptly returned to Coxsackie, where he served fifteen more months. Craig U. returned home to Massena in 1936 to find that the one industrial plant in town was calling back only those who had been previously laid off—and there was little off-season farm work to be had.[44] Benjamin G. wrote in 1939, "Everything seems to be at a standstill here in Troy as far as work is concerned and it is a very difficult thing to find."[45] Chief parole officer George Quinn acknowledged that Coxsackie was "confronted with the serious difficulty in securing employment as a result of present economic conditions." He observed that "many boys have been obliged to take whatever employment was offered regardless of their trade training."[46]

Faced with the great shortage of available work, Quinn relied heavily on the work programs of the New Deal, which served as a safety net for parolees from Coxsackie. Some went on WPA work projects while living at home, including

National Youth Administration work assignments.[47] By far the most common work program, however, was the Civilian Conservation Corps (CCC). Of the inmates in the case file sample released from Coxsackie between 1936 and 1941, 15 percent (19 of 128) spent some time working in a CCC camp. Perry R., an "essentially normal kid," was released on the day before Christmas, 1938. His parole officer, observing that "no offer of employment" had been secured, and that it was "not likely that one would be forthcoming," arranged for Perry to spend eighteen months in the CCC.[48] Coxsackie parolees went to camps across the United States, and most of the case files suggest a positive experience.[49] One wrote to his parole officer from his CCC camp at Niagara Falls: "I like it here because the views of Niagara Falls and other falls are something to see . . . I'll have something to talk about when I come home." When the CCC moved to bar parolees and probationers from entering the corps, Coxsackie parole officers simply advised released prisoners to avoid mentioning their parole status.[50]

To be sure, some reformatory inmates in the case files sample secured work in the trades for which they had trained at Coxsackie. Peter F. learned printing and, on his 1937 release from the reformatory, married and eventually found work as a printer—he wrote that it was exactly "the kind of work that I wanted."[51] A number of machine shop graduates in the case file sample found work as machinists. Max N. had chosen the machine shop "because I think there is greater possibility for me securing a job at home," and he found just such a position on his return to Buffalo.[52] Barry I., whose machine shop instructor described him as "one of the best prospects" he had ever seen, quickly secured work at a machine works in his hometown. An electric shop graduate, Donald S., confessed, "When I think of the trouble I have caused my people and the money they have spent on me I realize that I have been a jerk; I don't want to be a jerk anymore."[53] He embraced electrical work at Coxsackie and, after his release home, in Manhattan, where he secured work as an electrician's helper. Even some semiskilled training could connect young men to employment. Nicholas C. had trained in the kitchen, "which is semi-skilled and which offers the prospects of a job at a Rochester restaurant," which he secured while on parole; his work record was excellent—"he will eventually become a good cook"—and he contributed money to his parents and to his local Greek Orthodox Church.[54]

Trade training was no magic bullet, no guarantee of employment. Coxsackie inmates in the case file sample were frustrated by the limitations of their training in the outside world where more advanced certifications were required. Leonard J. secured a job in a tailor shop, thanks to a letter from his Coxsackie instructor, but was let go after just four days because he was "too inexperienced for the type of work required." Frederick K. wrote a discouraged letter to his parole officer: "I sent you a letter last week I told you about a job I might be able to get in the barber shop. I was given a try out but no soap. I couldn't get on the electric clippers. You know at the Inst. we didn't have electric clippers." Edwin M. wrote to the Coxsackie director of education, asking for some assistance in securing work: "Since my release, I have been offered various positions in barber shops here in town but have no proof of training. I would very much appreciate it if you would send me some kind of written certificate stating that I did have barber training for said period." The director replied in blunt terms: "I have looked up your school records which show that you are able to do good work on a helper's level, but you are definitely not a tradesman. You are smart enough to know this. We do not furnish educational records to former pupils. However, we shall be glad to furnish a detailed report about you on request from an employer."[55]

New York's liberal reform groups took seriously the job of placing young ex-prisoners in work situations. The Osborne Association, formed from the merger of Thomas Mott Osborne's National Society of Penal Information and his Welfare League Association, continued the latter's focus on aiding ex-prisoners. President Charles Osborne made clear in 1933 that traditional welfare agencies did not work well for young, single men just released from reformatories, "without definite family obligations." Osborne argued that the gap between release and eventual employment was a critical one, and urged the association to try to bridge that gap and allow young men to "reestablish themselves." The association's employment and relief secretary labored hard to help ex-offenders but faced daunting challenges in the midst of the Depression. In 1934, the secretary interviewed 429 men (some more than once) but was able to secure just 33 work positions. In 1939, the Community Service Society of New York partnered with the association to pay for a director of placement position, first held by Graves Moore. At times, association staff vented their frustration at the barriers to work for ex-prisoners; William Cox, a longtime Osborne associate, condemned the obstacles that "block the path of sincere endeavor." "Is this justice," Cox demanded to know. Must the young ex-offender, he asked, "forever be deprived of the right of opportunity to live a useful life because of youthful folly?"

In March 1936, the association partnered with Viola Ilma to create a vocational demonstration project, in which Ilma would make regular monthly visits to the New York City Reformatory at New Hampton and choose five young men for "employment placement and vocational guidance as well as intensive follow up work." A preliminary report showed that thirty-two of fifty-three program participants were working and doing well, far above the typical results for reformatory inmates, but the association was forced to discontinue the project in 1937 for lack of funds. In 1941, Elmira Reformatory organized a placement bureau, in conjunction with the Prison Association of New York and other agencies. The bureau was to concentrate on inmates who had been through the educational program and were qualified for "specific work situations."[56]

Even the wartime boom in industrial employment hardly ended the problems of securing employment. The Osborne Association continued to see hundreds of job-seeking former prisoners, including many rated 4F for military service, skilled workers whose felony convictions were hampering their ability to secure work, and (by 1944) growing numbers of dishonorably discharged servicemen. The director of vocational placement for the association, Robert Hannum, noted the "variety and seriousness of the adjustments our men must make when they 'hit the bricks,'" and hoped the wartime public would take the hard work of readjustment into consideration.[57] Throughout the postwar years, Coxsackie and various social service agencies would continue to try solving the problem of finding work for young reformatory parolees.[58]

The coming of World War II provided another option for young men pressed to find suitable work—military service. Of the young men in the case file sample released between the opening of the reformatory in 1936 and the end of the war in 1945, one in five (43 of 214) served in the military.[59] For a few, volunteering was a way of expressing a sense of manhood and patriotic duty. One week after Pearl Harbor, Stanley M. begged his parole officer to let him enlist: "I see that all my friends are joining the Army and they think I'm scared and I would like to show them that I am not scared, and I am writing you to see if I can join the Army, I see that all the others are doing their part and I would like to do my."[60] More often, the case files show voluntary military service as simply another work option for young men in unsatisfying life situations. For Benjamin G., tired of looking for work in Troy; for Irving J., weary of cleaning cesspools in the Bronx; for Melvin M., no longer wanting to recondition oil drums in Schenectady; and for Allen D., fired from his job in Manhattan for failing to pay union dues, volunteer service in the army beckoned as a more promising alternative.[61]

For other released prisoners, military service was a device by which they could be abruptly released from parole supervision. In September 1942, the superintendent wrote to all parolees, urging them to consider "how urgently our country needs every man who is capable of military service, to hasten the day of victory. The more each individual does, the sooner victory will come . . . if you wish to enter the service, a release from parole will be granted if the official request is made directly to the institution." By 1943, prisoners could be paroled directly into the military, and a branch draft board was set up at the reformatory. Even a "hard case" like Alex A., who had been sent to solitary confinement no fewer than seven times, was released to the army in 1943, after just fourteen months at the reformatory.[62]

For many Coxsackie prisoners in the case file sample, their adjustment to military life went as poorly as their adjustment to any other institutional setting. At least one-quarter of those in the sample serving in World War II (11 of 43) were charged with a serious crime or desertion while serving. This figure probably understates the total, for it includes only those instances where the misconduct was reported to the reformatory.[63]

Crime

The experience of Coxsackie's prisoners in military service is a reminder that they were being released from the reformatory just at the point of accelerating criminal careers. The reformatory was supposed to be an early and aggressive intervention in criminal careers, but Coxsackie was more often simply a stop along the way. Military enlistment during World War II competed with a potential return trip to the reformatory. The navy narrowly beat out Coxsackie for Edgar G., released on parole in 1943 to his parents' home in Syracuse. Edgar fought with his brother, stayed out all night, refused to pay board, and stole the family car. With his parole officer looking for him, he chose to enlist in the navy; his officer concluded, "From all indications it would seem a race between the Navy and a Violation of Parole Warrant and the Navy won."[64] Coxsackie beat the navy in the case of Neil K., paroled to his parents in 1942. Against the advice of his parole officer, Neil moved out of his parents' home into a residential hotel, which became his home base for a series of drunken parties and sexual liaisons with underage girls. Scheduled for induction into the navy, he was instead returned to Coxsackie for the final six months of his sentence.[65]

Just how many Coxsackie prisoners continued some involvement in the criminal justice system? The only systematic recidivism data comes from a study of prisoners that had been through the Elmira Reception Center, released in 1960, and the subject of a six-year followup conducted in late 1966. Table 6.1 shows that 60 percent of prisoners from Coxsackie were reconvicted in the six-year period following their release, and fewer than one in four avoided any sort of criminal justice entanglement.[66]

TABLE 6.1
Recidivism records in 1966 of Coxsackie inmates released in 1960

Criminal record	Number	Percentage
Total	215	100.0
No record	49	22.8
Parole violation or arrest only	37	1.2
Convicted	129	60.0
• Lesser offense / youthful offender	10	4.6
• Misdemeanor	60	27.9
• Felony	59	27.5

These numbers are consistent with the case file sample, in which 55 percent of the cases (205 of 376) give a clear indication of a subsequent arrest or return for parole violation. Of these cases, 128 were arrested, rather than being returned for parole violations (either because the offense was so serious or because it occurred after the end of parole supervision), with 105 sentenced to some period of confinement—ranging from short periods spent in local jails to long prison terms elsewhere.[67] The case file sample *understates* the extent of subsequent criminal justice involvement from 1945 forward, for two reasons. First, parole supervision moved to a state-level agency rather than remaining an institution-based operation, and the reporting of criminal offenses during and after the end of parole supervision was not systematic. Second, and more important, Coxsackie officials began to send a prisoner's *entire* case file when an inmate was transferred to another institution, or when he was subsequently sentenced to another New York prison. The pattern is quite striking: through early 1944, only 2 numbers were missing from a sample of 211 cases, but the sample of 161 subsequent cases included 92 missing case file numbers. Put another way, more than one-third (36%) of Coxsackie prisoners after mid-1944 are missing from the case files sampled. Since nearly all of those were missing because of disciplinary transfer or re-imprisonment, it is reasonable to assume the later files dramatically understate postrelease arrest and incarceration. Sorting the re-arrest numbers into pre- and post-1944 groups shows that 50 percent (105 of 211) of the earlier group recorded re-arrest, while only 14 percent (22 of 161) of the later group with missing files recorded a re-arrest. What is clear is that the level of criminality among ex-reformatory inmates was substantial and roughly comparable to contemporary rates of postrelease offending.[68]

In looking at arrest and imprisonment as part of the postrelease histories of Coxsackie inmates in the case file sample, some patterns emerge. Most notable are those cases in which low levels of employment and a pressing need for money resulted in new entanglements with the criminal justice system. Coming home at ages 18, 19, and 20, young men faced ever more demands for self-support, and low-level criminal activity remained an obvious option. Entering the bottom rungs of illicit enterprise was one way to do this; a young Sonny Carson left Coxsackie and began running a craps game, later recalling the pleasure of having real money coming in. Ernest N., newly married and unable to hold any job for long after his release, took to working for a policy racket that operated from the hotel where his father worked.[69] Mario F. wrote to another inmate about the "sweet little racket" that he and five other inmates from New York City had prepared when they all returned from Coxsackie.[70]

Gang members faced enormous challenges returning to their old neighborhoods. Coxsackie itself had been no holiday from the pressure of gang loyalty and gang violence, but if returning prisoners hoped to escape it once they came home, they quickly found that old ties were hard to sever.[71] Arthur, a 1946 Coxsackie parolee and a member of the Mysterious Fives gang, worriedly informed his parole officer that the gangs would be "after him," and that, in his Bronx neighborhood, gang membership was essential to survival. After being accosted and shot in the foot by an "enemy gang" three months after his parole, he "resumed relations" with the Mysterious Fives. In December 1946, Arthur and other members of the gang held up a Long Island dry cleaners and a liquor store. In the latter robbery, Arthur pistol-whipped the owner. Two days later, the police stopped Arthur and his friends (they were riding in a stolen car), and Arthur was eventually given a fifteen- to twenty-year sentence for assault and robbery.[72] Dhoruba Bin Wahad recalled a similar sort of pressure: "It happened fast, maybe a few weeks after I got out and was back in the Bronx. The simple fact was, I needed money. I had no job, nothing coming in. And I was back with my old cronies. And these brothers weren't jitterbugging no more; they were now full-fledged gangsters. Somebody came up with the idea to stick up this after-hours club in the Bronx. Being back in the hood, running with the boys again, I was down for that."[73]

Heroin led some Coxsackie parolees into what could be a decades-long revolving-door relationship to the criminal justice system. John Mack described coming back to New York City from Coxsackie in 1950 to find that his neighborhood was "flooded with heroin, as though it were coming out of the pavement."[74] Jack E., sent to Coxsackie for gang fighting in Harlem with the Socialistic Dukes, was paroled in 1944, after just twelve months in the reformatory. Following his release, Jack began using heroin regularly, and his postrelease record begins showing drug-related arrests and short-term incarcerations in 1948—five days in 1948, ten days in 1949, three months at Rikers Island in 1951, two years in state prison for felony possession with intent to sell in 1952, sixty days for possession in 1955, four months for petit larceny in 1956, five years in a federal penitentiary for narcotic sales in 1957, three heroin-related arrests in 1964 and 1965, six months for drug possession in 1966, and subsequent arrests in 1967 (possessing a needle), 1970 (drug possession), and 1976 (grand larceny)—at least twenty-eight consecutive years of drug-related involvement with the criminal justice system.[75]

Drifting was another postrelease path and, again, one that made young men quite vulnerable to arrest. For some young men, the lure was the freedom of the road—a choice that almost invariably brought them back into conflict with the law. Edward B. vanished within two weeks of his release in 1937, telling his family that he was "headed west." Later that year, police in Ohio picked up Edward as a vagrant, while he was riding the rails. Eventually, he made his way back to New Jersey, where he moved from place to place, and was jailed four times over the next five years. After a fifth arrest, for desertion, he vanished once again and was declared a fugitive. Richard F. arrived at Coxsackie a week after Edward and was released two months after him in 1937. Richard stayed at home for six months (acquiring and losing a job at Macy's, and being rejected for military service by the army) before disappearing. He wandered around, looking for work in Pittsburgh, Johnstown, and Philadelphia, before being arrested for vagrancy in the latter city. Philip D. also lasted about six months at home, with his grandparents in Newark, before leaving his job and family for Boston. After some time in that city, he made his way to Manhattan, where a detective arrested Philip for "offering to commit an indecent act for three dollars," for which he was returned to Coxsackie.[76]

Still others simply lacked the judgment or ability to function well on their own. Gregory V., diagnosed as feeble minded but retained at Coxsackie, told the following story of postrelease trouble: Gregory and a friend were enticed by an older man they both knew to steal a car and hold up a store. On their way to the store in the stolen car, they stopped at a gas station. The attendant asked the two a few leading questions. Gregory and his friend became scared and hit the attendant over the head with the handle from a gas pump. They fled the scene but ran out of gas in a lonely spot. To attract attention and get a ride, the two lit a small fire but burned the car completely. Convicted of grand larceny, Gregory went off to Napanoch, on the recommendation of the district attorney.[77]

In other cases, that same impulsivity and lack of judgment took terrible, tragic turns.[78] John Bender and Harold Elling were both Coxsackie parolees from Rochester, with frequent run-ins with the police both before and after their time in the reformatory. Bender was paroled to his parents in 1939 and given a job with the NYA. Within two months, he had been rearrested, after getting drunk, stealing a case of whiskey, and stealing a car—for which, unsurprisingly, he was returned for violation of parole. Bender was reparoled to his parents and an auto repair job in April 1941. By October, he and Elling decided to go hitchhiking, armed, with the idea of holding up drivers who stopped and taking their cars. When Paul Skaritza stopped, Bender and Elling ordered him from the car—Elling marched him down the road, knocked him down with the gun, and shot him in the head (to hear the gun go off, he later testified). Elling was sentenced to death, Bender to life imprisonment in Attica.[79]

For these veterans of the reformatory, the departure from Coxsackie was simply a graduation to the world of the adult criminal justice system, grinding in and out of local jails, or serving long sentences in state prisons. Coxsackie frequently refused to take parole violators back, transferring them up to the state prison level. The Coxsackie superintendent lectured Albert D. on his return: "You thought you were going to give yourself up and come back here and we would be nice and easy and treat you like a welcome guest. You parole violators have no privileges of any kind. You understand that?" But at least Albert was allowed back to the reformatory. Peter Y., who had been involved a highly publicized series of burglaries in Rochester in 1938, was refused entirely and given a ten-year sentence instead. Humberto R. was dismissed by Coxsackie as a "typical gangster" and was given a new sentence to Sing Sing. In general, if parolees were no longer of an appropriate age for Coxsackie or for another reformatory, they would be subject not to the typical reformatory sentence but to the "regular" sentence for the new crime they had committed.[80]

Young men released from Coxsackie too often found in postrelease life a continuation (or even an acceleration) of the strains and conflicts that had preceded their time behind bars. Even when new criminal justice entanglements were avoided, family frustrations played havoc with the process of reintegration, while limited job opportunities mocked the promise of vocational training. For many others, patterns of everyday life intersected with policing to ensure continued arrests and imprisonments. Collectively, the experiences of reformatory prisoners offer an early echo of Shadd Maruna's recent observation that "the situation facing recidivist offenders is something like a brick wall. It is surmountable but is enough of an obstacle to make most turn around and 'head back.' " Up against the wall while in Coxsackie's yard, ex-offenders found themselves up against another, no less formidable wall, once they left the reformatory.[81]

PART THREE

THE SLOW DEATH OF PRISON REFORM IN NEW YORK, 1944–1977

CHAPTER SEVEN

The Frying Pan and the Fire

The Reformatory in Crisis, 1944–1963

World War II resulted in a substantial reduction to New York's prison population, as military service drew away thousands of men who might otherwise have been incarcerated, including large numbers of parolees. As that population fell from a prewar peak of 18,400 prisoners to a wartime low of 14,894 in 1945, New York found itself able to lease a newly completed big house prison, Green Haven, to the federal government for confining deserters and soldiers convicted of crimes. In the midst of this decline, a worrisome countertrend of rising inmate populations emerged at Coxsackie and the other reformatories. A wave of adolescents came into the reformatory system, propelled by a rise in wartime delinquency and the resulting efforts to increase policing of youth crime and gang activity.[1]

At Coxsackie, the annual population survey recorded a rise from 1944 to 1945 of 25 percent (from 543 inmates to 680). Reformatory officials began purchasing additional dormitory beds and army cots that could be set up at night and taken down during the day. Coxsackie's dormitories were packed with new arrivals, their average population rising from forty to over seventy young men. Superintendent Scarborough complained of the many problems caused by the overcrowding, observing that "the general inmate morale has suffered considerably in those sections of the institution."[2]

Neither the practical challenge of finding beds and space, nor the challenges to inmate morale, troubled Coxsackie officials as much as their perceptions of the changing nature of the inmate population. Coxsackie during wartime began to shift its concerns from the problem of the *uneducable* inmate to the threat posed by the *ungovernable* inmate. As with the Napanoch solution to the uneducable inmate (see chapter 5), Coxsackie attempted to transfer away those young men who appeared to threaten the order of the institution. As they did, they began shifting ever-larger numbers of adolescents to other parts of the prison system. Even before World War II, a substantial minority (between 15% and 20% of the case file sample, for example) found themselves the subject of a transfer to another prison or state institution. Starting around 1944, Coxsackie employed transfers more aggressively; as many as one in three reformatory prisoners were transferred in the postwar period. In fact, institutional transfers were one of Coxsackie's most important resources for maintaining order and discipline.[3]

The practice of transfer also allows us to consider what aspects of inmate behavior and identity were most threatening to the institution. Just what could cause a prison like Coxsackie, which hardly shied away from tough, even brutal, internal discipline, to exile young men to other parts of New York's institutional system? This chapter shows that two issues emerged with particular force after World War II. First, the growing numbers of youth gang members, mostly from New York City, threatened to upset an already fragile racial order behind bars. Second, young heroin addicts, part of an epidemic of heroin use that swept New York City in the late 1940s, were being sent to Coxsackie after police crackdowns. Like the feeble-minded inmate, addicts were readily framed as the antithesis of suitable reform material.

As discipline problems grew, Coxsackie and state officials expanded their use of disciplinary transfer. In 1950, with the prison in a near-constant state of crisis management and grappling with the twin problems of youth gangs and heroin addiction, the state committed itself to designating a new "end of the line" prison at Great Meadow. This was a critical moment, as the state abandoned the idea, in place since the start of the reform movement in the 1930s, that there was a rehabilitative option for every adolescent offender. Designed to receive transfers from the reformatory populations at Coxsackie, Woodbourne, and Elmira, the Great Meadow prison would truly become the "fire" to the "frying pan" of reformatory life. Exiled together in one brutal, racist institution, the young men who disrupted Coxsackie helped to make Great Meadow ground zero of organized inmate resistance and political activism. New York's experience brings to mind Peter Zinoman's observation regarding Vietnamese colonial prisons: "By subjecting . . . colonial subjects with diverse regional backgrounds, social identities, and political commitments to the same terrifying ordeal, the prison system encouraged fraternal affinities and a sense of shared predicament that contributed to the formation of a national community."[4] Long before the Attica riot of 1971, even before the birth of a formal and organized movement for prisoner rights, the young men of the Coxsackie and Great

Meadow reformatories displayed an emergent political consciousness that, at times, came close to transcending the boundaries of race and ethnicity.

The Ungovernable, Part One—Coxsackie and Postwar Youth Gangs

The arrival of a new kind of youth gang member during World War II added a new layer to the social geography of the reformatory yard. Abubadika Sonny Carson recalled that the dominance of gang associations was something that prisoners "soon knew if you wandered there." Formerly divided largely by race, and to some extent geography, subsections of the yard's wall were now carefully divided around a Coxsackie-specific mixture of race, home city, neighborhood, and gang identifications. A teenage Sonny Carson quickly learned the vernacular map:

> On the righthand side of the yard, where the first group of blacks were located, you were told it was The Turks' turf. The Turks were from 118th Street in Harlem. A few feet on, the area belonged to the Brothers from Buffalo, Rochester, Syracuse, and all other upstate areas. Beyond them the area belonged to the Imperial Lords from the city. Next to them the Socialistics from downtown Harlem. Next to them were The Bachelors from 126th Street in Harlem. Next to them the Copians from Harlem.
>
> Then the widest sector in the center of this black-populated area was set aside for all the Brooklyn groups. Even though we were not united in Brooklyn, we were united in this place: The Robins, Beavers, Bishops, Socialistics, both Dukes and Gents, and every other gang from the Brooklyn vicinity. We intermingled and stood together against our foes.
>
> Next to our Brooklyn area were the Sabers; a few feet beyond them were The Chancellors and beyond them, ending our black area, The Slicksters, hated foes of the Sabers from 139th Street.

Carson, making his first trip into the yard, heard someone yell his name. He was "confronted with two of my fellow gang members, Brother Hassie, who already had a reputation for using his hands in combat, and Crip, who wasn't really crippled at all but walked as if he was." Hassie and Crip introduced Sonny to "all the people from Brooklyn . . . it was like old home week." He recalled later, "I was in good company, and when the whistle blew, I knew I had arrived."[5]

Nearly every postwar account of time served at Coxsackie mentions the prevalence and power of youth gangs in the reformatory. Coxsackie was recalled as "a prison full of gangbangers," serving a role that was an extension of what young men had experienced growing up: "Back then, before heroin came to dominate illegitimate capitalist activity in the ghetto, gangs served a different kind of purpose—especially for black males. They were an organization that taught young men codes of manhood; i.e., your word is your bond, loyalty—if someone lied to you, you confront them. That might seem like macho posturing in this day and age, but the gang did serve that purpose."[6] Lumumba Shakur, a leader of the New York Black Panthers, recalled much of the same when he arrived at the Woodbourne Reformatory in 1960, which he called a "gang-fighting haven." "I thought I stopped gang fighting in 1959," Shakur wrote, "but Woodburn [sic] changed all my thoughts about gang fighting again. During my first ten minutes in Woodburn the shit began."[7]

It was in the postwar period that Coxsackie acquired a new nickname—Bop City—that celebrated not just to the similarly named nightclub in the heart of Manhattan's commercial bebop jazz scene, but the "bop culture" that these new prisoners brought with them to the reformatory. As Eric Schneider and others have explained, the language of bopping was embraced by gang members (and adolescents) of all ethnic groups; to "bop" was to walk in the style of one listening to bebop itself, while "bopping" meant engaging in gang violence. If it was true, as Schneider argues, that "bop culture allowed adolescents to defy school and the labor market" and "to mock the symbols of the dominant culture," nowhere was this more intensely so than against the walls of Coxsackie.[8]

The surge of gang members into Coxsackie brought the already simmering racial tensions of the prison to a boil. Byron L., a member of the Harlem-based Turks, was denied parole in 1948 and the board took the unusual step of delaying his next hearing for one year (six months would have been typical) because of his conflicts with the "many Copians" in the prison yard.[9] But it was *interracial* conflict that spurred a decision, a year earlier, to begin transferring some of the Turks to the Elmira Reformatory. James J. was one of those identified for transfer. Sixteen years old and identified as "a leader of the colored group in the yard," James J. and several other Turks had been "trying to take over the [white] basketball court." The other Turks were shipped to Elmira. James remained at Coxsackie because he had been sentenced as a wayward minor, but his case file judges him to be "a problem case in anti-social attitudes," and concludes, "this present gang affair indicates he is not fit for release."[10]

The case file sample reveals the emergence of these new disciplinary transfers in the form of missing file numbers in the Coxsackie inmate records— these missing files were simply transferred, whole, to the new institution. The earliest disciplinary transfers appear to have been older parole violators, whom the reformatory began shipping out to the big house prisons. These seem to have begun in the fall of 1944, according to Coxsackie authorities, "to relieve the overcrowded conditions at this institution." Wallace T., who lasted only a single week on his parole, and whom authorities described as "cold, calculating," was transferred to Attica Prison. Leon W., an "agitator among the colored inmates," was sent to Clinton Prison. By the following year, with young men continuing to flood into the reformatory system at war's end, Coxsackie began transferring inmates in small groups; Melvin H. shipped out to Elmira in November, along with seven other prisoners, all of whom were designated "incorrigible" at Coxsackie.[11]

The Ungovernable, Part Two—Coxsackie and Heroin Users

The transfer solution was shortly applied to a second group of "ungovernable" reformatory inmates, young men who arrived at Coxsackie as heroin users. The first wave of postwar heroin-using reformatory inmates arrived between 1948 and 1951. By the time Francisco R. arrived at the Elmira Reception Center in April 1951, the professional staff there had already developed a great many ideas as to how a reformatory sentence could serve the interests of young heroin addicts. Francisco, 18, had been using "three or four caps" of heroin a day since he was 16. He had been arrested in his Bronx neighborhood, along with a "mixed race group" of boys, for robbing and trashing a grocery store. Francisco's mother felt he was "insane" and had brought him to the attention of the Community Service Society when he was only 10, because of his behavioral problems. The Reception Center sent Francisco along to Coxsackie, with a comprehensive set of treatment recommendations: "intensive and extensive psychotherapy . . . by a trained psychotherapist"; "extensive psychotherapy on the outside after release . . . psychotherapeutic social case work with the family to give them insight into the boy's real problem"; remedial education; social education "to feel secure"; and vocational "encouragement."[12]

Needless to say, Coxsackie was ill equipped to provide anything close to the intensive therapeutic program for Francisco that the Elmira Reception Center urged on them. Few if any public agencies *were* in that position as of 1951. Overwhelmed and uncertain how to respond, New York's network of social service provision often gave way to the criminal justice system. That year, for example, Angelo C. joined the Henry Street Settlement—one of Manhattan's best-known social work agencies for children. Angelo had a reputation as a "wise guy" veteran of state institutions, having served time at Warwick. He quickly attached himself to the older and rougher crowd at the settlement, got into several fights, and at one point threatened to "mop the floor" with any settlement staff that tried to keep him out. Most troubling for the staff, Angelo brought heroin into the settlement; he and his friends would lock themselves in the boys' toilet while they shot up. One evening, Angelo and his friends forced their way into the office of a young female social worker. While his friends taunted and heckled the young woman with sexually suggestive remarks, Angelo sat in the corner, his face flushed and his eyes glassy, watching the show. Not long thereafter, he robbed a man on the steps of the settlement, was reported to the police, arrested, tried, convicted, and sent to Coxsackie.[13]

By the early 1950s, Coxsackie housed about one hundred known heroin users at a time. Plans to segregate addicts within the reformatory were abandoned, largely because separate confinement of the young heroin user "only emphasizes his drug usage and leads to constant exchange of experiences about drugs." Although some of the addict prisoners were serious discipline problems, the more troubling aspect of this population was their propensity to be quickly returned for violation of parole. One-third of all parole violators (roughly twice their proportion of parolees) were drug users, and within a few years their numbers began to place some pressure on the system.[14] William G. was typical of the users caught in the revolving door of the criminal justice system. Paroled in 1952 to his father's custody, William had a postrelease job secured for him through the New York Employment Bureau, a job for which he had "little enthusiasm" or appreciation "of the interest in his behalf to obtain this job for him." Warned to stay away from his Coney Island hangouts and his old girlfriend, William appeared for his first day of work, but not his second or any other day of work. Skipping his first week's parole reporting, William was declared an absconder within two weeks. Tracked down in a neighborhood bar two months later, back on heroin, and with his now-pregnant girlfriend, William was quickly returned to Coxsackie.[15] This rapid rate of return led Coxsackie and the Division of Parole to set up an experimental project in 1956, in which heroin users returning to New York City would be specifically identified and tracked.[16]

In the meantime, the reformatory system struggled to understand just what addict prisoners needed, and whether or not they could—or should—be confined in traditional reformatories like Coxsackie. One case in particular highlights the great challenge heroin posed to the system. Miguel M. had arrived in New York City from Puerto Rico in 1936, when he was just 2 years old. By the summer of 1950, when Miguel was 15, he had begun using heroin with some friends in his Bronx neighborhood. His mother, as was so often the case, was the first line of response to Miguel's drug use. She had heard about the U.S.

Narcotics Hospital in Lexington, Kentucky, and tried to persuade Miguel at age 16 to voluntarily commit himself for treatment. He refused. Miguel's mother next turned to the New York City Youth Board to see if he might participate in an experimental program in individual psychotherapy. Once again, Miguel displayed no interest in the program, so his mother had him committed as a wayward minor. The court, apparently with the agreement of his mother, placed Miguel on probation and sent him to live with his father. The new arrangement proved no more satisfactory, and Miguel's father eventually threw him out of the house. Living on the street, stealing to support his habit, Miguel was arrested for breaking and entering and sent to the Elmira Reception Center in 1952.[17]

For Glenn Kendall and the reception center staff, Miguel was one heroin addict too many. Fed up with the revolving door, and no longer convinced that the reformatory system had much to offer users who were so quickly returning to drugs after release, the reception center staff poured out their feelings in Miguel's assessment. Their recommendation began by flatly asserting, "An experience in a correctional institution is not the solution to this youth's social adjustment problems." Why not? Miguel had no record of delinquency "prior to drug taking," the "present offense was motivated by money . . . for drugs," and he was "not basically a delinquent personality according to the psychiatrist." Instead of the reformatory system, Kendall and the ERC looked hopefully to Riverside Hospital on North Brother Island, where New York City had recently begun committing noncriminal adolescent heroin addicts for treatment.

In effect, the ERC staff signaled that they were done trying to manage heroin addicts, and that addict management should be the business of the public health system. But Miguel could not be transferred to North Brother Island. He had been convicted of a crime, and there was no alternative but to keep him in prison. What is more, Coxsackie authorities were strongly moved to disagree with Kendall and the ERC. "Further study of this case," Superintendent Donald Scarborough wrote to the ERC, "leaves one to feel that the Reception Center was not exactly justified in suggesting that this is the kind of case that should have gone to North Brother Island Hospital for treatment." Scarborough argued that Miguel was not "a case of drug usage alone," but that he had been "doing petty stealing over a considerable period" to support his habit. The superintendent also imagined that "further investigation" would almost certainly reveal that Miguel had sold heroin, as well as using the drug. "It is not within the intent of the North Brother Island project," he concluded, "to have persons of that kind there. That place is strictly for persons who have committed no offense other than the use of drugs alone."[18]

Scarborough's view of what qualified an adolescent for North Brother Island was exceedingly limited, and it is hard to imagine many young heroin users meeting the criteria of having never stolen to buy drugs or having never resold any of their supplies. But if his view was that heroin use was largely a problem for the criminal justice system, it did *not* follow that heroin users were somehow appropriate for Scarborough's particular corner of that system. In fact, Miguel was transferred after eight months at Coxsackie, sent to the Matteawan State Hospital after he began to hear voices and "act as if he is in a dream."[19] Released in late 1954, Miguel was arrested just a few months later on another breaking and entering charge, with his parole officer noting a suspicion that the young parolee was back on heroin—another turn of the revolving door that would continue to frustrate the state's efforts to manage addicts in the reformatory population.

The End of the Line—Great Meadow

By 1950, the twin problems of gangs and heroin could no longer be managed through the limited numbers of institution-to-institution transfers that Coxsackie could arrange. That year, Governor Thomas Dewey authorized, under pressure from the Department of Corrections, the creation of an interdepartmental working committee on youthful offenders. The committee was stacked with longtime DOC reform figures, including Walter Wallack, Donald Scarborough, Price Chenault, and Glenn Kendall.[20] Their final report, not completed until late 1952, proposed that Great Meadow Prison at Comstock be converted into a facility to handle those inmates who were "too tough" for Coxsackie and the other reformatories.[21] In early January 1953, Governor Dewey put the proposal in his annual message, and the legislature passed the requisite legislation in March.

The Great Meadow decision marks a momentous break in the history of the reform movement, which began after the riots of 1929. For the first time, reformatory officials—including many of those responsible for its original design—abandoned the pretense that there was a rehabilitative space for every adolescent prisoner and instead proposed the creation of an end-of-the-line facility.[22] The unrelenting campaign against youth gangs and heroin users had overwhelmed the reformatory system.[23] Now it was time to start removing inmates in large numbers, to expel the ungovernable along with the uneducable, in the hopes of saving the rest of the reformatory program.

The case files from Great Meadow (more often referred to as Comstock by prisoners) are invaluable in revealing what happened next, as each of the Woodbourne, Elmira, and Coxsackie case files they received reveals the patterns of experience and behavior that precipitated transfer.[24] The first group of eight inmates sent from Coxsackie give a preview of what was to come: a severe alcoholic serving a longer-than-average prison term of five years; a local boy who had helped plan an escape attempt (the idea was to move him away from the Coxsackie area); a heroin-addicted parole violator; three prisoners coming from long stays in isolation cells (including one who had gone "off his rocker" after having his parole deferred for nine months); and two file jackets that are now empty, the prisoner records having been transferred to adult prisons after subsequent criminal convictions.

The second group of transfers from Coxsackie consisted almost exclusively of heroin addicts, while many of the other early transfer groups included epileptic and mentally ill inmates. When one of these transfers, suffering from schizophrenia, arrived at Great Meadow, the institution's psychiatrist noted, "I cannot refrain from expressing my shock at seeing a boy like this in prison." A younger black prisoner had only recently returned to Coxsackie from Matteawan, where he had been sent with a diagnosis of schizophrenia. Transferred back to Coxsackie, he had become active in interracial conflicts, which was the immediate cause of his subsequent transfer to Great Meadow.

Interracial conflict at Coxsackie proved to be one of the main predictors of transfer to Great Meadow. By early 1954, the Commission of Correction was reporting an "inflamed atmosphere" at Coxsackie, with "considerable racial friction under the surface."[25] Not long thereafter, Coxsackie experienced a serious race riot on the baseball field between thirty-five black inmates and forty-five white inmates. The black inmates had possession of the softball field, while the white inmates claimed that the field was then theirs to use. The teams on the field refused to yield their ground, so one white inmate strode out on the field and lay down on the ground between the pitcher's mound and home plate. When the black inmates attempted to remove the white inmate, a general melee erupted between both groups. Five of the ringleaders of that battle were transferred to Great Meadow within two weeks of the fight. Other transfer files from the period indicate similar issues: "involved in a racial problem at Coxsackie"; "instrumental in some of the difficulty they had at that institution regarding racial difficulties"; and, "this inmate is one of several who have recently participated in racial agitation in the institution to the extent that there have been a number of black-white fights, reports of impending demonstrations, and other evidences of a tense situation." During 1955 alone, Coxsackie transferred (exclusive of mental hospital transfers) seventy-five prisoners, about the same number as departed at the maximum expiration of their sentences.[26]

Transferring all the most troubled, aggressive, and defiant adolescent offenders to a single prison created an explosive situation. Longtime Great Meadow warden Vernon Morhous retired at the end of 1954, unwilling or unable to take on responsibility for managing the prison as an end-of-the-line transfer institution; he was replaced by Joseph Conboy, the hard-nosed chief of custody from Coxsackie.[27] The young transfers understood just what Great Meadow was intended to be and, having already resisted the reformatory regime at Coxsackie, immediately began to organize further acts of resistance. Older inmates at Great Meadow claimed that the new, younger men "made them nervous" with their fighting and aggressive talk, which by the summer of 1955 began to include talk of a prison strike. Piri Thomas recalled "a grim-faced kid-con about eighteen or nineteen years old" saying, "Why won't it work? We stage a sit-down strike and demand to see the governor for better changes in this fucking prison."[28]

The strike came to pass on August 17, 1955, when 174 inmates gathered in an outside yard along the west wall and refused to go to dinner or to return to their cells. Piri Thomas (who appropriately observed that "a prison riot explodes like a boiler that's built up steam from a long way back"[29]) recalled "a few old-timers among the rioters" but that most were "grey-eyed, healthy kids looking for a rep or a blast out of boredom"—in other words, the transfer products of the reformatory system.[30] Thomas recalled "the struggle going on inside each inmate as we faced the decision of whether or not to tear loose from our lines and charge across to join the striking inmates huddled against the wall." Most did not. Those who remained up against the wall demanded to speak with the governor or with the commissioner of corrections. Commissioner Thomas McHugh arrived around midnight and got on a loudspeaker to promise inmates that he would speak with each of them individually the next morning, if they would return to their cells. He gave them five minutes. After counting down the minutes, McHugh then gave the signal for a contingent of more than two hundred New York state troopers and prison guards to move in and subdue the striking prisoners.[31] Thomas described the scene:

> A unified roar from both sides as they crashed together with the force of hate, anger, and frustration. The guards and troopers believed they were dealing with subhumans. I could see it in the carriage of their bodies and in the way they swung their clubs and rifle butts with deadly intent. The inmates met the onslaught manfully but were swallowed up in an ocean of guards' blue and troopers'

brown. Fighting was hand to hand. Gray bodies crumpled up and crashed limply on the green grass. The air was filled with screams and curses and a medley of orders being shouted on both sides.

The firm hand of prison authority, in suppressing the strike, had only begun to strike back. A wave of retributive violence was said to have continued "for hours, for days . . . the fury of reprisal was a monster unleashed . . . many inmates who had not participated in the strike, but who had at any time annoyed a guard, got broken heads and bruised bodies from surprise visits to their cells. It was the ideal opportunity for the guards to take care of past antagonisms."[32] As for the strikers, they were marched to cells, methodically beaten along the way—the injured and unconscious were laid out in a line—kept in a segregated part of the prison, their heads shaved, barred from doing anything but looking straight ahead and prohibited from talking with anyone. The conditions of their confinement were a haunting echo of the worst of the old nineteenth-century silent system, an almost instinctive reversion to the very conditions that had provoked early twentieth-century prison reformers.

The young inmates of Great Meadow, including the many transfers from Coxsackie (three of whom were among the strike leaders), clearly intended to be heard beyond the walls of the prison. Their choice of a strike, of physical resistance to the prison authority, grew out of what must be understood as a clear-eyed assessment that, in the reformatory world of 1955, there was simply no other immediate tool of resistance at hand. That they demanded to see the governor or the commissioner of corrections shows that they understood the political nature of their actions as well as the political nature of potential solutions. That Commissioner McHugh arrived from Albany in the middle of the night shows just how close they came to upsetting the entire institutional regime, or at least to having their voices reach out and beyond the reformatory walls.

But as much as these young men wanted their voices heard, they were not. In the immediate aftermath of the uprising, prison authorities assured reporters that, while prisoners had a "variety of complaints," these complaints had no coherent pattern. In fact, Commissioner McHugh went out of his way to render the strike unintelligible, observing to reporters that the trouble originated when the reformatory inmates heard radio news reports of a revolt at a Nebraska penitentiary; McHugh later assured the governor that the strike was "in large part spontaneous with little prior organization or planning."[33] McHugh also suggested that most of the strikers were unwilling participants, too fearful or cowed by a handful of leaders to break ranks and return to their cells. Media coverage of the Great Meadow strike largely reflected the state's version of events and applauded the vigorous repression of the uprising. Stafford Derby, New York bureau chief for the *Christian Science Monitor*, was hardly alone when he concluded, "Penologists may well check off the date of August 17, as one of their own in which a firm hand that was needed, was supplied."[34]

Building Separate Systems

In the wake of the 1955 Great Meadow uprising, the trends toward creating separate spaces within the reformatory system accelerated, as part of an increasingly desperate search for order. Almost immediately after the strike, Coxsackie resumed sending to Great Meadow a series of parole violators, heroin addicts, and the mentally disturbed. Above all, transfers continued to come from those prisoners who displayed too much hostility to prison authorities, or who participated in interracial fighting. One of the first poststrike transfers was Tom C., a parole violator "opposed to general education" and possessing "no vocational interests." Tom was ordered sent to Great Meadow following three fights in a row with black inmates at Coxsackie. Another poststrike transfer, Bradley S., went to Great Meadow after having been keeplocked indefinitely for interracial fighting and for "promoting racial agitation." Bradley's case file indicates that he "had been involved in a racial problem at Coxsackie . . . having been instrumental in some of the difficulty they had at that institution regarding racial difficulties . . . a ring leader in trying to stir up trouble . . . if any racial difficulties arise, he will be one of the first inmates to be held for questioning."[35]

When Bradley arrived at Great Meadow, he became one of the first prisoners at the prison to be given daily doses of Thorazine to control his behavior. Superintendent Conboy registered his dissatisfaction at the drugging, which seemed to him an unnecessary departure from the tried-and-true methods of physical discipline with which he was so familiar, but Bradley and others were soon on a daily regimen of pharmaceutical discipline. Like Bradley himself, the use of Thorazine to try to stabilize the racial order of the reformatory was transferred to Great Meadow from Coxsackie, where the practice was already well under way. Among those whose behavior precipitated drugging was 18-year-old Edward D., a white prisoner sent to Coxsackie from a Brooklyn court in 1955 for breaking and entering an office building with two friends. Like many prisoners at Coxsackie, Edward had been troubled and in trouble for many years. A "neglect case" since the age of 9, Edward spent five years at the Mission of the Immaculate Virgin on Staten Island. He accumulated a reputation for "vandalism and mischief" in the neighborhood and dropped out of the Williamsburg

Vocational High School after only a single term, working odd jobs prior to his arrest.

Edward quickly joined in the racial conflict at Coxsackie, accumulating fourteen formal disciplinary reports for "agitating his dormitory" and for interracial fighting. For an instance of the latter offense, Edward was keeplocked in his cell; his file contains the brief observation that this was the standard "policy when a negro and white inmate are involved in a fight." Just days after the fight, Edward was sent to the prison psychiatrist and placed on a daily regimen of 250 milligrams of Thorazine. Prison guards reported that while medicated, Edward "seems to be doped up, in a daze." Edward himself protested: "Pills don't help; make me sleep, is one thing they do, but I'm still going out of my mind." Eventually, Edward was moved off Thorazine and sedated with daily doses of Luminal (a barbiturate). According to the Coxsackie psychiatrist, these interventions hardly seemed to help. If anything, they intensified his already furious anger directed at the reformatory system. The psychiatrist described Edward as "belittling toward medication, towards psychotherapy, towards food, towards the institution."[36]

Whether out of animus toward the prisoners or desperation to save their reformatory program (or perhaps both), Coxsackie staff increasingly came to embrace the hope that it could transfer its way back to whatever prewar order it had once enjoyed. In 1958, the prison identified for transfer roughly two hundred inmates who had served two years or more. One of those transferred in that group recalled Captain Follette explaining to them that they were regarded as a bad example for the newer prisoners. In this instance, young men were sent all over the New York State system, including to Great Meadow, Napanoch, and several adult maximum-security prisons, including Auburn, Green Haven, and Attica.[37]

The result of this aggressive disciplinary transfer was that, by the 1960s, Coxsackie began to take on aspects of a demographic island within the New York reformatory system. White inmates were more than 60 percent of Coxsackie's inmates, even as the reformatory system neared parity between white and black at the start of the decade. In fact, the proportion of the white population at Coxsackie actually *increased* during the 1960s, even as black and Puerto Rican prisoners became a clear majority in the reformatory system as a whole.

Table 7.1 makes clear that Great Meadow continued to house a disproportionate number of black and Puerto Rican reformatory inmates. Half of all Puerto Rican reformatory inmates were housed in just two institutions by the

TABLE 7.1
Reformatory populations, by race, 1962–1968

Prison	% White, 1962	% Black, 1962	% Puerto Rican, 1962	% White, 1966	% Black, 1966	% Puerto Rican, 1966	% White, 1968	% Black, 1968	% Puerto Rican, 1968
Coxsackie	62.4	24.6	11.8	65.5	24.2	8.9	66.2	27.0	6.0
Elmira	48.1	38.1	13.2	47.5	38.9	13.0	44.6	43.9	10.4
Woodbourne	26.5	50.8	22.1	19.7	53.8	26.2	—	—	—
Gr. Meadow	38.9	47.6	12.9	32.2	53.1	13.8	24.8	59.2	26.2
Catskill	—	—	—	15.8	53.2	30.3	15.2	58.6	25.7
All reformatories	44.7	43.5	11.0	40.0	46.0	14.0	37.0	49.0	14.0

mid-1960s, Great Meadow and Catskill Reformatory. The latter institution operated on the site of what had been the Napanoch institution, which had closed when New York courts determined that the separate and indefinite confinement of defective delinquents was unconstitutional. Catskill replaced Woodbourne in 1967 as the reformatory of choice for adolescent males of "borderline or low normal intelligence," when Woodbourne was taken over by the Narcotic Addiction Control Commission as a treatment facility.

Consistent with the demographic shifts in reformatory populations, Coxsackie also became an outlier in terms of its proportion of prisoners from New York City. By 1962, only 45 percent of Coxsackie prisoners had been committed from New York City, compared with 57 percent at Elmira, 70 percent at Great Meadow, and 73 percent at Woodbourne. Remarkably, these differences also continued to grow during the sixties: by 1966, the proportion of New York City inmates at Coxsackie had dropped to 38 percent, and then to just 30 percent in 1968, astonishingly low compared to every other state reformatory. In short, as Coxsackie aggressively moved to purge its ranks of the uneducable and the ungovernable, it increasingly focused on housing white, upstate youth, leaving minority and New York City adolescents to fend for themselves at the end of the line.

Meanwhile, at Great Meadow, the strike of 1955 did nothing to change that prison's status as an end-of-the-line home for reformatory inmates, nor did it substantially modify the disturbing brew of racism, brutality, and conflict there. As at Coxsackie, prisoners being taken to disciplinary cells were routinely beaten (in a freight elevator, away from view) and held under the same stark conditions that had prevailed at Coxsackie.[38] When Stephen Chinlund arrived at Great Meadow in 1964, in conjunction with his work for Exodus House and the

East Harlem Protestant Parish, he knew it as a prison with "a reputation for being particularly tough," and a "well earned reputation for being more gratuitously tough than some other places." Chinlund recalled the vivid stories told of life at the end of the line:

> There were frequent confrontations between Officers and staff, since the youngest inmates were the most likely to rush into fights. Even then, there were stories about the Gladiators at Comstock, a group of Officers who would challenge an inmate to fight with fists. They would go to the basement and one of them would strip to the waist to fight the prisoner. If the prisoner chose not to fight, he would still be beaten up by the Officers. There were variations on that theme, but it was a tale retold for decades, a sad long chapter in the book of macho mania. Bones were broken; prisoners were killed. This was partly about sadistic revenge, fueled by public acceptance of the belief that prison should be hell.

Chinlund's account includes his first encounter with Warden Conboy, the man who had defined the custodial regime at Coxsackie before assuming the head position at Great Meadow. Conboy was, in Chinlund's account, "an angry man" who believed that it would be "better to have inmates and staff more frightened of him than of each other." Chinlund recounts the dialogue that followed his late arrival for an appointment with Warden Conboy:

> When I walked into his office, I extended my hand, but he just glowered.
>   "Sit down," he shouted. I sat down. "Who the hell do you think you are?"
> "I'm Stephen . . ."
> "I know what the hell your name is!"
> "I realize I'm late and . . ."
> "You're goddam right, you're late! Do you think we are here to wait on you?!"
> "No sir. I'm ready to stay over and come back tomorrow."
> "This is a fucking tough place to run and I don't need jerks floating in from New York City to make my life more complicated."
> "Yes sir, I understand, so I'll wait."
> "You're goddam right you'll wait, maybe forever!"
> "Yes, sir. I realize I'm here only if you . . ."
> "I don't know what the hell good you think you're doing visiting this human garbage in here. They aren't worth the powder it would take to blow them all to hell!" He was standing, glaring at me, waving his arms.

"Their mothers, sir, have given me . . ."

"I don't think they have mothers, these sons of bitches, and you make me as
sick as they do!" I started to get up.

"Sit down! I didn't give you permission to leave!"

"Yes, sir." I sat back down.

"You call yourself a minister."

"Yes, sir."

"What about all the good people you're supposed to be taking care of? What
are they supposed to do while you're here wiping the asses of these rotten
guys?"

"Sir, it's part of my job to . . ."

"I don't want to hear your bullshit."

I remained silent and let him go on talking. Slowly, he calmed down. Then,
suddenly he said, "OK, you can see your list. Get the hell out of my
office."[39]

Chinlund's account is consistent with another assessment of Great Meadow: "The
prison officials' attitude was that inmates were commodities, subhuman—a
means of employment."[40]

Great Meadow remained the focal point for political agitation among reformatory inmates, though the most serious conflicts were black against white
rather than expressions of interracial prisoner solidarity. Retrospective accounts
of life at Great Meadow during this period suggest that the official racism was
as bad, perhaps even worse, than what prisoners were experiencing at Coxsackie.
Lumumba Shakur, transferred to Great Meadow in 1961, at age 18, recalled that
the "racism at Comstock was naked," with numerous work assignments—
including the bakery, clerk positions, machine shop, and auto shop—effectively
closed to most black inmates. As at Coxsackie, black inmates were vastly over-
represented on assignments like the labor gang and the laundry. "There was,"
Shakur recalled, "a dual set of rules for everything in Comstock—one black and
one white."[41]

Piri Thomas reflected on the 1955 Great Meadow uprising, "If the majority of
inmates had joined in organizing the strike for prisoners' rights on that day in
August, 1955, it would have been an Attica, sixteen years before."[42] Whether that
was true is a question that has divided scholars. Ronald Berkman's account of
fifties-era prison riots de-emphasized politics, observing that, "what was at
stake in the riots of the 1950s was not the architecture of the house, but the way
it was kept."[43] On the other hand, Marie Gottschalk has observed, "The Nation

of Islam began organizing in an atmosphere that was already quite racially charged . . . Indeed, the state helped to politicize prisoners, especially around the issue of race."[44] The reformatory experience in New York reveals quite clearly that racism and harsh treatment behind bars helped spur the development of a collective political conscience.

Graduates of Coxsackie and Great Meadow came to link the reformatory system with systems of racial oppression and to believe that "rehabilitation is a myth and a lie," a pattern clearly visible by the time of the 1955 Great Meadow uprising.[45] Claude Brown recalled asking his friend Alley Bush, an ex-Coxsackie inmate and a Muslim, in the mid-1950s: "Damn, Alley, what the hell is going on in the jails here? It seems that everybody who comes out is a Muslim." Bush replied: "When you're in jail, man, you've got a lot of time to think about it. Then you can really see how this white man is fucking with you. The white cats in jail, man, they don't have to take all this shit that we have to take. They get the better jobs, and they get everything. It's just the black man, the black man, wherever he is, they're gon try and fuck with him."[46]

Reformatory inmates smuggled in copies of *Muhammad Speaks*, and the disciplinary cells became focal points of Muslim and black nationalist activists. "My first political education came at Comstock," recalled Sekou Odinga, who spent time in that reformatory before he joined Malcolm X's Organization of Afro-American Unity in 1965, then going on to organizing work with the Black Panther party in 1968. Other New York Black Panther leaders experienced similar forms of political education in the reformatory system. Over the course of Dhoruba Bin Wahad's journey through both Coxsackie and Great Meadow, he "began to reckon with a world he had not known existed—a world of theory, logic, and righteousness that, when combined with action, had the power to ignite a revolution." Lumumba Shakur believed that "the brothers became very nationalistic in Comstock," and that this was primarily concentrated among the reformatory-age transfer inmates, rather than the smaller population of older offenders from before Great Meadow changed status. "We would call the older brothers Uncle Toms," Shakur recalled, "and tell them that only uncivilized people and devils would run Comstock the way it was being administered."[47]

Claude Brown's old friend Alley Bush, who told him so many things about racism at the upstate reformatories, turned up at a raucous demonstration at the United Nations following the death of Patrice Lumumba in 1961. Reflecting on the publicity accorded the UN protest, Brown concluded, "It was a good thing for Alley, I suppose, because he was heard. He made the goddamn white man know that he was angry."[48] In his own way, Alley Bush was working on fulfilling the commitment to be heard made by a "youngblood" strike leader at Great Meadow facing transfer to an adult prison back in 1955: "They're doing us a favor by spreading us around. Wherever they send us, we'll get the shit going on again. It's a matter of dignity."[49]

By the early 1960s, the tensions and political unrest at Great Meadow were once again reaching the boiling point. Lumumba Shakur recalled that inmates "began talking about formulating some kind of action to redress and change the racial conditions of Comstock." He later wrote, "I must confess that we talked about action for a year, because somebody would always disagree with any method of action."[50] As had happened prior to the 1955 action, inmates debated just what to do to make themselves heard, and older inmates warned the young men against any sort of action against the system. Internal grievances against the reformatory system were increasingly linked to events occurring outside. In mid-September 1963, news of the terrorist bombing of the 16th Street Baptist Church in Birmingham, Alabama, "had a tremendous effect" on black inmates at Great Meadow. In response, a group of young men agreed to request shop and work assignments from which blacks had traditionally been excluded. None of the requests were granted, and the prisoners were told that the traditional reformatory policies would remain unchanged. A few days later, according to Lumumba Shakur, black inmates met and concluded, "The only way we are going to redress or change Comstock's racial situation is by violence—so let the shit hit the fan."

One month after the March on Washington and two weeks after the Birmingham bombing, a black inmate fought a white inmate over possession of a "white" handball court. At Great Meadow, the handball courts were the major site of outdoor recreation; twelve were reserved for white inmates, two for black inmates, and two for Puerto Rican inmates. The decision by one prisoner to deliberately violate the racial geography of Great Meadow's outdoor space was the trigger, intentional or not, for a major riot involving roughly 450 black and white Great Meadow inmates.[51] Prisoners demolished a guardhouse in the prison yard, using the timbers as weapons to battle each other and the officers.[52]

This time, even the Department of Corrections acknowledged (briefly) the more explicitly political dimensions of the conflict, with a spokesman indicating to at least one reporter that the underlying motivation was an expression of solidarity among black inmates for "the general movement of their race outside the prison walls."[53] This brief acknowledgment changed nothing about the prison system's response. "The next day," Shakur recalled, "everybody was locked in their cell all day and the correctional officers began beating brothers in their cells systematically." This time, a visit by the commissioner of corrections, Paul McGinnis, ended the beatings, and a decision was made to begin transferring the ringleaders of the action. The Department of Corrections ordered thirty Great Meadow inmates—black and white—to be transferred to various adult maximum-security prisons.[54] The department began planning the construction of yet another end-of-the-line prison, to be built from the ground up with the sole purpose of housing young men too tough for the current end of the line.[55]

By 1963, nearly three decades had passed since the opening of the New York State Vocational Institution. Within the Department of Corrections bureaucracy, the educational reformers of the New Deal–era system still held most of the critical positions. The reformatory system, still ostensibly organized around trade training and social education, remained at the center of New York's plan for dealing with the problem of the adolescent male under confinement. But the efforts to protect that legacy had produced disturbing consequences. Coxsackie itself increasingly tried to isolate itself from the larger system, removing various classes of inmates, in the hopes that somehow the institution could realize the reformist promises made at its opening, even as actual practice continued to mock the ideal. Along the way, New York abandoned the pretense that reform and rehabilitation were for every young man and created end-of-the-line institutions whose racism and brutality helped politicize a generation of prisoners.

Felipe Luciano, who served time in Coxsackie in the sixties, movingly describes his personal version of this larger process. As a young boy growing up in postwar New York City, Luciano reflected, "I was in love with Doris Day. I believed in Dwight Eisenhower. I loved Superman, Mighty Mouse, and My Friend Flicka. I didn't have a father, but Robert Young was my great daddy surrogate on the daily TV show, 'Father Knows Best.' We couldn't have dogs in NYC projects, but, in my fantasies, I lived with Lassie in the country and Rin Tin Tin on the frontier of America's West, fighting those evil Indians . . . For me," recalled Luciano, "America was a meritocracy and you could rise to any heights if you had the brains, the will, the talent." The reformatory at Coxsackie, on the other hand, offered a transformative experience of a different kind, one that came not from vocational training, but from watching "a young Jewish guy clasp his hands around a searing, hot steam pipe in his cell and burn his palms off just to get into the infirmary and not hear the silence of his jailroom," or seeing "a friend, Itchy, beaten so badly by prison guards his thigh and shin bones were broken." Coming home, in 1967, "for a young, black Puerto Rican like me . . . it was time to shit or get off the pot . . . I decided to shit and throw it at this government."[56]

As it had for so many other young men, Coxsackie instigated a political awakening for Felipe Luciano. After the reformatory, Luciano helped advance the radicalization of Puerto Rican activism in New York City as a founder of the Young Lords. In 1969, he gave a speech explaining the political position of the group, whose themes resonate with the experiences of many reformatory youth: "The conspiracy is evident, they want to chop us up. They don't want to let Puerto Ricans, they don't want to let New Yorkers or anyone else think that Puerto Ricans can think . . . So understand that this conspiracy is very related to you—I don't care who you are. But understand, when the repression hits, it may hit me, and then what the system tries to do is to isolate you from the masses of the people and then begins to knock you down as they did with the Panthers." As much as the reformatory experience may have helped crystallize this vision of repression, it also highlighted the need to recognize mutual humanity, to let voices be heard. "I believe," declared Luciano, "that everyone has the potential for being human—not Puerto Rican, not white, but human . . . Without that belief," he concluded, "revolutionaries cannot survive."[57]

Not every response to the reformatory system was explicitly political. Some expressed a powerful and profound rejection of what the state was doing to young offenders. At age 17, Armand Schaubroeck was sent to the Elmira Reception Center in 1962 to begin an indefinite three-year term, and he eventually served eighteen months in the reformatory. Upon his release, Schaubroeck poured out his feelings into his music, starting with garage-band recordings like "Lord My Cell Is Cold" (1963, with the band Kack Klick—a name that played off the prisoner nickname for Coxsackie, Cack) and "Babe We're Not Part of Society" (1965, with the band The Churchmice). By the late 1960s, Schaubroeck was developing an entire project around his Elmira experience, which at one point was to be the basis for an Andy Warhol film, and which eventually appeared as a pioneering proto-punk album, *A Lot of People Would Like to See Armand Schaubroeck . . . Dead.* The project's semi-autobiographical tracks (twenty-three in all) systematically dismantle the legitimacy of the reformatory system, while painting a haunting picture of the fight for survival. The protagonist declares, "I can beat this place" and "You won't find me swinging by my belt," but comes to the ultimate conclusion that "you can beat everything, but you can't beat time."[58]

Reformatory inmates were among the first to reject the thirties-era reformism on which Coxsackie was built, but they would not be the last. The rehabilitative framework that helped to perpetuate New York's reformatories was nearly out of time when Felipe Luciano, Armand Schaubroeck, and other young men returned home to describe and to fight the system. Already under siege by the start of the 1960s, the reformatory would be intellectually discredited and politically abandoned by the start of the 1970s. During that troubled decade, Coxsackie would lose its identity as a reformatory and undergo wrenching transformations.

CHAPTER EIGHT

Out of Time

Coxsackie and the End of the Reform Idea

Just as the Coxsackie reformatory would never have been constructed as it was without an underpinning of reform ideas, its eventual collapse was made possible—one might even say inevitable—by a dramatic retreat from those same ideas. Austin MacCormick's vision, a New Deal–era project deeply rooted in progressive-era reformism, fell so far out of favor that few even fully remembered its substance. Attacked from nearly all sides of the political spectrum, the rehabilitative ideal, as critics understood it, was declared dead and buried by the mid-1970s. By that time, Coxsackie was no longer a reformatory, its rhetorical ambitions for vocational training and educational uplift cast aside in favor of more explicitly "get tough" punishment rhetoric.

Of course, the end of the liberal ideal in corrections has been the subject of considerable scholarly attention for decades. Most studies argue that the rehabilitative ideals of liberal prison reform collapsed quite suddenly, with various explanations all centered around the late 1960s and 1970s: a reaction to prisoner uprisings; a more general reaction to the failures of modern liberalism at home and abroad; or a newly assertive conservatism in criminal justice policy, born of the quasi-populist law-and-order politics served up by Richard Nixon, Ronald Reagan, and George Wallace, among others.[1] The problem with each of these explanations is their over-attention to what might be called the "end stages" of liberal corrections' decline. The roots of that decline go back at least two decades before the bloody prison revolt at Attica in 1971. By the time Attica's D yard filled with prisoners, many of them veterans of the reformatory system, Austin MacCormick's ambitious vision of reform had already run its course.

Liberal Reform's Postwar Existential Crisis

Throughout the 1950s, as reformatory officials struggled to manage changing prison populations, liberal critics began directing ever-sharper critiques toward the reformatory concept itself. These critiques were, at this point, still embedded in the language of liberal reform; they could have pointed the way toward improving New York's response to the young adult offender and mitigating the worst aspects of reformatory life, which inmates already knew all too well. Instead, New York's prison administration embraced a rigid view of what constituted reform, hewing strictly to the education and reformatory-centered programs of the New Deal era. This rigidity made it difficult to adopt and adjust critical assessments or alternative policy proposals, which occasioned a sense of existential crisis rather than constructive engagement.

The decade began with the publication of the most significant liberal challenge yet to Coxsackie's educational program and, indeed, to the very idea of the reformatory. Bertram Beck, a social worker, prepared a report for the Community Service Society, made public the first week of January 1951.[2] During World War II, Beck had worked for the military in the mental hygiene unit at Drew Field in Tampa. In follow-up work he conducted in conjunction with the Menninger Clinic, Beck was highly critical of therapeutic work done in an "authoritative" setting. Such settings, he concluded, were almost inevitably hostile to the aims of effective treatment and intervention, despite any good intentions. "The measure of authoritarianism," Beck argued, "is not the manner in which the authority is exercised nor the degree to which it is exercised. It is the implied power and the potential power of the authority that counts." He cautioned readers to consider "the threat that may be constituted by the psychiatric approach" and to come to terms with the idea that "the question of the patient's assuming responsibility for his own life plans, which is so pertinent in the non-authoritarian setting, is almost completely beside the point in military casework."[3]

Beck then applied his emerging anti-authoritarian critique of institutions to the reformatory. In this, he was hardly alone. Indeed, as early as 1937's *Youth in the Toils*, liberal critics of the reformatory had counseled against the construction of any more "Coxsackies" in New York State. But World War II sharply accelerated the liberal critique of the reformatory, as it merged with broader liberal concerns about the authoritarian state.[4] Not surprisingly, these early critics emphasized the distortions in social organization produced by prison life. F. E. Haynes, writing in 1948, concluded: "The prison community with its conniving, its perversions, and exchange of crime techniques re-enforces the behavior tendencies which society wishes to prevent. We cannot expect to break down anti-social habits in an atmosphere that is distinctly anti-social."[5] One of Haynes's students, writing during the war, claimed inmate-on-inmate aggression was the product of autocratic systems.[6]

In this context of rising anti-authoritarian critique of state interventions, Bertram Beck was commissioned to produce a major study of the treatment of adolescent criminal offenders. To complete his work, Beck was given extensive access to the programs at Elmira and Coxsackie. His final report, however, was a stinging indictment of the reformatory system, and Beck saved his harshest criticisms for the educational reformers and the institutions they had created and still administered.[7] Beck described Coxsackie and Elmira as having an appearance to "oppress the spirit and freeze the heart of the youngster . . . they loom like avenging hands out of the peaceful countryside." How could the reformatory, dominated by "the eternal lock," ever fulfill its supposed commitment to democratic education? "How to rehabilitate in an atmosphere so ridden by custody and dominated by instruments of oppression," Beck concluded, "is indeed a problem." Where MacCormick had placed his faith in the ability of good people to remake the prison, Beck was quick to claim that the failures of Coxsackie were not those of its personnel: "This situation is not the fault of the institutional administration, nor of the custodial officers themselves. They are all trapped by the nature of the established program." Beck concluded that Coxsackie and Elmira were not particularly bad reformatories, nor ones in which brutality played much of a part in institutional life, but they were "exactly what might be expected of a peno-correctional philosophy which is in transition between a goal of punishment and one of treatment."[8]

Prison educators, Beck argued, were fundamentally unable to deliver on their promise of rehabilitation. In part, he concluded, educators were increasingly dressing up their programming with the language of mental health fields, borrowing the terms of psychology "without borrowing the knowledge." As for the many specific diagnostic evaluations undertaken at the Elmira Reception Center, each with their own specific recommendations for the treatment of young men, Beck found these quite detached from reality: "Treatment is prescribed by the various departments and then by the program committee in separate and distinct areas as if one gave a youngster vocational medicine, religious medicine, recreational medicine, all in separate doses with one area of personal development quite unrelated to the other."[9]

Beck's final report made two substantive suggestions for New York's approach to the young male offender. On the one hand, he urged institutional authorities to shift away from educational programming toward a program of mental health interventions. Beck was so critical of the existing reformatories, however, that his second suggestion was to shift New York's resources away from grim prison facilities. As Beck observed, "Greater masses of institutional brick and mortar have been accepted without trial of more promising measures of rehabilitating young offenders."[10] This shifting of resources away from prison would be particularly valuable, he argued, in cases who "have never been in custody before and who could be expected to benefit by a program which was enabled to place less emphasis on security and more on rehabilitation." To meet this goal, Beck was inclined toward youth work camps, modeled after the forestry camps being developed in California, which were rooted in the Civilian Conservation Corps experience. His report praised the California forestry camps he had visited: "Such camps could certainly teach the habit of work, but, more important, they could provide the setting where treatment, directed toward counteracting the wellsprings of criminal behavior, might be conducted."[11]

The publication of Beck's report prompted a furious response from New York's reformist prison administrators, the first public split between the correctional reformers and critics from the left. Elmira superintendent Leroy Weaver attacked the report's endorsement of forestry camps, noting that young men from urban areas needed training for the jobs to which they would return, and that "they can't learn that in a lumber camp." Elmira Reception Center (ERC) director Glenn Kendall discounted Beck's call for greater reliance on psychology and psychiatry: "They are not the complete cure for the ills of the juvenile penal system." In their zeal to discredit Beck's work, Kendall and Weaver nearly recapitulated the same hostile language with which conservatives had attacked MacCormick two decades earlier. They denounced the "theoretical and fantastic ideas promoted," in their words, "by inexperienced social workers who have failed through their harebrained, coddling ideas."[12]

The strain in relations between the reform regime and liberals on the outside was never really resolved. Both sides agreed to attend a Welfare Council meeting in March, aiming for some measure of reconciliation. Instead, the meeting further highlighted the points of disagreement. Price Chenault represented the Division of Education at the meeting, looking to defend "education, vocational training, religion and other disciplines in our institutions."[13] Most notable, in light of the reform regime's beginnings, Austin MacCormick sided against the state. He testily responded to Weaver that it "ill becomes the superintendent of the Elmira Reformatory . . . to brand the sound and sensible ideas of the Community Service Society report as 'theoretical and fantastic ideas.' "[14]

Later that year, MacCormick gave up on New York altogether, joining the faculty of the new School of Criminology at Berkeley, where he remained for the rest of the decade, urging colleagues interested in constructive reform programs to come to California.

Within the state correctional bureaucracy, Beck's call for a new emphasis on psychiatry and mental health work was largely ignored, but the work camp idea was harder to dismiss. Key constituencies within state government began to push for the creation of these camps, despite the resistance from the reform regime. In 1955, the Governor's Youth Commission recommended the creation of a forestry conservation camp for adolescent male offenders (ages 16 to 21), drawn from the ranks of the most promising reformatory inmates. New York's conservation commissioner joined the call, approaching the Department of Corrections for help in maintaining the huge forests planted by CCC workers in the 1930s. With the reformatories struggling to manage the growing ranks of "uneducable" and "undesirable" minority youth, the forestry camps appeared to be another way of salvaging at least one segment of the young offender.

The first camp opened the following year, in 1956, at an old CCC camp set in the middle of a 40,000-acre forest. The humble group of buildings that became known as Camp Pharsalia may have housed only a tiny fraction of the adolescent male prison population, but it posed a much larger existential threat to the reformatory system.[15] Although historian Volker Janssen has called California's forestry camps "the penal welfare state's liberal reform treatment for the ghetto," the concept aroused considerable hostility from reformatory interests in New York State.[16] After all, nothing about the camps reflected the worldview of the prison educators that dominated the Department of Corrections. The camps offered little or no formal educational programming, emphasized work habits rather than vocational training, and reintroduced aspects of military drill that the reformatories had seemingly purged from the system back in the thirties.

Though the Department of Corrections resisted any dramatic expansion of camp populations, the state did add a second camp (Camp Monterey) in 1958, and two more in 1960, after Governor Nelson Rockefeller enthusiastically embraced the concept.[17] The governor and other state politicians found the camps to be a fine spot for a political drop-in, members of the press in tow.[18] Indeed, the camps received consistently good press; stories tended to emphasize the positive qualities of the campers and the healthy and supportive relations between the camps and members of nearby communities—quite a contrast to the reformatories, which received little or no press coverage, save for brief coverage of prisoner disturbances. A district forester for the state, who had worked with the old CCC camp, praised the young men and found "no grousing or complaining like there was in the CCC camps; it's the greatest thing that has happened to conservation here."[19] As for the young men, media accounts suggested that they seemed "genuinely happy to be working in the woods instead of being behind bars" in Elmira or Coxsackie.[20]

For the first time since they opened, Coxsackie and the other reformatories were no longer the institutions of first choice for the most promising young men. Having spent the postwar years desperately transferring undesirable youth to end-of-the-line institutions, Coxsackie and Elmira now found themselves losing the most desirable prisoners to the camps. Even more galling, the camp directors managed to secure for themselves the ability to come into the reformatories to select the inmates they wanted, through a "special screening process."[21] Throughout the late fifties and the sixties, Coxsackie and the reformatories lost a number of their most tractable prisoners to the camps.

The existential crisis of the period came into clearest relief with the case of Roger V., a would-be college student.[22] A 17-year-old from a rural upstate county, just two credits short of his high school graduation, Roger joined a group of friends in holding up a couple at gunpoint. Although the trial judge at sentencing agreed to designate the entire group as youthful offenders, he sent Roger and one co-defendant off to the Elmira Reception Center. At sentencing, the judge made the case that "great leniency" was expected by the family and the community, but that this leniency would have been just the sort of response that led the young men astray in the first place.

Roger arrived at the Elmira Reception Center in 1956, at a challenging moment for the reformatory system. With racial unrest, inmate uprisings, and growing doubts about the effectiveness of correctional education, the external critique of incarceration began to creep into the evaluative work conducted at the ERC. As much as any other case, Roger seemed to provoke questions at the reception center about whether *any* reformatory sentence was appropriate. Staff psychologist Chauncey Martin judged Roger to be "not a very serious case from the standpoint of personality deviation . . . he should be released as soon as possible so he may return to complete his high school work and go on to college." Even Glenn Kendall, a staunch defender of the reformatory system, was led to conclude, "There is nothing to be gained by longer incarceration, very early release is recommended." Roger should be sent to Coxsackie and then released in no more than six months' time, Kendall observed, so that he could be home for the start of the 1957 school year.

The uneasiness expressed at the ERC provoked Coxsackie officials. Superintendent Donald Scarborough sided with the trial judge and complained to Kendall and the ERC that an early release would be just the sort of preferential handling that "had gotten the inmate in trouble in the first place." Scarborough resisted the six-month limit on incarceration, pointedly writing to Kendall, "It is the understanding of the committee that no recommendation from the Reception Center is a binding one; that it is not the desire of the Reception Center to have us rubber stamp any decision made there." When Roger made his first appearance before the Coxsackie program committee, reformatory officials declined to certify him for the parole board.

Roger's failed appearance before the program committee prompted a new round of intense debate over Coxsackie and the role of the reformatory. Back home, his father began to apply significant pressure on the Department of Corrections in Albany. Interestingly, a counter-campaign of sorts emerged from Roger's hometown. The vice-principal of the high school, for example, wrote to Superintendent Scarborough, urging him not to give into the pressure for Roger's release, but to "set a firm example." Albany caved fairly quickly, however, issuing a ruling that the Coxsackie program committee could not withhold certification in light of the ERC's recommendation. The ruling prompted a flurry of animated correspondence between Scarborough and Commissioner McHugh.

At the heart of Roger's case was a question as painful to reformatory officials as it was simple—was time spent at Coxsackie harmful to an otherwise normal and well-adjusted boy? The reception center seemed to imply as much, Superintendent Scarborough's correspondence reveals that the implication was not lost on him: "The point which has bothered me more than anything else . . . is the implication (I have never seen it stated directly, and I doubt if anybody has thought of it that way) that it is going to be in some manner harmful for youth of basically sound background, to spend a little time in the institution . . . If there is anything these two youths need, it is to learn something of self-discipline; to respect the rights of others, and to realize they are no better than many other people. Thus, it is my firm conviction that a few months here will actually be beneficial." Scarborough wrote to the program committee a memo that actually reversed the reception center's implication, noting, "We have to decide whether these youths, because of their smirking attitude would be harmful to the institution and to the other inmates, who are perhaps more naïve." Meanwhile, educational supervisor George Drojarksi stirred the pot a bit, pointedly writing to the reception center, asking Kendall for guidance on the specific courses he felt the two young men should be taking while at Coxsackie.

In the end, despite the tensions between Elmira, Albany, and Coxsackie, and despite an apparently underwhelming performance before the program committee, Roger was held for the May parole board, and then for the August parole board, which released him in September, in time for the new school year. He was given exceedingly strict parole supervision by the standards of the case file sample—his parole file runs to fourteen pages, all of which was reported back to Coxsackie. Reformatory officials could learn every detail of Roger's postrelease life, even the name and residence of his senior prom date. Still, as with many Coxsackie parolees, the highly specific parole terms weren't strictly enforced— caught driving without a license, for example, Roger was retained on parole. By the time his period of supervision expired, Roger was a student at a prestigious university and married, with a baby.

Though Roger spent only a short time at Coxsackie, his presence managed to roil the reformatory system and raise some fundamental questions about what institutions like Coxsackie were trying to do. For critics, both outside and to some extent inside the system, large artificial institutions like Coxsackie could do no "normal" young man any good at all. For the defenders of the reformatory, the educational and vocational opportunities offered at Coxsackie were *most* appropriate for the "normal" young men of the system. As they attempted to purge the reformatory of the drug addicted, the gang affiliated, the mentally unstable, and a largely minority population of the "uneducable," Roger and his kind were just the sort of young to benefit from their educational discipline. To suggest otherwise, in 1957, was to suggest that there was nothing to fight for and preserve. In response, the reformatory system at last began to undertake a scheme to prove its own effectiveness.

Does It Work? The Reception Center Research Project

When the Elmira Reception Center opened in 1945, part of its formal mission was to conduct research: into the causes of delinquency, the effectiveness of the center's diagnostic tools, and the effects of subsequent reformatory programming. In fact, when Governor Dewey's Interdepartmental Committee on Delinquency first proposed the center in 1943, it strongly urged an evaluation "after a reasonable period of operations."[23] Just one year into ERC operations, center personnel began planning for just such an evaluation study, going so far as to prepare a coding plan for prisoner data. But the study never moved beyond the preliminary stages, largely because the center lacked sufficient state-funded staff positions. The professional staff of the ERC that might have engaged in careful study were, instead, confronted with the day-to-day challenges of processing large numbers of young men every month.

Over the course of the ERC's first two decades, more than thirty-two thousand prisoners were processed through the facility, while research ambitions went largely unrealized. An external study of young offenders, completed in 1953, called on the state to more carefully assess the differences, if any, between the programming recommendations of the center and the actual program assignments prisoners experienced at the reformatories. This project was never undertaken. The Great Meadow uprising followed soon thereafter, and Commissioner McHugh complained that the department had been "operating blindly without even minimum research facilities."[24] In response, the state legislature finally authorized a Division of Research, and the Department of Corrections hopefully suggested that with the division in place, "voluminous data, long unused for lack of trained people to analyze it, can eventually be utilized now in thoughtful modification of existing programs and in realistic planning for new ones."[25]

The quest for program evaluation was, above all, a quest to affirm the value of correctional education. Commissioner McHugh said as much, speaking in 1955, when he asked, "Can it be proven that the investment the State is making in correctional education is a good one?" But even with the Division of Research in place, progress toward real evaluation was painfully slow for those who had invested so much in the state's reformatory system for young male offenders. Division staff, led by Herbert L. Bryan, spent much of their time responding to data requests from the DOC and the federal Bureau of Prisons, responding to special legislative requests like creating a database on all serious sex offenders, and working on creating an IBM punch card system for collecting data on every prisoner entering and leaving DOC institutions.[26]

The only substantial research on correctional education conducted by the state appeared in early 1961, a study of educational achievement of male adolescent offenders while under institutional custody.[27] The following month, the DOC published a related study, in conjunction with the Division of Parole, to measure educational achievement and parole adjustment, one that found no real connection between academic progress behind bars and success after release.[28] Although the report suggested that it was "almost axiomatic" that educational programs aided parolee success, the actual data suggested that this was mostly true of prisoners who arrived at the reformatory with a high level of educational attainment (a small portion of the reformatory population).

In the wake of the educational attainment study, calls from within the Department of Corrections for a comprehensive and definitive study of reformatory impact grew even more urgent. The Division of Research observed, "We do not have sufficient information to clearly evaluate the progress and potential of vocational training . . . In order to get this," the Division noted, "we must set up basic data . . . this is long overdue." In 1965, the Department of Corrections began to prepare for the design of a twenty-year plan, alongside its planning for the upcoming fiscal year. As part of the process, the department finally committed itself to a full-scale program evaluation. The context was clear: "Many of the administrative personnel in the Department have lived with the Reception Center operations since its conception and birth. Their views and interpretations of any research findings on the Center should be invaluable and time is running out on their availability for explanations and interpretations."[29] *Time is running out*—the veterans of the 1930s, including Glenn Kendall, Walter Wallack, and Price Chenault, understood that mandatory retirement would remove them from active roles in reformatory administration by the end of the decade. This study would represent their final and best chance to defend the reformatory system they had built.

The first written proposal for the study, seeking special state funding, suggested a three-to-five-year project conducted using a sample of case files from the thirty-two thousand young men processed by the ERC between 1945 and 1965. The department noted, "A major issue in correctional research today is how to validate the relative emphasis to be given custody and treatment . . . we lack not only sufficient evidence on the extent to which existing systems rehabilitate their subjects but also comparative evidence to support the efficacy of current theories of treatment . . . the Reception Center Research Project represents, among other things, an effort to make a scientific and objective assessment of the results obtained by New York's correctional system in rehabilitating the young male offender."[30] For the first time, the pitch to the legislature worked, and what became known as the Reception Center Research Project received a substantial funding commitment: $50,000 for FY 1966–1967, and another $100,000 for FY 1967–1968, with a request pending for a continuation of funding in FY 1968–1969. The legislative support allowed the Division of Research to support a project staff of five full-time researchers and four professional consultants.

The first stage would consist of a preliminary study to demonstrate the feasibility and utility of the project. The preliminary study included a statistical overview of the ERC cases between 1945 and 1965, as well as a small pilot postrelease

survey. The postrelease pilot was based on a sample of 220 young men who had
been through the ERC and then released from a department institution in 1960.
Research staff located roughly six in ten of the men in the sample group, and
95 percent of those located agreed to participate.[31] The survey interviews were
conducted by parole officers paid "on an extra-service basis" to assist with the
project.

The pilot study was to have been the basis for a much larger postrelease
study, one that would have conducted similar survey interviews with a 10 percent sample of the entire population of 32,000 ERC inmates. The full-scale
project plan had four phases: an analysis of the precommitment characteristics
of the center's diagnostic findings and recommendations; an evaluation of subsequent institutional treatment and custody in relation to the center's findings
and recommendations; a similar evaluation of parole experience; and a determination of recidivism prior and subsequent to center commitment as well as a
current personal interview with located subjects to appraise socio-economic adjustment and the effect of the correctional process on that adjustment.

The pilot project was nearing completion in early 1967 when Department
of Correction officials assembled for their legislative budget hearing with
the Ways and Means Committee. Commissioner Paul McGinnis arrived asking
the state for additional educational and guidance positions, observing, "In our
treatment . . . we place a great emphasis on education, in all its aspects, for there
is convincing evidence that our inmates are generally under educated." The legislators pushed back against the budget requests. Longtime legislative budget
consultant Howard "Red" Miller, secretary to Ways and Means, pressed McGinnis
on the need for expanding the commitment to educational programs. McGinnis
protested: "If we didn't have education, what would we have? You have to take
education as the basic, the fundamental leg of this whole rehabilitation program."
When Miller responded, "I think we ought to have more evidence of this," Mc-
Ginnis promised that when the Reception Center Research Project was finished,
"you are going to have definite evidence of it. I hope so. I really hope you do,
because I hope his study will show what we are doing at the Reception Center
and what we are doing in the institutions with these people after they leave has
been helpful to them and had done the job on the rehabilitation we hope we are
doing."[32]

McGinnis managed to use the word "hope" four times in his reply, consistent with the department's growing sense that the future of the reformatory
program would depend on positive research results. For Vito Ternullo, representing the Division of Education at the hearing, a comment from Miller that

the department should wait for the results of the study before moving into "phase two" of program investment was a bit too much: "We have been in phase one for about 40 years now, and this is our problem . . . we have asked for money for research time and time again." Even Ternullo, however, conceded that the results of the study were hard to predict with any certainty. "This study . . . is going to be a terrific boost, one way or another . . . if you were to ask me whether [correctional education] was really effective in terms of recidivism, I couldn't give you an answer, obviously, because we have nothing to back us up on except some educated guesses." Herb Bryan, representing the Division of Research, promised the pilot study would be done soon and in the meantime offered up a single happy case: "I don't want to gold the lily, but the first case I looked at that came in that they had located upstate was a youngster who is 28 now and married and has four children. He is working as a manager of the computer center, and, interestingly enough, he built his own home, which he values at $18,500. He made $7,000 in 1966."[33]

The full study was never completed. The pilot project was completed in April 1967, two months after the legislative budget hearing. Later that year, research staff selected the 10 percent sample from reformatory case records and microfilmed copies of the case files (the microfilm can be found today at the New York State Archives). While the case files were being assembled, the research staff received the unwelcome news that the federal Office of Law Enforcement Assistance had rejected their application for project funding (there is no record of why the grant request was turned down). By the time of the Department of Corrections 1968 budget hearing, prison officials were no longer talking about the research project, and there was a noticeable absence of research and education staff at the hearing. The Reception Center Research Project, understood as the last and perhaps best chance to demonstrate the positive impact of the reformatory system, was gone. Overwhelmed by events, the defenders of correctional education and the reformatories had run out of time, and the critics now took center stage.

The Governor's Special Committee

Even as the Department of Corrections began planning the Reception Center Research Project, the reformatory system faced growing scrutiny from a state government previously deferential or simply inattentive. Long inactive, the Senate Committee on Penal Institutions began to rouse itself in 1966, with committee chairman Robert Lynch arranging for actual committee meetings and tours of "as many penal institutions as possible." Those inspections were undertaken by a freshman senator, John R. Dunne, whose resulting report adopted a critical tone regarding the state's "determined although sometimes futile effort" in the area of correctional education.[34]

By 1968, Dunne had become chairman of the Penal Institutions Committee and was now holding public hearings in Albany and New York City on the causes of criminal recidivism and the role of penal institutions in managing the problem. These hearings opened up a public discussion regarding prisons that had been mostly muted since the 1930s. Dunne himself was intrigued by the idea of using work-release programs to move criminal offenders from institutional to community settings. While the Community Service Society—the organization that had funded Bertram Beck's work—professed itself "delighted" with the proposals and with the "enlightened and tireless" Dunne, the response from within a defensive Department of Corrections was more hostile. Commissioner McGinnis doubted that work-release programs in California "would withstand critical analysis," and argued that federal work-release programs were for "an entirely different type of offender than on average we deal with."[35] All of this was followed by the standard defense of correctional education programs, a mark of just how rigid state correctional policy had become by 1968, unwilling or unable to integrate alternative strategies for handling criminal offenders.

The reformatory system was also under siege from the executive office. Here, too, gubernatorial interest in corrections re-emerged in the 1960s after a long period of inattention. In 1965, Governor Nelson Rockefeller assembled a Governor's Special Committee on Criminal Offenders and directed them to identify new and more imaginative approaches to the prevention of recidivism. Chaired by Department of Corrections Paul McGinnis and parole board chairman Russell Oswald, the special committee was stocked with high-level state correctional and welfare service administrators.

After about a year of the committee's efforts being expended in several evaluative, legislative, and programmatic directions, Rockefeller narrowed their mandate to the production of a detailed report assessing the state's post-adjudicatory system. The creative forces behind the report's production were Executive Director Peter Preiser, Assistant Director John V. Delaney, and Deputy Assistant Director Douglas S. Lipton. The committee's *Preliminary Report* appeared in early 1968, advertised as "the first modern comprehensive rationalization of the New York correctional system."[36]

Part one of the report, largely authored by Peter Preiser, went directly after the conceptual underpinnings of the New York prison system, "because the

Committee was unable to find a comprehensive focused statement of the principles of the system anywhere." The committee's own discussion of these principles—rather immodestly described in the report as "a landmark presentation"—were antithetical to many of the presumptions of the Austin MacCormick–era reformatory system. The report questioned the value of the wayward minor and youthful offender classifications, under which so many young men had entered the reformatory system. In the application of such categories, the report concluded, "The basis for the adjudication and the basis for the disposition are not rationally related to each other." Youthful offenders "must trade the risk of a heavy sanction for the boon of exemption," and in the process, minor offenders ended up swept into the reformatory system, while the most serious offenders would not be granted the same status and thus would head straight into the adult prison system.[37] The critique of artificial juridical categories extended to the entire concept of the reformatory itself; in a revised system, the report suggested, there should "no longer be artificial ... distinctions between types of institutions."[38] These distinctions were reflective of a system "bound in by a particular image which is a heritage of the past."[39]

Most important, part one of the report re-introduced the concept of retribution into state-level policy discussions, a direct response to the growing public unhappiness with rising crime rates. The criminal sanction, said the report, must have "a sufficient degree of unpleasantness" to "reinforce the confidence of the public in the fact that the state is determined to uphold norms, through a demonstration of action taken against wrongdoers."[40] Using a bit of tortured sociological analysis, the report denied that this public demonstration of determination to combat crime was retributivist, claiming instead that it was merely the "prevention of anomie" caused by the state not meeting "the retributive feelings of the public."[41]

Austin MacCormick, by now returned to New York from Berkeley, reacted strongly to this re-introduction of retributivist language in the *Preliminary Report*. Both before and after the report's publication, MacCormick criticized the approach of the special committee. Karl Menninger wrote to MacCormick, asking "what we ought to think about the Committee Report of the Governor's Special Committee on Criminal Offenders ... Has it got a chance? Has it got your approval? Has it got our support?"[42] MacCormick replied that the report was too scholarly and dense for legislators, with an "indefensible" emphasis on the prevention of anomie.[43] As a member of the Citizens Advisory Committee, he took his concerns directly to Preiser, telling him, "It means in plain language that if a judge thinks an offender is a good risk for probation, he must think twice before he puts them on probation and must worry that the public will think that he and all judges are being too soft on criminals. It is a concept you find only in a 'dollar-ditch-water' sociological treatise."[44]

In his meeting with the governor's committee, MacCormick was particularly incensed by the idea that "the state must take the retributive feelings of the public into account . . . if you are going to sell this idea on the present attitude of American people on crime, kowtowing to it, falling in line with it and the old ideas of retributive punishment, I would not be willing to help." To which the committee replied, "Like it or not, that is not the mood of this state." Florence Kelley, administrative judge of New York City's family court, at the same meeting argued that giving way to the anomie concept would "make the system crumble." Liberal administrators like herself were starting to be "brainwashed" on the idea of returning to definite sentences, and "this time I'm really going to fight . . . I think we are too concerned with what the community thinks."[45]

The tremendous fluidity of thinking about corrections and punishment in the late sixties rendered the report contradictory and incoherent (multiple authorship did not help). For instance, although the report called clearly for the re-introduction of a retributivist rationale, it also offered up the outline of what it contended would be an entirely new approach to rehabilitative services. Calling for centralized and more powerful diagnostic centers, the report proposed an unwieldy set of "fourteen fundamental characteristics [that] can be postulated as being both social impedimentia and crime related."[46] These fourteen "may appear singly, or in combination of two, three, or four in one individual offender at one time" and were matched up with an even more unwieldy list of fifteen basic treatment options.[47] The central diagnostic centers would create a "unified file" that would contain all the "data and the background material for the development of the diagnostic and treatment profile. This would then be summed up by use of a coding system."[48] The proposed plan for "a unified post-adjudicatory treatment agency" must surely rank as one of the most convoluted pieces of policy recommendation ever generated. It illustrates the extent to which progressive and New Deal reformism had devolved into a set of quasi-scientific recidivism-prevention impulses that, when fully expressed, had a farcical quality.

MacCormick was aghast at the proposal and observed, correctly, that it bore little or no relation to practical governance. "This whole system of places where you go for diagnoses and the board is there deciding something, and then somebody up on Albany deciding for children and another board for youths and another for adults," he wrote to Menninger, "my God, you just don't run a correctional department that way. Where are they going to be while they are going through this lengthy diagnostic process? They are going to go home and wait for the decision to find out what they need done to them."[49] MacCormick tartly chided the committee in person, observing that the *Preliminary Report* "amounted to very tedious reading, even for a retired professor of criminology who has had to read many a graduate thesis."[50]

Little of the specific treatment program apparatus proposed in the *Preliminary Report* was ever implemented. Indeed, in spelling out the complicated mechanisms required to diagnose and treatment criminal offenders, the report's authors may have done more to illustrate just how unlikely implementation of a medical treatment model in corrections would be. The most influential dimension of the *Preliminary Report*, however, had nothing at all to do with the unwieldy treatment proposals but instead directly challenged the extent to which the state's reformatory system had ever rehabilitated anyone and questioned the degree to which it ever could. In this challenge lay all the elements of a worldview that, by the mid-seventies, would be distilled into the pessimistic catchphrase "nothing works."

Freedom Rider: Robert Martinson on the Road to "Nothing Works"

If Austin MacCormick could, in some sense, be described as the architect of New York's reformatory system, Robert Martinson could be described as the architect of its destruction. This credits both with more individual responsibility than either really bore, but both were the most influential public faces of their respective intellectual and policy positions. A criminologist trained at the UC Berkeley School of Criminology, Robert Martinson arrived in New York in 1967, recruited to the governor's special committee to work under the direction of Deputy Assistant Director Lipton. Martinson assisted in the preparation of a massive review of correctional program evaluations published since 1945. His work on the special committee helped influence a sharply negative critique of the reformatory system in the *Preliminary Report* and launched Martinson on a career as the highest-profile critic of rehabilitation.

The road traveled by Robert Martinson to the governor's special committee serves as a case study in the disenchantment of the postwar left with the liberal state and with the development of neoconservative approaches to punishment. As a young undergraduate at the University of California, where he received his degree in 1949, Martinson became actively involved in left-wing student politics and activism on the Berkeley campus. Part of the anti-Stalinist Trotskyite student left, Martinson was an active member of the Socialist Youth League. The central fight of his young political career involved the battles over a faculty loyalty oath introduced around the time of his graduation. Martinson led the fight against the anticommunist oath requirement, defending academic freedom against the encroachments of state politics.

The oath fight was a notably bitter episode in the history of campus anticommunist politics, and Martinson was discouraged by the failure of students and faculty to defeat the efforts of the regents to terminate nonsigning faculty. *Cold War on the Campus*, a pamphlet Martinson authored in 1950, was "dedicated to those students and faculty members of the University of California who have had the honor of being casualties of the Cold War on Campus." He decried the extent to which "a barracks discipline, a regime of fear and distrust cripples an educational institution" and compared this to the manner in which fascist Germany and Stalinist Russia "encased their artists, scientists and intellectuals in uniforms and forced them to subordinate their ideas to the demands of the totalitarian state." Stalinism embodied "reactionary social aims and totalitarian methods," Martinson argued, and it would be particularly tragic to adopt these in the service of the anticommunist policing of university faculty. He denounced the "liberal inquisition" led by Sidney Hook and others and urged upon students the realization that any compromise would constitute a "death blow" to academic freedom.[51]

Martinson remained at Berkeley throughout the remainder of the decade, developing his critique of all forms of totalitarian structures. He completed a master's degree in sociology and social institutions in 1953. His thesis, "The Role of the Communist Party in the Spanish Civil War: A Study in Totalitarian Organization," examined the role of the party as part of a larger examination of "the modern totalitarian 'movement.'" Spanish communists, he felt, had undergone a kind of transformation under Soviet influence, and what remained by the late 1930s was "the Russian pressure instrument with its definitely rigidified and ordered structure."[52] In Martinson's view, rigid organization rendered the party "more and more impermeable to the influence of popular pressure," even as it became "highly skilled in mass manipulation and organization."[53] Martinson was particularly struck by the extent to which the party began to attack its own allies and employ the apparatus of the police state to imprison and torture left-wing dissidents.[54]

Martinson spent the decade following the completion of his master's degree as a sometime student and well-known peace activist in Berkeley. Cutting a striking figure, he participated in nearly every significant local political protest. He made a run for mayor in 1959, opposing the incumbent, retired UC vice president Claude Hutchinson. Running as the candidate of the United Social-ist Action Party, Martinson was handily defeated in the April elections. In 1961, Martinson joined other civil rights activists in one of the early groups of Freedom Riders, traveling to Mississippi to protest racial segregation. He was among those Riders arrested in Jackson, Mississippi, and eventually trans-ferred to the maximum-security unit of Parchman State Farm—the state's notorious prison farm. As had many civil rights activists before him, Martin-son went to prison and, in the process, discovered some realities of life in institutional confinement.[55]

For Martinson, the salient part of Parchman was not the racism or the bru-tality, but the "absurd quality" of institutional life, with its strange web of "min-ute rules" governing every aspect of daily existence. In fact, he observed that the daily order that the Riders organized for themselves at Parchman was not really of their own making but "dovetailed with [that of] the guards' and [was] partially built upon it." Sitting in cell five with another Rider, Martinson observed that almost every decision—making the bed or refusing to make it, eating breakfast or refusing to eat it, returning the tray or refusing to return it—was oriented around the guards' own rules and expectations for behavior. Even the social bonds of the Riders behind bars, he felt, had the "special quality" of an "indig-enous solution to life in such a unit."[56]

As Martinson forged the link between prison systems and the authoritarian regimes he had condemned in his political youth, he also grew disenchanted with the newer dimensions of radical politics. Working on his doctorate through the School of Criminology (from which Austin MacCormick had retired in 1960), Martinson's peace activism now included implicit criticisms of New Left political tactics. Writing in the *Nation*, Martinson observed, "The anxieties of the atomic age have begun to penetrate every city, village, and hamlet in Amer-ica." He approvingly noted the work of the Eugene, Oregon, Steering Commit-tee for Peace, which "broke with the traditional conception that peace is the monopoly of the Left" and instead tried to speak for the community as a whole. "Peace advocates," Martinson argued, "must win over the vast, uncommitted, but politically decisive middle ground which will only respond negatively to hys-teria, alarums, and mindlessness." Civil disobedience, he concluded, "a respon-sible and appropriate response for the civil-rights struggle in the South," might become "gauche and self-defeating when carried over uncritically to the peace field."[57]

By the time of the Berkeley Free Speech Movement in 1964, Martinson had become disenchanted with the emergent New Left, and the veteran peace activist committed himself to completing a dissertation in criminology. Working primarily in California institutions, Martinson's work before arriving in New York was profoundly critical of criminal justice systems, vigorously rejecting what he regarded to be the organizational rigidity and managerialism of liberal corrections. His work was also part of a larger explosion in social science, "guided by a reaction against the unabashed and unexamined moralism of early American social science."[58] From this perspective, for example, the value of reformatory education could not and should not be rooted in any moral sense of the good to be gained through education—the old Deweyan-MacCormick view—but only in empirically measurable positive outcomes. Focusing on anything beyond recidivism was becoming, for critics, a mark of evasion and incompetence.[59] An emphasis on outcomes and process meant that the substantive values behind the rehabilitative program became less important. The procedural values of the rehabilitative regime—emphasizing a heightening of state power, informality and discretion, and a minimization of due process—were woefully out of step with an emerging embrace of a new rights-oriented constitutionalism.[60]

By 1966, Martinson had settled on a preliminary label for what he was observing: treatment authoritarianism. The "problem of transforming men," he argued, had become so central to prison administration that treatment interests had taken over the "sphere hitherto ruled over by the uniformed officer class." In other words, the compulsion to remake the criminal offender had produced a system of control that could be remarkably punitive for those prisoners who ran afoul of its demands. The "medical police" of the modern age had replaced more primitive correctional forms, Martinson argued, and could make "Orwell's 1984 seem like a pleasant dream"—the very work he had invoked in discussing the Spanish Communists in his 1953 master's thesis.[61]

Just as Martinson's reflections on Parchman Farm largely passed over racism and physical brutality, his reflections on the modern prison dismissed the relevance of more traditionally brutal dimensions of punishment. "Those who will push and preach for the prison to become a 'hospital,'" he suggested in a 1966 article, would have society "use the iron compression chamber of prison life to screw down upon the helpless, the aged, the misfits, the liars, the psychopaths, the drop-outs, and those who have almost accidentally got cause [sic] up in the correctional stream." On the other hand, he felt, a purely custodial approach to imprisonment should not be regarded as inherently severe: "*custodians need not be punitive*" (emphasis in original).[62]

A year after that essay appeared in print, Martinson headed east to join the staff of the governor's special committee, to help explore the committee's preliminary sense that "there was no available guidance on the question of what has been shown to be the most effective means of rehabilitation." The task, Martinson recalled, was "to remedy this defect in our knowledge; our job was to undertake a comprehensive survey of what was known about rehabilitation."[63] Martinson's job was to examine published evaluations of correctional rehabilitation programs, completed and published between 1945 and the end of 1967. A total of 231 studies were eventually compiled, containing between them 285 separate treatment findings. Consistent with the emerging critical social-scientific perspective, the project excluded measures of anything beyond recidivism: the impact of programs on adjustment to prison life, vocational success, educational achievement, personality and attitude change, or general adjustment to the outside community. Instead, the study dealt "only with the effects of rehabilitative treatment on recidivism, the phenomenon which reflects most directly how well our present treatment programs are performing the task of rehabilitation."[64]

With respect to the extant research literature, the *Preliminary Report* got right to the point:

> For the purpose of setting these matters in the proper context, it is important to stress the fact that at the present time we do not have any organized collection of information—nor do we believe that a collection of information exists anywhere—to form a gauge or set of gauges by which we can judge the effectiveness of any program operated by the Department, or by any other State or local agency that administers post-adjudicatory treatment. In other words we presently have no reliable basis for stating whether anything any correctional agency in the country is doing at the present time is helping to prevent recidivism. In fact, some of the information that we do have shows that application of some of the most 'advanced' treatment techniques on an across-the-board basis (i.e. to undifferentiated groups of offenders) may actually increase the likelihood of recidivism for some offenders.[65]

Nor were vocational and educational programming spared the general critique. The report made the case that there was "no reliable evidence anywhere" to show that these efforts had any effect "on reducing recidivism." In fact, the report invoked one of the department's own studies—the 1961 report on educational attainment and parole adjustment—to demonstrate the limited impact. For the tottering correctional education regime, the *Preliminary Report* offered this devastating conclusion: "Unless we utilize these programs in accordance with a rational design for prevention of recidivism . . . we may think of them only as methods of utilizing inmate time for constructive purposes."[66]

The Elmira Reception Center came in for withering criticism. The *Preliminary Report* observed that the process of managing the adolescent offender "does not constitute a system for formulating and pursuing specific treatment goals within the framework of an overall, centrally controlled, diagnostic-based plan." As Bertram Beck had argued, the reception center was conceptually "isolated from the rest of the system." It produced a product, in the form of the detailed program recommendations, "which other institutions may accept or reject, and receiving no feedback to help refine its diagnostic techniques . . . where its recommendations are not followed, its effort is largely futile . . . where its recommendations are followed . . . it has no way of applying experience to refine or correct itself." The *Preliminary Report* also offered up an implicit criticism of the Reception Center Research Project, observing, "Without any centralized control, the prognosis for any type of systematic evaluative research on treatment effectiveness is quite poor."[67]

Although the *Preliminary Report* reflected deep skepticism about the potential of rehabilitative programs to accomplish the reductions in recidivism that would justify their existence, it did not quite offer the full-blown attack that Martinson himself wanted to deliver. As he later observed, the careful systematic review of research studies that he undertook with Douglas Lipton lacked a powerful policy conclusion, one that he then took it upon himself to supply. In doing so, he completed the conceptual bridge to the intellectual position that helped enable the modern age of mass incarceration.

The great, painful irony of Robert Martinson's life story (and many other public and academic figures for whom he stands in as a representative) is that the attack on rehabilitation was not at all intended to support an expansion of imprisonment. On the contrary, Martinson believed that, shorn of its rehabilitative justification, the prison would lose its place in American society and gradually be replaced by noncustodial alternatives. All that remained for critics of the prison, then, was to give the whole pathetic apparatus one final shove and condemn the entire rehabilitative enterprise.[68] Martinson, with plenty of company, did just that, making his now-famous case that "rehabilitation is a social myth" and that "nothing works."[69]

To make this case, Martinson first needed to deny one of the central premises of MacCormick-style reformism—that the most serious harms of imprisonment were caused by idleness, indifference, and cruelty. Like many of his contemporaries, Martinson argued that old-fashioned ideas of harsh justice had largely been banished, leaving the prison field entirely to treatment-custody bureaucracies. Actual brutality was a self-serving myth perpetuated by those same bureaucracies. Indeed, the treatment prison was worse than supposedly now-extinct systems of harsh justice: "A relatively brief prison sojourn today may be more criminogenic than a much longer and more brutal sojourn a century ago . . . the early prisons left physical and mental scars but did not inhibit the offender from productive work, marriage, family."[70]

In the wake of the Attica uprising, Martinson decried the entire range of groups who attached themselves to the rioters—"posh white radicals . . . poverty lawyers, radical intellectuals, upper-middle-class legal professionals, reporters, mass media specialists . . . politicians dependent upon the inner-city black and Puerto Rican vote . . . members of revolutionary sects, academic guerillas and a few students."[71] He argued, "This movement incorrectly interprets convict insurrection as a response to 'racism' and 'brutality.'"[72] Martinson's position was, in essence, a denial of the actual reformatory experience at Coxsackie and elsewhere, a forcible muting of the horrific experiences of thousands of young men.

Martinson also needed to take his criticism of rehabilitative programs a step further than the suggestion that they had not been shown to work and make the case that they *could not* work. Far from being a misinterpretation of Martinson's research, the "nothing works" phrase was a reasonably accurate reflection of his many public statements. The high-water mark of this effort was the 1974 publication, in the *Public Interest*, of the essay "What Works?—Questions and Answers about Prison Reform." Here, he concluded, "With few and isolated exceptions, the rehabilitative efforts that have been reported so far have had no appreciable effect on recidivism."[73] The more than two hundred evaluation students, he concluded, "give us little reason for hope . . . Maybe," he wrote, "our programs are simply not yet good enough, but more likely . . . there is a more radical flaw in our present strategies—that education at its best, or that psychotherapy at its best, cannot overcome, or even appreciably reduce, the powerful tendency for offenders to continue in criminal behavior."[74]

So where ought prisons and punishment turn next? Here, Martinson embraced a return to determinate sentencing and fixed periods of confinement for the most serious offenders. "If we can't do more for (and to) offenders," he wrote, "at least we can safely do less."[75] High-risk offenders could be housed in prisons "which are nothing more (and aim to be nothing more) than custodial institutions." Toward that end, he happily related, "lawyers and criminologists are returning to the long-deserted classical trail."[76] Martinson was hardly alone in his embrace of classical punishment. Even the venerable Correctional Association of New York, in 1978, dismissed concerns that this might lead to worse conditions:

> Determinate sentencing is criticized out of fear that its adoption may result in prisons becoming more overcrowded and inhumane than they already are . . . Because determinate sentencing is generally viewed as rejecting the philosophy of rehabilitation, it is feared that the adoption of a determinate system will undercut the rationale for prison programs, and thus cause them to be reduced . . . while it is possible that prisons may become more harsh under a determinate scheme, that result is hardly mandated and would be contrary to the emphatic urgings of those recommending a determinate scheme. Prisons are already intolerably harsh; what is required is that they become more humane and decent.[77]

Martinson, at least until the mid-1970s, remained absolutely convinced that he was helping to end the reliance on the prison as a locus of punishment. Writing in 1972, he argued that the disintegration of the correctional treatment model was a necessary prerequisite for a "social planning" phase of development in which "prisons are necessary to some stages of civilization but can be gradually replaced by milder forms of control to the degree permitted by democratic crime prevention."[78] In the grandiose language that would have been absolutely familiar to anyone who had known the young socialist, the long-time peace activist, the Freedom Rider, and—above all—the committed anti-totalitarian, he wrote: "The long history of prison reform is over. On the whole the prisons have played out their allotted role. They cannot be reformed and must gradually be torn down . . . We shall be cleansed of the foreign element of forced treatment with its totalitarian overtones . . . The myth of correctional treatment is now the main obstacle to progress; it has become the last line of defense of the prison system; it prevents the sound use of resources to balance public protection and inmate rights; and it diverts energy away from defending democracy through widening opportunity. It is time to awake from the dream."[79]

Life for Robert Martinson was its own kind of dream for a short time. Now a member of the sociology faculty at the City University of New York, he enjoyed a remarkable wave of public attention and popular approval. In a 1975 *60 Minutes* interview with Mike Wallace, he reiterated his view that rehabilitative programs had "no fundamental effect on the recidivism rate of people." Wallace replied, "No effect at all?" To which Martinson responded, "No effect, no basic effect."[80] To a *People* magazine reporter in early 1976, he suggested that his attacks had thrown criminal justice into "a state of extreme intellectual crisis."

Institutions like reformatories had been designed "to handle boy scout offenders, mildly criminal types, but now we are dumping serious criminals onto this
system . . . No wonder people think it's a farce."[81]

A postprison vision for criminal justice proved to be its own sort of dream,
one that faded quickly in the politics of the seventies. Harsh justice proved not
to have been dead and buried; by the end of the decade, a new era of punitive
punishment and prison expansion was clearly beginning to take shape. Given a
substantial grant from the National Institute of Law Enforcement and Criminal
Justice to undertake a massive new meta-analysis and create the Center for
Criminal Justice Planning, Martinson disavowed his earlier methodology. Conscious of the direction in which the attack on rehabilitation was taking criminal
justice, he no longer excluded all but controlled studies and instead embraced a
much larger sample of research reports, encompassing 555 research studies
published since 1945. Preliminary findings appeared in late 1976, but a series of
personal and administrative conflicts plagued the center and the project, and no
final study ever appeared.

By the time Martinson's final publication appeared in the *Hofstra Law Review* in 1979, he had completely recanted his earlier position on rehabilitation.
Noting that it "was misleading to judge criminal justice on the basis of . . .
merely the experimental (evaluation) research," he revisited his earlier conclusions. He had "thought it important" that his earlier conclusion be made public
and debated and, Martinson now ruefully noted, "it surely was debated." With
an almost desperate directness, he wrote: "On the basis of the evidence in our
current study, I withdraw this conclusion. I have often said that treatment added
to the networks of criminal justice is 'impotent,' and I withdraw this character-
ization as well." His final published sentence offered up a plea for a more
thoughtful approach to prison programs: "Those treatments that are helpful
must be carefully discerned and increased; those that are harmful or impotent
eliminated."[82]

Austin MacCormick and Robert Martinson serve as bookends to New York's
reformatory era. Although they each spent the decade of the fifties on the Berkeley campus, there is no evidence of any meaningful interaction between the
two. Each left California for New York in the 1960s, MacCormick to try to sustain liberal prison reform, and Martinson to try to end it. Neither man lived to
fully appreciate the direction in which American penal policy was headed.

MacCormick spent the last years of his life commuting from his Connecticut
home into New York City, the elder statesman returned to serve as executive
director of the Osborne Association, the outgrowth of his work decades earlier

with his mentor. He published an influential monograph against the death penalty, continued to visit state prison systems to support reformist policies, and supported continued investments in programs for juvenile offenders and for the support of prisoners postrelease. His pioneering educational work of the 1930s, however, was already fading into obscurity—work more cited than actually read—by the time of his death in October 1979.

Robert Martinson's work, in contrast, stubbornly refused to fade into obscurity, even as the man himself struggled to maintain his position in the criminal justice field. No longer the public figure he had been only a few years earlier, Martinson was denied tenure at CUNY and suffered a series of personal setbacks. Apparently haunted by the rise of a new, punitive approach to punishment, and his own connection it, he wrote the *Hofstra Law Review* essay as a little-noticed attempt to put the cork back into the bottle. Two months before MacCormick's death, Martinson took his own life.[83] "Nothing works"—his argument, if not his exact words—lived on, however, at the heart of the new prison politics.

CHAPTER NINE

Floodtide

Coxsackie and Post-Reformatory Prison Politics, 1963–1977

In late 1962, Glenn Kendall became Coxsackie's third superintendent since the reformatory's opening. He came to the institution as one of the pioneers of New York's reformatory movement. He had gone to Wallkill Prison from Teachers College, in 1935, to conduct some of the first experimental educational programs, became one of the founding administrators of the Division of Education, and then became the first and only director of the Elmira Reception Center until moving to Coxsackie. And now, after twenty-seven years in the state system, Kendall was finally given the chance to administer one of the reformatories.

Kendall observed a deeply divided institution when he arrived. Educators, shop teachers, and counselors labored, as they had always done, to instill in young men any number of personal qualities they were seen as lacking: intellectual curiosity, public-spiritedness, work discipline, and more. Their students, in turn, continued to respond with a profound ambivalence to reformatory programming. Eager to learn and acquire desirable skills, they nonetheless responded with deep skepticism about both the capacity and the willingness of New York to provide these. Time and again, Kendall observed, the group logic of the inmate social system fought "the regular program" of the reformatory, and heaped contempt on the "squares" that bought what Coxsackie was selling.[1]

If prisoners shared a common hostility to the reformatory, Kendall discovered that this was still undercut by deep and profound racial conflict. "Race segregation is still strong" at Coxsackie, he observed, noting that old-timers on the staff claimed that it had existed since the beginning of the institution. Even the water fountains, he reported, were clearly demarcated by the prisoners for black and for white use. It is hard to estimate just how surprising the race conflict would have been to a system veteran like Kendall, but there is no question that he deeply objected to its existence. The "great emphasis on race prejudice" at Coxsackie, he warned, was in direct contrast to "the official policy and procedures of no segregation or discrimination." Reformatory officials, said Kendall, had been far too willing "to ignore the whole business" rather than address the conflict head on.[2] One of his first actions was to order the creation of multiple outdoor yards, through which various housing divisions would rotate. In this way, he attempted to destroy what he called the yard-centered "padded" subculture of the reformatory, in which the single main yard was carved up into racially and geographically specific pads owned by various groups of inmates. Kendall also encouraged discussions, led by both teachers and willing guards, on the "evils of segregation and discrimination," designed to counter the prevailing attitudes of reformatory inmates.[3]

Kendall also sought to soften the hardest edges of the reformatory regime. Being witness to the physical brutality perpetuated by guards against the young men at the Nebraska reformatory where he first worked had left a lasting impression on Kendall. It was "a horrible experience," the new superintendent recalled, "and I've never forgotten it." For the first time, prisoners in solitary confinement at Coxsackie were to be given an educational program, to break up the harsh effects of their isolation. Under Kendall's leadership, the flow of new programs continued as it had before: intensive psychotherapy for drug-addicted inmates, a new Explorer post for the reformatory, group counseling programs, and more. Where policies seemed counterproductive, Kendall worked to change them—one of his early decisions was to end the long-standing rule that chapel attendance was mandatory, a rule that was increasingly being resisted by reformatory inmates.[4]

Kendall and the liberal reformers with which he came of age were bound together by a shared vision of a prisoner's worth and humanity as well as a commitment to creating a space in which young men could develop the qualities of constructive citizenship. But there was simply no way that this vision could be realized in the context of a single reformatory. Even if Kendall had been able to overcome the resistance of prisoners and guards, which he could never wholly do, much of the effort to sustain Coxsackie continued to involve preserving the institution as disproportionately white and upstate. The pursuit of a reformworthy population during Kendall's tenure (see chapter 7) was an important part of what was ultimately a failing attempt to keep the politics of punishment at bay. By the time Kendall reached his mandatory retirement age in the summer of 1969, the New York State Vocational Institution had only eighteen months left as a reformatory but years of painful transition ahead as the vestiges of the reform idea were swept away by the mass incarceration floodtide.[5]

Reformers in the Political Wilderness

The core elements of liberal reform in the New York prison system remained a strong presence in the Division of Education, the Elmira Reception Center, and the state reformatories—but they increasingly found themselves politically isolated both inside and outside the prison system. Prison reform rapidly faded as an issue after the Elmira Reception Center opened, with years of policy drift and fiscal inattention. Veterans of the prison system during this period recalled that state budgets were not at all satisfactory, and that the correctional system was systematically underfunded by the legislature.[6] One post-Attica review concluded that the Department of Corrections was "unable to plan, to implement, or to evaluate new programs or to monitor the individual components of the system. Each facility was an isolated, autonomous fiefdom that used its limited resources primarily to tighten security."[7] The Prison Association of New York glumly observed that if all the recommendations of all the studies made since 1930 had been acted on, New York's correctional system would be among the most outstanding in the nation. That it was not seemed painfully obvious.[8]

Governors Averell Harriman (1955–1958) and Nelson Rockefeller (during his first two terms in office, 1959–1966) demonstrated no particular interest in corrections. Harriman returned the Democrats to the executive mansion, but his one term in office scarcely reminded anyone of the Roosevelt-Lehman years. Faced with massive Republican majorities in both legislative houses, a Democratic policy apparatus woefully underdeveloped since Lehman's departure, and his own instinctive caution, few major legislative initiatives were forthcoming— his major area of interest was mental health, where he devoted his limited funds for new program development.[9] As for Rockefeller, one insider observed, "The governor's primary area of interest was the State University system . . . so no special attention was given to the Correction Department budget . . . when things are going smoothly, there is no need to get involved in program change, nor is there any need for the Governor's special involvement."[10] The person charged with making things go smoothly was Paul D. McGinnis, appointed commissioner of corrections by Harriman and reappointed by Rockefeller. McGinnis, according to a veteran of prison politics in New York, "had a reputation for 'keeping expenses down' and 'things quiet' within the institutions," all of which meant little understanding or sympathy for new program investment.[11]

The New York legislature proved just as disinterested in correctional matters under Harriman and Rockefeller. The legislature, dominated by Republicans, had little interest in promoting an expansion of liberal prison programs, though they were far more likely to ignore than attack rehabilitative efforts. The Senate Penal Institutions Committee, which would eventually become a center of political activity, was for most of this period inactive. One aide recalled, "All correspondence from inmates was immediately discarded in the waste paper basket."[12] Charles McKendrick, educator, prison administrator, and liberal stalwart within the Department of Corrections, recalled that prior to 1967, he had never once been contacted by the state legislature, never been asked for any information, and never had a single state legislator visit his institutions.[13]

But if drift and inattention were the hallmarks of state politics, there were certainly signs that the growth of liberal policy had come to an end. The fate of youth courts reveals growing political resistance to the expansion of reform. A system of statewide youth courts had been first proposed in 1942 as part of the Youthful Offender Act. Based on the pioneering efforts in New York City, these youth courts would have focused exclusively on adolescent offenders. The youth courts failed to make it into the final 1942 legislation; it took repeated efforts and fourteen more years before the legislature finally passed the 1956 Hughes-Farbstein Act, authorizing a separate youth court in every county in the state. Opponents delayed implementation by placing a hold on the act in early 1957, and then another hold in 1958. Critics, like the County Judges Association, decried the "flood tide" of adolescent crime, arguing that the youth court looked "like a further invitation for more young people to become criminals . . . extend a certain immunity to a greater number of persons responsible for a major portion of our crime, further clog our courts and add more labor to undermanned police departments."[14] The senate and gubernatorial campaigns of 1958 were replete with charges and counter-charges over the state's growing crime problem, and the youth court rapidly lost its appeal.[15] In early 1961, the youth court legislation, which had never been implemented, was repealed by the legislature.[16]

Like tremors before an earthquake, the reformatory system of the 1950s and 1960s revealed signs of the coming era of mass incarceration. While overall prison populations remained relatively stable, growing numbers of young offenders were being swept into the system, based on their involvement in drug or gang activity. The designation of Great Meadow as an end-of-the-line institution revealed the limits of liberal ideals when confronted with large numbers of socially marginal inmates. Likewise, while the Rockefeller drug laws of 1973 are commonly seen as a pioneering step away from a rehabilitative logic for drug offenders and toward social exclusion, treatment interventions had been declared off-limits for gang members and criminal offenders since at least the North Brother Island experiment.[17]

What appear, at first glance, to have been stable prison population levels before 1973, turn out to mask a growing use of incarceration as a tool of social policy. In adopting civil commitment for narcotic addicts in 1966, for example, the Narcotic Addiction Control Commission (NACC) took over one of the New Deal–era reformatories—Woodbourne—to house the many young men caught up in the system. Longtime addiction researcher Herman Joseph recalled, "The addicts called the facilities 'candy-coated jails' . . . and that is a very apt description." Woodbourne was thus "converted" from a reformatory to a treatment facility, but with the same restrictions on inmates, the same layout, and even the same custodial staff (who remained in the employ of the Department of Corrections). The young inmates may have no longer counted as state prisoners, but this was a distinction without difference.[18] Meanwhile, the New York City correctional system was staggering under a wave of short-term jail commitments, the product of aggressive policing of the city's serious drug and crime problems. Overcrowded to the point of ungovernability, the city correctional system began shipping city prisoners to state facilities, a practice that added to the challenges of managing the state prison system.[19] Even the Elmira Reception Center, by 1969, housed overflow inmates from New York City.

Coxsackie's formal existence as a reformatory ended on January 1, 1971, with the creation of the Department of Correctional Services. The legislation that created the DOCS was widely mocked at the time for the many symbolic changes it introduced (including changing "prisons" to "correctional facilities" and "wardens" to "superintendents"), but it was hardly congenial to the older reform interests in the state. Indeed, it essentially dismantled the old reformatory system. No longer would the reformatories and the Elmira Reception Center function as an independent network within the larger state system. The New York State Vocational Institution became the Coxsackie Correctional Facility and was designated a general confinement institution, more specifically a "medium security" facility. (Elmira and Wallkill also became medium security; Woodbourne, for the moment, remained with the NACC; Great Meadow become maximum security; and Catskill housed overflow New York City inmates.) The DOCS also largely completed the sweep of any reformist veterans out of positions of authority within the system, though retirement and death had been taking many of them out of the system already.[20]

The 1971 legislation produced profound bureaucratic disarray throughout the entire prison system. The post of deputy superintendent was replaced by three new positions: deputy superintendent of programs, deputy superintendent of security, and deputy superintendent of administration. The superintendent position was removed from the civil service lists, and the person could be hired and fired at will by the commissioner of corrections, which theoretically gave Albany more power but actually just weakened the superintendent's position and gave more power to local political interests, especially correctional officers. And it would be the correctional officers, working with the state legislature, who would lead the charge in redefining prison politics.

The Rebellion of the Guards

When Coxsackie opened, prison guards there and elsewhere in the system had very limited political power within their institutions and almost no external political presence. In the absence of any labor organization or collective bargaining, custodial staff was almost entirely at the mercy of wardens and superintendents, who wielded considerable power with little external oversight. Liberal reformers had been no more interested in empowering the guards than any other prison administrators had been. The creation of the Central Guard School was effectively a bid to exert even closer control over guard selection, training, and behavior.

Of course, prison guards *were* deeply embedded in their local communities, and it is there where their earliest, quite modest forms of political influence may be detected. At Coxsackie, guards were part of local bowling leagues, softball teams, fraternal organizations, American Legion posts—connections that paid off in 1942 following some escape attempts at the reformatory, including one in which two young men stole saddle horses used by guards to patrol the perimeter of the farm land, and another in which four inmates attacked a guard to obtain a set of keys.[21] A local Greene County grand jury, undoubtedly with strong feelings for the guards, convened to make recommendations for the reformatory administration. Their report recommended that parole violators not be returned to Coxsackie, since "there are no walls" and the institution was "not properly equipped to handle more serious cases." Further, they urged hiring more guards at the institution and modifying the buildings to eliminate routes of escape.[22]

There is little indication that the grand jury recommendations were followed in any respect, and guard influence at Coxsackie remained limited until the emergence of a coherent union movement. The earliest stirrings of labor organization date at least to 1953, when the American Federation of State, County, and Municipal Employees (AFSCME) began to organize prison guards, though it did not have the right to collectively bargain labor contracts. An AFSCME committee investigated prison disturbances and concluded, "Low morale, inadequate pay and poor working conditions among the guard personnel [were] largely responsible." The first local was established at Sing Sing in 1953, and within a short time, AFSCME Council 50 represented security personnel throughout the New York prison system. Almost immediately, Council 50 demanded the establishment of a forty-hour workweek for guards, pointing out that this had been achieved in private industry since before the war.[23]

Salary disputes occupied Council 50 much of the time. Prison guards were bitterly unhappy about Civil Service Commission decisions in 1954–1955 placing them in salary grade 11, rather than the requested grade 14. At that point, guard salaries began to seriously lag those of other prison employees, as well as those of New York City guards. Council 50 condemned the denials of salary grade changes as "cruel and heartless disregard of loyal, underpaid state workers."[24] A year later, guards seeking "dignity and job protection" marched on the state capitol, carrying signs demanding wage increases and a state-funded life insurance policy, along with more general recognition of their worth as "first class citizens."[25]

Years of frustration with the Civil Service Commission came to a head in 1965, with the denial of yet another appeal. The Department of Corrections' rejected appeal is a poignant reminder of the liberal framework that still dominated the Albany administration. Referring to the classification dispute as "perhaps the most important matter that has faced us in many years," the department attacked the commission for "improper, inconsistent, illogical, [and] arbitrary and capricious conclusions." The department pointed out in the appeal that guards remained stuck at grade 11, while teachers were at grade 12 and senior teachers at grade 15. "There are very few, if any, Correction Officers who are not actively and directly involved in a corrective and rehabilitative approach with all inmates . . . Education in its various forms is the driving core of the rehabilitative program," the department noted, and "educational programs in correctional institutions could not survive one day without the efforts of the Correction Officers."[26]

The failure of the Department of Corrections to use the rhetoric of rehabilitation to obtain better pay for guards pushed Council 50 further toward direct political action. Pickets went up in 1965 at a series of institutions, including Coxsackie, protesting the civil service denial of a grade increase. Early in 1966, Council 50 wrote to every state legislator, warning of "a condition of maximum low morale among the state correction officers."[27] The overwhelming focus of labor activity in this period was on the bread and butter issues surrounding wages, hours, and the other terms and conditions of employment, but there were some signs that guards were beginning to define internal prison policy as a negotiable condition of employment. From the beginning of the reform period in New York, a substantial proportion of guards had resisted the imposition of extensive prison programs; the Central Guard School had been both an acknowledgment of this and an attempt to overcome that resistance. Among the high-profile educational reformers in prison administration was Charles L. McKendrick, a product of the Central Guard School who had been identified by the leading reformers as a kindred spirit and promoted steadily up through the system (while he pursued a master's and a doctorate at Teachers College). Following two racial disturbances at Napanoch in 1960, Council 50 publically attacked Superintendent McKendrick for showing "too much leniency toward the prisoners"—while McKendrick dismissed the attack as part of Council 50's ongoing public push for salary increases.[28]

These were minor skirmishes. It was not until 1969 that AFSCME finally won the right to represent correctional officers in the bargaining of new state contracts. At about the same time, correctional officers broke away from Council 50, which represented multiple categories of state employees, to start Council 82, composed largely through not exclusively of prison custodial workers.[29] The first contract negotiations brought forth a torrent of officer demands over long-ignored aspects of their work lives: "improvements in salary, promotion, hours of work, retirement benefits, health and life insurance, special disability provisions, vacations, holidays, personal and sick leave, seniority, coffee breaks, and uniform allowances."[30] The earliest grievances at Coxsackie were likewise mostly grounded in day-to-day work issues: employees working two shifts within a twenty-four-hour period without receiving overtime, inadequate lighting for the employee parking lot, inadequate compensation for travel time from Albany to Coxsackie, and so on.[31]

The 1971 restructuring of the prison system produced considerable chaos and weakened traditional warden and superintendent authority, pushing Council 82 much further in the direction of demanding greater institutional control for officers and lobbying for prison policy changes. In the wake the Attica riot that same year, Council 82 presented the state with seven specific demands and threatened a system-wide lock-in of prisoners.[32] At the heart of their demands was the quest to secure for officers a greater role "in determining what levels of security are required in each institution, how much inmate movement can be tolerated, which posts must be covered if the prison is to run a full schedule, and how security resources are to be deployed."[33]

These demands were largely focused on the internal politics of prison governance, but Council 82 assumed a more substantial role in state-level prison politics as well. Russell Oswald recalled that officers of the 1950s and 1960s "were not politically oriented insofar as they did not use the press as their public arena or inform the press as to trouble within the institutions . . . . [Commissioner] McGinnis exerted too strong a control for that to occur."[34] While Oswald overstated the matter, it is true that correctional officers' political interventions stayed largely behind bars.

Among the most important early successes for Council 82 involved their fight to deny Herman Schwartz nomination to head the State Commission of Correction. Governor Hugh Carey appointed Schwartz to head the commission, a prison watchdog organization of sorts. The announcement, in August 1975, was a low-key affair, which drew only modest press coverage and garnered generally favorable reviews.[35] Many correctional officers, however, were enraged by Schwartz's appointment and determined to prevent his confirmation by the senate. Most recalled Schwartz's role in the Attica uprising as one of the first and most important outside intermediaries with the inmates in D yard. Although he had shown unquestionable courage at Attica, his willingness to negotiate with the prisoners, his concern for their well-being, his efforts to secure legal amnesty for most of the men involved, and above all his condemnation of the "inhumanity that men perpetuates against his fellow man in the name of justice" made Herman Schwartz the object of unrelenting hostility from officers. Council 82 made his defeat their number one political priority. John Burke, of the Council 82 Correction Policy Political Committee, wrote to legislators condemning Schwartz's "ultra-liberal philosophies." The nominee, wrote Burke, was "more concerned with the rights of criminals . . . than he is of the rights of victims of crime and the Correction Officers who work in the prisons and happen to be law-abiding citizens and tax payers." His confirmation, legislators were warned, would have a "demoralizing effect on the silent majority of society."[36]

In response to the furor, state senator Ralph Marino, head of the Committee on Crime and Correction, proposed hearings ("we have to see whether he's gone too far").[37] Three days of contentious hearings in late February revealed just how much Schwartz had become "a symbol of the liberal attitude toward prison administration" and a lightning rod for conservative criticism of the penal system. Ultimately, the nomination failed, hinging on Marino's deciding vote, which he withheld because he felt Schwartz's record "indicates a propensity toward an inmate's point of view above and beyond his position as Correction Commissioner."[38] Liberals bemoaned the result; Tom Wicker called the defeat "one more entry in a long record of contempt and disregard by the state for its prisons and their inmates," one that "raises the question of whether any real improvement in prison conditions is politically possible."[39]

Correctional officers celebrated the defeat of Schwartz and continued to press their advantage with the state and individual institutional administrators. Council 82 executive director Carl Gray declared: "We are not patsies and we are not brutes and we will not take abuse from anyone."[40] Officers at Napanoch staged a wildcat strike in 1976 to force the institution to permit an institution-wide frisk for weapons, contrary to policy but strongly urged as a security measure. Council 82 dismissed prioritizing anything but security: "The present situation is one of warehousing only. Rhetoric about rehabilitation and programs are only that."[41] Thomas Coughlin became corrections commissioner in 1979, in the wake of a systemwide work stoppage by correctional officers. In his view, "The correction officers had received no real benefits from the Attica riot and they felt they were being ignored . . . I decided to bring some balance into the system by responding to the group I would consider my constituency—the correction officers and especially the union, because they were an organized, cohesive group—an enduring force."[42] An enduring force—nowhere was this truer than behind the walls of Coxsackie, where years of conflict came to a head in 1977 and provided the correctional officers with the definitive opportunity to put an end to what was left of the institution's reform legacy.

The War of 1977

As a reformatory, Coxsackie had managed for years to control what sorts of prisoners it received, through the screening processes at the Elmira Reception Center and the extensive use of disciplinary or program transfers. Once Coxsackie lost its status as a reformatory in 1971 and became just another medium-security prison in the larger system, it lost all control over the inmate pipeline. As a consequence, the transition toward a largely African American and Puerto Rican population that had been taking place elsewhere in the system over the course of the entire postwar period took place almost instantly at Coxsackie. The inmates remained, for the time being, largely between 16 and 18 years of age, but now they were overwhelmingly young men of color. As late as 1969, white inmates accounted for more than 60 percent of the prison population at the institution; less than a decade later, they accounted for no more than 15 percent of the total. Guards told observers that the "character" of the population had changed in recent years, and this was at least partly a euphemism for the declining presence of white, upstate youth.

Guards were not wholly wrong, however, to point out that there were some changes afoot in the prison population. With Coxsackie no longer part of a self-contained reformatory network within the prison system, it began receiving a much greater variety of inmates, including those with more serious criminal records. In addition, the rapid growth of the overall prison population in the 1970s, combined with the desire to implement a "fluid" system organized by security level, resulted in the Department of Correctional Services transferring large numbers of inmates every day, just to match the supply of prisoners with available prison space. One legislative report estimated that as many as five hundred state inmates were in transit on buses on any given day—the equivalent of one medium-size prison in the system.[43] As a consequence, correctional officers felt that Coxsackie had large numbers of transient inmates with no attachment to prison programs as well as more serious offenders who presented a security risk. The prison farm, once the pride of the institution, was barely functioning by 1977—when Coxsackie tore the barn complex down in 1981, it had to import minimum-security inmates from Camp Summit to do the job.[44]

Unfortunately, critics charged, elements of the correction officer workforce at Coxsackie responded to these dramatic changes by accelerating the systematic abuse of prisoners. Now, more than ever, verbal abuse and physical brutality were said to have taken on strongly racial elements. Attorney Elizabeth Gaynes, who entered Coxsackie as a representative of Prisoners Legal Services in late 1976, observed the inability, as she saw it, of the older officers, "to adjust to these inmates." According to Gaynes, Coxsackie featured "physical and verbal abuse by corrections officers, particularly white officers against black inmates," and did so at "a much higher percentage than I have encountered at other prisons." She later testified, "I have been told by guards that my clients are animals, retards, black bastards, lower then animals; that 'these people aren't like us,' that I must be unable to sleep at night knowing I'm helping these niggers." Commission of Correction chairman Stephen Chinlund, who had replaced Herman Schwartz, further acknowledged that the actions of the most racist elements of the guard force had created a split, even "among captains, lieutenants, and sergeants, leaving the line staff in a difficult position of not knowing who to follow and what to do."[45]

Violence against inmates, as before, tended to concentrate around solitary confinement, and inmates were beaten when taken to solitary, much as they had been for decades.[46] It did not help matters much that, at some points in the early 1970s, there was not a single black officer at Coxsackie. One of the early black officers, Dirome Williams, observed that racism was prevalent: "I'm used to feeling alienated. I have a better rapport with most prisoners than with most guards." When asked if officers routinely beat inmates, he admitted, "The honest truth is, yes, they do."[47] Even Commissioner of Corrections Benjamin Ward, appointed in 1975, acknowledged, "there is racism in the prison system, and it's obviously a problem at Coxsackie."[48]

Coxsackie's prisoners were, in turn, as angry and politicized as their reformatory counterparts had been in years previous. Just as the correctional officers discovered, the prisoners had learned to take their case to the media and to outside advocacy groups. Days after the bloody retaking of Attica prison in 1971, one Coxsackie inmate wrote: "We are the victims of mental harassments, intimidations and threats. Brothers are denied the right to convene together under the Islamic doctrines . . . They have a form of Jim Crow sub-rules here, which they use to suppress us . . . We need your help Brother. It's time Black people start sticking together, fighting together, and dying together, if need be."[49]

Prisoners at Coxsackie engaged in a series of protests around labor behind bars. In 1972, kitchen workers, angry over their low wages (at that point, between 25 and 40 cents per day), went on strike. The resulting conflict included two incidents in which windows were broken and toilets damaged in housing units, and authorities used tear gas on about eighty inmates to restore order. One prisoner, already in solitary confinement, was gassed after he "began shouting and threatening guards."[50] Work stoppages at Coxsackie continued to be a tool of resistance in other circumstances as well. When authorities instituted a rule, in 1973, that inmates be required to eat all the food they took at the prison mess hall, prisoners refused to work once again.[51]

Black inmates, who for decades had been subject to attacks and beatings from the majority white reformatory population, began to return the violence. Now overwhelmingly in the minority, white inmates found themselves vulnerable and victimized. Even a prisoners' attorney conceded that, since black inmates "cannot act against the white guards . . . they coerce white prisoners to give up their commissary, take property, provoke fights, and so forth." One thing had not changed—Coxsackie was still at the boiling point of racial conflict, and still more so than the so-called "adult" prisons in the system.[52]

January 1977 brought three new developments that would intertwine with one another over the course of the year and lead to a final reckoning for what was left of the old reformatory's liberal legacy. In the second week of January, Vito Ternullo was appointed superintendent of Coxsackie, switching institutions with Superintendent Theodore Reid. Ternullo was well known to the veteran staff of Coxsackie, and his appointment immediately raised concerns among ranks of the correctional officers. As much as anyone, Ternullo was identified with the educational reform regime. He had begun his career at Coxsackie as a teacher in 1950, briefly moved to the Albany office, and then returned to Coxsackie in 1956 as a guidance supervisor and then director of education. In 1960, Ternullo returned to Albany, where he rose through the ranks to head of the Division of Education in 1969—the same post previously occupied by Glenn Kendall and Price Chenault, and the post at the very heart of the reform network in New York. When the division ceased to exist after the 1971 reorganization, Ternullo took on a series of warden and superintendent positions.[53]

Ternullo was, by most accounts, a hard-working, serious prison administrator, who tried his best to sustain a reformist orientation at Coxsackie, despite many obstacles. Elizabeth Gaynes of Prisoners Legal Services, a fierce critic of New York's prisons, called Ternullo accessible and fair, someone from whom she "got honest, immediate answers, thorough investigations, undivided attention, and kept promises." Like the reform figures who had built Coxsackie, Ternullo believed that prisoners had real capacity for growth and development— and that communication and humane treatment were essential parts of that process. He gave full support to the institution's educational and vocational offerings. Ternullo further determined to supplement underdeveloped prison programs by encouraging volunteer services at Coxsackie.[54]

From the correctional officers' point of view, one of Ternullo's most objectionable decisions was to cultivate the Inmate Liaison Committee (ILC). In the wake of the Attica uprising, ILCs had been organized at institutions as a way of managing inmate grievances and communicating with the administration. Each institution, of course, would end up determining whether the ILC would be a fully functioning part of prison operations or a dead letter. Ternullo gave the ILC its own office and granted them the privilege of direct phone communication with the superintendent's office. As one supervising officer pointed out, "My COs don't have that privilege."[55] Although the ILC claimed to be functioning effectively, stopping fights and serving a peacekeeping function, officers saw prisoners being given a wholly inappropriate opportunity to challenge institutional policies and practices—precisely the sort of dispute that had brought down Thomas Mott Osborne and the Mutual Welfare League over six decades earlier.

Within days of Ternullo's arrival, a second critical event set the tone for the year to come. On January 19, two prisoners apparently attacked an officer, Jose

Colon. What happened next became the subject of intense and bitter dispute for months to come. Most accounts describe one of the inmates being taken to solitary and beaten by a large group of officers. Prison authorities, including at least one representative from the central offices in Albany, happened to discover the beating in progress. Attorney Lewis Oliver claimed that the prisoner's hands were strapped together, his pants down, and his shirt being ripped off while other officers kicked and beat him. One lieutenant, George Frees, was heard to yell, "Shove the motherfucker in the corner, if he moves, kill him."[56]

In the aftermath of the beating, the department chose to bring charges only against Frees. Frees was not disciplined but was required to admit having "acted in a manner not normally expected of a supervisor." From the prisoners' perspective, this amounted to nothing more than a slap on the wrist—the beatings at Coxsackie had been, ever so briefly, exposed to the central administration and then largely ignored. When Frees was appointed, in June, as chairman of the Adjustment Committee (responsible for disciplining inmates), it marked "the end of respect for the prison discipline process by the prisoners." Inmate Lewis Oliver claimed, "Every prisoner who comes before the committee knows that Frees is morally corrupt and not worthy of respect."[57]

From the officers' perspective, the reaction to Frees was equally incomprehensible. The inmate being beaten had, after all, just been accused of attacking a correctional officer. Superintendent Ternullo had reportedly refused to speak with Frees afterward, or allow him into his office, and almost certainly supported charges being brought in Albany. Frees's tires were slashed in the employee parking lot. A group of officers' wives charged that all the staff involved in the beating were "hounded, harassed, and threatened with being brought up on charges."[58] The conflict between Frees and Ternullo took on aspects of an open power struggle between two longstanding elements of the reformatory—the educational and rehabilitative structure and the discipline-oriented guard force.

Just five days after the Frees incident, on January 24, Council 82 began negotiations with New York over a new contract for correctional officers. The negotiations kicked off "with an exchange of demands submitted by both sides" and continued on through February and March.[59] During the negotiations, reports of attacks by prisoners on correctional officers surged, and the correctional officers took their case to the media. Coxsackie officers demanded a shakedown search of the entire institution, threatening to take "appropriate action" if Ternullo did not respond. Union local president William Tobin charged that officers were "confronted with knives, razor blades and homemade blud-

geons, while the system does nothing to protect us."[60] Tobin told another reporter that the conditions at Coxsackie were "the worst it has been in 12 years."[61]

Department of Corrections spokeswoman Ruby Ryles complained to the
press that "every possible incident, including those so minor that they wouldn't
have been reported in the past," was being reported as negotiations continued
for a new guards contract with the state, a charge categorically denied by Council 82 field representative Robert Walker. Council 82 policy chairman Robert
Maloney did, however, request that all local officers "send to me any material
they may have or are able to obtain in regards to the above items including number of officers hurt, amount of time lost, number of inmates involved in assaults."[62] Certainly the inmates felt that the contract negotiations were a high
point of tension with the officers, and that guards looking for "good press and
pressure for their negotiations" were either initiating or blowing up incidents
with prisoners.[63]

As negotiations wore on, Council 82 locals began to threaten a strike if collective bargaining reached an impasse. Union locals at the former reformatories
were among the most militant and helped precipitate a major crisis in April.
Negotiations over a new contract had been brought to a conclusion and approved
18 to 5 by the union negotiating committee when three Council 82 locals sought
a court injunction against the agreement. Although union leadership managed
to thwart the tactic at the last minute, Council 82 entered a period of instability,
during which time more conservative elements clearly gained an upper hand;
Executive Director Gray resigned before the end of the year.[64]

The conflict at Coxsackie spilled over into state politics. Following a mess
hall riot in March, in which four correctional officers were injured, state assemblyman Clarence D. Lane called for an investigation of conditions at the prison,
citing public "outrage" over "privileged treatment" given inmates.[65] Lane's
charges prompted Commissioner Ward to concede that the public was "right-
fully outraged over the privileged treatment presently extended to hardened
criminals at our state corrections facilities."[66] Lane pushed state senator Ralph
Marino to hold hearings on Coxsackie, supported by seven other Republican
assemblymen. Critics called the hearings a "political charade" and an attempt
by Republican politicians to embarrass a Democratic administration.

Into the middle of this tumultuous year, the Department of Corrections
dropped a bomb on Coxsackie with its preliminary budget proposal for the
coming fiscal year. In the budget, Commissioner Ward proposed significant
cutbacks to prison programming, most notably ending the practice of all-day
programming, which had been the norm at Coxsackie since 1935. In a June 16

memorandum, Ward stated, "It is my firm intention to reduce the cost of Corrections," and "any program that calls for a full day of academic or vocational schooling with industrial or maintenance work is to be recommended for elimination." Industrial production, on the other hand, "should be expanded" throughout the system.[67] Deputy Commissioner Mark Corrigan called for a "moratorium on the seemingly endless consideration of correctional rehabilitation," noting, "all we have discovered about rehabilitation is that we are not doing it." New York prisons, Corrigan argued, must undertake a "shift away from the issue of rehabilitation."[68]

For the former reformatories, the focus on cost reduction and prison industries threatened to finally dissolve what remained of the distinction between their institutions and big house prisons like Auburn or Clinton (where Ward's proposal would have little or no impact). Prisoners were "well acquainted with the evils of economic exploitation and the coercion of their labor for minimal reward," observed one critical response, meaning the proposal would not be "well received by those whose consent is necessary for its implementation."[69] Leon Van Dyke, an educator, prominent Albany civil rights figure, and employee of the Department of Correctional Services, attacked the proposal as a justification for a custodial model of correction, "under the guise of saving money." Van Dyke doubtless spoke words that program staff in Coxsackie would have seconded when he concluded, "Within the DOCS there are sensitive, intelligent persons (working as guards and counselors, administrators and secretaries) who agonize over the present situation. But they will remain silent and frustrated as long as they feel that no one cares, or that they may lose their job for being honest. These people are as brutalized by the system as the inmates."[70]

These were the feelings that led to the December radio announcement at Coxsackie, announcing the end of full-day programming in strongly negative terms and setting off the hostage-taking incident the following day (see introduction).[71] The end of the hostage episode marked the definitive point at which the institution finally turned away from whatever liberal ambitions had once animated Coxsackie; however lightly these ambitions had touched the lives of some prisoners, it had nonetheless been a struggle to extinguish them. The state sent in an "executive team" to restore order to the prison, removed Ternullo as superintendent and several of his close aides as well.[72] His departure was universally mourned among prisoners' rights organizations; Elizabeth Gaynes declared his removal to have been a "victory for those who believe that the corrections officers should be able to hold life or death grips on the policies, programs, and administration of a prison." She concluded, "By the removal of

Mr. Ternullo," the department "has rewarded the Coxsackie officers for their insubordination, violence and racism." Ternullo had not been lenient, one prisoner observed; he had merely been a human being: "There doesn't seem to be any place for human beings in the Department of Corrections."[73]

Behind prison walls, the dismantling proceeded apace. "Guards have the power now," inmates reported, and the officers reminded prisoners that "Ternullo ain't here no more." The prison was locked down for three days, while more security staff was added, new regulations imposed, and troublesome inmates transferred out of the institution. The old Inmate Liaison Committee was disbanded, its prized office taken away, and some of its members transferred out of the institution. Over the protests of some program staff, volunteer programs were either scaled back or eliminated.[74] New security measures included an end to freedom of movement around the institution, with escort squads now required to march prisoners in double-file lines from one area to another; a new alarm system; and a block-housing system that allowed for more inmates to be forcibly or voluntarily confined to cells.[75] Frees's Adjustment Committee, which in December had adjudicated 273 cases and handed down 116 days' worth of solitary confinement, handled 743 cases in January and imposed 528 days of solitary.[76]

Senator Marino and the Crime and Correction Committee scheduled public hearings on Coxsackie for mid-February 1978 and made certain that they would serve as a strong endorsement of a get-tough approach to prisoners and prison administration. At the hearings, the committee subjected Commissioner Ward to some extremely harsh questioning; this despite Ward's continued eagerness to criticize Ternullo and liberal corrections. "All of us instinctively know," Ward testified, that prisoners were confined for the purposes of punishment, and not to be rehabilitated. Once again, he called for abandoning "the fiction of rehabilitation," on the grounds that it "will stop inmates from being outraged when we tell them we're rehabilitating them but really only discipline." He criticized Coxsackie for attempting to be "some kind of reform school spin-off" instead of providing stricter security and supervision, placing blame squarely on the remnants of the old reform system, rather than on custodial staff.[77] Employing convoluted logic, Ward claimed that the real source of anger among Coxsackie inmates was not racism, brutality, harsh discipline, or regimentation—but the hypocrisy of a system that claimed to be helping inmates. This revolt against hypocrisy, he claimed, was "the same thing youth experienced in the Columbia University riots or the Vietnam protests."[78]

Most other participants at the hearing issued more straightforward calls for cracking down on resistant prisoners and soft administration. Senator Marino, reviewing Ternullo's rules for negotiating with prisoners who did not want to leave their cells, opined: "If I tell an inmate to get the hell out of a cell he ought to go get out of a cell, and if not get a couple of guards to take him out." Assemblyman Clarence Lane condemned the Ternullo approach to running Coxsackie, observing, "Your philosophy and policy are powder puffs. When the facility deteriorates to the point where people are afraid to go to work in the morning, it is a bad situation."[79]

The real stars of the Marino hearings were the officers' wives. Not long before the hearings, roughly forty women whose husbands worked in prisons (mostly at Coxsackie) gathered at St. Patrick's Elementary School in Catskill to form a new organization, the Coxsackie-Hudson Women for Correction Reform. Assemblyman Lane and Council 82 local head Valentine Kriel were also in attendance. Lane happily reported that the new Coxsackie superintendent was "hard nosed and stiff armed" and that Coxsackie was "on the road to recovery." Despite Lane's assurance, the women were primarily concerned about preparing for the hearings; their two primary goals were the removal of Ward and the restoration of the death penalty in New York State.[80]

As members of the Coxsackie-Hudson Women for Correction Reform picketed outside the Legislative Office Building in Albany, their representatives entered Hearing Room A to deliver the most forceful attacks of the entire proceedings. Everything that officers were unable to say, their spouses delivered directly to the state senators. "The Department," they testified, "has taken all the respect and controls from the Correction Officer whether he's experienced or 'New Jack' . . . A carpenter can't build a house without a hammer," they argued, "and a Correction Officer can't run a division without disciplinary controls." They mocked the pretense of inmate programs, questioning "what inmate picnics, inmate parties, free busing for inmate visitors, free housing for inmate conjugal visits, free box lunches for inmate visitors, free postage and social security checks for inmates have to do with rehabilitation . . . If their families couldn't help these inmates for the 16, 18, 25, 35 or even 50 years they already spent with them, what good is a monthly visit."[81] Commissioner Ward received the same unsparing treatment. Noting that Coxsackie's farm, "once a show place," had "deteriorated into a neglected eye-sore," the officers' wives mocked Ward's observation that city boys shouldn't have to work on the farm since it has no relevance to city life: "Perhaps they should practice muggings and rapings— which is what, in fact, they do since the officers are prevented from and forbidden to do their jobs."[82] This was the officers' viewpoint, raw and unfiltered, and it dominated the proceedings.

Back at Coxsackie, inmates were reportedly feeling "lousy, depressed, and scared." Inmate Terry Stanford declared the "peace" at the prison to be a façade: "You scare people enough and you get control over them. They've got control right now. But that's all it is, control. There's no respect. There's tension and fear. It works now because the fear is new. Eventually you're not afraid. And then you'll fight. It can happen here again."[83] And, in one sense, Stanford was right—Coxsackie would and does remain a troubled and dangerous institution.

In less than a decade after Glenn Kendall's retirement, the New York State Vocational Institution and the other reformatories had been erased from the correctional landscape. The structures were still there, of course, but none of them was ever again anything but a small part of a rapidly growing prison system for adult male offenders. As the Coxsackie Correctional Facility became, first, a medium-security prison and later a maximum-security facility, visitors could read the inscription "New York State Vocational Institution" above the front entrance without any idea of what that might have meant. The continuity of the physical structure should not be mistaken for political continuity. Though prison programs would (and do) continue at Coxsackie, the politics of punishment—both inside and outside the walls—were resolved decisively in favor of custodial interests. Liberal ambitions had given birth to the reformatory, and reform-minded staff had battled for decades to realize those ambitions behind bars. The failures of liberalism behind bars were more notable than were its successes, but the ultimate defeat of reform mattered as well. The new dominance of prison administrative regimes centered on security and custody helped pave the way for the era of mass incarceration.

The Ghost of Prisons Future

In 1986, Robert A. Mathias, director of the Budget Education Project for the Correctional Association of New York, prepared a detailed report on the future of prison populations in New York State. In the report, entitled "The Road Not Taken: Cost-Effective Alternatives to Prison for Non-Violent Felony Offenders in New York State," Mathias attempted to paint a dark picture of where the state might be headed if decisive actions to reduce the use of imprisonment were not taken. This was no abstract concern; correctional policy debates in the years since Coxsackie's turbulent 1977 had been increasingly consumed by the scale of imprisonment question.

In 1980, Governor Hugh Carey, faced with rising inmate numbers and over-crowded institutions, proposed a prison-building campaign of $275 million, to add four thousand new beds by 1984.[1] By 1981, this had morphed into a massive $500 million prison bond initiative, placed before New York State voters in November. The bond money was to support, among other things, the construction of brand-new facilities alongside Wallkill, Woodbourne, and Coxsackie. The prison bond fight was a lengthy and bitter contest between the advocates of new construction (including the state's correctional officers) and a broad coalition of reform groups opposed.[2] Groups like the Correctional Association of New York protested, "New York State can no longer afford the human and dollar costs that accompany a policy of continued expansion of imprisonment as the primary tactic in the battle against serious crime" while New York City mayor Ed Koch argued, "When someone who's convicted of a vicious crime is in jail for that period of time, he or she is not committing a crime."[3] In the end, the bond issue went down to a razor-thin defeat at the polls—only to have the state respond by finding other sources of new construction funds and begin an unprecedented prison-building boom.

So Mathias had reason to be concerned, in 1986, about where prison populations in New York were headed. He warned readers that the state had taken the
path through the criminal justice system and turned it into "a costly superhigh-
way crowded with travelers bound for one destination—prison." Mathias observed the state's "frantic struggle" to house all these prisoners and asked readers
to conjure up a nightmare vision of New York's penal future. Citing a recent report suggesting that the state might be housing as many as 46,000 inmates by
1992, Mathias warned, "While we are haunted by the costs of prisons past and
present, the specter of prisons yet to come may prove even more frightening . . .
Like the terrifying vision presented to Scrooge by the ghost of Christmas future,"
he concluded, "the scenario we have sketched [of 46,000 prisoners by 1992] is not
inevitable."[4] Mathias's vision of prisons to come may have been terrifying—but it
dramatically *underestimated* the future growth of prison populations in New York.
By 1992, New York State had more than 61,000 prisoners held in state facilities,
and by the end of the century, that figure had topped 72,000.

Given the enormity of mass incarceration in New York State and elsewhere,
it is hardly surprising that the terms of public discussion shifted heavily in the
direction of scale and scope, and away from prison programs and conditions of
confinement. A wave of important social scientific work described the outlines
of this hugely important social trend, attempted to sort out its causes, and
considered its implications for various communities. Indeed, scholars made the
case that mass imprisonment was a social policy moment whose power and
significance rivaled that of anything else in twentieth-century American experience.[5] It was no surprise, then, that historians would come eventually, though
belatedly, to the mass incarceration moment.[6]

But with the focus so squarely on the post-seventies penal system, it seems
reasonable to ask whether the so-called liberal era in prison history holds any
relevance for studies of contemporary corrections. The historical experience of
New York's reformatories reveals some essential lessons for students of prison
history generally and for anyone interested in the organization and administration of penal systems.

The Origins of Mass Incarceration

New York's reformatory experience makes it abundantly clear that the roots of
mass incarceration, and the corresponding crisis of prison liberalism, are substantially deeper than is commonly understood. At the rhetorical level, the con-
cepts bundled together by the phrase "law and order" were not simply conjured
up in the sixties by opportunistic politicians, but were deeply embedded in

prison politics. Denigrations of prisoner worth, a disregard for citizenship and community integration, and an emphasis on retributive sanctioning—these were hallmarks of New York's prison politics in the twenties, and they never really went away. Coxsackie was built to keep these impulses at bay, but get-tough politics entered the reformatory on the day it opened, carried up Highway 9W by the custodial staff making the trip from the old House of Refuge. Countervailing liberal politics could be found as well, in the Division of Education, the Central Guard School, and the program staff, but these interests were never completely dominant behind bars.

Even at the level of state politics and policy, it is hard to see liberalism dominant after World War II. To be sure, reformers dictated much of correctional policy during the Roosevelt and Lehman governorships, but they reached their high-water mark of influence before the end of World War II. In the years that followed, drift and indifference were more common than active resistance to prison liberalism, but the fears of youth crime in postwar New York effectively halted further expansion of reformist correctional policy. The twin challenges of gang violence and heroin in the immediate postwar period were accompanied by a decided shift toward tougher and more control-oriented prison policy; if the scale of these challenges was not enough to provoke mass incarceration, the political impulses were already crystal clear.

The creation of the Great Meadow end-of-the-line reformatory in 1953 is perhaps the most obvious transition point between the ambitions of the New Deal–era reformers and the racially charged fears of youth crime that spurred policy in the postwar period. New York abandoned the faith that reform could fit every young offender and embraced instead a strategy of isolating and segregating those who could not be governed in the community or at Coxsackie. Great Meadow looks strikingly like today's "warehouse" prisons as described by Loic Wacquant: "race-divided and violence-ridden . . . geared solely to neutralizing social rejects by sequestering them physically from society."[7] Coxsackie's uneducable and ungovernable youth are a useful reminder that prison systems are part of a larger political process, and that progressive rules and rhetoric can give way quickly when confronted with subjects perceived to function outside the limits of social citizenship—precisely the observation made so often by scholars of postindustrial mass incarceration in the United States and of colonial penal regimes globally.[8]

The Failures of Prison Liberalism

It is not enough to understand the era of mass incarceration as a triumph of conservative politics, for it was also built on the deep limitations of the liberal prison. These are limitations with which we must reckon, even though (perhaps because) much remains in the worldview of progressive prison reformers that seems attractive and even radical by contemporary standards. Anthropologist Lorna Rhodes has perceptively observed: "Failures of imagination . . . may be failures to see how many imaginations are at play."[9] If so, then the greatest failure of New York's reformers was an inability to fully confront the power of race and racism in the lives of their prisoners, or in the day-to-day operations of the reformatories they constructed. One searches in vain for extended discussions of race in the work of Austin MacCormick or his contemporaries, save for their investigations of southern penal systems. Blindness to issues of race ultimately rendered institutions like Coxsackie incapable of responding appropriately, or even humanely, to the young men they housed.

A related blind spot for New York's liberal reformers was their desperate need to preserve their programs by removing subjects who could not benefit from, or who threatened, their efforts. It is worth noting that the state committee that recommended the creation of the Great Meadow option included many stalwarts of reform within the Department of Corrections. The history of reform seems clear—every Coxsackie begat a Great Meadow, a Napanoch, or a Woodbourne, where threatening young men were shunted off to be warehoused, or worse. If young men of color being confined for drug offenses, swept up in a seamless web of community-level surveillance that took them from home to school to prison, sounds familiar today, it should be remembered that this is also the story of the postwar liberal reformatory. Khalil Gibran Muhammad has persuasively argued, "Racial liberalism foundered on the shoals of black criminality," and it is not hard to see this at play in the New York experience.[10] Long before Attica or Rockefeller drug laws, a basic framework for mass incarceration took shape on the streets of New York City, in Albany, and behind the walls of reformatories like Coxsackie. The prisoners of D yard at Attica were veterans of that system, and their frustration and rage was partly rooted in the experiences of the teenage years, when many first learned what racism really meant.

Coxsackie had such a hard time adapting to the changing racial composition of the prison population partly because the liberal prison reformers had a hard time adapting to anything at all. Time and again, the reform regime in New York refused to deal with external changes, instead assuming a rigid and unproductive stance. Coxsackie was built for the young men of the Depression era, designed to feed prisoners back into their communities as skilled tradesmen, or at least prepare them for industrial employment upon release. But, for many of the reformatories' graduates, postwar urban economies mocked the ambitions of industrial employment, and local communities increasingly lacked the work opportunities for which young men had been trained. As numerous scholars have shown, the failures of prison liberalism went hand in hand with postwar urban crisis and industrial decline. Given opportunities to rethink reform and to adapt to changing conditions, New York's reformers instead clung to the New Deal–era system they had constructed, leaving real change to be eventually realized by their opponents.

Recovering a Lost Vision

Given the failures of liberal reform, it may seem incongruous to suggest that we also try to recover something of the breadth and scope of the progressive ambition for prison reform, but this study suggests that there is much to be gained from a reappraisal. To begin with, the reform visions Ben Shahn tried to capture in his Rikers Island mural are much broader than we commonly understand. One of the unfortunate legacies of the Martinson-era debates over rehabilitation is a continued fixation on "objective" measures of success, especially recidivism rates. Defenders of rehabilitative programs have chosen, for more than three decades now, to keep fighting Martinson on his own turf—that prison programs can only be justified by objective measures of policy impact. Where reform interests have been successful with this approach, it has succeeded in helping to claw back much-needed room for prison programs. But a fixation on "evidence-based" corrections continues to sideline any other elements of the older, progressive, New Deal–era vision, particularly ones that cannot be quantified: humanity, compassion, communication, and more.[11]

Progressives were less interested in the "what works?" question that Martinson brought to the forefront. They argued, instead, for the inherent virtue in offering educational opportunity, even when it did not result in immediate, measurable effects. It is no surprise, perhaps, that educational programming declined most precipitously in the era of mass incarceration. Conservative critics attacked prison education, not for the failures to prevent recidivism, but for the undeserved benefits educational programs accorded to prison inmates.[12]

In fact, it is worth remembering that terms like rehabilitation scarcely mattered in the Osborne-MacCormick universe; if there was something like a rehabilitative concept, it amounted, more or less, to providing prisoners the resources they needed to fully realize their potential and to accept the community membership being offered to them. As simple as it sounds, Osborne and Mac-Cormick wanted to explore the obstacles to doing well, not only so that prisons could help, but also so that the ways in which prisons and the criminal justice system actively hindered could be understood and altered. As both men often observed, precious little separated the prisoner from the free citizen. Given the same opportunities for the realization of a satisfying means of living, and freed from needless restraint, the criminal offender would make his own way in the world.[13]

Voices Behind Bars

Prison politics tell us a great deal about the larger social contexts in which they are produced—but they are also shaped by, and lived by, real people. This study represents a modest effort toward bringing those who live and work behind bars back into the historical conversation. This includes the reform-minded administrators, teachers, and vocational instructors who attempted to realize the ambitions of Coxsackie. It also includes, to an extent, the reformatory guards and officers. I have, in other work, delved more closely into the work lives of correctional officers, and there is almost certainly more to be said about the men who worked at Coxsackie.[14] Most of all, this work acknowledges the voices of those kept in confinement. One of the great constants of imprisonment is the struggle to be heard. At times, rioting and violence become the only instrument loud enough to register beyond the prison walls, and even then only dimly understood.

Internal prison politics at Coxsackie, and elsewhere, were profoundly shaped by the clash of interests among inmates, among prison staff, and between inmates and staff. Like all politics, these never had a static quality but were instead a fluid and dynamic process at work. And, of course, internal prison politics was never separable from external politics. Prisoners brought with them their own understanding of race, manhood, and the legitimacy of the criminal justice system; officers brought much of the same with them—and everyone strove to make connections with political interests on the outside as a way of advancing their own interests and position behind bars.

The young men who lived through Coxsackie were all changed, in some way, by that moment in life. Very few of them ever recorded their feelings about the reformatory. Most, being still very young after their release, moved on to new stages of life where a reformatory experience was either irrelevant or embarrassing and certainly not the stuff of public reflection. But their experiences deserve to be heard, if for no other reason than that we must acknowledge what we have done, and continue to do, in the name of punishment and correction.

Abbreviations

AMC	Austin MacCormick Collection
CCF	Coxsackie Case Files
CCJR	New York State Coalition for Criminal Justice Records
CCP	Carnegie Corporation Papers
FDR	Franklin D. Roosevelt Papers as Governor of New York
HLP	Herbert H. Lehman Papers
HMP	Howard F. Miller Papers
JRDP	John R. Dunne Papers
LHP	Louis Howe Papers
OFP	Osborne Family Papers
SBP	Sanford Bates Papers

Preface

1. Mike Stobbe, "Ugly Past of U.S. Human Experiments Uncovered," *Associated Press*, 27 Feb. 2011; Irving Gordon, Hollis S. Ingraham, and Robert F. Korns, "Transmission of Epidemic Gastroenteritis to Human Volunteers By Oral Administration of Fecal Filtrates," *Journal of Experimental Medicine* 86 (1947): 409–22. For a provocative historical study focusing on medical experimentation behind bars, see Allen M. Hornblum, *Acres of Skin: Human Experiments at Holmesburg Prison* (London: Routledge, 1999).

Introduction · The Ashes of Reform

1. "Prison Kidnapers Hope Effort Yields Changes," *Plattsburgh Press-Republican*, 6 Dec. 1977, 7.

2. In 1975, corrections commissioner Benjamin Ward fired a prison teacher at Eastern for being a Grand Dragon of the New York State Klan and ordered others to quit the Klan or leave their jobs. There is ample evidence for Klan activity at Eastern. See Juanita Diaz-Cotto, *Gender, Ethnicity, and the State: Latina and Latino Prison Politics* (Albany: SUNY Press, 1996), notes on 123–24. Not long before the hostage incident, Eastern inmates had formed the John Brown Anti-Klan Committee and released a press packet naming thirty-five officers as Klan members or sympathizers. Persistent stories arose of officers engaged in "night riding" at Eastern, wearing white sheets and hoods late at night

as a means of intimidation. See Tom Wicker, "Catch-22 Behind Bars," *Times-News*, 1 June 1979, 2.

3. "Prison Kidnapers Hope," 7.

4. Frederic U. Dicker, "Ward Answers His Critics on Coxsackie Security," *Albany Times-Union*, 11 Jan. 1978, n. p.

5. Annabar Jensis, "Legislators Grill Ward at Committee Hearings," *Greene County News*, 16 Feb. 1978, 1.

6. Ted Conover, *Newjack: Guarding Sing Sing* (New York: Vintage Books, 2001).

7. Tracy Huling (producer), *Yes, in My Backyard* (Galloping Girls Productions and WSKG Public Broadcasting in association with the Independent Television Service and Eastern Educational Network, 1998). Tracy Huling, "Building a Prison Economy in Rural America," in *Invisible Punishment: The Collateral Consequences of Mass Imprisonment*, ed. Marc Mauer and Meda Chesney-Lind (New York: New Press, 2002).

8. Unlike Coxsackie, the House of Refuge has been well chronicled. See Robert S. Pickett, *House of Refuge: Origins of Juvenile Reform in New York State, 1815–1857* (New York: Syracuse University Press, 1969).

9. Gustave de Beaumont and Alexis de Tocqueville, *On the Penitentiary System in the United States* (Philadelphia: Carey, Lea & Blanchard, 1833).

10. Alexander W. Pisciotta, "Treatment on Trial: The Rhetoric and Reality of the New York House of Refuge, 1857–1935," *American Journal of Legal History* 29 (1985); Alexander W. Pisciotta, "The Theory and Practice of the New York House of Refuge, 1857–1935" (Ph.D. diss., Florida State University, 1979).

11. Society for the Reformation of Juvenile Delinquents, *One Hundred and First Annual Report of the House of Refuge* (New York: House of Refuge Printing Class, 1925).

12. Steven Schlossman and Alexander Pisciotta, "Identifying and Treating Serious Juvenile Offenders: The View From California and New York in the 1920s," in *Intervention Strategies for Chronic Juvenile Offenders: Some New Perspectives*, ed. Peter Greenwood (New York: Greenwood Press, 1986), 34.

13. See Society for the Reformation of Juvenile Delinquents, *One Hundred and Seventh Annual Report* (New York: House of Refuge Printing Class, 1932); Schlossman and Pisciotta, "Identifying and Treating Serious Juvenile Offenders," offer an interesting comparative perspective. Only 7% of new commitments at the Whittier State School in California were 16 or 17 years of age; well over half (56%) of all new commitments to the House of Refuge were in that age group.

14. Harry M. Shulman, *From Truancy to Crime—A Study of 251 Adolescents: A Report of the Sub-Commission on Causes and Effects of Crime* (Albany: J. B. Lyon Company, 1928).

15. Frank Tannenbaum, *Crime and the Community* (Boston: Ginn and Company, 1938), 74–75.

16. Howard Mingos, "East River Islands Viewed As Possible Parks," *New York Times*, 15 June 1924, xx–3.

17. "Wants City Islands Made Playgrounds," *New York Times*, 25 Sept. 1926, 16. The park idea was revived by Parks Commissioner Moses, who announced in 1934 his intention to convert Randall's Island into a public park and to demolish the old House of Refuge complex. "Huge Island Park Planned For City," *New York Times*, 15 May 1934, 23.

18. "Tri-Borough Bridge to Cost $24,625,000," *New York Times*, 25 March 1927, 23.

19. "Asks State to Drop House of Refuge," *New York Times*, 19 Nov. 1928, 21. The author of the report was state budget director Joseph H. Wilson. The next month, the Prison Association of New York authored a resolution urging the closure of the House of Refuge.

20. Randall's Island today generally reflects Moses's plan, or at least some aspects of it. The Triborough Bridge complex has its critical hub on the island, which is also home to many public parks. On the site of the House of Refuge, or at least very nearby, was Downing Stadium, a track and field stadium opened in 1936 in time for the Olympic trials.

21. Funds for Warwick's construction were designated from the annual public improvement bond issue for 1930. See "Metropolitan Area To Get $35,000,000," *New York Times*, 16 Jan. 1930, 17; on the Coxsackie site, see "Roosevelt Approves Site For Reformatory," *New York Times*, 16 July 1932, 2.

22. "45 Boys Break Jail in Uprising," *New York Times*, 2 Sept. 1934, 1.

23. "Inquiry Begun In Riot At Randall's Island," *New York Times*, 4 Sept. 1934. One member of the House of Refuge board blamed the disciplinary environment and urged the Commission of Correction not to import the old disciplinary staff to the new institution. The transcript of Helbing's interview is in Philip Klein and Leonard W. Mayo, *Recommendations for the Administration of the New York State Vocational Institution* (22 March 1935), box 1, series 1, Leonard Mayo Papers, Social Welfare History Archives, University of Minnesota Libraries.

24. For a comprehensive text written from this perspective, see Blake McKelvey's tellingly sub-titled *American Prisons: A History of Good Intentions* (Montclair, N.J.: Patterson Smith, 1977).

25. David J. Rothman, *Conscience and Convenience: The Asylum and Its Alternatives in Progressive America*, revised ed. (New York: Aldine de Gruyter, 2002); David J. Rothman and Sheila M. Rothman, *The Willowbrook Wars: Bringing the Mentally Disabled into the Community*, revised ed. (New Brunswick, N.J.: Transaction Publishers, 2005).

26. Erving Goffman, *Asylums: Essays on the Social Situation of Mental Patients and Other Inmates* (Garden City, N.Y.: Anchor Books, 1961). Reviewers failed to connect *Conscience and Convenience* with its most obvious intellectual inspiration, in part because (oddly) Goffman's work is never mentioned in the original edition of *Conscience and Convenience*. But the connections between the two are considerable. Both served on the Committee for the Study of Incarceration, and a number of Rothman's earlier publications had explicitly credited the influence of Goffman's concept of the total institution, embracing the functionalist position that all such institutions, regardless of apparent differences in mission or program, were possessed of the same internal structure and dynamic. Rothman observed that Goffman made a convincing case that brutalization and humiliation were "inherent in institutions, which by their nature are infantilizing or corrupting." David J. Rothman, "Of Prisons, Asylums, and Other Decaying Institutions," *Public Interest* 26 (1972): 13. Through this extension of Goffman's work, Rothman sought to demonstrate "the inherent and unalterable defects of reform through incarceration." David J. Rothman, "Prisons: The Failure Model," *Nation*, 21 Dec. 1974, 657.

27. Andrew Scull, "The Lives of the Cell," *Nation*, 14 June 1980, 795.

28. For a comprehensive treatment more recent than Rothman's, see Andrew J. Polsky, *The Rise of the Therapeutic State* (Princeton, N.J.: Princeton University Press, 1993).

29. Of these threads, the question of decency and compassion is largely forgotten today, in part because reform efforts so often ended up producing conditions (such as they did at Coxsackie) that were far from decent or compassionate. Still, progressive sensibilities squared up against the rhetoric of harshness and toughness that would deny citizenship to criminal offenders. Michael Tonry, "Unthought Thoughts: The Influence of Changing Sensibilities on Penal Policies," *Punishment & Society* 3 (Jan. 2001): 167–81, offers one of the few extended reconsiderations of this thread. See also, Michael Tonry, *Thinking about Crime: Sense and Sensibility in American Penal Culture* (New York: Oxford University Press, 2004).

30. This approximates David Garland's concept of "penal-welfarism," first explored in *Punishment and Welfare: A History of Penal Strategies* (Aldershot, Hants, UK; Brookfield, Vt.: Gower, 1985), an account of its development in the early twentieth-century.

31. Recent work has begun to draw a clearer picture of the significance of punitive politics during the "liberal" era of crime and punishment. Most notable among recent works is Marie Gottschalk, *The Prison and the Gallows: The Politics of Mass Incarceration in America* (Cambridge; New York: Cambridge University Press, 2006). An extraordinarily rich account of the battle between reformers and punitive interests can be found in Estelle B. Freedman's *Maternal Justice: Miriam Van Waters and the Female Reform Tradition* (Chicago: University of Chicago Press, 1996).

32. Rebecca McLennan has drawn the most complete picture to date of what she calls "penal managerialism," and usefully distinguishes it from punitive traditionalism. McLennan makes the case that it effectively replaced the older, progressive vision of "New Penology." Rebecca McLennan, *The Crisis of Imprisonment: Protest, Politics, and the Making of the American Penal State, 1776–1941* (New York: Cambridge University Press, 2008). I argue that the older vision continued to find active political expression during and well beyond the 1930s.

33. The variability of prison governance within single-state systems is a theme I developed earlier in William R. Wilkinson, John C. Burnham, and Joseph F. Spillane, *Prison Work: A Tale of Thirty Years in the California Department of Corrections* (Columbus: Ohio State University Press, 2005).

34. Peter Zinoman, *The Colonial Bastille: A History of Imprisonment in Vietnam, 1862–1940* (Berkeley: University of California Press, 2001), 16. Zinoman's pioneering study has been joined by a wealth of excellent works on the colonial prison. The best of these include Daniel V. Botsman, *Punishment and Power in the Making of Modern Japan* (Princeton, N.J.: Princeton University Press, 2005), and the essays collected in Florence Bernault, ed., *A History of Prison and Confinement in Africa* (Portsmouth, N.H.: Heinemann, 2003).

35. See, for example, Mary Gibson, "Global Perspectives on the Birth of the Prison," *American Historical Review* 116 (Oct. 2011): 1040–63.

36. Rebecca McLennan, "Punishment's 'Square Deal': Prisoners and Their Keepers in 1920s New York, *Journal of Urban History* 29 (July 2003): 597–619; Rebecca M. McLennan, *The Crisis of Imprisonment: Protest, Politics, and the Making of the American Penal State, 1776–1941* (New York: Cambridge University Press, 2008).

37. McLennan's fruitful focus on labor has echoes in the more recent work of Volker Janssen, "When the 'Jungle' Met the Forest: Public Work, Civil Defense, and Prison Camps in Postwar California," *Journal of American History* 96 (Dec. 2009): 702–26, and

Heather Ann Thompson, "Why Mass Incarceration Matters: Rethinking Crisis, Decline, and Transformation in Postwar American History," *Journal of American History* 97 (Dec. 2010), 703–716. Thompson's work, like McLennan's, is highly attuned to the complex politics of imprisonment, both inside and outside the prison itself. On racism, crime, and punishment beyond the southern experience, the literature has been rapidly growing, though it tends to focus more on scale and organization than on the details of penal governance. Most notable among recent works is Michelle Alexander, *The New Jim Crow: Mass Incarceration in the Age of Colorblindness* (New York: New Press, 2010).

38. Mary Ellen Curtin, "State of the Art: The New Prison History," *Labor: Studies in Working-Class History of the Americas* 8 (fall 2011), 97–111.

39. McLennan, "Punishment's 'Square Deal,'" 599. Steven Schlossman was among the first historians to show the complexities and contradictions of criminal justice operations, and that "social reform is always contested and negotiated, and that, at the least, it is a two way street." Steven L. Schlossman, *Transforming Juvenile Justice: Reform Ideals and Institutional Realities, 1825–1920* (DeKalb: Northern Illinois University Press, 2005), xxv. Along the same lines, Frank Dikötter observed, "Many historians have written about the prison in society, but we also need a history of society in the prison," particularly one that goes beyond a simple dichotomy of resistance and accommodation. Frank Dikötter, "Introduction," in *Cultures of Confinement: A History of the Prison in Africa, Asia, and Latin America* (New York: Cornell University Press, 2007), 11.

40. For another perspective, see David W. Wolcott and Steven L. Schlossman, "In the Voices of Delinquents: Social Science, The Chicago Area Project, and a Children's Culture of Casual Crime and Violence," in *Science in the Service of Children: Perspectives on Education, Parenting, and Child Welfare*, ed. Emily Cahan, Barbara Beatty, and Julia Grant (New York: Teachers College Press, 2006).

41. Ann Chih Lin, *Reform in the Making: The Implementation of Social Policy in Prison* (Princeton, N.J.: Princeton University Press, 2000). Lin makes a powerful case that, "whether specific policies are effective at reintegrating prisoners into society is an important question. But no answer to it can be found if the policies in question are never implemented, do not function as designed, or are changed beyond recognition. Before it is possible to test 'what works?,' one must ensure that the conditions for a fair test exist" (p. 10–11).

42. The Woodbourne quotation echoes words posted at an eighteenth-century Dutch workhouse, recorded by John Howard: "Fear not: I mean not vengeance, but your reformation. Severe is my hand, but benevolent my intention." Quoted in John Howard, *An Account of the Principal Lazarettos in Europe* (London: J. Johnson, D. Dilly, and T. Cadell, 1791), 73.

43. On the question of torture behind bars in a contemporary context, see Anne-Marie Cusac, *Cruel and Unusual: The Culture of Punishment in America* (New Haven, Conn.: Yale University Press, 2009).

Chapter 1 · The Reformer's Mural

1. Arthur Bartlett, Profiles, "The Four-Eyed Kid," *New Yorker*, 26 May 1934, 26. A sample of the national press coverage of the raid can be seen in the Associated Press reporting, such as the front page coverage in "World's Worst Prison," *Dubuque (Iowa) Telegraph*

Herald and Times-Journal, 25 Jan. 25, 1934, 1. MacCormick's raid on the Welfare Island Penitentiary proved to be a remarkably durable story, particularly his role in exposing the influence of politically connected inmates like Joseph Rao. A version of this story was featured in Seymour J. Ettman, "Hell in Mid-Channel," *Headquarters Detective* (Oct. 1940), which itself followed up the Hollywood film version of the story, *Blackwell's Island* (starring John Garfield) in 1939.

2. Rikers was finally completed in 1935. The Welfare Island Penitentiary was torn down a year later.

3. The Maine quote is MacCormick's, from his 1956 Bowdoin Institute Lectures, lecture 2, page 11, Austin MacCormick Collection, Newton Gresham Library, Sam Houston State University (hereafter AMC).

4. See Alejandro Anreus, ed., *Ben Shahn and the Passion of Sacco and Vanzetti* (New Brunswick, N.J.: Rutgers University Press, 2001). The series brought him to the attention of Diego Rivera, who took Shahn on as one of several assistants for his work on the RCA Building at Rockefeller Center.

5. Memorandum to Mayor LaGuardia from Ben Shahn and Lou Block, in Deborah Martin Kao, Laura Katzman, and Jenna Webster, *Ben Shahn's New York: The Photography of Modern Times* (Cambridge, Mass.: Fogg Art Museum, 2000). See also, Howard Greenfeld, *Ben Shahn: An Artist's Life* (New York: Random House, 1998).

6. For more on Ben Shahn, see Frances Kathryn Pohl, *Ben Shahn* (San Francisco, Calif.: Pomegranate, 1993); Susan Chevlove, *Common Man, Mythic Vision: The Paintings of Ben Shahn* (Princeton, N.J.: Princeton University Press, 1998). A comprehensive and outstanding review of Shahn's New York work, including the Rikers mural, can be found in Kao, Katzman, and Webster, *Ben Shahn's New York*.

7. Lou Block was an important muralist in his own right. Details of his contributions to the Rikers project are to be found in the Lou Block (1895–1969) manuscript collection at University of Louisville Special Collections and Libraries.

8. Clarke A. Chambers offered any early and influential argument for continuity between the progressive moment and the New Deal era in *A Seedtime of Reform: American Social Service and Social Action, 1918–1933* (Minneapolis: University of Minnesota Press, 1963).

9. The most comprehensive study of the George Junior Republic is still Jack M. Holl, *Juvenile Reform in the Progressive Era: William R. George and the Junior Republic Movement* (New York: Cornell University Press, 1971). The George Junior Republic inspired the work of Homer Lane at the Little Commonwealth for 13- to 19-year-old delinquents in Dorset, England. See Judith Stinton, *A Dorset Utopia: The Little Commonwealth and Homer Lane* (Norwich, UK: Black Dog Books, 2005).

10. Donald Lowrie, *My Life in Prison* (New York: Mitchell Kennerley, 1912).

11. Ibid., 3.

12. See Donald Lowrie, *My Life Out of Prison* (New York: Mitchell Kennerley, 1915), 333. Winthrop D. Lane, writing in "Thomas Mott Osborne," *Nation*, 10 Nov. 1926, 478, captured the idea well: "To Mr. Osborne self-government was a means of making prisoners better; it was a therapeutic agent. It was not a concession to imagined rights of prisoners, as some people thought . . . to him self-government was a means of training people in the art of living in concert."

13. The story of Osborne, the Mutual Welfare League, and Sing Sing has been told many times, and it is not my intent to fully recapitulate it here. It was the basis for two admiring books: Rudolph W. Chamberlain, *There is No Truce: A Life of Thomas Mott Osborne* (New York: Ayer Publishing, 1935) and Frank Tannenbaum, *Osborne of Sing Sing* (Chapel Hill: University of North Carolina Press, 1933). More recently, the episode plays an important role in McLennan's *Crisis of Imprisonment*, which is a most thorough account.

14. McLennan, *Crisis of Imprisonment*, 441. Robert Perkinson, in *Texas Tough: The Rise of America's Prison Empire* (New York: Macmillan, 2009), 196, makes essentially the same case, that "penological visionaries in the mold of Davis and Osborne gained little traction in the so-called lawless decade."

15. McLennan, *Crisis of Imprisonment*, 443. McLennan correctly observes that while Osborne's work helped lay the foundation for the managerial prison, such a system of governance was anathema to Osborne himself. One need only observe that Osborne was no fan of Warden Lawes, or vice versa. An entertaining account of Lawes's views on Osborne, one mostly sympathetic to Lawes, is in Ralph Blumenthal, *Miracle at Sing Sing: How One Man Transformed the Lives of America's Most Dangerous Prisoners* (New York: St. Martin's Press, 2004). Interestingly, Shahn and Block interviewed Lawes for their mural project as well, and they shared Osborne and MacCormick's disregard for the self-publicizing Sing Sing warden, calling him "as phony as a twelve-dollar bill." Greenfeld, *Ben Shahn*, 106.

16. Those who worked with Osborne felt that, even in his lifetime, few fully understood the breadth of his work. As MacCormick's collaborator put it, "Let us record our protest against a too narrow view of Mr. Osborne's interest in prisons." The "League Idea" was constantly an issue, but Garrett observed that Osborne was interested in "every other phase of prison activity as anyone must be who has seen the problem both as an inmate and as an administrator." Paul W. Garrett, "Report to the Board of Directors," 1926, folder 1, box 11, AMC.

17. The newest and most insightful reading of Osborne's work is Kevin P. Murphy, *Political Manhood: Red Bloods, Mollycoddles, and the Politics of Progressive Era Reform* (New York: Columbia University Press, 2008).

18. Austin H. MacCormick, "Crime and Delinquency, Prevention and Control," Bowdoin Lecture Series, lecture 2, 8, AMC.

19. Ibid., 8.

20. MacCormick was apparently unaware that Osborne's Auburn self-commitment had not been done anonymously. The inmates at Auburn were largely aware of who Osborne was, which Osborne believed (and MacCormick would later ruefully agree) was a more effective way for getting information about prison conditions.

21. On the relationship between Roosevelt and Osborne, see Kenneth S. Davis, *FDR: The Beckoning* (New York: Putnam, 1971), 277–83.

22. Thomas Mott Osborne to Austin H. MacCormick, 20 Dec. 1916, box 132, Osborne Family Papers, Special Collections Research Center, Syracuse University Library [hereafter OFP].

23. Thomas Mott Osborne to C. W. Carroll, 18 Oct. 1919, box 143, OFP.

24. Frank Tannenbaum, *Wall Shadows: A Study in American Prisons* (New York: Putnam, 1922), 149.

25. Thomas Mott Osborne, *Within Prison Walls* (London; New York: D. Appleton and Company, 1914), 16. It is worth noting that Shahn's photographs of inmates consistently showed them to be merely the "wayward sons and brothers" of society, rather than exaggerating their features. Kao, Katzman, and Webster, *Ben Shahn's New York*.

26. Osborne, *Within Prison Walls*, 10, 296.

27. This notion of self-government as self-discipline remained a potent one in the interwar years. In 1934, Federal Bureau of Prisons chief Sanford Bates praised the Soviet Union's Bolshevo Commune: "A large proportion had no desire to leave the colony. They earn standard wages, work every day, and bring up their families, and are free from restraint. Why should they want to go out? . . . You would not believe it unless you went there that the place could exist without a club or brass button in the outfit. You can say that it was a show place. But I had a hard time getting them to show it to me. There is food for thought in that experiment." Osborne Association, annual report, 1935, 20, AMC. The Bolshevo Commune was one of the largest of the so-called Makarenko colonies. See Thorsten Eriksson, *The Reformers: A Historical Survey of Pioneer Experiments in the Treatment of Criminals* (New York: Elsevier, 1976). MacCormick echoed his mentor in a letter to Osborne, relaying a visit to San Quentin Prison: "The more I see of men in confinement, the more I am committed to self-government as the saving principle." Austin H. MacCormick to Thomas Mott Osborne, April 23, 1919, box 147, OFP.

28. Paul W. Garrett and Austin H. MacCormick, *Handbook of American Prisons and Reformatories, 1929* (New York: National Society of Penal Information, 1929).

29. Austin H. MacCormick, untitled manuscript, n. d., 17a, AMC.

30. See Thomas Mott Osborne to Josephus Daniels, 2 July 1917, OFP.

31. See the reconstructed mural in Kao, Katzman, and Webster, *Ben Shahn's New York*, 230–41.

32. *Ben Shahn* exhibition catalog, Kennedy Galleries, 1969, plate 10.

33. See, for example, Diana L. Linden, "Ben Shahn's New Deal Murals: Jewish Identity in the American Scene," in Chevlove, *Common Man, Mythic Vision*, 37–66.

34. Austin H. MacCormick, *The Education of Adult Prisoners: A Survey and a Program* (New York: National Society of Penal Information, 1931), 11.

35. MacCormick, "Crime and Delinquency, Causation," Bowdoin Lectures, lecture 1, 37, AMC.

36. MacCormick, *The Education of Adult Prisoners*, 33, 404–405.

37. Diane Ravitch, *Left Back: A Century of Battles Over School Reform* (New York: Simon and Schuster, 2001), 81–86.

38. MacCormick, *The Education of Adult Prisoners*. See also Tannenbaum, *Crime and Community*, and John Dewey, *Human Nature and Conduct* (New York: Holt, 1922).

39. John Dewey, *Democracy and Education: An Introduction to the Philosophy of Education* (New York: Macmillan, 1916); Angela Cross-Durant, "John Dewey and Lifelong Education," in *Twentieth Century Thinkers in Adult and Continuing Education*, ed. Peter Jarvis (London: Routledge, 1991).

40. Notable books followed Dewey's *Democracy and Education*, including James Harvey Robinson's *The Mind in the Making* (New York: Harper, 1921), the British Institute of Adult Education's *The Way Out: Essays on the Meaning and Purpose of Adult Education* (London; New York: Oxford University Press, 1923), Eduard Lindeman's *The Meaning of*

Adult Education (New York: New Republic, 1926), and Dorothy Canfield Fisher's *Why Stop Learning?* (New York: Harcourt, Brace, 1927).

41. See Richard J. Altenbaugh, *Education for Struggle: The American Labor Colleges of the 1920s and 1930s* (Philadelphia: Temple University Press, 1990).

42. For further discussion of Smith and the Bryn Mawr School, see Joyce L. Kornbluh, *A New Deal for Workers' Education: The Workers' Service Program, 1933–1942* (Urbana: University of Illinois Press, 1987), 16–17.

43. To understand these efforts in a larger context, see Leon Fink, *Progressive Intellectuals and the Dilemmas of Democratic Commitment* (Cambridge, Mass.: Harvard University Press, 1997); his treatment of South Carolina educational reformer Wil Lou Gray offers a generally sympathetic account, though Fink sees a retreat from the more radical social-restructuring goals over the course of the 1920s.

44. Harold W. Stubblefield and Patrick Keane, *Adult Education in the American Experience: From the Colonial Period to the Present* (San Francisco, Calif.: Jossey-Bass, 1994).

45. Within the field of education history, the legacy of Carnegie and the AAAE is vigorously debated. See, for example, Stubblefield and Keane, *Adult Education in the American Experience*, 194. See also E. C. Lagemann, "The Politics of Knowledge: The Carnegie Corporation and the Formulation of Public Policy," *History of Education Quarterly* 27 (summer 1987): 205–220.

46. See, for example, Benjamin C. Gruenberg, *Science and the Public Mind* (New York: McGraw-Hill, 1935); Ira De A. Reid, *Adult Education Among Negroes* (Washington, D.C.: The Associates in Negro Folk Education, 1936); and Benson Y. Landis and John D. Willard, *Rural Adult Education* (New York: Macmillan, 1933). The AAAE also played a role in cultivating the careers of important women in the field of adult education, including Dorothy Canfield Fisher, Mary L. Ely, and Lucy Wilcox Adams.

47. His first, informal, report went to Morse Cartwright in October 1928. See Austin H. MacCormick to Morse A. Cartwright, 2 Oct. 1928, box 2, AMC.

48. MacCormick, *The Education of Adult Prisoners*, 41.

49. Ibid., 44. MacCormick notes that the federal Smith-Hughes Act of 1917, while providing a great deal of financial support for worker education and training, was by statute not available to institutions for delinquent, dependent, or defective youth and adults.

50. Ibid., 21.

51. Ibid., 202.

52. Ibid., 190. For more on the extent to which the Danish folk schools had captured the progressive imagination, see Daniel T. Rodgers, *Atlantic Crossings: Social Politics in a Progressive Age* (Cambridge, Mass.: Harvard University Press, 1998).

53. MacCormick, *The Education of Adult Prisoners*, 49. MacCormick opposed Snedden's argument that vocational training should be narrowly cast. He did support the vocational high school concept, though he argued that it should not be "an inferior grade of education" and should have just as varied a program as any high school. MacCormick, "Crime and Delinquency, Prevention and Control."

54. MacCormick, *The Education of Adult Prisoners*, 12.

55. Alain Locke made the same argument in 1933 about adult education: "The mind of the adult must be met in terms of its living, even if parochial and one-sided interests, and then gradually led out into a broader, wider and even deeper point of view." For

Locke and the question of African American adult education, this meant fully engaging, not ignoring, "racial problems and interests." See Eunice Barnard, "The New Thirst for Adult Education Is Being Discovered by High-Pressure Sales Organizations, Association Head Warns," *New York Times*, 28 May 1933, E7.

56. MacCormick, *The Education of Adult Prisoners*, 4.

57. New York State Prison Survey Committee, *Report of the Prison Survey Committee* (Albany: J. B. Lyon, 1920); New York State Legislative Committee on Prison Industries, *Report of Committee on Industries* (1913).

58. Walter M. Wallack, Glenn M. Kendall, and Howard L. Briggs, *Education within Prison Walls* (New York: Teachers College, Columbia University, 1939), 29–30.

59. MacCormick, *The Education of Adult Prisoners*, 204.

60. Ibid., 215.

61. MacCormick allowed a similar role for religion in rehabilitation: "Religion of the true sincere type that becomes part of one's being and is not a matter of dogma, not a matter of outward conformity [sets] up one of the strongest bulwarks against delinquency and crime or indeed human maladjustment." MacCormick, "Crime and Delinquency, Prevention and Control."

62. *Handbook of American Prisons and Reformatories, 1926* (New York: National Society of Penal Information, 1926), 55.

63. MacCormick, *The Education of Adult Prisoners*, 182.

64. MacCormick placed two conditions on the photographs: first, that Shahn secure permission of inmate subjects before taking their photos and, second, that Shahn not publish the photos themselves.

65. Deborah Martin Kao, "Ben Shahn and the Public Use of Art," in Kao, Katzman, and Webster, *Ben Shahn's New York*, 62.

66. Osborne Association, annual report (1936), 24.

67. David L. Angus and Jeffrey Mirel, *The Failed Promise of the American High School, 1890–1995* (New York: Teachers College Press, 1999), 63.

68. MacCormick, "Crime and Delinquency, Prevention and Control." The gap issue spurred the creation of vocational high schools as a bridge between skilled trades and the departure from school. See a discussion of the vocational guidance movement in Joseph F. Kett, *Rites of Passage: Adolescence in America 1790 to the Present* (New York: Basic Books, 1977). Grace Palladino observes: "The Great Depression had finally pushed teenage youth out of the workplace and into the classroom . . . In the process, adolescents had become an age group and not just a wealthy social class, a shift that helped to create the idea of a separate, teenage generation." Palladino, *Teenagers: An American History* (New York: Basic Books, 1996), 5.

69. Ilma was a strong proponent of encouraging the expansion of CCC forestry camps to include vagrant and delinquent youth. She wrote: "The very nucleus that the nation depends upon for the future must starve or develop into criminality . . . Camps would give them a chance to rebuild themselves, get a mental rest, let their confidence return with their health." Viola Ilma, *And Now, Youth!* (New York: Robert O. Ballou, 1934), 23–24. Ilma's work is a fascinating, earnestly pro-Roosevelt pamphlet. See also MacCormick, "Youth and Crime," Osborne Association, *Report for Year 1936*, 21–22. Ilma later became director of the Young Men's Vocational Foundation, with Eleanor Roosevelt as a board member.

70. MacCormick, "Youth and Crime," 18–29.

71. Max Grunhut, *Penal Reform: A Comparative Study* (Oxford: Clarendon Press, 1948), 228.

72. Austin H. MacCormick, "Existing Provisions for the Correction of Youthful Offenders," *Law and Contemporary Problems* 9 (autumn 1942), 594.

73. Franklin E. Zimring, *The Changing Legal World of Adolescence* (New York: Free Press, 1985).

74. Shulman, *From Truancy to Crime*, 81.

75. MacCormick, "Existing Provisions for the Correction of Youthful Offenders," 591.

76. Ibid.

77. Memorandum from Ben Shahn and Lou Block to Fiorello LaGuardia, in Kao, Katzman, and Webster, *Ben Shahn's New York*. The memo indicated that, over the course of their conversations with Austin MacCormick, Dean George Kirchwey, William B. Cox of the Osborne Association, and Warden Lewis Lawes, "we abandoned the idea of dealing with the history of penology. We felt that the murals would have more force if they treated only with prisons of our own time, both of an unenlightened nature and those which have been administered by individuals who believe in the need for penal reform."

78. See Kao, Katzman, and Webster, *Ben Shahn's New York*.

79. Laura Katzman, "'Mechanical Vision': Photography and Mass Media Appropriation in Ben Shahn's Sacco and Vanzetti Series," in *Ben Shahn and the Passion of Sacco and Vanzetti*, 58.

80. See the mural reconstruction in Kao, Katzman, and Webster, *Ben Shahn's New York*.

81. *Ben Shahn* exhibition catalog, Kennedy Galleries, 1969.

82. Kao, Katzman, and Webster, *Ben Shahn's New York*, 240.

83. Austin H. MacCormick, untitled manuscript, folder 1, box 8, AMC.

84. Burt M. McConnell, "Barbarism to Convicts," *Nation*, 10 Nov. 1926, 479–80.

85. Tannenbaum, *Wall Shadows*, 154–55.

86. For a more general description of the NSPI's activities, see Paul W. Garrett, "Report to the Board of Directors," 1926, folder 1, box 11, AMC.

87. Ibid., 3.

88. Frank Tannenbaum, *Darker Phases of the South* (New York: Putnam, 1924), 86.

89. MacCormick, "Crime and Delinquency, Correctional Training and Treatment," Bowdoin Lecture Series, lecture 3, 5, AMC.

90. Tannenbaum, *Darker Phases of the South*, 113.

91. National Commission on Law Observance and Enforcement [Wickersham Commission], *Report on Penal Institutions, Probation, and Parole* (Washington, D.C.: U.S. Government Printing Office, 1931).

92. Austin MacCormick, report to the 1934 annual meeting, Osborne Association, AMC.

93. Lowrie, *My Life in Prison*, 51, 69.

94. Tannenbaum, *Darker Phases of the South*, 74.

95. Austin H. MacCormick to Thomas Mott Osborne, 23 April 1919, box 147, OFP.

96. MacCormick, *The Education of Adult Prisoners*, xxxv.

97. Austin H. MacCormick to Thomas Mott Osborne, 1 Feb. 1920, box 152, OFP.

98. Garrett and MacCormick, *Handbook of American Prisons and Reformatories* (1929), xxxviii; Walter Wallack, *The Training of Prison Guards in the State of New York* (New York: Teachers College, Columbia University, 1938). One consequence of this view was a general tendency to recoil against indictments of the prison system that were seen as overbroad or too generalized. Sinclair Lewis presented a graphic version of prison life in *Ann Vickers* (1933), in which the title heroine is a bold reforming pioneer in women's correctional vocational education, whose book *Vocational Training in Women's Reformatories* becomes a widely read success. E. R. Cass, of the Prison Association of New York, reviewed the novel in the *Journal of Criminal Law and Criminology* [!] and complained that Lewis had done reformers a disservice by painting the prison picture with too broad a brush. He wrote: "More good would have been served if the author had departed even slightly from his iconoclastic style and given more credit where credit is due." E. R. Cass, "Ann Vickers" [Review], *Journal of Criminal Law and Criminology* 24 (Nov.–Dec. 1933): 814–17.

99. Austin H. MacCormick, "There is No Truce" [Review], *Columbia Law Review* 35 (June 1935): 958–60.

100. Austin H. MacCormick to Thomas Mott Osborne, 23 Jan. 1920, box 152, OFP.

101. Austin H. MacCormick to Thomas Mott Osborne, 22 Feb. 1920, box 152, OFP. "We have bucked up against a blanker wall than the bigotry of the civil population with regard to state prisons . . . We tried to chew solid stone and only a rock-crusher can do that." Not long thereafter, Osborne wrote to MacCormick (March 1, 1920, box 152, OFP): "The way things are turning out, I advise you very strongly to send in your resignation at once. I am getting out of here just as soon as I can and things are looking pretty black for the future. You and I will both want to be able to speak the truth about the Navy."

102. The Naval Welfare League at Portsmouth was dismantled, as were shipboard versions of the same. Captain Clark Stearns, who had toured naval facilities with Mac-Cormick, was removed from his command of the USS *Michigan*. Navy Secretary Edwin Denby blasted the system as "soviet" and called for a return to the firm disciplinary regime.

103. MacCormick, "Crime and Delinquency, Correctional Training and Treatment," 8–9.

104. Thomas Mott Osborne to Austin H. MacCormick, 2 Nov. 1923, box 2, AMC.

105. MacCormick, "Crime and Delinquency, Correctional Training and Treatment," 9a, 9b.

106. Ibid.

107. Austin H. MacCormick to Thomas Mott Osborne, 29 Dec. 1924. A brief exchange of telegrams in the first week of January 1925 indicate that Osborne was willing to consider coming out to Colorado as deputy warden. In the end, no offer was forthcoming. The exchanges are in box 2, AMC.

108. Austin H. MacCormick to Thomas Mott Osborne, 19 Jan. 1925, box 2, AMC.

109. "M'Cormick Assails Hoover on Parole," *New York Times*, 15 Oct. 1937, 13.

110. "Head G-Man 'No Cream Puff,'" *Christian Science Monitor*, 9 Nov. 1937, 7. The Hoover-MacCormick exchange should be read in light of Murphy, *Political Manhood*.

111. "M'Cormick Assails Hoover on Parole."

112. Lowrie, *My Life Out of Prison*, 149.

113. Chamberlain, *There Is No Truce*, 341–42.

114. MacCormick, "There is No Truce."

115. The rejection was big news in the art world. See Philippa Gerry Whiting, "Speaking About Art: Rikers Island," *American Magazine of Art*, 28 Aug. 1935.

116. "Anti-Social Move Seen in Relief Art," *New York Times*, 9 May 1935, 13.

117. Ibid.

118. Ibid.

119. Edward Alden Jewell, "Sketches Stress New Prison Policy," *New York Times*, 10 May 1935, 19.

120. Greenfeld, *Ben Shahn*, 110–11.

121. Ibid., 109.

122. Ibid.

123. Shahn and Block, as well as Audrey McMahon, corresponded with Walter Thayer, Commissioner of the New York State Department of Corrections, in the summer of 1935. See Kao, Katzman, and Webster, *Ben Shahn's New York*, 135.

124. Austin H. MacCormick to Thomas Mott Osborne, Jan. 26, 1925, box 2, AMC.

125. Austin H. MacCormick, "Planning for Tomorrow and Thereafter," *Prison World* (Sept.–Oct. 1944): 8–9, 27.

Chapter 2 · A New Deal for Prisons

1. Austin H. MacCormick, "Crime and Delinquency, Correctional Treatment and Training." His Bowdoin lecture contains an interesting reflection on the 1929 riots at Leavenworth Penitentiary, and the extent to which the riots were a kind of focusing event that pushed federal reform spending through Congress. The Leavenworth riot "in a sense cleared the air, it scared the living daylights out of Congress; we had the backing of the president and an excellent attorney general by this time and we were able by talking about the riot and using it as a thing to scare them, to get appropriations such as nobody had ever got before . . . we were able in one year virtually to transform the whole federal prison system, at least to begin its transformation." Likewise, William Cox (executive secretary of the Osborne Association), wrote in the association's 1932 annual report that these riots "although disastrous in themselves . . . served to call attention to the futility of administering prisons on a purely custodial and punitive level."

2. The term "rehabilitative regime" is used in Pamela L. Griset, *Determinate Sentencing: The Promise and the Reality of Retributive Justice* (Albany: SUNY Press, 1991). See also Vanessa Barker, *The Politics of Imprisonment: How the Democratic Process Shapes the Way America Punishes Offenders* (Oxford; New York: Oxford University Press, 2009).

3. Clinton Prison, annual report (1928), in Clinton Prison Annual Reports, 1922–1953, New York State Library.

4. "3 Convicts Killed, 20 Hurt, 1,300 Riot at Dannemora, Set Fire and Storm Walls," *New York Times*, 23 July 1929, 1.

5. "2 Die as Convicts Burn Auburn Prison," *Rochester Evening Journal*, 29 July 1929, 1.

6. McLennan, *Crisis of Imprisonment*, 196.

7. Blumenthal, *Miracle at Sing Sing*, praises Lawes's efforts as warden. See also Lewis E. Lawes, "Are We Coddling Our Prisoners at Sing Sing?" *Prison Journal* (April 1922): 12–16. The manner in which Lawes continued Thomas Mott Osborne's Mutual Welfare League was especially objectionable to MacCormick, who concluded in 1929 that the

league's importance "as a strong moral force in the prison . . . has practically disappeared." Garrett and MacCormick, *Handbook of American Prisons and Reformatories* (1929), 715.

8. "Baumes Board Asks 84 Curbs on Crime," *New York Times*, 2 March 1927, 1.

9. "The Baumes Law," *Prison Journal* (Oct. 1927): 17–19.

10. "Pictures Prisons Filled With 'Lifers,'" *New York Times*, 17 Feb. 1928.

11. Blumenthal, *Miracle at Sing Sing*, 95.

12. Al Smith was deeply committed to the idea of prison reform. David R. Colburn persuasively makes this case in "Governor Alfred E. Smith and Penal Reform," *Political Science Quarterly* 91 (1976): 315–27. Still, Smith's efforts to stamp his imprint on the prison system failed to match his enthusiasm. Perhaps the most lasting of Smith's contributions to New York's prison reform program was his recommendation to rely on bond issues, rather than current revenues, to finance new prison construction. The long reluctance to do this had resulted in the massively overcrowded conditions in the twenties, and the embrace of long-term financing created the conditions for the state's prison construction boom in the thirties, without which the reform regime could not have sustained itself.

13. Blumenthal, *Miracle at Sing-Sing*, 99.

14. E. R. Cass, "Penal Legislation in New York, 1921," *Prison Journal* (July 1921): 11.

15. Garrett and MacCormick, *Handbook of American Prisons and Reformatories*, 671.

16. See Wallack, *Training of Prison Guards*, 10.

17. Ibid., 15; Garrett and MacCormick, *Handbook of American Prisons and Reformatories*, 683–94. See also MacCormick, *The Education of Adult Prisoners*, 288–89.

18. Chamberlain, *There is No Truce*, 8.

19. "Mutiny at Auburn Put Down by State Police; Fatalities Placed at 9," *Schenectady Gazette*, 12 Dec. 1929, 1.

20. Herbert H. Lehman to Allan Nevins, memorandum, 4 Jan. 1962, and Herbert H. Lehman to Allan Nevins, letter, 16 March 1961, Herbert H. Lehman Papers, Special Correspondence Files, Rare Book and Manuscript Library, Columbia University Library [hereafter HLP].

21. F. Raymond Daniell, "Hold Warden Hostage," *New York Times*, 12 Dec. 1929, 1; "Prison Riot Broken; 9 Dead," *Chicago Daily Tribune*, 12 Dec. 1929, 1.

22. "Three Found Guilty of Auburn Murder; 3 Others Acquitted," *New York Times*, 16 Feb. 1930, 1. Four inmates in all were charged with murder and acquitted; the various trials gave extensive public airing of the many complaints prisoners had with how Auburn Prison was run.

23. In *The Big House* (1930), prisoners were involved in a prison break whose details were clearly based on the Auburn riot. The film received an Academy Award nomination for best picture, and screenwriter Frances Marion won an Oscar for her work. See Robert L. Hilliard, *Hollywood Speaks Out: Pictures That Dared to Protest Real World Issues* (Chichester, UK; Malden, Mass.: Wiley-Blackwell, 2009), 63–81.

24. "A Dramatic Talkie; Ruth St. Clair Pleads to be Saved from Her Life Sentence," *New York Times*, 24 Feb. 1930.

25. Women's clubs sent a large number of letters and petitions to Governor Roosevelt. See, for example, "Rochester Club Women Protect Life Term for Shoplifter," *Rochester Evening Journal*, 10 Feb. 1930, 1.

26. Spencer Miller was head of the Workers Education Bureau, and an active figure in adult education reform. Thomas S. Rice was a Brooklyn lawyer who made something of a career out of promoting conservative crime control.

27. "Sees Baumes Laws as State Liability," *New York Times*, 25 March 1930, 20; Rice's performance also included a discussion of the first fourth-strike sentence handed down under the Baumes Laws, given to a "Negro" whose offenses consisted in getting intoxicated, stealing cars, and speeding through town with them. Rice contended that he was "more of a danger to us than ten professional gunmen."

28. "Prison Riots May Be Caused By Baumes Law," *Pittsburgh Press*, 30 July 1929, 13.

29. Franklin D. Roosevelt, Office of the Governor to Editor, *Lexington Leader*, 10 Aug. 1929, "Herbert H. Lehman," series 1: correspondence, box 48, Franklin D. Roosevelt, Papers as Governor of New York, Franklin D. Roosevelt Library [hereafter FDR].

30. "Louis Howe," series 1, box 41, FDR.

31. Felix Frankfurter to Franklin D. Roosevelt, 25 July 1929, folder 5, box 7, Sanford Bates Papers, Newton Gresham Library, San Houston State University [hereafter SBP]; Adolph Lewisohn wrote a long memo along the same lines to Lieutenant Governor Lehman. Adolph Lewisohn to Herbert H. Lehman, 11 Sept. 1929, HLP.

32. Franklin D. Roosevelt to Felix Frankfurter, 5 Aug. 1929, in *Roosevelt and Frankfurter: Their Correspondence, 1928–1945*, ed. Max Freedman (Boston: Little, Brown, 1968), 42–43.

33. "Osborne Paid High Tribute by Roosevelt," *Washington Post*, 13 Nov. 1933, 3. Osborne's sons remained political supporters of Roosevelt. See Lithgow Osborne to Franklin D. Roosevelt, 15 April 1930, series 1, box 60, FDR.

34. See Adolph Lewisohn to Franklin D. Roosevelt, 8 Nov. 1929, and Franklin D. Roosevelt to Adolph Lewisohn, 14 Jan. 1930, series 1, box 49, FDR. See also, from the same correspondence, Adolph Lewisohn to Franklin D. Roosevelt, 18 March 1930.

35. Sam Lewisohn to Franklin D. Roosevelt, 15 Jan. 1931, series 1, box 49, FDR.

36. Franklin D. Roosevelt to Adolph Lewisohn, 9 Dec. 1929, series 1, box 49, FDR.

37. See Alfred Rollins, Jr., *Roosevelt and Howe* (New York: Knopf, 1962), 273–74, and Frank Freidel, *The Triumph* (Boston: Little, Brown, 1956), 95–97.

38. "Says Crowding Led to Prison Revolts," *New York Times*, 20 Sept. 1929.

39. "Dr. Thayer on the Job," *New York Telegram*, newspaper clipping sent by Walter Thayer to Franklin D. Roosevelt, series 1, box 78, FDR.

40. "Dr. W. N. Thayer Jr., Penologist, Dies," *New York Times*, 7 Jan. 1936, 21.

41. Roosevelt's initial search for committee members focused on well-known corporate figures. See E. R. Cass to Louis McHenry Howe, 27 Feb. 1930, box 20, Louis Howe Papers, Franklin D. Roosevelt Library [hereafter LHP].

42. Franklin D. Roosevelt to Marshall Field, 14 March 1930, box 20, LHP.

43. Freidel, *The Triumph*, 126–28.

44. Franklin D. Roosevelt to Sam Lewisohn, 19 Feb. 1931, series 1, box 49, FDR.

45. "Humanization of Prisons Vital to Crime Cure, Says Lewisohn," *Rochester Evening Journal*, 16 Feb. 1931, 25.

46. "College Lectures Held Prison Need," *New York Times*, 11 Jan. 1932, 23.

47. Reducing the size of prisons was a key component of reformist thought during this period. See, for example, John Callender, "Planning the Fall of the Bastille," *Survey*, June 15, 1931: "Designed functionally the prison of the future will bear little resemblance

to the Bastille of the last hundred years. It will probably suggest a hospital or school or small community rather than a fortress . . . 500 is about the ideal size." A clipping of the article was sent to Roosevelt by George Gordon Battle, president of the National Committee on Prisons and Prison Labor, series 1, box 58, FDR.

48. "Elmira Reforms Education System," *New York Times*, 27 Feb. 1933; New York State Commission of Correction, *Sixth Annual Report* (1932).

49. Walter M. Wallack, *A Preliminary Report on an Educational Project at Elmira Reformatory,* Special Report by the Commission to Investigate Prison Administration and Construction (Albany: J. B. Lyon, 1933), 6; See also Howard L. Briggs, *A Handbook of Methods for Vocational Teachers* (New York: New York State Department of Correction, Division of Education, 1938).

50. Wallack, *Preliminary Report on an Educational Project,* 17–22.

51. Austin H. MacCormick, untitled manuscript, n. d., 24a, AMC.

52. Commission for the Study of the Educational Problems of Penal Institutions for Youth, *Preliminary Report to His Excellency Governor Herbert H. Lehman* (New York: Commission, 1934), 3.

53. Sam Lewisohn to F. P. Keppel, 25 June 1934, series 3: grants, folder 32, box 153, Carnegie Corporation Papers [hereafter CCP]; N. L. Engelhardt to Sam A. Lewisohn, 25 May 1934, CCP. The Carnegie grant was renewed in 1935, based on a recommendation from Morse Cartwright at the AAAE. See Cartwright to F. P. Keppel, 24 Oct. 1935, CCP.

54. An additional $7,000 came from the New York Foundation, and then a large contribution of $100,000 came from the Works Progress Administration as part of funds provided to New York State for adult education programs. "WPA to Help Prisoners," *New York Times*, 5 Feb. 1936, 10.

55. Susan Sheehan, *A Prison and A Prisoner* (Boston: Houghton Mifflin, 1978), 83. Hopkins spelled out his vision in *Prisons and Prison Building* (New York: Architectural Book Publishing, 1930).

56. Walter M. Wallack, "Wallkill, A Medium Security Prison," *Prison World* (May–June, 1940): 29–30.

57. Sheehan, *A Prison and a Prisoner,* 190.

58. Glenn M. Kendall, *Organization and Teaching of Social and Economic Studies in Correctional Institutions* (New York: Teachers College, Columbia University, 1939), 68–83.

59. Minutes of the meeting of the Commission for the Study of Educational Problems of Penal Institutions for Youth, 26 June 1935, New York State Library. See also New York State Commission for the Study of the Educational Problems of Penal Institutions for Youth, *Progress Report Number 2 of the Educational Project at Wallkill State Prison Covering the Period May 10 to June 20, 1935.*

60. In 1947, Woodbourne was redesignated as an institution for 16- to 21-year-olds of "borderline" intelligence (defined as IQ scores in the 71 to 85 range).

61. F. C. Helbing, "Proper Guard Attitudes and Relations Toward Young Offenders," in Wallack, *Training of Prison Guards,* 316.

62. When Walter Wallack went on to a position as superintendent of Wallkill in 1940, he was replaced as director of education by former assistant director Glenn Kendall, and Kendall in turn was replaced by Price Chenault (who had started as director of education at Coxsackie). All three men were nationally known prison educators, found-

ers of the American Prison Association's Committee on Education and later the Correctional Education Association. Between Wallack, Kendall, and Chenault, the pioneer reform group ran the Division of Education from its establishment in 1935 to its effective dissolution in 1970.

63. Wallack, Kendall, and Briggs, *Education within Prison Walls*, 34.

64. Ibid.

65. Paul D. Meunier and Howard D. Schwartz, "Beyond Attica: Prison Reform in New York State, 1971–1973," *Cornell Law Review* 58 (1972–1973): 938.

66. "Ray Corsini: A Life that Spans an Era," *Psychologist* 37 (fall/winter 2002): 68–77.

67. New York State Department of Corrections Division of Education, *Progress Report 1942–1943* (New York: Department of Corrections, 1943).

68. New York State Department of Corrections, *Annual Report (Fiscal Year 1937–1938)* (New York: Department of Corrections, 1938), 29.

69. Ibid., 35, 43.

70. See Walter M. Wallack, "The Service Unit," in *Contemporary Correction*, ed. Paul W. Tappan (New York: McGraw-Hill, 1951), 141–53. See also Walter M. Wallack and John J. Sheehy, "The Service Unit as Part of the Prison Program—Part I," *Prison World* (Nov.–Dec. 1948): 6–7, 23–24.

71. Minutes of the meeting of the Commission for the Study of Educational Problems of Penal Institutions for Youth, June 26, 1935, New York State Library.

72. Wallack, *Training of Prison Guards*, 38.

73. "Big Albany Bills Sped to Passage," *New York Times*, 18 April 1935, 2.

74. "Assails Long Hours for State Workers," *New York Times*, 26 Jan. 1932, 14; Harry L. Bowlby, "Prison Guards' Long Hours," *New York Times*, 12 April 1935, 22.

75. "Prison Guards to Be Graduated," *New York Times*, 21 June 1937, 21.

76. Wallack, *Training of Prison Guards*, 41–43, 57–59.

77. Austin H. MacCormick, "Trends in Correctional Treatment," in Wallack, *Training of Prison Guards*, 219, 223; Frank L. Christian, "What Can the Guard Contribute to the Treatment Program of the Institution?" in Wallack, *Training of Prison Guards*, 262.

78. Glenn M. Kendall, "Guard Training—A Continuous Project," *Prison World* (Sept.–Oct. 1941): 6.

79. Ibid., 6; Wallack, in "Wallkill, A Medium Security Prison," says that 682 recruits passed though the Central Guard School between 1936 and 1940; by late 1941, more than 1,100 recruits and in-service trainees had passed through the Central Guard School.

80. New York State Department of Corrections, Division of Education, *Report of Progress in Educational Programs, 1942–1943* (New York: Department of Corrections, 1943), 1–4. For more on the revised program, see "Personnel Training," *Correction* 15 (July 1948): 12–14.

81. Leonard V. Harrison and Pryor McNeill Grant, *Youth in the Toils* (New York: Macmillan, 1938), 137. See also New York Law Society, *The Forgotten Adolescent: A Study of the Pre-Trial Treatment of Boys Charged with Crime in New York City* (New York: New York Law Society, 1940).

82. "Dewey Eases Lot of Wayward Boys," *New York Times*, 15 Nov. 1940, 14; "Curran Denies Dewey Set Court Precedent," *New York Times*, 17 Nov. 1940, 2. Dewey and Chief Magistrate Henry H. Curran fought for some time over who would take leadership of the

youthful offender issue; this political contest informed much of the state-level handling of the youthful offender legislation. See also "New Group to Aid Young Offenders," *New York Times*, 1 March 1941, 13, in which Curran complained to reporters, "I don't understand where Dewey gets off appointing a committee to solve what he calls a 'problem' . . . This isn't Dewey's problem—it's the Legislature's responsibility." Paul Blanshard called the issue the "knottiest and most vital" issue for the 1942 legislative session. Paul Blanshard, "Adolescents Pose Problem," *New York Times*, 17 Nov. 1941, C18.

83. "Dewey Seeks To Aid Young Lawbreakers," *Christian Science Monitor*, 11 Dec. 1940, 7.

84. William Draper Lewis, "Treatment of Youth Convicted of Crime," *Federal Probation* 4 (May 1940): 20–23. John R. Ellington, "The Youth Authority Plan: Its Development and Prospects," in Tappan, *Contemporary Correction*, 124–39. The committee was formed in 1938 and submitted its model Youth Correction Authority Act that same year. For more on the ALI, see Alex Elson, "The Case for an In-Depth Study of the American Law Institute," *Law and Social Inquiry* 23 (July 1998): 625–40.

85. Glenn Kendall, "Reception Centers," in Tappan, *Contemporary Correction*, 107–123.

86. In 1940 the ALI also helped in the production of a radio series, *Youth in the Toils*. Episodes included "Boys Beyond the Law" (a young boy as he turns into a hardened criminal), "Girls Beyond the Law" (a young woman who starts as a shoplifter, enters a life of crime, and becomes pregnant), "A New Guy Joins the Club" (youth lured into a life with the gangs), and "Classrooms of Crime" (in jail for six months on suspicion). This thirteen-part series aired over the Blue Network of NBC, on Mon. evenings from 7:15 to 7:30. MacCormick himself presented one of the episodes.

87. "Albany Bill Backs Court for Youths," *New York Times*, 28 Jan. 1942, 20.

88. "Call Youth Court A Plan to 'Coddle,'" *New York Times*, 25 March 1942, 24.

89. "Dewey Signs Bills to Cut Youth Crime," *New York Times*, 18 April 1943, 7. Arlene Wolf, "New York's Youthful Offender Law Can Clear Characters," *Reading Eagle*, 16 July 1946, 19; W. Charles Barber, "Youthful Offender Law Misunderstood," *Newburgh News*, 24 April 1956, 4.

90. An ambitious earlier attempt to extend this principle of indeterminacy to most adult offenders failed in 1934, vetoed by Governor Lehman in the face of extensive police, judicial, and prosecutorial opposition. See "Fowler Praises Lehman For Parole Veto," *Rochester Evening Journal*, 16 May 1934, 102; "They're Not Ready For It," *Rochester Evening Journal*, 17 May 1934, 8; "The Parole Bill," *New York Times*, 12 April 1934, 22; "Corrigan Urges Parole Bill Veto," *New York Times*, 6 May 1934, 20; "Governor Vetoes Quick Parole Bill," *New York Times*, 16 May 1934, 1.

91. The quote comes from the January 12, 1957, draft of the ALI report on "Sentencing and Treatment of Young Adult Offenders," SBP.

92. Austin H. MacCormick to O. B. Ellis, 4 March 1958, folder 4, box 10, AMC.

93. Division of Education, *Progress Report 1942–1943*.

94. Robert W. Potter, "Dewey Aides Urge reforms in Attack on Juvenile Crime," *New York Times*, 11 March 1945, 1.

95. Richard N. Smith, *Thomas E. Dewey and His Times* (New York: Simon and Schuster, 1982).

96. Glenn Kendall, "The Elmira Reception Center," *Prison World* (March–April 1946): 8–9, 27.

97. Ibid.

98. Kendall, "Reception Centers," 107–123.

99. "Elmira Reception Center," *American Journal of Correction* 23 (1961): 38.

100. Kendall, "Reception Centers."

101. Ibid., 123.

Chapter 3 · *Adolescents Adrift*

1. Case file A, box 270, Coxsackie Case Files, New York State Archives [hereafter CCF]. The case files are drawn from a 5% sample of the entire run of Coxsackie case files held at the state archives. The names associated with each case file are pseudonyms, used to protect the identity of the young men at Coxsackie. The reference to the Coxsackie Case Files includes the box number, but not the specific file number. Since the file number is the inmate's prisoner number, this would also potentially compromise the identity of a prisoner. The sampled files from each box are lettered in sequence, lettering that corresponds to a list of prisoner numbers in my possession. When references to Coxsackie prisoners come from published sources, such as newspaper articles or court cases, I have used their real and full names. Pseudonyms are identifiable by the use of first name and last initial.

2. Evan Hunter, *Blackboard Jungle*, 50th anniversary ed. (New York: Simon and Schuster, 2004), 34–35.

3. Glenn M. Kendall, "Some Characteristics of Reception Center Youths (With Special Reference to the Field of Recreation)," *Journal of Correctional Education* 3 (July 1955): 43.

4. Ibid.

5. Case A, box 270, CCF.

6. Isidor Chein, Donald L. Gerard, Robert S. Lee, and Eva Rosenfeld, *The Road to H: Narcotics, Delinquency, and Social Policy* (New York: Basic Books, 1964), 120.

7. Chein et al., *Road to H*, 121. Young men in the drug-using groups had family members with police records in 25% and 30% of the cases. The study also compared the extent of family alcoholism. The control group (12%) and the drug-using groups (8% and 20%) were both well below the 27% of Coxsackie inmates with alcoholic family members.

8. Case I, box 100, CCF.

9. Case F, box 210, CCF.

10. Frank S., case C, box 220; Walter B., case A, box 260; Walter M., case D, box 250, all in CCF.

11. Case E, box 160, CCF.

12. Case I, box 160, CCF.

13. Case H, box 90, CCF.

14. Case J, box 140, CCF.

15. Case J, box 140, CCF.

16. The quoted phrases come from, in order, case M, box 80; case A, box 110; case B, box 110; case E, box 110; case I, box 110; case J, box 170; case O, box 120; case H, box 140; case L, box 140; and case C, box 200, all CCF.

17. Case A, box 100, CCF.

18. Case G, box 110, CCF.

19. The achievement test scores for reading averaged 8.5 grade. Leonard S. Black, "An Inmate's-Eye View of Himself and the Public School," *Journal of Correctional Education* 9 (Jan. 1957): 9–12.

20. Rocky Graziano, *Somebody Up There Likes Me: The Story of My Life Until Today* (New York: Simon and Schuster, 1955), 25.

21. Black, "An Inmate's-Eye View," 9–12.

22. Mwlina Imiri Abubadika, *The Education of Sonny Carson* (New York: Norton, 1972), 16; Bertram M. Beck, *Youth within Walls: A Study of the Correctional Treatment of the 16- to 21-Year Old Male Offender in New York State Institutions With Recommendations for Future Development* (New York: Community Service Society, 1950), 21.

23. Case A, box 260, CCF.

24. John Modell, *Into One's Own: From Youth to Adulthood in the United States, 1920–1975* (Berkeley: University of California Press, 1991), 125. See also Ruth E. Eckert and Thomas O. Marshall, *When Youth Leave School* (London; New York: Regents' Inquiry, McGraw-Hill, 1938) and Donald E. Super and Robert D. Wright, "From School to Work in the Depression Years," *School Review* 49 (Jan. 1941): 17–26.

25. Bonnie Stepenoff, *The Dead End Kids of St. Louis: Homeless Boys and the People Who Tried to Save Them* (Columbia: University of Missouri Press, 2010), 109.

26. New York State Commission of Corrections, *Annual Report for 1939–1940* (New York: New York State Commission of Corrections, 1940), 37.

27. Ernest N., a non-sampled case file from box 30, CCF.

28. Eric Schneider, *Vampires, Dragons, and Egyptian Kings: Youth Gangs in Postwar New York* (Princeton, N.J.: Princeton University Press, 2001), 193.

29. New York Law Society, *The Forgotten Adolescent: A Study of the Pre-Trial Treatment of Boys Charged With Crime in New York City* (New York: New York Law Society, 1940), 58.

30. Case G, box 110, CCF.

31. "Slight Increase in State's Arrests for Major Crimes in 1950 Accounted for by Increased Narcotics Arrests," *Correction* 16 (Jan. 1951): 14–15.

32. Harrison and Grant, *Youth in the Toils*, 37.

33. Abubadika, *Education of Sonny Carson*, 40.

34. "Stabber Wins Suspension of Prison Term," *Schenectady Gazette*, 15 Feb. 1938, 4; "Police Squad Closes in and Seizes a Prowler," *Auburn (NY) Citizen-Advertiser*, 15 Nov. 1937, 5; "Youth Seized on Mail Box Charge, Sentenced," *Binghamton Press*, 11 Feb. 1935, 5.

35. Chein et al., *Road to H*, 139.

36. Case A, box 80, CCF.

37. For a provocative contemporary version of this idea, see Victor M. Rios, *Punished: Policing the Lives of Black and Latino Boys* (New York: New York University Press, 2011).

38. Irwin August Berg, "Comparative Study of Car Thieves," *Journal of Criminal Law and Criminology* 34 (1943–1944): 392–396. Leonard D. Savitz, "Automobile Theft," *Journal of Criminal Law, Criminology, and Police Science* 50 (July–Aug. 1959): 132–43.

39. "Slight Increase in State's Arrests for Major Crimes in 1950 Accounted for by Increased Narcotics Arrests," *Correction* 16 (Jan. 1951): 14–15.

40. Savitz, "Automobile Theft."

41. James E. Bulger, "Automobile Thefts," *Journal of Criminal Law and Criminology* 23 (Jan.–Feb. 1933): 806–810.

42. Non-sampled case file, box 240, CCF; David Wolcott, *Cops and Kids: Policing Juvenile Delinquency in Urban America, 1890–1940* (Columbus: Ohio State University Press, 2005), 180. As John Modell observes, "When families had to cut back, the realms in which they were most able to economize were precisely those areas that had become in the last decade so important to the new adolescent styles of life: recreation, automobiles, and clothing." Modell, *Into One's Own*, 129.

43. This is consistent with the observation made by Richard Wedekind in "Automobile Theft, The Thirteen Million Dollar Parasite," *Journal of Criminal Law, Criminology, and Police Science* 48 (1957–1958): 443–46: "Most authorities agree that a majority of automobile thefts are perpetrated by juveniles with no intention of selling the stolen cars or converting them to their own use permanently."

44. Harrison and Grant, *Youth in the Toils*, 29.

45. William J. Davis, "Stolen Automobile Investigations," *Journal of Criminal Law and Criminology* 28 (Jan.–Feb. 1938): 720–38. It is worth noting that joyriding was defined as larceny in the New York State penal laws. Superintendent Helbing was no fan of joyriding prosecutions. He argued that "the real evil" of joyriding was the conviction of young men on grand larceny charges; he urged the state to pass a law mandating the locking of car doors. See "Locked Auto Seen Curb on Delinquency," *Rochester Democrat Chronicle*, 6 Dec. 1939, 1.

46. See, generally, Schneider, *Vampires, Dragons, and Egyptian Kings*, on the development and nature of postwar youth gangs in New York City.

47. Case I, box 170, CCF.

48. Case H, box 270, CCF, and case A, box 330, CCF.

49. Tamara Myers, "Embodying Delinquency: Boys' Bodies, Sexuality, and Juvenile Justice History in Early-Twentieth Century Quebec," *Journal of the History of Sexuality* 14 (Oct. 2005): 383–414.

50. The growing concern over adolescent sex offenses should be balanced against Stephen Robertson's argument in *Crimes Against Children: Sexual Violence and Legal Culture in New York City, 1880–1960* (Chapel Hill: University of North Carolina Press, 2005) that mid-century America began to normalize adolescent sexual activity, moving toward what he calls a "new leniency" (p. 199). Robertson (p. 182) explicitly links New York's youthful offender legislation to this trend. One might consider that both could be true—an increased level of policing might well have gone hand in hand with a system that treated defendants as less mature and culpable than in the past.

51. Case A, box 200, CCF, and case L, box 70, CCF.

52. Case C, box 270, CCF.

53. Schneider, *Vampires, Dragons, and Egyptian Kings*, 134–135, also found that New York City gang members "assaulted male homosexuals, and some gang members engaged in same-sex relations, usually with [an] older male in exchange for cash or drugs."

54. Graziano, *Somebody Up There Likes Me*, 85.

55. Cases B and C, box 230, CCF.

56. Case E, box 320, CCF.

57. Glenn M. Kendall, "Correctional Institutions and the Youthful Drug Addict," *Journal of Correctional Education* 8 (April 1956): 52; 1951 was the peak year in this first

heroin epidemic, and the ERC percentage of heroin users gradually declined to about 10% in the 1955–1956 fiscal year. Austin MacCormick downplayed the narcotics problem, calling it a "temporary phenomenon," "Narcotics Addiction Called Exaggerated," *New York Times*, 26 May 1951, 19. Still, the 1951 case files show many of these heroin admissions. See, for example, cases A and B, box 300, CCF.

58. Case D, box 250, CCF.

59. Chein et al., *Road to H*, chapter 2 ("Neighborhood Distribution of Drug Use") offers reasonably definitive evidence that 1951 was the peak year for new cases of adolescent heroin use in this first postwar epidemic.

60. Graziano, *Somebody Up There Likes Me*, 122.

61. New York Law Society, *Forgotten Adolescent*, 6; Harrison and Grant, *Youth in the Toils*, 55.

62. See T. J. English, *The Savage City: Race, Murder, and a Generation on the Edge* (New York: William Morrow, 2011), 61: "Youth officers from the NYPD were liable to give an ass-whupping to any gang kid they caught—black, white, or Latino—but Negro gangs presented a special problem"; see also Schneider, *Vampires, Dragons, and Egyptian Kings*, 205: "Instead of enforcing the peace, nightstick justice reinforced resentment and ethnic hostility."

63. *New York v. Valletutti*, 78 N.E. 2d 485 (1948).

64. Dominic J. Capeci, *The Harlem Riot of 1943* (Philadelphia: Temple University Press, 1977) covers this territory well. See also Wendell E. Pritchett, *Brownsville, Brooklyn: Blacks, Jews, and the Changing Face of the Ghetto* (Chicago: University of Chicago Press, 2003).

65. Abubadika, *Education of Sonny Carson*, 21.

66. Pritchett, *Brownsville, Brooklyn*, 90–92. Martha Biondi, *To Stand and Fight: The Struggle for Civil Rights in Postwar New York City* (Cambridge, Mass.: Harvard University Press, 2006), 70, confirms that police beatings were routine.

67. The denial of legitimate access to family by the police emerges in Graziano, *Somebody Up There Likes Me*; Abubadika, *Education of Sonny Carson*; and in the cases discussed in Harrison and Grant, *Youth in the Toils*.

68. Jake LaMotta, *Raging Bull: My Story* (Englewood Cliffs, N.J.: Prentice-Hall, 1970), 30.

69. New York Law Society, *Forgotten Adolescent*, 8.

70. Harrison and Grant, *Youth in the Toils*, 36.

71. Ibid., 67.

72. Graziano, *Somebody Up There Likes Me*, 124.

73. New York Law Society, *Forgotten Adolescent*, 14–15, 46.

74. Ibid., 50.

75. Graziano, *Somebody Up There Likes Me*, 111; Sheehan, *A Prison and a Prisoner*, 179.

76. *New York v. Losacco*, 173 NYS 2d 920 (1958). See also *New York v. Jardine*, NYS 2d 454 (1960), also involving a Coxsackie prisoner, in which a New York court ruled: "The mere physical absence of a defendant's lawyer at the time of entry of a guilty plea does not vitiate the conviction."

77. Case A, box 80, CCF.

78. *State v. Giaccio and Panzella*, 96 NYS 2d 912 (1950).

79. Ibid.

80. Harrison and Grant, *Youth in the Toils*, 95.

81. *Gayes v. State of New York*, 332 U.S. 145 (1947).

82. Harrison and Grant, *Youth in the Toils*, 43.

83. Case G, box 160, CCF.

84. "Boy is Morally Ill, Judge Tells Brooklyn Court," *New York Amsterdam News*, 4 Nov. 1944, 4B.

85. "Mercy is Refused Trio Who Confess Many Burglaries," *Utica Observer Dispatch*, 20 Feb. 1936, 17.

86. LaMotta, *Raging Bull*, 36.

87. Case F, box 100, CCF.

88. Case A, box 140, CCF.

89. Case B, box 200, CCF.

90. Case M, box 100, CCF.

91. Case G, box 100, CCF.

92. Jacob Miller, *Untouchable* (Bloomington, Ind.: Xlibris, 2011), 190–91.

93. New York State Commission of Correction, *Twenty-Ninth Annual Report* (New York: Commission on Correction, 1955).

94. "State Study Asked on Sex Offenders," *New York Times*, 7 March 1948, 46.

95. New York State Department of Corrections, Bureau of Research, *Characteristics of Inmates Under Custody* (New York: New York State Department of Corrections, 1962), 11.

96. Case I, box 200, CCF.

97. Case H, box 260, CCF.

98. Case G, box 200, CCF.

Chapter 4 · *Against the Wall*

1. Graziano, *Somebody Up There Likes Me*, 121.

2. Ibid., 118–19.

3. The phrase comes from pseudonymous Frankie Moreno, who took the big train ride in the early 1960s. See Miller, *Untouchable*, 189.

4. The idea that prison life could be transformative (and not in a positive way) and produce prison-specific social relations has a long intellectual genealogy, going back at least to progressive era commentators such as Kate Richards O'Hare and Thomas Mott Osborne. Donald Clemmer was among the first to embed this thought in a more sophisticated social-scientific theoretical framework when he adapted social learning theory to explain what he called "prisonization." Donald Clemmer, *The Prison Community* (Boston: Christopher, 1940). Clemmer's prewar model was further developed in Gresham Sykes, *The Society of Captives: A Study of a Maximum Security Prison* (Princeton, N.J.: Princeton University Press, 1958), and still further in Erving Goffman, *Asylums: Essays on the Social Situation of Mental Patients and Other Inmates* (New York: Doubleday, 1961). Not long after Goffman's work appeared, a counter-trend of work stressing the importation of preprison values, attitudes, and cultures appeared. Notable among these early works was Rose Giallombardo, *Society of Women: A Study of a Women's Prison* (New York: Wiley, 1966). By the 1970s, these two literatures were each sufficiently well developed that they were cast as competing models. See Charles W. Thomas, "Theoretical Perspectives on Prisonization: A Comparison of the Importation and Deprivation Models," *Journal*

of Criminal Law and Criminology 68 (March 1977): 35–45. Curiously, the era of mass incarceration has not been kind to research in this area. There has been less work than the subject deserves, and too much devoted to relatively narrow (though measurable) questions about prison discipline. See Matt DeLisi, Chad R. Trulson, James W. Marquart, Alan J. Drury, and Anna E. Kosloski, "Inside the Prison Black Box," *International Journal of Offender Therapy and Comparative Criminology* 56 (June 2012): 1186–1207.

5. Abubadika, *Education of Sonny Carson.*

6. Graziano, *Somebody Up There Likes Me,* 121.

7. Miller, *Untouchable,* 196–97.

8. Case J, box 40, CCF.

9. T. J. English, *Savage City,* 141.

10. Miller, *Untouchable,* 196–97.

11. Harrison and Grant, *Youth in the Toils,* 109.

12. Abubadika, *Education of Sonny Carson,* 45.

13. A secure outdoor athletic field was finally completed in 1952. See "Around the DOC," *Correction* 17 (Aug. 1952): 16.

14. Abubadika, *Education of Sonny Carson,* 50.

15. Ronald Casanova and Stephen Blackburn, *Each One, Teach One: Up and Out of Poverty: Memoirs of a Street Activist* (Austin, Tex.: Curbstone Press, 1996), 43.

16. Gail W. Sullivan, *Tears and Tiers: The Life and Times of Joseph "Mad Dog" Sullivan* (New York: Felon Entertainment, 2006), 24.

17. Schneider, *Vampires, Dragons, and Egyptian Kings,* 87.

18. Philip Klein and Leonard Mayo quizzed Superintendent Helbing before the opening of Coxsackie on the matter of racial segregation, and he assured them that inmates would not be segregated behind bars. The nature of the question clearly implied that racial segregation had been the norm at the House of Refuge. See Leonard Mayo and Philip Klein, *Recommendations for the Administration of the New York State Vocational Institution* (22 March 1935), appendix, 13, box 1, series 1, Leonard Mayo Papers, Social Welfare History Archives, University of Minnesota Libraries. There is some evidence that racial segregation in cell and dormitory assignments continued at Coxsackie and ample evidence of informal racial rules concerning many institutional assignments. Harrison and Grant, *Youth in the Toils,* 104: "The Negroes have their own dining hall, a separate section in the auditorium, and separate tiers of cells."

19. LaMotta, *Raging Bull,* 63.

20. Ben H. Bagdikian, *Caged: Eight Prisoners and Their Keepers* (New York: Harper & Row, 1976), 249.

21. Carl Weiss and David James Friar, *Terror in the Prisons: Homosexual Rape and Why Society Condones It* (Indianapolis, Ind.: Bobbs-Merrill, 1974), 220.

22. Casanova and Blackburn, *Each One, Teach One,* 53.

23. Harrison and Grant, *Youth in the Toils,* 105.

24. Charles McGregor and Sharon Sopher, *Up From the Walking Dead: The Charles McGregor Story* (New York: Doubleday, 1978), 303.

25. Harrison and Grant, *Youth in the Toils,* 117.

26. Schneider, *Vampires, Dragons, and Egyptian Kings,* 41.

27. New York State Commission of Correction, *Twenty-ninth Annual Report* (New York: New York State Commission of Correction), 445.

28. Diaz-Cotto, *Gender, Ethnicity, and the State*, 67.

29. LaMotta, *Raging Bull*, 43.

30. Richard Jacoby, *Conversations with the Capeman: The Untold Story of Salvador Agron* (Madison: University of Wisconsin Press, 2000), 148.

31. Case L, box 160, CCF.

32. Case P, box 160, CCF.

33. LaMotta, *Raging Bull*, 59.

34. Well-known professional fighters, such as Joe Louis, were held in great esteem. Former heavyweight champion James Braddock even visited Coxsackie to give an exhibition. Paul Grondahl, "Boxing 'Cinderella' Remembered on Film and in Real Life," *Albany Times Union*, 3 March 2005, n. p. Earl W. was disciplined for cutting out a picture of Ezzard Charles knocking out Sam Baroudi, in the bout where Baroudi had been killed. Case H, box 200, CCF.

35. According to one ex-Coxsackie inmate, each of the reformatories developed their own particular fighting style: "They were prison martial arts, not traditional styles." The styles included the "Woodbourne shuffle," which involved getting close to an opponent; the "Comstock style," which involved "the use of dirty fighting techniques"; and the "Coxsackie style," a kind of close-quarters wall fighting. Legend had it that Floyd Patterson's famous "peekaboo" boxing style came from Coxsackie, though Patterson took up the sport during a stay at the Wiltwyck School for juvenile delinquents and was never a prisoner at Coxsackie. See Anne Darling and James Perryman, "Karate Behind Bars: Menace, Or Means of Spiritual Survival," *Black Belt* (July 1974): 16–21.

36. Harrison and Grant, *Youth in the Toils*, 105, 109.

37. Piri Thomas, *Seven Long Times* (New York: Praeger Publishers, 1974), 80.

38. Case A, box 260, CCF.

39. Miller, *Untouchable*, 198, 200.

40. Harrison and Grant, *Youth in the Toils*, 104–106.

41. Sullivan, *Tiers and Tears*, 25.

42. Sullivan, *Tiers and Tears*, 24: "The Gees were supposedly the elite of the white fighting force, though probably almost half either knew someone from the street or paid five or ten cartons of cigarettes for the distinguished honor of standing with the Gees. There were really only a handful of dudes who could really thump (fight). The rest were phonies and were getting a free ride through the joint on their reputation."

43. Lucky's story is told in Bagdikian, *Caged*, 242–67.

44. *Rodriguez v. New York*, 2 NYS 2d 167 (1938).

45. Case A, box 380, CCF.

46. Regina Kunzel, "Situating Sex: Prison Sexual Culture in the Mid-Twentieth-Century United States," *GLQ: A Journal of Lesbian and Gay Studies* 8 (2002): 253–70, and, more recently, Regina Kunzel, *Criminal Intimacy: Prison and the Uneven History of Modern American Sexuality* (Chicago: University of Chicago Press, 2011).

47. Case J, box 120, CCF.

48. There are occasional observations regarding prison guards propositioning adolescent inmates, though these do not appear systematically. See, for example, Abubadika, *Education of Sonny Carson*, 53.

49. Case A, box 340, CCF; case L, box, 120, CCF.

50. LaMotta, *Raging Bull*, 63.

51. It should be noted that by the 1950s, the Elmira Reformatory had established a distinct special training unit for "passive homosexuals"—that is, those prisoners actively and willingly serving the passive role in sexual encounters.

52. Case F, box 370, CCF.

53. Non-sampled case, box 310, CCF.

54. Harrison and Grant, *Youth in the Toils*, 100.

55. Thomas, *Seven Long Times*, 80.

56. Case F, box 350, CCF.

57. Case F, box 170, CCF.

58. For an example of the argument that institutions for youth created the punk role, see Albert J. Reiss, "Sex Offenses: The Marginal Status of the Adolescent," *Law and Contemporary Problems* 25 (Spring 1960): 309–333, 321.

59. LaMotta, *Raging Bull*, 52; case K, box 160, CCF.

60. Weiss and Friar, *Terror in the Prisons*, 220.

61. McGregor and Sopher, *Up From the Walking Dead*, 303.

62. Felipe Luciano, "Part 2," *Lords of East Harlem*, Aug. 12, 2009, http://felipeluciano.wordpress.com/2009/08/12/part-2/

63. Case A, box 80, CCF.

64. Case E, box 200, CCF. Likewise, Cornelius N. wrote, "I am being bulldozed and picked on . . . my life is being made miserable here . . . now a place like Sing Sing I would be more guarded there . . . I'm not asking you, I'm begging you on my knees to please send me to a different Institution." Case D, box 20, CCF.

65. Thomas, *Seven Long Times*, 75.

66. Weiss and Friar, *Terror in the Prisons*, 172.

67. Thomas, *Seven Long Times*, 139.

68. Case G, box 20, CCF.

69. Case B, box 350, CCF.

70. Harrison and Grant, *Youth in the Toils*, 113–115.

71. Miller, *Untouchable*, 192.

72. Case L, box 120, CCF.

73. Case L, box 120, CCF. Leonard P.'s case is hardly singular. Joseph M., according to his case file, "was given to aggressive homosexual behavior" and was sent to solitary indefinitely for allowing two other inmates to sodomize him in the tool room. Joseph slashed his wrists on several occasions, before being transferred to Napanoch as a "borderline mental defective." Case M, box 140, CCF.

74. LaMotta, *Raging Bull*, 41.

75. "Helbing Outlines Value of Scouting at Annual Session," *Kingston (NY) Daily Freeman*, 23 Jan. 1941, 1.

76. "Helbing's Farewell Message Bears Guidance for All Youth and Parents; Reveals 'Goal,'" *Greene County Examiner-Recorder*, 7 Aug. 1941, 1.

77. Principal keeper was the title for the chief custodial officer in New York prisons. Philip Klein and Leonard Mayo, authors of the report, hoped as well that the principal keeper position would be downgraded below the level of assistant superintendent in the Coxsackie administrative organization. This did not happen, either, and the head of custody remained the effective number-two figure in the reformatory. See Klein and Mayo, *Recommendations for the Administration of the New York State Vocational Institution.*

78. Abubadika, *Education of Sonny Carson*, 51–52. See also, "George Cochran Retires from Post at Institution," *Greene County Examiner-Recorder*, 24 Feb. 1949, 1.

79. Eugene W. Morrell, "Rehabilitation through Custody," *Correction* 17 (Sept. 1952): 3–4.

80. Harrison and Grant, *Youth in the Toils*, 100.

81. LaMotta, *Raging Bull*, 53.

82. Gertrude Samuels, "A New Lobby—Ex-Cons," *New York Times*, 19 Oct. 1969, SM36.

83. Graziano, *Somebody Up There Likes Me*, 141.

84. Any undercounting results from one of two factors. First, in the case file sample are inmates who case records are incomplete, often because they were transferred to another institution, or because part of their file was passed along to another prison when they were re-incarcerated. In such cases, it is reasonable to speculate that at least some had been assigned to disciplinary cells while at Coxsackie. Second, the reporting of disciplinary cell assignment cannot be assumed to have been complete. Most of the time, a notation of such an assignment appears in the disciplinary record, but there is no reason to believe that every disciplinary action was properly recorded.

85. Abubadika, *Education of Sonny Carson*, 55–56.

86. Miller, *Untouchable*, 200.

87. Weiss and Friar, *Terror in the Prisons*, 172.

88. John Mack, "An Open Letter to the Parole Board," *Village Voice*, 9 Aug. 1976, 8.

89. Case P, box 160, CCF.

90. Bagdikian, *Caged*, tells Lucky's story of going to the hole for fighting a white inmate: "He was stripped of all his clothes and put naked into the barren cage. There was no mattress and no blanket on the slab bed. After three days he was given clothes, a mattress and a blanket. He considered himself fortunate. It was warm weather, so he did not get the 'cold shoulder'—a custom that forced the naked prisoner to open the window in winter on pain of being beaten" (p. 250). It is worth noting that the elements in these inmate narratives from Coxsackie echo those in similar narratives from the old-line, big house prisons in New York. See, particularly, *Wright v. McMann*, 387 F.2d 519 (1967), a case from Clinton Prison that helped open the federal courts to New York State prisoners.

91. Sullivan, *Tiers and Tears*, 25–26. Joseph Sullivan, by the 1970s, was working as a mob hitman. Convicted of three murders in 1982, he remains in a New York prison, serving a life term. What makes Sullivan's account of Coxsackie brutality particularly interesting is that he named names: Captain Follette, Captain LaVallee, and Sergeant Fritz, all of whom, he stated, went on to become wardens in the New York State prison system. Captain Follette refers to Harold W. Follette, who did become warden of Green Haven Prison, having been promoted first to principal keeper at Clinton Prison in 1960, following five years as a captain at Coxsackie. See "Prison Warden Named," *Watertown Daily Times*, 18 Sept. 1965, n. p. According to Stephen Chinlund, Follette "had a reputation for being vicious," and when he arrived at Green Haven, the prisoners initiated a hunger strike, in the hopes that "they might somehow make him go away." Chinlund's account of how that strike was broken featured the same crawling and animal noises as in Sullivan's account. See Stephen Chinlund, *Prison Transformations: The System, the Prisoners, and Me* (Bloomington, Ind.: Xlibris, 2009). Captain LaVallee refers to Joseph

Edwin LaVallee, who later became warden of Clinton Prison. It was LaVallee who brought Follette to Clinton Prison as the principal keeper. With LaVallee as warden, Clinton became a center of conflict with the Black Muslims. See, for example, "Prisoner Group Held Anti-White," *New York Times*, 31 Oct. 1959. According to a 1975 Jack Anderson column, LaVallee was known as "the godfather" in Clinton, and inmates complained of being "beaten, hosed down, harassed and subjected to degrading regulations such as repetitive rectal searchers." Jack Anderson and Les Whitten, "Inhuman Conditions Reported in Prison," *St. Petersburg Times*, 21 Nov. 1975, 18. Sergeant Fritz refers to Harry Fritz, who became warden of Auburn Prison at the start of the 1970s, and who later became warden of Coxsackie (see chapter 8). He was known in both places as a traditional, pro-discipline prison administrator.

92. Mack, "An Open Letter to the Parole Board," 8.

93. Claude Brown, *Manchild in the Promised Land* (New York: Macmillan; Toronto: Collier Macmillan, 1965), 239.

94. English, *Savage City*, 65. Dhoruba Bin Wahad became a Muslim while in prison for the first time, undergoing an awakening of political consciousness that was occurring throughout the reformatory system in the 1950s and 1960s, and which would find full expression still later in the adult prisons.

95. Sullivan, *Tiers and Tears*, 24; Case A, box 80, CCF.

96. Case I and case K, box 120, CCF.

97. Case H, box 110, CCF.

Chapter 5 · Reform at Work

1. Wallack, Kendall, and Briggs, *Education within Prison Walls*, iii.

2. Price Chenault, "Areas of Agreement and Disagreement between Correctional Educators and Wardens," *Journal of Correctional Education* 5 (Jan. 1953): 7.

3. Lin, *Reform in the Making*, 12.

4. Wallack, Kendall, and Briggs, *Education within Prison Walls*, 165.

5. Ibid., 173–74.

6. Ibid., 128–33.

7. New York State Vocational Institution, *Third Annual Report* (New York: New York State Vocational Institution, 1938), 4–5; Frederick Helbing, Donald D. Scarborough, and Ray P. Grabo, *A Preliminary Report of Educational Activities at the New York State Vocational Institution, Sept. 1–1935–Jan. 31, 1936* (New York: New York State Department of Corrections, 1936).

8. New York State Department of Corrections, Division of Education, *Annual Report for Fiscal Year 1938–1939* (Albany: J. B. Lyon, 1939), 34. This classification disparity was finally adjusted in the 1940–1941 fiscal year; see Division of Education, *Annual Report for Fiscal Year 1940–1941* (Albany: J. B. Lyon, 1941), 34. Still, the 1942–1943 report recounted an appeal by the Division of Education to the Division of the Budget for higher salaries, with current salary levels "not at all commensurate with the duties and working conditions inherent in institutional teaching." New York State Department of Corrections, *Report of Progress in Educational Programs, 1942–1943* (Albany: J. B. Lyon, 1943), 31.

9. Wallack, Kendall, and Briggs, *Education within Prison Walls*, 166.

10. The economy program reduced state contributions to local public school systems as well; see "N.Y. School Budget Is Slashed; Cut in Aid from State Blamed," *New York Times*, 26 July 1939, 1.

11. Division of Education, *Annual Report for Fiscal Year 1938–1939*, 32–33. See also Wallack, Kendall, and Briggs, *Education within Prison Walls*, 68.

12. *Future Plans and Costs for Education in Institutions in the New York State Department of Corrections* (Ossining, N.Y.: Sing Sing Printing Class, 1941).

13. New York State Department of Corrections, Division of Education, *Report on Progress in Educational Programs, 1942–1943* (Albany: J. B. Lyon, 1943), 31.

14. See "Record of Interview," March 22, 1939, CCP.

15. Division of Education, *Report on Progress in Educational Programs, 1942–1943*, 32.

16. Bertram Beck, *Youth within Walls*, 21.

17. Division of Education, *Report on Progress in Educational Programs, 1942–1943*, 7.

18. Untitled manuscript, folder 2, box 3, AMC.

19. "Lack of Teachers Closes Coxsackie Shops and Classes," *Civil Service Leader*, 10 Oct. 1961, 20. For the assessments of the Commission of Correction, see the *Twenty-Seventh Annual Report* (pp. 152–53), the *Twenty-Ninth Annual Report* (pp. 172–73), the *Thirty-First Annual Report* (pp. 160–61), and the *Thirty-Second Annual Report* (p. 160).

20. The Commission for the Study of the Educational Problems of Penal Institutions for Youth [Engelhardt Commission], *Report to His Excellency Governor Herbert H. Lehman* (Albany: J. B. Lyon, 1937), 17.

21. Helbing, Scarborough, and Grabo, *A Preliminary Report of Educational Activities*, 11.

22. Kendall, *Organization and Teaching of Social and Economic Studies*, 128.

23. Ibid., 50.

24. Beck, *Youth within Walls*, 25.

25. The impetus for the course had been a working committee's conclusion that "the present generation of youth" had been greatly influenced by the "low state" of public and private morality. "Department of Correction Launches Intensified Program of Training in Morals and Ethics throughout Its Institutions," *Correction* 17 (Oct. 1952): 3–4.

26. On the Cold War–era character guidance program, see Lori Lyn Bogle, *The Pentagon's Battle for the American Mind* (College Station: Texas A&M University Press, 2004).

27. New York State Commission of Correction, *Twenty-Seventh Annual Report* (New York: Commission of Correction, 1953), 152–54; Glenn Kendall, "Some Trends in Correctional Education," *Journal of Correctional Education* 6 (July 1954): 39–41.

28. Chenault, "Areas of Agreement and Disagreement," 8.

29. Price Chenault, "New Developments in Social Education in Correctional Educations," *Journal of Correctional Education* 6 (Oct. 1954): 69. Price Chenault, "Developing Education in a Correctional Setting," *Journal of Correctional Education* 15 (Oct. 1962): 16.

30. Price Chenault, "Treatment Techniques," *Prison World* (Nov.–Dec. 1947): 13–14.

31. Division of Education, *Report on Progress in Educational Programs, 1942–1943*; Black, "An Inmate's-Eye View," 9–12; and Kendall, *Organization and Teaching of Social and Economic Studies*, 73.

32. Kendall, "Some Trends in Correctional Education," 40.

33. Chenault, "New Developments in Social Education," 70; John Severance, "The General Education Department of the Elmira Reception Center," *Journal of Correctional Education* 8 (April 1956): 33–35.

34. P. E. Hagen, "Some Problems of an Educational Worker in an Institution," *Journal of Correctional Education* 9 (Oct. 1957): 88–92.

35. Kendall, "Some Characteristics of Reception Center Youths," 43.

36. Case D, box 10; case H, box 10; case J, box 10; case C, box 120; case H, box 200, all CCF.

37. Helbing, Scarborough, and Grabo, *A Preliminary Report of Educational Activities,* 17; see also New York State Vocational Institution, *Fourth Annual Report,* 46–47; and Division of Education, *Annual Report 1938–1939,* 50.

38. Case K, box 280; case D, box 350; case D, box 300, all CCF.

39. Felipe Luciano, "The Song of Joe B," *New York Magazine,* 25 Oct. 1971, 49.

40. "Joe Bataan: The Boogaloo Godfather Tells of His Transition from Street Thug to Cherished Icon of Latin Music," *Red Bull Music Academy* (2006), www.redbullmusic academy.com/lectures/joe-bataan—extraordinary-joe.

41. Abubadika, *Education of Sonny Carson,* 52–53.

42. Margaret C. Hannigan and William T. Henderson, "Narcotic Addicts Take Up Reading," in *Bibliotherapy Sourcebook,* ed. Rhea Joyce Rubin (Phoenix, Ariz.: Oryx Press, 1978), 281–86.

43. Wallack, Kendall, and Briggs, *Education within Prison Walls,* 29.

44. Howard L. Briggs, "Selecting Vocational Education Material," *Journal of Correctional Education* (Jan. 1949): 16–24, 20.

45. New York State Commission of Correction, *Twenty-Ninth Annual Report,* 172–73, indicates that the carpenter shop was about 40% maintenance work, upholstery 80–90%, and the paint shop 90%. The tailor shop, in 1955, set a production record of 10,775 pieces of clothing, pillowcases, sheets, and towels.

46. Not until 1955 did the State Commission of Correction recommend paying Coxsackie inmates, "in view of the production character of some of the vocational shop activities." Commission of Correction, *Twenty-Ninth Annual Report,* 175. Starting the following year, Coxsackie prisoners finally began to receive five cents a day in wages.

47. Case I, box 100, CCF.

48. Non-sampled case file, box 30, CCF.

49. Case A, box 100; case A, box 310; case B, box 110; case A, box 150, all CCF.

50. Case J, box 180, CCF.

51. Raymond Corsini, "Vocational Interests of Juvenile Delinquents," *Journal of Correctional Education* 3 (Jan. 1951): 11–16.

52. "Correctional Institution Farms," *Correction* 16 (Aug. 1951): 14–15.

53. Beck, *Youth within Walls,* 24. Case H, box 210, includes an explicit statement of reformatory policy in this regard.

54. New York State Commission of Correction, *Thirtieth Annual Report* (New York: Commission of Correction, 1956), 176.

55. Case I, box 150, CCF; case L, box 150, CCF.

56. Case D, box 250, CCF.

57. Non-sampled case file, box 360, CCF. Coxsackie introduced the "Waiting on Table" program in 1952. The content of the course included "the qualifications of a

waiter, getting ready for work, taking and filling orders, service during the meal, meeting emergencies, and employer-employee relationships." "N.Y.S.V.I. Offers Course on 'Waiting on Table,'" *Correction* 17 (Oct. 1952): 13.

58. Non-sampled case file, box 360, CCF.

59. Non-sampled case file, box 390, CCF.

60. New York State Commission of Correction, *Twenty-First Annual Report* (New York: Commission of Correction, 1947), 74; John B. Costello, "Institutions for Juvenile Delinquents," in Tappan, *Contemporary Correction*, 352; New York State Commission of Correction, *Twenty-Eighth Annual Report* (New York: Commission of Correction, 1954), 167.

61. Glenn Kendall, "Application of Basic Principles of Administration and Supervision to the Conduct of a Correctional Institution Educational Program," *Journal of Correctional Education* 10 (Oct. 1958): 104–107.

62. Thomas, *Seven Long Times*, 93–94.

63. Ibid., 94.

64. Case I, box 140, CCF.

65. Case F, box 40, CCF.

66. Case D, box 300, CCF.

67. Case D, box 340, CCF.

68. Heather Ann Thompson, "Rethinking Working-Class Struggle Through the Lens of the Carceral State: Toward a Labor History of Inmates and Guards," *Labor: Studies in Working-Class History of the Americas* 8 (Fall 2011): 15–45.

69. See Price Chenault, "Psychiatry in the New York State Department of Correction," *Correction* 13 (July 1948): 3, 5, 7, 11. See also Paul Wegner, "Social Rehabilitation from the Psychiatric Point of View," *Prison World* (July–Aug. 1944): 11, 26. V. C. Branham, "The Psychopathic Delinquent," *Prison World* (Sept.–Oct. 1940): 21–22, 84, calls for a separate institution for psychopathic inmates in New York.

70. Alexander W. Pisciotta, "The Theory and Practice of the New York House of Refuge, 1857–1935" (Ph.D. diss., Florida State University, 1979), 184.

71. Hyman Goldstein, "Vocational Guidance of the Underprivileged," *Industrial Arts and Vocational Education* 30 (1941): 45–46.

72. William Argento viewed Coxsackie's immigrant and minority prisoners as having a lower native intelligence, while Howard Gondree published work expressing deep skepticism over what "adolescent training schools" like Coxsackie could successfully accomplish. On Argento, see Nicole Rafter, *Creating Born Criminals* (Urbana and Chicago: University of Illinois Press, 1997), 19. On Gondree, see Howard E. Gondree, "Institutional Training Should Prepare for Parole," *Federal Probation* 31 (1951): 31–34.

73. Raymond J. Corsini and Gregory A. Miller, "Psychology in Prisons, 1952," *American Psychologist* 9 (May 1954): 184–85; "Ray Corsini: A Life That Spans an Era," *Psychologist* 37 (fall/winter 2002): 68–77. See also Walter B. Martin, "Common Sense Psychiatry," *Prison World* (Jan.–Feb. 1942): 9–10, and Bertram Pollens, "The Plain English of Psychology," *Jail Association Journal* (July–Aug. 1939): 7. Guard responses to disturbed inmates employed far less complex language than that of the mental health professionals— "inmate is either a complete jerk or else passing himself off as one" with lots of "screwball behavior" (Ronald M., case C, box 240, CCF); speaking of Edward Z., a 17-year-old from Rochester, who eventually received fifteen formal disciplinary reports, for

disobedience, insolence, refusing to work, idleness, contraband, failure to obey orders, smoking, gambling, and leaving his work assignment: "Putz is no good. Putz knows that he is no good. Putz knows that I know he is no good." Case E, box 300, CCF.

74. See Louis N. Robinson, "Institutions for Defective Delinquents," *Journal of Criminal Law and Criminology* 24 (July–Aug. 1933): 352–99.

75. Prior to becoming an institution for defective delinquents, Napanoch was known as the Eastern New York Reformatory. For more on the early history of Napanoch, see Alexander W. Pisciotta, *Benevolent Repression: Social Control and the American Reformatory-Prison Movement* (New York: New York University Press, 1994).

76. Rafter, *Creating Born Criminals*, 216.

77. IQ testing was universal at Coxsackie from the day it opened in 1935; in February 1938, the New York State prison commissioner ordered that psychologists in all institutions immediately conduct IQ tests on all fourteen thousand inmates in their institutions. See New York State Department of Corrections, *Second Annual Report of the New York State Vocational Institution* (New York: Department of Corrections, 1937), 51, and *Third Annual Report of the New York State Vocational Institution* (New York: Department of Corrections, 1938), 39.

78. Case J, box 160, CCF.

79. Glenn M. Kendall, "The Mental Defective in Correctional Institutions: From the Standpoint of Classification," *Journal of Correctional Education* (Jan. 1949): 11–15, quotation on 15.

80. Case I, box 30, CCF.

81. Case H, box 10; case H, box 50; and case M, box 140, all CCF.

82. Cases I and J, box 20, CCF.

83. McCartney intended every transfer to Napanoch to be held for the rest of their lives under supervision, recommended more cases for transfer than were ever actually undertaken, and even attempted to have inmates at the expiration of their sentences sent to Napanoch (see, for example, the case of Richard F., case H, box 10, CCF). McCartney, in *Understanding Human Behavior* (New York: Vantage Press, 1956), placed a heavy emphasis on heredity, observing, "intelligence is fixed at conception" (p. 19). His view was highly racialized—"This has nothing to do with training. It is a question of breeding" (pp. 20–21). McCartney also concluded that true educational success required at least an IQ of 120. No inmate tested that high.

84. Sullivan, *Tears and Tiers*, 26.

85. Rafter, *Creating Born Criminals*, 220. Courts never challenged the authority of prison officials to transfer inmates for disciplinary reasons. Indeed, in *New York v. Glowacki* (1940), the court argued that transfer offered "the superintendent an opportunity to clear out the rotten apples, leaving the sound ones in the barrel." See John S. Broude, "Use of Involuntary Inter-Prison Transfer as a Sanction," *American Journal of Criminal Law* 3 (fall 1974): 117–64.

86. This concept was subjected to an early and devastating attack by Michael Hakeem, "A Critique of the Psychiatric Approach to Crime and Correction," *Law and Contemporary Problems* 23 (1958): 650–82.

87. James L. McCartney, "Classification of Prisoners," *Psychiatric Quarterly* 7 (1933): 369–77; "Psychiatrists in Correctional Institutions," *American Journal of Psychiatry* 117

(Feb. 1961): 754; and "The Evaluation of Classification in Prisons," *American Journal of Orthopsychiatry* 4 (April 1934): 225–32.

88. Case D, box 180, CCF.

89. Case C, box 20, CCF.

90. *Joseph P. Scott v. New York,* 322 NYS 2d 247 (1971).

91. See "Freeing Madman Scored," *New York Times,* 10 Sept. 1952, 26; "Record of Killer in Asylum Opened," *New York Times,* 6 Sept. 1952, 12; the state was sued over Jones's release, and the court found Matteawan to be in "a deplorable condition of over-crowding and understaffing." *Yula P. St. George, as Administratrix of the Estate of Frank St. George, Deceased, Claimant, v State of New York,* 118 NYS 2d 596 (1953). The case attracted national attention within the psychiatric profession. See Winfred Overholser, "The Present Status of the Problems of Release of Patients from Mental Hospitals," *Psychiatric Quarterly* 29 (Jan. 1955): 372–80.

92. "Dr. Charles Cuccio," *Schenectady (NY) Daily Gazette,* 3 Oct. 2001, 13. Elmira had established an early group therapy program the previous year. Paul E. Plowitz, "Psychiatric Service and Group Therapy in the Rehabilitation of Offenders," *Journal of Correctional Education* 2 (1950): 78–80.

93. Cases D, F, and J, box 280, CCF.

Chapter 6 · *A Conspiracy of Frustration*

1. Gertrude Samuels, "A New Lobby—Ex-Cons," *New York Times,* 19 Oct. 1969, SM46.

2. Abubadika, *Education of Sonny Carson,* 56.

3. English, *Savage City,* 179–80.

4. Brown, *Manchild in the Promised Land,* 237.

5. Case E, box 200, CCF.

6. Harrison and Grant, *Youth in the Toils,* 123–27.

7. Never-paroled inmates generally included the most serious disciplinary problems at the institution. Earl W., warned before his first hearing that "your actions will govern what our decision at that time will be," and before his next that "if you work for a break, you don't have to ask for one," accumulated twenty-seven disciplinary reports (the third highest of any prisoner in the case file sample) and was never paroled. Within a year of his release, Earl was headed to Sing Sing after pleading guilty to a new burglary charge. Case H, box 200, CCF.

8. *New York v. Glowacki,* 174 Misc. 415; 22 NYS 2d 22 (1940).

9. Case D, box 170, CCF.

10. Case F, box 170, CCF.

11. Cases A and B, box 180, CCF.

12. Case H, box 200; cases F and H, box 210, all CCF.

13. Case A, box 160, CCF.

14. Indeed, he was held—the program committee held him for three more months before a successful parole hearing. Case F, box 230, CCF.

15. Case A, box 300, CCF.

16. English, *Savage City,* 117.

17. Mack, "An Open Letter to the Parole Board," 8. See also Lumumba Shakur's account of facing the parole board at Great Meadow in 1963. Asked if he was sorry for his

original offense, and if he would "disavow and renounce the Black Muslims and black nationalism," Shakur refused and had his parole denied. Kuwasi Balagoon, *Look for Me in the Whirlwind: The Collective Autobiography of the New York 21* (New York: Random House, 1971), 243.

18. Case G, box 30, CCF.

19. Case D, box 20, CCF.

20. Case A, box 320, CCF.

21. Case D, box 60, CCF.

22. Case F, box 200, CCF.

23. Case F, box 20, CCF.

24. Case E, box 50, CCF.

25. Case A, box 360.

26. Case E, box 360, CCF; case F, box 90, CCF.

27. Case D, box 150, CCF.

28. Cases D and E, box 40, CCF.

29. Case J, box 100, CCF.

30. Case G, box 10, CCF.

31. Case B, box 20, CCF.

32. Case F, box 100, CCF.

33. Case A, box 10, CCF.

34. See cases D and E, box 270, and case B, box 20, all CCF.

35. Case H, box 300, CCF.

36. Wallace Gillpatrick, "The Outmate," *Proceedings of the Annual Congress of Correction of the American Prison Association* (New York: American Prison Association, 1917), 259.

37. Case C, box 10, CCF.

38. Case I, box 200, CCF.

39. Case B, box 30, CCF.

40. Case J, box 140, and case J, box 80, CCF.

41. Case C, box 100, CCF.

42. Case C, box 60, CCF.

43. Case A, box 10, CCF.

44. Case E, box 10, CCF.

45. Case C, box 30, CCF.

46. New York State Department of Corrections, *First Annual Report of the New York State Vocational Institution* (New York: Department of Corrections, 1936), 27.

47. Case F, box 30, and cases C and H, box 50, CCF.

48. Case E, box 60, CCF.

49. Case files include prisoners sent to camps in Oregon (case E, box 60, CCF) and Nevada (case L, box 90, CCF). There were some exceptions. Mario A. was expelled from a CCC camp for encouraging the men in the camp to go on strike. See case I, box 70, CCF). Jack W. (case B, box 60, CCF) was stabbed to death on the day he left a CCC camp in Utica.

50. As a consequence, parolees from Coxsackie continued to go into the CCC through early 1941. For more on the issue of parolees in the CCC, see Margot Canaday, *The Straight*

State: Sexuality and Citizenship in Twentieth-Century America (Princeton, N.J.: Princeton University Press, 2009), 120.

51. This inmate was inducted into the army a year after finding work as a printer and was killed in action in July 1944.

52. Case A, box 100, CCF.

53. Case F, box 280, CCF.

54. Case C, box 300, CCF.

55. Case F, box 320; case N, box 100; case C, box 180; all CCF. This policy doesn't seem to have been followed consistently. Near the end of his term as superintendent of Coxsackie, Glenn Kendall cheerfully supplied former prisoner Gordon M. with a certificate of accomplishment in electrical work, noting, "I hope this certificate will be of help to you. Good luck!" Case A, box 240, CCF.

56. See the reports of the Osborne Association for the years 1933, 1934, 1936, and 1939, all presented at the annual meetings of the Osborne Association, in AMC; Cox quote comes from the 1934 report, page 8; "Elmira Reformatory, Elmira," *Prison World* (Jan.–Feb. 1942), 26.

57. Robert Hannum, "Report of Robert Hannum, Director of Vocational Placement, for the Year Ending December 31, 1944," Osborne Association (Jan. 5, 1945), unpublished manuscript, SBP.

58. See, for example, the effort by Coxsackie to establish a vocational placement program for reformatory parolees by working with unions and business. See New York State Commission of Correction, *Thirty-First Annual Report* (1957), 165; and New York State Commission of Correction, *Thirty-Second Annual Report* (1958), 165. As late as 1969, Price Chenault remained committed to expanding inmate vocational and postrelease employment opportunities. See Glenn Kendall to Lithgow Osborne, March 18, 1969, AMC.

59. For inmates in the case file sample released during the war itself, the percentage serving in the military was slightly higher, at 26% (27 of 103).

60. Case M, box 100, CCF.

61. Case C, box 30; case D, box 50; case O, box 140; and case B, box 150, all CCF. For draftees, wartime service interrupted more promising marriage and work situations. Peter F., pleased with his work as a printer in Albany, was married early in 1942. "We both know," Peter wrote his parole officer, "that our getting married will not stop me from going in the draft. I have a good job and am working steady and feel that we can get along on this." Two months later, Peter was inducted into the army, and he died in military service in July 1944. See case A, box 20, CCF.

62. Case A, box 150, CCF.

63. See case E, box 50 (sentenced to U.S. military prison at Green Haven); case G, box 60 (under psychiatric evaluation in an army hospital following unspecified criminal conduct); case E, box 80 (arrested for robbery while in U.S. Army); case F, box 80 (given a four-year sentence as a U.S. Army deserter); case F, box 90 (given a five-year sentence as a military deserter); case N, box 90 (sentenced to five to ten years in Sing Sing after induction into the U.S. Army); case D, box 120 (sentenced by military for being AWOL and escaping confinement); case E, box 140 (under psychiatric observation at a naval hospital); case R, box 170 (charged with being AWOL); case H, box 220 (charged with being AWOL).

64. Case E, box 160, CCF.

65. Case F, box 120. Consider also the case of Howard G., "one of the most capable bakers that has been trained in this institution." Paroled in 1940, rearrested for petty larceny but acquitted, he enlisted in the army in late 1940 but stole the family car and disappeared before actually reporting for duty. Returned to Coxsackie for violation of parole, Howard was released in early 1942 to serve several months of military time for desertion. He was drafted by the army in 1943 but was sentenced to a five- to ten-year term in Sing Sing before he could report for duty. Case N, box 90, CCF.

66. A study conducted by the DOC of 950 adolescent males paroled from reformatories between June 1957 and May 1958, showed that 371, or 39.1%, were returned for violation of parole (the subgroup of Coxsackie inmates returned for violation of parole was also 39%). See Russell G. Oswald and Paul D. McGinnis, *Parole Adjustment and Prior Educational Achievement of Male Adolescent Offenders, June 1957–June 1961* (Albany: New York State Division of Parole, 1961).

67. The Oswald-McGinnis study also found no statistically significant differences between parole completers and parole violators, based on IQ, race, age, or educational progress while confined in reformatories.

68. The literature on prison reentry has become quite robust. Jeremy Travis notes that "the odds against successful reentry are daunting," and that two-thirds of released prisoners will be arrested for one or more crimes. Travis, *But They All Come Back: Facing the Challenges of Prisoner Reentry* (Washington, D.C.: Urban Institute Press, 2005), particularly chapter 5, "Prisoner Reentry and Public Safety," which offers a useful overview of the contemporary research literature on postrelease criminality.

69. Case A, box 30, CCF.

70. Case K, box 180, CCF; "30 Robberies Laid to Brooklyn Pair," *New York Times*, 24 May 1952), 12.

71. Jake LaMotta recalled deciding to pursue boxing upon his release from Coxsackie and facing the anger of his best friend, who challenged him: "What are you gonna do for eating money? Join your old man in the peddling business?" Likewise, he angered the local mobster who wanted to represent him: "Want to make it own your own yet? You know what you can make on your own, don't you Mister Chump? Nothin', that's what!" LaMotta, *Raging Bull*, 74, 80.

72. Ralph S. Banay, *Youth in Despair* (New York: Coward-McCann, 1948), 59–60.

73. English, *Savage City*, 180.

74. Mack, "An Open Letter to the Parole Board," 8.

75. Case I, box 170, CCF.

76. Cases C and H, box 100, CCF; case A, box 50, CCF.

77. Case E, box 30, CCF.

78. See case B, box 180, in which Warren W. was convicted for beating a man to death two years after his parole from Coxsackie, a crime for which he could give no explanation.

79. "To Die For $11 Robbery," *New York Times*, 19 March 1942, 16; *New York v. Bender*, 176 NYS 2d 27 (1958); *New York v. Bender*, 37 NYS 2d 227 (1942); *New York v. Elling*, 46 NE 2d 501 (1943). In a similar vein, Bernard Berman was convicted of first-degree murder in Erie County in 1944, a conviction later overturned because of a coerced confession (1965) in the case of *New York v. Augello and Berman*, 265 NYS 2d 509. There is considerable

evidence that Berman, Joseph Augello, and their wives had committed a series of crimes. A gasoline ration book found in their possession after the Syracuse murder and robbery belonged to a Cleveland, Ohio, man who had been held up, robbed, and left tied to a tree. Other holdups in Utica and Albany were linked to the foursome. See " 'Honeymoon Bandits' Crime Wave Betrayed by Red Coat," *Milwaukee Sentinel*, 16 Jan. 1944, 8. Augello pled insanity at their trial, and the two men were convicted in March 1944. See "Augello, Berman Found Guilty of Tavern Slaying," *Grape Belt and Chautauqua (NY) Farmer*, 10 March 1944, 1. The two participated in a mass escape from the Erie County jail while in custody. They were picked up trying to board a freight train at a railyard east of Buffalo, shivering and hanging on to the sides of a tank car. See "Three of Eight Prisoners Nabbed by Sheriff's Staff," *Avon (NY) Herald News*, 10 Feb. 1944, 1.

80. Case C, box 10; case G, box 20; case B, box 30; all CCF. See the case of James Watkins, on parole from Coxsackie in 1942, then convicted of second-degree assault and sentenced to five to ten years. *People of New York ex rel. James Watkins v. Robert E. Murphy, as Warden of Auburn State Prison*, 3 NY 2d 163 (1957). For more on the practice, see New York State Division of Parole, *Twenty-Seventh Annual Report of the Division of Parole, State of New York* (Albany: J. B. Lyon, 1957), 155.

81. Shadd Maruna, *Making Good: How Ex-Convicts Reform and Rebuild Their Lives* (Washington, D.C.: American Psychological Association, 2001), 55.

Chapter 7 · The Frying Pan and the Fire

1. Schneider, *Vampires, Dragons, and Egyptian Kings*, 57, points out, "The wartime juvenile crime wave was produced as much by the effort to curb youthful behavior as by the growth of misbehavior itself," though he also acknowledges that wartime disruptions to family and community provided opportunities for adolescents to exercise a newly rebellious attitude. See chapter 2, "Discovering Gangs," more generally.

2. "Population Trends in New York Prisons," *Journal of Criminal Law and Criminology* 37 (Nov.-Dec. 1946), 32; MacCormick, "Existing Provisions for the Correction of Youthful Offenders," 588–99.

3. Coxsackie was hardly unique in this regard. Given how significant disciplinary transfers were as a resource of control for prison authorities more generally, it is surprising that they have received virtually no attention from prison historians.

4. Zinoman, *Colonial Bastille*, 4.

5. Abubadika, *Education of Sonny Carson*, 51.

6. English, *Savage City*, 60, 65.

7. Balagoon, *Look for Me in the Whirlwind*, 176–77.

8. Schneider, *Vampires, Dragons, and Egyptian Kings*, 163.

9. Case C, box 220, CCF.

10. Case H, box 180, CCF. James was held until the maximum expiration of his sentence.

11. See case H, box 70; case L, box 160; case P, box 160; all CCF.

12. Case G, box 300, CCF.

13. Case F, box 350, CCF; Angelo was a serious disciplinary problem and held for the maximum expiration of his sentence.

14. The Department of Corrections would not send those convicted of drug sale violations to Coxsackie; in 1955, eighty-three young men convicted of narcotic sale offenses

went to Elmira, while none at all went to Coxsackie. See New York State Commission of Corrections, *Twenty-Ninth Annual Report*, 444.

15. Case B, box 300. William, on his return to Coxsackie, was held for the maximum expiration of his sentence.

16. New York State Division of Parole, *Twenty-Seventh Annual Report*; Legislative Document No. 119 (1957), 14–20.

17. Case C, box 320, CCF.

18. Case C, box 320, CCF.

19. Case C, box 320, CCF.

20. Glenn Kendall felt the youthful offender designation was being poorly used by the courts, resulting in Coxsackie receiving large numbers of young men "who are so seriously disturbed or so badly conditioned that the chances for rehabilitation are small indeed." Glenn Kendall, "Youth Offender Procedures—The Reception Center," paper delivered at the 41st Annual State Conference of Probation Officers, West Point, New York, Oct. 20, 1949, unpublished manuscript, AMC.

21. "Dewey to Ask Aid for Young Felons," *New York Times*, 5 Jan. 1953, 15. The solution of transferring Coxsackie inmates to Great Meadow persisted for years. Not until 1976 did that transfer relationship finally break down; in an effort to "improve the reputation" of Great Meadow, transfers began going to Green Haven instead. See Sheehan, *A Prison and a Prisoner*, 71. Sheehan also refers to Great Meadow as the "garbage dump" of the state prison system (p. 3).

22. The search for an end-of-the-line solution for adolescent offenders had at least two parallels in postwar New York social policy. In the juvenile system, the state took over the old New York City Reformatory at New Hampton in 1957, with the intention of using the institution to house youths too aggressive for the juvenile reform schools at Warwick and Industry. In a second parallel development, the New York City school system responded to delinquency and youth violence with the creation of the "600" schools for troubled youth, and a smaller number of "700" schools for older delinquent students. For more on the 600 schools, see the excellent study by Daniel Hiram Perlstein, *Justice, Justice: School Politics and the Eclipse of Liberalism* (New York: Peter Lang, 2004).

23. Emma Harrison, "Youth Board Sifts Work Camp Plans," *New York Times*, 28 Aug. 1957, 29.

24. I was fortunate that the inmate case files from Great Meadow extended just far enough chronologically to capture the shift to a transfer institution. These cases are all drawn from boxes 314–320 of the Great Meadow Inmate Case Files at the New York State Archives. I reviewed every file in these boxes, not all of which were transfers from Coxsackie. Some came directly from the Elmira Reception, others from Elmira and Woodbourne, and a few from the maximum-security prisons. It should be noted, however, that more came from Coxsackie than anywhere else.

25. New York State Commission of Correction, *Thirtieth Annual Report*, 175.

26. New York State Commission of Correction, *Twenty-Ninth Annual Report*, 442–43.

27. Conboy would remain as the warden of Great Meadow until his retirement in 1972. His retirement was preceded by another major disturbance. See Emanuel Perlmutter, "Guards Put Down Disorder in Great Meadow Prison," *New York Times*, 16 Sept. 1971, 49. Scott Christiansen recalled a visit to Great Meadow right around the time Conboy retired, observing that the warden appeared to be "a relic from another century" who

offered commentary on "how to handle the coloreds." See Scott Christiansen, *With Liberty for Some: 500 Years of Imprisonment in America* (Hanover, N.H.: University Press of New England, 2000), xi.

28. Thomas, *Seven Long Times*. One of Thomas's friends, Bayamon, warned the younger cons: "You cats better believe it, you can pick up all the sticks and stones you want and do all kinds of numbers with your fists, but you better dig that it's gonna take more than heart to go against guards and state troopers and, dig it, even the armed forces if need be. They'd send planes in to strafe this fucking place if they had to. I'm in for the idea, but not for it coming out of thin air" (p. 189).

29. Thomas, *Seven Long Times*, 209.

30. Piri Thomas, *Down These Mean Streets* (New York: Knopf, 1967), 283.

31. The Comstock riot is well described by Piri Thomas in *Seven Long Times* and *Down These Mean Streets*. See also, "Clubs Quell Riot in Upstate Prison," *New York Times*, 19 Aug. 1955, 40.

32. Thomas, *Seven Long Times*, 214.

33. For the Associated Press coverage of the Great Meadow riot, see "Convicts Riot is Broken Up," *Milwaukee Journal*, 18 Aug. 1955, 9. See also "Clubs Quell Riot in Upstate Prison"; "Prisons Chief Calls Riot 'Spontaneous,'" *New York Times* 28 Aug. 1955, 58.

34. Stafford Derby, "A Firm Hand Needed—And Supplied," *Christian Science Monitor*, 12 Sept. 1955, 16.

35. "Keeplocked" refers to the practice of keeping an inmate confined in his cell for disciplinary reasons. Keeplocked inmates could not participate in the regular daily schedule of prison activities. Great Meadow Case Files, boxes 318 and 320.

36. Case C, box 380, CCF.

37. Sullivan, *Tears and Tiers*, 26.

38. English, *Savage City*, 65–66. By the 1960s, Great Meadow prisoners in disciplinary cells were also having their heads shaved bald, according to one account.

39. Chinlund, *Prison Transformations*, 47–48, 167.

40. Balagoon, *Look for Me in the Whirlwind*, 184.

41. Ibid.

42. Thomas, *Seven Long Times*, 219.

43. Ronald Berkman, *Opening the Gates: The Rise of the Prisoners' Movement* (Lexington, Mass.: Lexington Books, 1979), 39.

44. See Gottschalk, *Prison and the Gallows*, 171–76. That the concentration of disaffected minority youth under racially discriminatory conditions should have produced political consequences is not surprising. This is consistent with basic argument made by Daniel Kryder that wartime mobilizations during World War II fundamentally altered the American racial dynamic and gave momentum to the movements for civil rights and racial equality. The prison was simply another setting in which the configuration of race in America was reshaped. See Daniel Kryder, *Divided Arsenal: Race and the American State During World War II* (Cambridge: Cambridge University Press, 2000).

45. The quote comes from Lumumba Shakur, in Balagoon, *Look for Me in the Whirlwind*, 180. This is not unlike the Harlem activists Martha Biondi has studied, who "discursively linked police brutality in New York to southern lynching and racist violence, but they offered a distinct analysis of urban police brutality." Biondi, *To Stand and Fight*, 70.

46. Brown, *Manchild in the Promised Land*, 326.

47. English, *Savage City*, 66–67. Bin Wahad also read the work of J. A. Rogers, a pioneering scholar of African history and anthropology. According to *Savage City*, Rogers's writings "were so prized in prisons that inmates painstakingly copied his pamphlets by hand so that more inmates could have access to them" (p. 66).

48. Brown, *Manchild in the Promised Land*, 332–33; see also "Riot in Gallery Halts U.N. Debate," *New York Times*. 16 Feb. 1961, 1.

49. Thomas, *Seven Long Times*, 219. For Dhoruba Bin Wahad, the turning point came after Malcolm X's assassination. While still a prisoner in Great Meadow, in 1965, he changed his name from Richard Earl Moore to Dhoruba al-Mujahid Bin Wahad. See English, *Savage City*, 115.

50. Balagoon, *Look for Me in the Whirlwind*, 242–43.

51. "Prison Racial Fight Injures 23 Upstate; 450 Join in Melee," *New York Times*, 23 Sept. 1963, 22. Conboy observed to reporters, "The whites consider certain courts their domain and the Negroes consider certain courts to be their own." "Handball Game Turns into Riot at Prison," *Amsterdam Daily Democrat*, 28 Sept. 1963, 1.

52. "Prison Racial Fight Injures 23 Upstate," 22.

53. The quote comes from the Associated Press coverage of the riot; see "Racism Linked to Prison Riot," *Spokane Daily Chronicle*, 28 Sept. 1963, 18.

54. "State Transfers 30 Rioters from Racially-Torn Prison," *Auburn (NY) Citizen-Advertiser*, 17 Oct. 1963, 7.

55. Barbara Lavin McEleney interviewed Vito Ternullo, a longtime ally of the reform interests within the New York State Department of Corrections. Ternullo believed that the growth in black and Puerto Rican inmates was the number one issue for security personnel in the New York State system and was one motivator behind their push for new institutions in the system, a push that began with the adoption of Great Meadow as a transfer reformatory and developed into the proposal for a further-down-the-end-of-the-line prison in 1963. That prison was not constructed, in part owing to the modest declines in overall prison population. See Barbara Lavin McEleney, *Correctional Reform in New York: The Rockefeller Years and Beyond* (Lanham, Md.: University Press of America, 1985).

56. Felipe Luciano, "1969," *Lords of East Harlem* (2009), http://felipeluciano.word press.com/2009/08/11/hello-world.

57. Felipe Luciano, "Speech by Felipe Luciano, New York State Chrmn., Young Lords Organization, at the First Spanish Methodist Church in El Barrio (111th St. & Lexington) on Sun., December 21, 1969," in *The Young Lords: A Reader*, ed. Darrel Enck-Wanzer, Iris Morales, and Denise Oliver-Velez (New York: New York University Press, 2010), 208–212.

58. Armand Schaubroeck's recordings remain as powerful as ever, though not nearly as well-known as they should be. The best overview of his Elmira project is Elwood Mole, "Armand Schaubroeck Steals," *Perfect Sound Forever* (April 2006), www.furious.com /perfect/armandschaubroeck.html.

Chapter 8 · Out of Time

1. The crisis of the liberal prison is well documented, but the deep roots of that crisis are not well understood. Francis Cullen and Karen E. Gilbert, in *Reaffirming Rehabilitation* (Cincinnati, Ohio: Anderson, 1982), 82, assumed the dominance of liberalism in

corrections into the late sixties: "Rehabilitation thus remained unchallenged as the dominant correctional ideology. There seemed to be little chance that there would be a call either to revert to the punitive principles of bygone days or to abandon the quest to build upon the foundation of the therapeutic state." Recent historical scholarship has begun to develop a clearer picture of the significance of conservative politics during the "liberal" era of crime and punishment. Michael W. Flamm, *Law and Order: Street Crime, Civil Unrest, and the Crisis of Liberalism in the 1960s* (New York: Columbia University Press, 2005) is a useful account, particularly as it explores the 1950s-era foundations of law-and-order politics. See also Gottschalk, *Prison and the Gallows*, and Theodore Hamm, *Rebel and a Cause: Caryl Chessman and the Politics of the Death Penalty in Postwar California, 1948–1974* (Berkeley: University of California Press, 2001).

2. Bertram M. Beck, *Youth within Walls*.

3. Bertram M. Beck, *Short-Term Therapy in an Authoritarian Setting* (New York: Family Service Association of America, 1946), 7, 35.

4. David Ciepley, *Liberalism in the Shadow of Totalitarianism* (Cambridge, Mass.: Harvard University Press, 2006), 162.

5. F. E. Haynes, "The Sociological Study of the Prison Community," *Journal of Criminal Law and Criminology* 39 (Nov.–Dec. 1948): 432–40, 435.

6. Norman Polansky, "The Prison as an Autocracy," *Journal of Criminal Law and Criminology* (May–June 1942): 16–22; see also K. Lewin, R. Lippitt, and R. K. White, "Patterns of Aggressive Behavior in Artificially Created Social Climates," *Journal of Social Psychology* 10 (1939): 271–99; Gresham Sykes, "The Corruption of Authority and Rehabilitation," *Journal of Social Forces* 34 (1955): 257–62.

7. Lucy Freeman, "State Prisons Seen Lax Toward Youth," *New York Times*, 5 Jan. 1951, 15.

8. Beck, *Youth within Walls*, 18–19, 32.

9. Ibid., 24, 27.

10. Ibid., 17.

11. Ibid., 42.

12. "Youth Work Camps Held Undesirable," *New York Times*, 8 Jan. 1951, 18.

13. "Grave Mistakes Seen in Youth Psychiatry," *New York Times*, 8 March 1951, 31. E. R. Cass represented the Prison Association of New York. Bertram Beck attended, as did Austin MacCormick.

14. "Aiding Youthful Prisoners," *New York Times*, 19 Jan. 1951, 24.

15. Edward Hudson, "Young Offenders to Get Camp Term," *New York Times*, 17 Aug. 1955, 22.

16. Janssen, "When the 'Jungle' Met the Forest," 706.

17. Peter Kihss, "Rockefeller Seeks More Work Camps for Delinquents," *New York Times*, 9 Sept. 1959, 1.

18. Warren Weaver, Jr., "Campers Uphold Governor's Idea," *New York Times*, 3 Oct. 1959, 1.

19. Emma Harrison, "Work Camp Boys Find New Lives," *New York Times*, 4 Sept. 1957, 35.

20. "Young Offenders Work in Camps," *New York Times*, 7 Dec. 1958, 154.

21. "50 Offenders Going to Forestry Camp," *New York Times*, 27 Aug. 1955, 17. See Milton Bracker, "Governor Hints State May Widen Youth-Camp Plan," *New York Times*,

7 Sept. 1959, 1; Robert Alden, "A Work Camp Assessed: Better Boys, Better Forest," *New York Times*, 7 Sept. 1959, 1.

22. The entire discussion of Roger V.'s case comes from case B, box 380, CCF.

23. This quote comes from the original 1965 study proposal, part of the New York State Department of Corrections records at the New York State Archives.

24. "Corrections Chief Will Ask Fund Rise," *New York Times*, 6 Nov. 1955, 38.

25. New York State Department of Corrections, *Your New York State Department of Correction and the Challenge of Delinquent Youth* (New York: Department of Corrections, 1955), 6.

26. *Characteristics of Inmates Under Custody* in New York State Correctional Institutions (Dec. 31, 1962), Department of Corrections, Division of Research (New York State Department of Corrections, 1963). The IBM punch card data were collected and maintained by the division, who systematically compiled information on every inmate entering and leaving the Department of Corrections. First published in 1963 and collected for 1962, the punch card data were collected at some point between the authorization of the division in 1954 and the 1962 collection, but exactly when is unclear.

27. The push for a research division goes back at least to a 1952 Prison Association of New York report, which called for the creation of a division of research. See "Prison Study Unit for State Asked," *New York Times*, 4 Feb. 1952, 10. Back in 1955, Commissioner Thomas McHugh had sounded the call for "careful research." "Correctional Education Looks Ahead" *Journal of Correctional Education* (Oct. 1955): 70. During this period, department officials routinely decried the lack of resources for research programs. Reports of program success tended to take the form of case reports of positive accomplishments, such as Price Chenault, "The Illiterate Who Would Be a Reader," *Journal of Correctional Education* (July 1965): 5–12.

28. New York State Division of Parole and New York State Department of Corrections, *Parole Adjustment and Prior Educational Achievement*.

29. New York State Department of Corrections, *Annual Report* (1963), 33.

30. New York State Department of Corrections, *Correction* (1967), 12.

31. The initial sample of 220 cases was reduced to 186 by eliminating deceased, fugitives, and former Elmira Reception Center prisoners who were living out of New York State. Of the 186, a total of 112 were located in time to complete the pilot project in 1967, and 106 of those agreed to participate in the study, reflecting a generally quite agreeable response of former inmates (though it is obviously hard to speculate on the actual response of ex-prisoners to being contacted for the project).

32. Legislative Budget Hearing, Department of Corrections, 20 Feb. 1967, series 3, box 5, Howard F. Miller Papers (hereafter HMP), M. E. Grenander Department of Special Collections and Archives, University at Albany, State University of New York.

33. Ibid..

34. Robert E. Lynch to John R. Dunne, 18 Feb. 1966, Penal Institution Committee Files, John R. Dunne Papers (hereafter JRDP), M.E. Grenander Department of Special Collections and Archives, University at Albany, State University of New York.

35. Statement by Paul D. McGinnis, Commissioner of Correction, State of New York at a Public Hearing of the New York State Senate Committee on Penal Institutions, Albany, 27 March 1968, Penal Institution Committee Files, JRDP.

36. *Preliminary Report of the Governor's Special Committee on Criminal Offenders* (New York, 1968).

37. Ibid., 45–46.

38. Ibid., 57.

39. Ibid., 212.

40. Ibid., 29.

41. Ibid.

42. Karl Menninger to Austin H. MacCormick, 18 March 1969, AMC.

43. The same may be seen in MacCormick's response during a meeting of the Crime Control Council, *Citizens Advisory Committee of the Governor's Special Committee on Criminal Offenders* (St. Albans, New York, 1968), held at the Roosevelt Hotel.

44. Crime Control Council, *Citizens Advisory Committee of the Governor's Special Committee on Criminal Offenders*, 13.

45. Ibid., 33–34, 36. Meanwhile Donald H. Goff of the Correctional Association of New York rather lamely praised the report, which "we believe will set guidelines for the next 50 years." Ibid., 60. For works opposing the discretion that lay at the heart of the rehabilitative regime, see Kenneth Culp Davis, *Discretionary Justice: A Preliminary Inquiry* (Baton Rouge, La.: Louisiana State University Press, 1969), and Marvin E. Frankel, *Criminal Sentences: Law without Order* (New York: Hill and Wang, 1973).

46. *Preliminary Report*, 301–302. The list included inadequacy, immaturity, dependency, ill equipped in social skills, ill equipped in education, vocational maladjustment, cognitive deficiency, compulsive pathology, organic pathology, antisocial attitudes, career commitment, catalytic impulsivity, habitual impulsivity, asocial attitudes.

47. Ibid., 307.

48. Ibid., 311.

49. Ibid., 26.

50. Crime Control Council, *Citizens Advisory Committee of the Governor's Special Committee on Criminal Offenders*, 12.

51. Bob Martinson, *Cold War on the Campus* (New York: Socialist Youth League, 1950); see also Robert Martinson, letter to the editor, *New International* (Sept.–Oct. 1952), 265–67.

52. Robert Magnus Martinson, "The Role of the Communist Party in the Spanish Civil War" (M.A. thesis, University of California, Berkeley, 1953), vi.

53. Ibid., 189.

54. Ibid., 190.

55. Numerous scholars have observed a connection between civil rights and prison activism, usually observing that the legal branches of the civil rights movement turned to prison litigation as more and more activists went to jail. See, for example, Gottschalk, *Prison and the Gallows*, 177. On the other hand, Martha Biondi, *To Stand and Fight*, 71, perceptively suggests that civil rights attorneys had often acted as public defenders, suggesting a path from jail to civil rights, rather than the other way around.

56. Robert Martinson, "Solidarity Under Close Confinement: A Study of the Freedom Riders in Parchman Penitentiary," *Psychiatry* (May 1967): 132–48.

57. Robert Martinson, review of *Where It's At: Radical Perspectives in Sociology*, by Steven E. Duetsch and John Howard, eds., *American Sociological Review* 35 (Dec. 1970):

1103–1104. For more on the process by which left-wing anti-Stalinists embraced conservative politics, see Alan W. Wald, *The New York Intellectuals: The Rise and Decline of the Anti-Stalinist Left from the 1930s to the 1980s* (Chapel Hill: University of North Carolina Press, 1987).

58. Jerome H. Skolnick and Elliott Currie, *Crisis in American Institutions* (Boston: Little, Brown, 1970), 1.

59. Sociologist Donald Cressey succinctly laid out the critical perspective: "A research study which seemed to show that attending a prison school had little or no effect on the reformation of criminals would not necessarily lead to abandoning the school program. Rather, the 'intangible benefits' of education would probably be enumerated . . . in our society, education is a Good Thing, and schools must be maintained in prisons and justified as corrective ('good' men are educated; therefore, to make bad men good, educate them) whether or not there is any scientific evidence of their effectiveness." Donald R. Cressey, "The Nature and Effectiveness of Correctional Techniques," *Law and Contemporary Problems* 23 (autumn 1958): 754–71, quotation on 760. See also Joseph W. Eaton, "Symbolic and Substantive Evaluative Research," *Administrative Science Quarterly* 6 (March 1962): 421–42.

60. Ciepley, *Liberalism in the Shadow of Totalitarianism,* 194, see also 240–41.

61. Martinson argued that California was a model of the modern alliance between treatment professionals and prison administrators, where "centralized control was combined with efficient classification . . . middle management was trained in group treatment techniques and custodial ranks were indoctrinated with the new perspective which came to be called the 'correctional therapeutic community.'" Robert Martinson, "The Paradox of Prison Reform—I, The Dangerous 'Myth,'" *New Republic,* 1 April 1972, 24.

62. Robert Martinson, "The Age of Treatment: Some Implications of the Custody Treatment Dimension," *Issues in Criminology* 2 (fall 1966): 281.

63. Robert Martinson, "What Works?—Questions and Answers about Prison Reform," *Public Interest* 35 (Spring 1974): 22–54, 23.

64. Ibid., 24.

65. *Preliminary Report of the Governor's Special Committee on Criminal Offenders,* 197–98.

66. Ibid., 200–201.

67. Ibid., 224.

68. The general liberal-radical revolt against the rehabilitative ideal has been well described already, though it has not often been linked to the developments of the postwar period. See Francis Allen, *The Decline of the Rehabilitative Ideal: Penal Policy and Social Purpose* (New Haven, Conn.: Yale University Press, 1981); for contemporary expressions of the sentiment, see Erik Olin Wright, ed., *The Politics of Punishment* (New York: Harper and Row, 1973); American Friends Service Committee, *Struggle for Justice: A Report on Crime and Punishment in America* (New York: Hill and Wang, 1971).

69. Lucia Mouat, "Penal Reforms Come—But Too Slowly," *Christian Science Monitor,* 19 Jan. 1973, 2.

70. Martinson, "The Paradox of Prison Reform—I," 25.

71. Martinson, "The Paradox of Prison Reform—III, The Meaning of Attica," *New Republic,* 15 April 1972, 19.

72. Ibid., 19.

73. Martinson, "What Works?" 25.

74. Ibid., 49. The larger project, once published, was commonly, if inaccurately, referred to as "the Martinson Report." For a vigorous early critique from within the correctional bureaucracy, see Ted Palmer, "Martinson Revisited," *Journal of Research in Crime and Delinquency* (1975): 133–52.

75. Martinson, "What Works?" 48.

76. Ernest van den Haag and Robert Martinson, "Review of *Deterrence: The Legal Threat in Crime Control*, by Franklin E. Zimring and Gordon J. Hawkins," *Contemporary Sociology* 3 (Sept. 1974): 454–56.

77. Report of the Special Committee on Criminal Sentencing, *Correctional Association of New York*, 8–9.

78. Martinson, "The Paradox of Prison Reform—I," *New Republic*, 1 April 1972.

79. Martinson, "The Paradox of Prison Reform—IV, Planning for Public Safety," *New Republic*, 29 April 1972, 23.

80. Francis Cullen, Paula Smith, Christopher Lowenkamp, and Edward J. Latessa, "Nothing Works Revisited: Deconstructing Farabee's Rethinking Rehabilitation," *Victims and Offenders* 4 (2009): 101–123.

81. Lee Wohlfert, "Criminologist Bob Martinson Offers a Crime-Stopper: Put a Cop on Each Ex-Con," *People*, 23 Feb. 1976.

82. Robert Martinson, "New Findings, New Views: A Note of Caution Regarding Sentencing Reform," *Hofstra Law Review* 7 (winter 1979): 243–58, 254, 258.

83. "It Has Come to Our Attention," *Federal Probation* 43 (1979), 87. Martinson remains a figure of some mystery, with many accounts of his death failing to even correctly identify the year in which he committed suicide.

Chapter 9 · Floodtide

1. Glenn M. Kendall, "The Anatomy of a Youth Reformatory Sub-Culture," *Proceedings of the Ninety-Fourth Annual Congress of Correction* (Washington, D.C.: American Correctional Association), 178–91, 189.

2. Ibid., 189.

3. Ibid., 190.

4. Howard Lewis, "A New Chance for Community Failures," *Knickerbocker News*, 29 March 1964, 13A; Dick Weber, "New Dope Cure at Coxsackie," *Knickerbocker News*, Feb. 1963, 3B; Howard Lewis, "A Crucial Time at Coxsackie," *Knickerbocker News*, 26 May 26 1964; "Explorer Post Formed at Area Institution," *Kingston Daily Freeman*, 20 November 1967, 21.

5. This account of the Coxsackie experience reinforces Marie Gottschalk's essential observation that "remarkable transformation took place in the interest groups and social movements involved in criminal justice" during this period. See Gottschalk, *Prison and the Gallows*, 40.

6. See, for example, Paul D. Meunier and Howard D. Schwartz, "Beyond Attica"; specific testimony to this effect came from Wim Van Eekeren, deputy commissioner of administrative services, and from Frank Daley, director of the budget.

7. Meunier and Schwartz, "Beyond Attica," 928–29.

8. "Youthful Offenders," *New York Times*, 14 Feb. 1956, 28.

9. Rudy Abramson, *Spanning the Century: The Life of W. Averell Harriman, 1891–1986* (New York: William Morrow, 1992), particularly chapter 20, "Governor," and pp. 516–533.

10. Barbara Lavin McEleney, *Correctional Reform in New York*, 29–30; McEleney's fine account employs interviews with a number of important figures from the period.

11. Ibid., 22.

12. Ibid., 32, quoting a former legislative aide to the committee.

13. Ibid., 32.

14. "Wider Youth Law Asked by Judges," *New York Times*, 8 Dec. 1957, 75.

15. See "Hogan Says G.O.P. Shams on Crime," *New York Times*, 7 Oct. 1958, 26; Warren Weaver, Jr., "Rockefeller Charges Rival Harms State Crime Fight," *New York Times*, 8 Oct. 1958, 1; "G.O.P. is Accused of Lag on Crime," *New York Times*, 9 Oct. 1958, 29. Rockefeller blasted Harriman, for example, for being slow to build more camps of the Camp Pharsalia model; see, "Queens Children Mob Rockefeller," *New York Times*, 30 Oct. 1958, 25.

16. Layhmond Robinson, "Mayor's Auto Ban Backed in Albany," *New York Times*, 23 March 1961, 25; "Rockefeller Signs Youth Act Repeal," *New York Times*, 30 March 1961, 21.

17. For an important review of the Rockefeller laws, see Julilly Kohler-Hausmann, " 'The Attila the Hun Law': New York's Rockefeller Drug Laws and the Making of a Punitive State," *Journal of Social History* (fall 2010): 71–96.

18. Prison population totals also miss developments like the court rulings that required the state to largely empty its institutions for the criminally insane. At the start of 1966, Matteawan and Dannemora housed 2,597 prisoners, a number that had been reduced to 998 by the spring of 1968, as prisoner inmates were shifted to state hospitals.

19. The New York City jail uprisings of August and October 1970 were the most notable product of this overcrowding. One of the most useful accounts of the 1970 jail rebellions is Diaz-Cotto, *Gender, Ethnicity, and the State*, 35–45.

20. Walter Wallack reached mandatory retirement in 1966 and departed Wallkill Prison; Price Chenault reached mandatory retirement in 1970.

21. "Escaped Hunt Selves; Caught," *Greene County Examiner-Recorder*, 21 May 1942; "Foiled Inmates to Face Grand Jury Here," *Greene County Examiner-Recorder*, 5 March 1942, 1.

22. "Grand Jury Asks Steps to Protect People of Area," *Greene County Examiner-Recorder*, 24 Dec. 1942, 1.

23. "40 Hour Week Is Stressed to Help Morale of Guards," *Kingston Daily Freeman*, 1 March 1955, 5.

24. "Prison Local Hits Pay Plan," *Newburgh News*, 3 March 1958, 6.

25. "500 In March Asking State Pay Increase," *Yonkers (NY) Herald Statesman*, 3 March 1959, 12.

26. J. Earl Kelly, director of classification and compensation, "Appeal to the State Civil Service Commission in Connection With Title of Correction Officer and Related Titles After Denial of Reallocation Request," 23 Aug. 1965, 21, Council 82 Papers.

27. John R. Martin, "Council 50 to New York State Senators and Assemblymen," 24 Jan. 1966, JRDP.

28. "13 Unions Again Hit Napanoch," *Newburgh-Beacon News*, 13 Oct. 1960.

29. Jerry Wurf to Al Wurf, Sept. 2, 1969, series 2, box 3, Council 82 Papers.

30. James B. Jacobs and Norma Meacham Crotty, "Collective Bargaining in New York State Prisons," in *Guard Unions and the Future of the Prisons* (Ithaca: Institute of Public Employment, New York State School of Industrial and Labor Relations, 1978), 10–39.

31. Contract negotiations, 1969, items of locals, series 2, box 1, Council 82 Papers.

32. Diaz-Cotto, *Gender, Ethnicity and the State*, 104.

33. Correction Policy Committee, 1971–1972, series 2, box 2, Council 82 Papers.

34. The literature on public employees, correctional officers, and the labor movement is small but helpful: Joseph E. Slater, *Public Workers: Government Employee Unions, the Law, and the State, 1900–1962* (Ithaca, N.Y.: ILR, 2004); Paul D. Staudohar, "Prison Guard Labor Relations in Ohio," *Industrial Relations* 15 (May 1976): 177–90; Jacobs and Crotty, *Guard Unions and the Future of the Prisons*; John M. Wynne, Jr., "Unions and Bargaining Among Employees of State Prisons," *Monthly Labor Review* (March 1978): 10–16.

35. Linda Greenhouse, "Correction Bill Signed By Carey," *New York Times*, 13 Aug. 1975, 1.

36. John Burke to Honorable J. J. Marchi, 8 March 1976, series 2, box 1, Council 82 Papers. One union member put it this way: "I was one of the most vocal opponents Mr. Schwartz had or ever will have in his life—he was an ultraliberal, sick member of our society while local correction officers are conservative and vehemently opposed to Schwartz because of his behavior at Attica and his views on rehabilitation." Jacobs and Crotty, *Guard Unions and the Future of the Prison*, 35.

37. Linda Greenhouse, "Senators Cool to Correction Chief," *New York Times*, 26 Jan. 1976, 45.

38. Linda Greenhouse, "Schwartz Appears Headed for Defeat as Correction Chief," *New York Times*, 4 March 1976, 1, 29. Senator Edwyn Mason accused Schwartz of caring more for "the incorrigibly depraved than for the state's law abiding citizens." Linda Greenhouse, "Politics and Little More Stopped Schwartz," *New York Times*, 11 April 1976, 146.

39. Tom Wicker, "Attica and Schwartz," *New York Times*, 29 Feb. 1976, 15.

40. "Statement by Carl F. Gray, Executive Director Security and Law Enforcement Employees Council 82, AFSCME, AFL-CIO, before the Senate Standing Committee on Crime and Correction, 30 March 1977," series 2, box 1, Council 82 Papers.

41. Council 82, "New York State Correctional System" (1976), series 2, box 2, Council 82 Papers.

42. McEleney, *Correctional Reform in New York*, 136.

43. *Crisis Management: The State of Corrections in New York State*, Report of the Assembly Republican Task Force on the Corrections Crisis (22 March 1983), 2.

44. Correctional Services News (July 1981), box 5, Correctional Association of New York Papers, M. E. Grenander Department of Special Collections and Archives, University at Albany, State University of New York.

45. Lewis B. Oliver, Jr., "Summary of Testimony," series 5, box 1, New York State Coalition for Criminal Justice Records (hereafter CCJR), M.E. Grenander Department of Special Collections and Archives, University at Albany, State University of New York.

46. The accounts of violence against inmates were consistent with what had been reported for years, but prisoner charges were now given a more public airing. One inmate

cautioned legislators, "When they talk about special housing they don't mention the beating you get on the way up." Annabar Jensis, "Legislators Grill Ward At Committee Hearings," *Greene County News*, 16 Feb. 1978, 1, 8. In June 1977 four officers were involved in an assault on inmate Jerome Handy, who was badly beaten. Handy was charged with assault but acquitted by a Greene County jury in June in a rare defeat for officers in the local criminal justice system. See Oliver, "Summary of Testimony" CCJR.

47. Jeff Sommer, "Coxsackie: A Look Inside," *Knickerbocker News*, 1 March 1978. In 1974, Coxsackie had only six Spanish-speaking officers in the institution; see John E. Van De Car, Director of Manpower and Employee Relations to Thomas Holland, Chairman of the [Council 82] Corrections Policy Committee, Correctional Policy Committee Meetings, 1974, series 2, box 2, Council 82 Papers. Correctional officers were not particularly concerned about the lack of diversity among them, arguing that it was a natural effect of the location of state prisoners and the standards of merit-based civil service. "No one from the minority groups is being discriminated against" was the position of the officers; John J. Panella to State Senator John Dunne, 12 July 1967, Penal Institutions Files, JRDP. Bryant Collins, "Where I'm Comin' From," *New York Amsterdam News*, 5 Feb. 1972, A1, pointed out that Coxsackie had just one black guard at the start of 1972, David Harris, and he was being transferred, leaving no black guards at all at the former reformatory.

48. Jeff Sommer, "Correction Chief Ties 'Politics' to Coxsackie's Troubles," *Knickerbocker News*, 2 March 1978, 13A.

49. Ahbegee Abdul, "West Coxsackie Plea," *New York Amsterdam News*, 18 Sept. 1971, A7.

50. "Cells Are Searched After Disturbances at a Prison Upstate," *New York Times*, 9 April 1972, 57.

51. "Prisoners Stop Work in Food Dispute," *New York Times*, 11 Aug. 1973, 23. A spike in protests coincided with the arrival of Harry Fritz as superintendent, which represented a huge victory for the custodial staff. Fritz had been a sergeant at Coxsackie back in the 1950s and had risen through the custodial ranks to the position of warden. He had been known as a tough-minded officer when he was first at Coxsackie (harsher assessments came from the inmates; see chapter 5); moreover, he had long been active in promoting the labor interests of correctional officers. Fritz arrived after serving as warden of Auburn during its 1970 uprising, which he blamed in testimony to the state legislature on the "permissive attitude" of the previous administration. See "Prison Practices Aired As 9 Testify At Hearing," *Schenectady Gazette*, 17 Dec. 1970, 9.

52. Oliver, "Summary of Testimony," CCJR; Oliver observed that "being so young, the Coxsackie blacks do not have the maturity to understand that all whites are not bad and keep their reactions [to official racism] from being generalized to all whites, including fellow prisoners."

53. "Area Men Score on Job Test," *Newburgh (NY) Evening News*, 15 Dec. 1971, 9.

54. Elizabeth Gaynes described the basis for officers' resentment: "Perhaps Mr. Ternullo's alleged leniency refers to the large number of volunteer programs he permitted and encouraged to supplement the limited programs which the budget and central office offer. Or maybe it's the emphasis he placed on education. Or the display of inmate art on his office walls. Perhaps the respect he received from inmates and their attorneys discredited him." Elizabeth A. Gaynes, "Summary of Testimony," series 5, box 1, CCJR.

55. Among the ILC's objectionable behavior, they apparently selected the film *Texas Chainsaw Massacre* to be shown. Permission to do so was only revoked after protests from correctional officers. Annabar Jensis, "New Warden and Policies for Coxsackie Institution," *Greene County News*, 26 Jan. 1978, 1, 3.

56. Gaynes, "Summary of Testimony," CCJR.

57. Oliver, "Summary of Testimony," CCJR.

58. "Statement of Officers Wives," *Greene County News*, n. d. 1978, n. p., series 5, box 1, CCJR.

59. Council 82 Executive Board Files, minutes, 24 Jan. 1977, series 1, box 1, Council 82 Papers.

60. "Coxsackie Guards Demanding Search," *Newburgh (NY) Evening News*, 27 Jan. 1977, 7.

61. "Coxsackie Guards Tell of 14 Attacks," *Schenectady Gazette*, 25 March 1977, 2.

62. Memorandum, Robert Maloney, policy chairman, 4 April 1977, series 2, box 2, Council 82 Papers.

63. Gaynes, "Summary of Testimony," and Oliver, "Summary of Testimony," CCJR.

64. In April 1979, Council 82 reversed its tentative acceptance of a state contract, leading to a systemwide strike later that month, led in part by the resistance of union locals at Elmira, Great Meadow, and Coxsackie. The Elmira local had successfully sued to enjoin the implementation of the 1977 contract agreement between Council 82 and the state; Jacobs and Crotty, *Guard Unions and the Future of the Prison*, 17. Two years later, the union did renege on an agreement because of locals' discontent, which precipitated a full-blown prison officers' strike. See Richard J. Meislin, "Prison Guards' Chief Jailed as Strike Enters 9th Day," *New York Times* 28 April 1979, 1, 28. Officers there claimed, "In five or six years it will be renamed 'the Elmira Recreational Facility,'" and "the prisoners up there have it better than we do." See also Alan Richman, "Striking Guards Say They Are the Prisons' Real Inmates," *New York Times* 27 April 1979, B1. The state refused to reopen negotiations, which led to the strike. Sheila Rukle, "Talks Begin in Strike by Prison Guards," *New York Times* 21 April 1979, 26.

65. "Group Wants End to Big Prisons," *Hudson Register Star*, 15 March 1977, n. p.

66. Ibid.

67. Memorandum from Benjamin Ward, commissioner, Department of Correctional Services, 16 June 1977, series 5, box 1, CCJR.

68. "Work Mandated, Study Voluntary," *Albany Times-Union*, 25 June 1977, 8.

69. Memorandum from John Ives, community coordinator, Judicial Process Commission, 12 Aug. 1977, CCJR.

70. Memorandum, Leon Van Dyke, New York State Department of Correctional Services, 1977, CCJR. Van Dyke was an educational specialist in the department, and a civil rights activist in the Albany area. Prison programs were already understaffed and overworked. Elizabeth Gaynes called the counselors, "the most concerned, dedicated, hardworking and cooperative counselors I have ever encountered in the correctional system." Their caseloads, she observed, were "so outrageous that they cannot possibly be as accessible as necessary." "Summary of Testimony," CCJR.

71. In November, Coxsackie Civil Service Employees' Association Local 162, issued a strongly worded memorandum in opposition to the proposed program changes at the institution: "The memorandum misquoted and misrepresented the proposed program,"

and the negative radio announcement preceded the hostage event. See New York State Coalition for Criminal Justice, "Coalition Demands Full Disclosure on Coxsackie," 13 Jan. 1978, series 5, box 1, CCJR.

72. R. Victor Stewart, "Albany Recalls Coxsackie Chief," *Knickerbocker News*, 9 Jan. 1978, n. p. The immediate aftermath of the hostage event scarcely reduced tensions at Coxsackie. The Inmate Liaison Committee went from cell to cell, along with the volunteer services director (McKinley Johnson) to collect care packages for the prisoners being held in solitary confinement, to the outrage of correctional officers.

73. Gaynes, "Summary of Testimony," CCJR.

74. Jeff Sommer, "Peace a Façade in Troubled Jail," *Knickerbocker News*, 28 Feb. 1978, 1.

75. Annabar Jensis, "Committee to Call Ward Back Again," *Greene County News* 16 Feb. 1978, 1, 8.

76. Jeff Sommer, "Coxsackie, A Look Inside," *Knickerbocker News*, 1 March 1978. Coxsackie union local head Valentine Kriel reported, "There is no more Inmate Liaison Committee running the Institution and Volunteer Services has been disbanded for the present"; the new deputy for security was Donald Pierce, formerly a captain at Coxsackie. Annabar Jensis, "New Warden and Policies for Coxsackie Institution," *Greene County News*, 26 Jan. 1978, 1, 3.

77. Frederic U. Dicker, "Security Tightens at Coxsackie," *Albany Times-Union*, n. d., n. p., series 5, box 1, CCJR. Frederic U. Dicker, "Ward Answers His Critics on Coxsackie Security," *Albany Times-Union*, 11 Jan., 1978, n. p., series 5, box 1, CCJR.

78. Jeff Sommer, "Corrections Chief Ties 'Politics' to Coxsackie Troubles," *Knickerbocker News*, 2 March 1978, 13A; see also Jeff Sommer, "Coxsackie: A Look Inside," *Knickerbocker News*, 1 March 1978, 1.

79. Annabar Jensis, "Legislators Grill Ward at Committee Hearings," *Greene County News* 16 Feb. 1978, 1.

80. Annabar Jensis, "Correction Officers Wives Organize Lobbying Group; To Demonstrate in Albany," *Greene County News*, 2 Feb. 1978, n. p., series 5, box 1, CCJR.

81. "Statement of Officers Wives," *Greene County News*, 16 Feb. 1978, 1, 9.

82. Ibid. In New York City, police officers' wives took a similarly active role in their political struggles. See Daniel J. Walkowitz, "Patrolling the Borders: Integration and Identity in the New York City Police Department, 1941–1975" (Ph.D. diss., New York University 2000). See also, William J. Bopp, *The Police Rebellion: A Quest for Blue Power* (Springfield, Ill.: Charles C. Thomas, 1971).

83. Jeff Sommer, "Peace a Façade in Troubled Jail," *Knickerbocker News* Feb. 28, 1978. The New York State Coalition for Criminal Justice questioned whether prisoners were being made scapegoats in an election year. New York State Coalition for Criminal Justice, "Coalition Demands Full Disclosure on Coxsackie," 13 Jan. 1978, series 5, box 1, CCJR.

Conclusion · The Ghost of Prisons Future

1. Selwyn Raab, "Carey Offers 275 Million Plan to Expand State Prisons," *New York Times*, 6 June 1980, B1.

2. The New York State Coalition for Criminal Justice Records (CCJR), housed at the M.E. Grenander Department of Special Collections and Archives, University at Albany, State University of New York, provide comprehensive coverage of the prison bond fight.

3. Dorothy J. Gaiter, "Controversy Intensifies on Prison Bond Issue," *New York Times,* 1 Nov. 1981, 53.

4. Robert A. Mathias, *The Road Not Taken: Cost-Effective Alternatives to Prison for Non-Violent Felony Offenders in New York State* (New York: Correctional Association of New York, 1986).

5. Some of many outstanding explorations of the consequences and impact of mass incarceration: Alexander, *New Jim Crow;* Todd R. Clear, *Imprisoning Communities: How Mass Incarceration Makes Disadvantaged Neighborhoods Worse* (Oxford; New York: Oxford University Press, 2007); Megan Comfort, "Punishment Beyond the Legal Offender," *Annual Review of Law and Social Science* 3 (2007): 271–96; Steven Raphael and Michael A. Stoll, eds. *Do Prisons Make Us Safer? The Benefits and Costs of the Prison Boom* (New York: Russell Sage, 2009); Bruce Western, *Punishment and Inequality in America* (New York: Russell Sage, 2006).

6. See, especially, Alex Lichtenstein, "A 'Labor History' of Mass Incarceration," *Labor* 8 (2011): 5–14, and Thompson, "Why Mass Incarceration Matters."

7. Loic Wacquant, "Deadly Symbiosis: When Ghetto and Prison Meet and Mesh," *Punishment and Society* 3 (2001): 95–133, 109. See also John Irwin, *The Warehouse Prison: Disposal of the New Dangerous Class* (Los Angeles, Calif.: Roxbury, 2001).

8. For broad version of each argument, see Alexander, *New Jim Crow,* and Zinoman, *Colonial Bastille.*

9. Lorna A. Rhodes, *Total Confinement: Madness and Reason in the Maximum Security Prison* (Berkeley: University of California Press, 2004), 223.

10. Muhammad, *Condemnation of Blackness,* 13.

11. For an important, and useful, overview of evidence-based corrections, see Doris Layton MacKenzie, "Evidence-Based Corrections: Identifying What Works," *Crime and Delinquency* 46 (Oct. 2000): 457–71.

12. Michelle S. Phelps, "Rehabilitation in the Punitive Era: The Gap Between Rhetoric and Reality in U.S. Prison Programs," *Law and Society Review* 45 (2011): 33–68.

13. Perhaps the closest, and most promising, approximation of the old Osborne-MacCormick approach to the criminal offender might be psychologist Tony Ward's "Good Lives Model" of rehabilitation. In the Good Lives Model, "an individual is hypothesized to commit criminal offences because he lacks the capabilities to realize valued outcomes in personally fulfilling and socially acceptable ways." See, for example, Tony Ward, Ruth E. Mann, and Theresa A. Gannon, "The Good Lives Model of Offender Rehabilitation: Clinical Implications," *Aggression and Violent Behavior* 12 (2007): 87–107; for a broader overview, see Tony Ward and Shadd Maruna, *Rehabilitation: Beyond the Risk Paradigm* (New York: Routledge, Chapman and Hall, 2007).

14. See, for example, Wilkinson, Burnham, and Spillane, *Prison Work.*

The inmate case files from the Coxsackie and Great Meadow reformatories constitute the single most important source of information for this project. These were transferred to the New York State Archives by the New York State Department of Corrections as part of a massive deposit of institutional case files that total more than 2,500 cubic feet of paper materials. Most of the files cover the period from the 1920s to the mid-1950s. The New York State Archives also house files from after the mid-1950s, but these are microfilmed copies of sampled records and were not used in this study. Taken together, the case file collection represents an extraordinary window into the operations of mid-century American corrections. Because the New York State Department of Corrections operated such a wide range of institutions, these files can provide historians with valuable details on almost every kind of correctional operation: maximum-security prisons for adult men; institutions for women; facilities for the criminally insane and for "defective" delinquents; and the reformatories. These records have not been used nearly as often as they should, and many have never been examined; they represent a historical treasure of the first order.

The Coxsackie records include approximately 7,500 case files, relating to inmates with consecutive numbers between #1 and #10362. The first of the case files are actually House of Refuge files, covering the young men who were removed from that institution and sent upstate in 1935. The last of these case files cover admissions from 1956, though the actual coverage of institutional operations inside those files extends to about 1960. The Great Meadow records include approximately 6,200 case files of inmates housed at the institution between 1915 and 1956, with consecutive numbers between #7764 and #20540. It was my good fortune that these case files extended just into the period after Great Meadow had been converted into an end-of-the-line reformatory; these Great Meadow files are nearly all files of prisoners transferred from Elmira, Woodbourne, and Coxsackie. Spotting the files from Coxsackie was a simple matter of looking for the original Coxsackie inmate number on the top of the file itself.

Each individual case file, particularly from the reformatories, constitutes a massive record in and of itself, dozens of pages in length (the most substantial of the files could often include more than one hundred pages of material). The files represent a particular moment in the history of corrections, when reform-minded administrators strove to accumulate as much information as possible about a prisoner's past, about the details of their work and behavior while in confinement, and (in some cases) about their histories after release. We shall not see anything like them again in correctional practice. Today, huge paper files have largely been supplanted by electronic records, and much of these are pared-down bureaucratic management tools rather than substantive case files. At Coxsackie, a typical case file begins with an institutional photograph on the inside front cover and a prisoner information card, both collected upon the prisoner's entrance into the reformatory. Case files often include records from the sentencing court, including results of presentencing investigations. After the opening of the Elmira Reception Center, every case file includes the evaluation records from the ERC, sent along with the prisoner. Case files include seemingly endless records of prisoners' educational work, typically long checklists of worksheet units completed as well as monthly evaluations. Case files also include prisoner disciplinary records, psychiatric records, the records of the program and adjustment committees that pre-evaluated prisoners for parole, and (before 1945) parole records themselves. Unfortunately, once the state centralized parole services, ending the practice of reformatories like Coxsackie operating their own parole departments, the parole records in the files generally disappeared. The sheer size of the collection, coupled with the limitations on recording prisoner names imposed by the University of Florida Institutional Review Board (which precluded photocopying prisoner records), necessitated my sampling the range of files from 1935 to 1956. I sampled every tenth box (of more than three hundred boxes of case files) and reviewed every other file in each of the boxes I pulled, for an overall sample of approximately 5 percent of the total. For the few boxes of relevant Great Meadow case files, I reviewed every single file of prisoners transferred from Coxsackie.

Unfortunately for this study, the incredible richness of the case file collections in the New York State Archives is not matched by the quality of the Department of Corrections records more generally. Institutional records, especially for the mid-twentieth century, are very spotty. The 392 cubic feet of Coxsackie case files, for example, represent the total of deposited institutional records for the reformatory. The same holds true for Great Meadow and Woodbourne. The records of the central Department of Corrections offices in Albany are likewise sparse and offered little that was directly useful to this study. The New York State Library, however, contains a marvelously complete record of official Department of Corrections publications. The most important of these, for the purposes of this study, were the annual reports of the Coxsackie reformatory; the annual reports of the State Commission of Correction; various annual and monthly publications of the Department of Corrections; and the many reports generated by the Lewisohn and Engelhardt commissions in the 1930s.

Researchers interested in New York State correctional history generally will be heartened by the incredibly extensive collections housed at the M. E. Grenander Department of Special Collections and Archives at the University of Albany, State University of New York. Reflecting the longstanding importance of academic programs in criminal justice at that university, this archive contains several vitally important collections for this study. The first are the records of the Correctional Association of New York, successor to the venerable Prison Association of New York. The oldest and, at times, most influential reform organization in the state, the Prison Association of New York involved itself in almost every significant issue related to prison policy. The second collection is the records of Council 82, Security and Law Enforcement Employees, AFSCME. Few areas of prison history are as poorly covered as the story of prison guards and correctional officers, and the implications of unionization in the modern period are particularly in need of research and study. The Council 82 records are a remarkably detailed record of the organization's operations from its genesis in the late 1960s though the mid-1980s. They contain executive committee minutes, legal files, subject files, and a reasonably comprehensive collection of Council 82 publications. The third significant source is the records of the New York State Coalition for Criminal Justice, an extraordinary collection of material from one the state's leading reform organizations in the 1970s and 1980s. Formed in the aftermath of the Attica prison riot, the New York State Coalition for Criminal Justice left records that provide comprehensive coverage of every significant political issue relating to corrections in this period. At moments of crisis within particular prisons, like Coxsackie in 1977, these files provide helpful context and insight. One of the richest areas of this collection, only briefly used in this study, covers the organization's fight against prison expansion in New York State, particularly in the early 1980s, when the future of mass incarceration was coming into view but much of the actual expansion had not yet taken place. The M. E. Grenander collection also includes extensive coverage of New York State politics; the most significant collection, in terms of prison history, are the John R. Dunne Papers, which cover the career of the New York state senator most engaged with questions of prison conditions during the tumultuous late 1960s and early 1970s.

The life and career of Austin MacCormick deserve more attention from historians. Toward the end of his life, MacCormick arranged for his papers and books to be donated to the Newton Gresham Library of Sam Houston State University. The choice of institution may seem odd, until one recalls that (like the University of Albany) Sam Houston was a pioneer in criminal justice education, with the College of Criminal Justice among the first in the nation to offer a Ph.D. in the field. Moreover, Austin MacCormick's good friend George J. Beto, former director of the Texas Department of Corrections, was one of the founders of the Sam Houston program. Beto arranged not only for the deposit of MacCormick's papers, but also for those of the first two directors of the Federal Bureau of Prisons, Sanford Bates and James B. Bennett. Together, these three collections offer an impressive window into the world of mid-century prison reform, at least from the point of view of the reform-minded prison administrator. The papers of Bates and Bennett, not much used in this project, will be a wonderful resource for future historians. MacCormick's papers cover many aspects of his storied career. This collection does not provide extensive coverage of MacCormick's early work with Thomas Mott Osborne, but fortunately, there is the massive collection of Osborne's own papers. These are housed as part of the Osborne Family Papers at Syracuse University. They cover his late career—the decade from his resignation at Sing Sing to his death in 1926—remarkably well, and this is a period that deserves closer study from historians.

The review of prison politics in this work tends to be focused, especially in the later period, on the state legislature, the officers' union, the Department of Corrections, and the institutions themselves. The politics of the earlier period in this study, during which the reformatory system took shape, was also influenced by governors Roosevelt and Lehman. Fortunately, the Franklin D. Roosevelt Collections at the Franklin D. Roosevelt Presidential Library and Museum in Hyde Park, New York, contain a significant amount of material related to the prison issue during FDR's time as New York governor. The Herbert H. Lehman Collections of the Columbia University Rare Book and Manuscript

Library contain somewhat less directly useful material on prison politics, but they are still worth consulting.

A few regularly published journals from this period, read straight through, amount to a fairly complete record of mainstream prison reform and practice. *Jail Association Journal, Prison World,* and *American Journal of Correction* are the various titles of the same journal regularly published by the American Correctional Association. The *Prison Journal* is another important source, in consistent publication since 1921. Less prison-focused but very comprehensive is the *Journal of Criminal Law and Criminology,* known as the *Journal of the American Institute of Criminal and Criminology* from 1910 to 1931, the *Journal of Criminal Law and Criminology* from 1931 to 1951, and the *Journal of Criminal Law, Criminology, and Police Science* from 1951 to 1972. Students of correctional education should pay particularly close attention to the *Journal of Correctional Education,* published by the Correctional Education Association. In its early years, the journal was dominated by New York prison educators, and it effectively chronicles the development of the field. Finally, the Correctional Education Association emerged out of a standing committee of the American Prison Association (later the American Correctional Association), a group whose published annual proceedings are a useful guide to the evolution of prison administration.

A series of published works from the reform period are required reading for scholars of prison reform in the modern United States. Thomas Mott Osborne's *Within Prison Walls* (New York: D. Appleton and Company, 1916) and his less well-known *Society and Prisons: Some Suggestions for a New Penology* (New Haven, Conn.: Yale University Press, 1916) are both good starting places. Highlights from the work of Osborne-inspired reformers include: Donald Lowrie, *My Life Out of Prison* (New York: M. Kennerley, 1915); Frank Tannenbaum, *Wall Shadows: A Study in American Prisons* (New York: Putnam, 1922); Frank Tannenbaum, *Crime and the Community* (Boston: Ginn and Company, 1938); and Austin MacCormick, *The Education of Adult Prisoners: A Survey and a Program* (New York: National Society of Penal Information, 1931).

Highlights from the secondary literature on American correctional history in its progressive, liberal period must certainly begin with David J. Rothman, *Conscience and Convenience* (New York: Aldine de Gruyter, 2002). It isn't the last word on the subject, despite being treated that way for many years, but it remains an essential starting point. Reconsiderations of modern punishment worth consulting include David Garland, *Punishment and Welfare: A History of Penal Strategies* (Aldershot, Hants, UK; Brookfield, Vt.: Gower, 1985), and Michael Tonry, *Thinking About Crime: Sense and Sensibility in American Penal Culture* (New York: Oxford University Press, 2004). From there, historians have begun to take the history of this period in different conceptual directions. For a study that emphasizes the deep roots of today's punitive approach to punishment, readers should consult Marie Gottschalk, *The Prison and the Gallows: The Politics of Mass Incarceration in America* (Cambridge; New York: Cambridge University Press, 2006). The study that finally drew historians' attention back to the centrality of labor to northern prison regimes is Rebecca M. McLennan, *The Crisis of Imprisonment: Protest, Politics, and the Making of the American Penal State, 1776–1941* (New York: Cambridge University Press, 2008). Gender and masculinity are given their proper due in Kevin P. Murphy, *Political Manhood: Red Bloods, Mollycoddles, and the Politics of Progressive Era Reform* (New York: Columbia University Press, 2008). The most serious consideration of therapeutic interests in bureaucratic context is Andrew J. Polsky, *The Rise of the Therapeutic State* (Princeton, N.J.: Princeton University Press, 1993); although I do not agree with all of its conclusions, its conceptual foundations are fascinating and essential reading for historians of rehabilitative systems. Race has too often been left out of the history of the modern "reform" prison, better explored in histories of "southern" prisons (both the U.S. and global South), but readers interested in an important reconsideration should consult Khalil Gibran Muhammad, *The Condemnation of Blackness: Race, Crime, and the Making of Modern Urban America* (Cambridge, Mass.: Harvard University Press, 2010). The colonial prison study that helped inspire my own work, and that remains one of the most sophisticated treatments of imprisonment, is Peter Zinoman, *The Colonial Bastille: A History of Imprisonment in Vietnam, 1862–1940* (Berkeley: University of California Press, 2001). Finally, two works of special note. I have been both moved and inspired by Estelle B. Freedman, *Maternal Justice: Miriam Van Waters and the Female Reform Tradition* (Chicago, Ill.: University of Chicago Press, 1996), an exceptionally fine treatment of an individual prison reformer from this era. The work that represents the foundations of my own development as a scholar, and reveals just how complex and confounding criminal justice is when examined up close and from the front lines, is Steven L. Schlossman, *Transforming Juvenile Justice: Reform Ideals and Institutional Realities, 1825–1920* (DeKalb: Northern Illinois University Press, 2005).